—ANTIQUE— FURNITURE EXPERT

—ANTIQUE— FURNITURE EXPERT

PETER PHILIP
GILLIAN WALKLING

CONSULTANT EDITOR

JOHN BLY

CENTURY

London Sydney Auckland Johannesburg

First published in 1991 by Century,
an imprint of
Random Century Group Limited,
Random Century House,
20 Vauxhall Bridge Road,
London SW1V 2SA

Random Century Australia Pty Ltd,
20 Alfred Street, Milsons Point,
Sydney 2061, Australia

Random Century (NZ) Ltd,
18 Poland Road, Glenfield,
Auckland 10, New Zealand

Random Century South Africa Pty Ltd,
PO Box 337, Bergvlei, 2012 South Africa

A catalogue record for this book is
available from the British Library

ISBN 0 7126 5100 4

Conceived, edited, designed and produced by Duncan Petersen Publishing Ltd,
54 Milson Road, London W14 0LB

Filmset by SX Composing Ltd, Rayleigh, Essex

Originated by Regent Publishing Services, Hong Kong

Printed in Italy by G. Canale & C. SpA, Turin

Editorial director	Andrew Duncan
Assistant editor	Kate Macdonald
Index	Rosemary Dawe
Art director	Mel Petersen
Designers	Chris Foley and Beverley Stewart
Picture research	Catherine Palmer and Gillian Walkling

Line illustrations by Sandra Ponds and Will Giles

Graham Child (Alpha Antique Restorations, High Street, Compton, Newbury, Berkshire)
gave invaluable advice for the section on recognizing woods.

Using this book

This is a reference book designed to be consulted as and when needed – much as a field guide to birds. The point of its systematic analysis is to help the layman identify furniture without having to assimilate masses of information in advance. To make this possible, some repetition has been necessary.

While you can use the book without prior knowledge of antiques, you will find it easier and more interesting to use if you first read the guides to periods and styles at the start of each of the European, English and New World sections; also the advice on recognizing woods on pages 8-15, and on finishes, page 16.

Within each of the European, English and New World sections, the furniture is arranged alphabetically by type – starting with beds and ending, typically, with tables.

For each type of furniture, there is a generally chronological sequence, period by period, starting with the earliest, ending with the latest. However, this chronological sequence is sometimes broken in order to group like with like or to assist the pagination.

Don't forget that there is an illustrated glossary of technical terms on pages 329-317.

In the interests of saving space for essential information, the authors have sometimes described the construction by shorthand – typically 'usual methods of the day'. A full description of the methods of the day will be found on a neighbouring page.

On pages 323-333 there is a deliberately brief and selective guide, type by type and period by period, to prices reached at auction and in salerooms.

The term 'European' is used to describe furniture originating on the European mainland in order to distinguish it from 'English'. 'English' assumes furniture made in all parts of the British Isles.

CONTENTS

INTRODUCTION

WHAT IS AN ANTIQUE

Until about 1870, the word 'antique' was used to describe things appertaining to ancient Greece and Rome – what we now call antiquities – while what we term antiques were known then as curios or curiosities. From then until about 1980, an antique came to mean any artefact over 100 years old, though purists have set earlier, arbitrary datelines, such as the long-revered 1830.

Since 1980, the unofficial trend has been towards defining an antique as anything made before the outbreak of the Second World War. The pre-war world was in many ways very different from the one we live in today, and in taking 1940 as the cut-off point, this book recognizes that there is now a serious collectors' market in early 20thC furniture.

Designers and craftsmen are disinclined to recognize time barriers. They borrow ideas from all kinds of sources, and the wise collector or home-maker likewise cultivates an eclectic taste, discreetly mixing together pieces from many places and different periods, not forgetting the hi-tech equipment of the present day – some of which is undeniably elegant.

Stool sold by a London store from 1884 onwards, made in ancient Egyptian style.

TOWN AND COUNTRY

Mixing furniture of different periods and nationalities is a fairly safe bet, so long as the pieces exhibit roughly the same degree of sophistication. Country cousins do not always mix happily with city types. It is not a matter of money.

Vernacular furniture often finds itself out of place in an aristocratic ambience, even though it can now cost as much, and in some cases more, than its ormolu-mounted equivalent. A good oak Welsh dresser of around 1800 can cost as much as a Sheraton mahogany sideboard of the same date; a well-carved French Provincial commode can fetch as much as one made by a Paris *ébéniste*, while a simple Shaker sewing chest can bring more at auction in the USA than the rest of them put together.

An oak Welsh dresser, about 1800.

Regency mahogany sideboard, about 1810.

In a wide-ranging book of this kind, it has not been feasible to devote as much space to vernacular furniture as the present market in it deserves; but the ways in which it has related to (or has ignored) city fashions and changes of style, at various times and places, have been noted, and typical examples from many regions are illustrated.

EXPERT ADVICE

Country furniture is a specialized subject, and those attracted to it are well advised to seek out dealers and auctioneers with a detailed knowledge of their regional types. The same applies to sophisticated, mainstream furniture. There are still a few dealers surviving with an

Country-made oak bed, late-17thC.

encyclopaedic knowledge that covers just about everything from fine furniture to vintage cars, but even they will admit, under pressure, that they can no longer keep up with market fluctuations. Specialization is the order of the day.

Inexperienced buyers, armed only with a smattering of book-learning and driven by a hunger for a home furnished with antiques, often pay out substantial sums for pieces that take their fancy, but which carry no worthwhile guarantee. At least until they have acquired a good working knowledge by dint of studying the things themselves, as well as by reading books such as this, buyers should ask themselves whether it might not be better to pay a little more – even a little too much – for the right thing, guaranteed by a reputable expert, than to grub around for so-called bargains that turn out to be 'wrong' (trade euphemism for fake). Generally speaking, a detailed invoice from an established dealer is a much safer form of protection than any description in an auctioneer's catalogue.

The larger firms of auctioneers retain specialists in various fields, who are willing to give advice if it is sought, but the laws affecting the sale of goods by auction vary greatly from country to country and are often very vague. The salerooms do, however, provide splendid opportunities for examining furniture in detail by taking out drawers and turning things upside down in a cavalier fashion that would annoy any self-respecting dealer, if it were to be attempted in his gallery without prior permission.

INVESTMENT

Too much has been made in recent years of the 'investment potential' of antiques. It is true that, for the most part, they have performed very well indeed in the long term, but no one can be sure that prices are going to rise without check. Some will fall from time to time, either because a fashion changes or for extraneous economic reasons; but antique furniture is always worth something, which is more than can be said for many of its modern equivalents.

If, when it finally has to go, an antique shows a decent financial gain, that is a bonus. The real dividend on the original investment is the pleasure it has given. If profit is the main motive, the activity should be acknowledged as speculation, with all the inherent risks that it entails. Speculation is for dealers, investment for collectors and home-lovers – but seen in terms of quiet satisfaction rather than cash in the bank. Happy hunting.

Peter Philp
Gillian Walkling

May 1991

Part-18thC Chippendale sofa, upholstered with older fragments of tapestry.

RECOGNIZING WOODS

An ability to recognize the woods used in a piece of furniture is a great help in assessing its age, place of origin and relative value, but even professionals are sometimes bemused when faced with a rarity.

The descriptions which follow, (arranged alphabetically), taken with the selection of illustrations, can only be a starting point for acquiring an expertise in recognizing woods. There is no substitute for practice and experience.

Much depends on the direction in which the timber has been sawn: a board with the grain running lengthwise would look very different from a piece cut from the same tree but across the grain, to exhibit the annual rings, or from the gnarled growths that produce burr (or 'burl') woods, used mainly for veneers.

As a first step, it is worth becoming familiar with the appearance of as many raw woods as possible, but bearing in mind that they change colour dramatically by treatment with oil, wax, varnish and stain. On each of the following three pages, and on pages 14-15, pairs of circular photographs illustrate just how dramatic this difference can be for four commonly encountered types of wood.

Not only man-made finishes, but natural agents can dramatically change the appearance of raw wood. Strong sunlight will bleach them, a smoky atmosphere may darken them; even in ideal conditions, they are mellowed by age until, finally, by combining some or all of these influences with an accretion of honest dirt, they acquire that magic glow, deep and rich – hard to describe and hard to fake – called 'patina'.

With the exception of the hardwoods used for Chinese furniture – a specialized subject not covered in these pages, with a vocabulary all its own – the following list includes most timbers likely to be encountered in the search for antique furniture in Europe, including the British Isles, and North America.

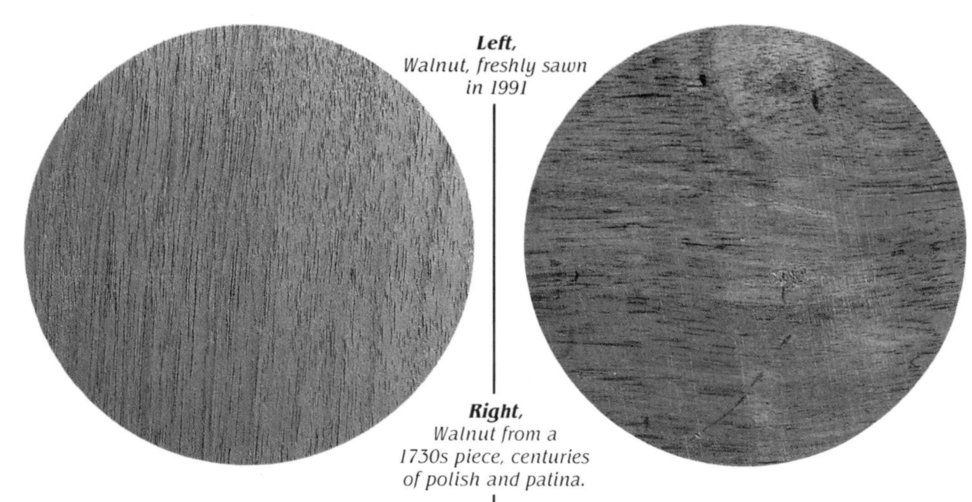

Left, *Walnut, freshly sawn in 1991*

Right, *Walnut from a 1730s piece, centuries of polish and patina.*

Acacia Introduced to Europe from North America. Dull yellow with brown markings. Used in the 18thC, as a substitute for banding satinwood.

Alder Grows in marshy soil, resists wet rot. Used for rails of stick-back chairs as an alternative to beech or birch.

Alkanet The henna plant; tincture of alkanet root is used to stain linseed oil dark red – the usual way of darkening mahogany in the 18thC. (In the 19thC potassium dichromateand potassium permanganese replaced alkanet.)

Amaranth See **Purpleheart.**

Amboyna Grown in the West Indies. Yellow-brown 'bird's eye' figure, used as veneer.

Apple Used by English country craftsmen in the 17th- 18thC for chair frames, spindles.

Arbutus See **Strawberry wood**.

Ash Widely grown. Very pale yellow with long, irregular brown grain. Tough, pliable, much used for country furniture, for example, the backs of Windsor chairs.

Avodiae From the Ivory Coast. Golden yellow, highly figured. Often mistaken for satinwood. Used as veneer in the 19thC. Very small pores; polishes beautifully.

Basswood See **Lime**.

Beech Grows world-wide. Brownish-white with distinctive speckles. Much used for seat-rails because it will not split easily when tacked; also for areas intended for gilding, and turned legs of country chairs.

Birch Common in Europe and America. Pale yellow. 'Satin birch' veneer with rippled markings is a substitute for satinwood. Birch rods, strong and pliable, are used for bentwood furniture. A common material for plywood.

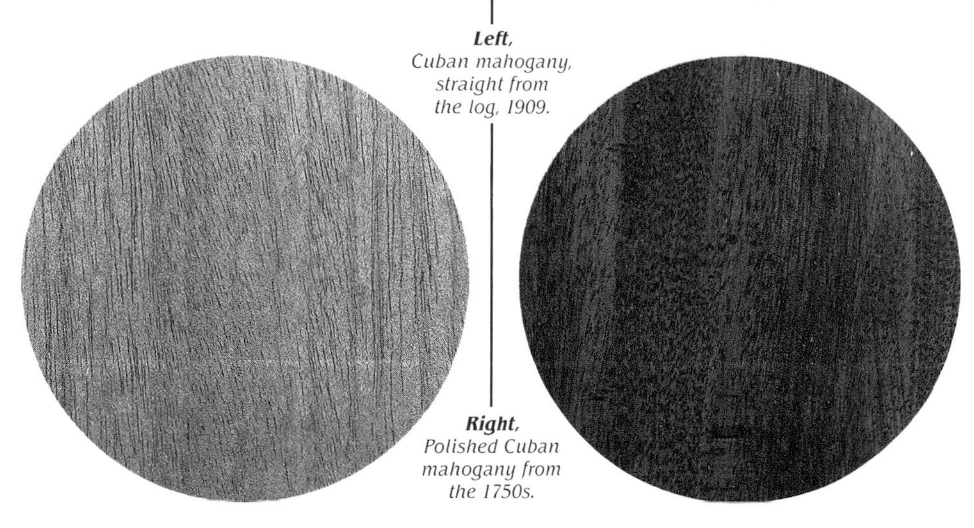

Left, *Cuban mahogany, straight from the log, 1909.*

Right, *Polished Cuban mahogany from the 1750s.*

Bog Oak Oak that has been buried in peat bog and become almost black; used for solid inlay in the 16th-17thC and for ornately carved furniture in the 19thC.
Bog Yew Irish yew, blackened by burial in peat bog, used in the same way as bog oak in the 19thC.
Bois Clairs Various pale woods, for example satin birch, cherry, fashionable in the Biedermeier period.
Bois Durci Wood-based plastic material, invented in France 1855, used to imitate carved ebony ornamentation on furniture.
Bois Violet See **Kingwood.**
Box Widely grown as shrubs or hedges, its narrow diameter makes it suitable for

Tulipwood, freshly sawn in 1991 – almost garish purple streaks.

stringing – narrow inlaid lines. Very pale, close-grained, and very hard.
Brazilwood (Braziletto) Bright orange with dark red stripes. Used for inlay in the 17thC; occasionally for marquetry in the 18th-19thC.
Burr ('burl' in the U.S.A.) Cut from abnormal growths on trunks or roots of trees – walnut, yew, elm, oak, ash. Usually cut into veneers but curiously marked pieces are sometimes used in the solid by country craftsmen, for example as seats of chairs.
Butternut Variety of American walnut used for much country furniture.
Calamander See **Ebony**. Also known as **Coromandel**.
Camphor From the East Indies. Pale brown, not strongly marked. Used for clothes chests because of its moth-repellant aroma, also for early-19thC portable writing desks, military chests.
Canary Pale wood, usually cut into veneers, stained red and used as a substitute for mahogany. Figure lacks depth.
Cane Obtained from rattan palm grown in Malay Peninsula. Split cane first imported into Europe mid-17thC, used by specialist cane-chair makers.
Cedar West Indies, Honduras: red-brown, open-grained, aromatic; used for chests, shelves in linen cupboards, drawer sides in the mid-18thC. Virginian pencil cedar (close-grained) used mainly for small drawers and pigeon holes in bureaux. See

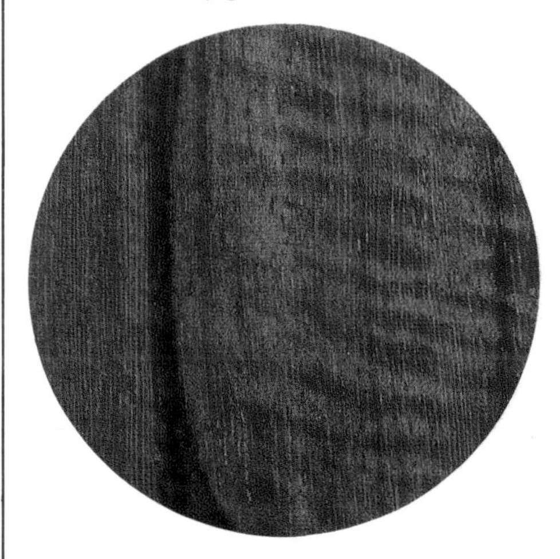

Tulipwood from an 18thC piece, showing the original finish.

also **Juniper.**
Cherry Widely grown. Yellow/pink/brown. Wild cherry (*merisier*) much used by country craftsmen, especially in France, Austria; also for Biedermeier furniture.
Chestnut Sweet (Spanish) chestnut, light brown, widely used in 17thC and later as an alternative to oak. Horse chestnut is light yellow with a pink tint, close-grained, soft, used for turning and carving.
Citrus (lemon wood) Mediterranean. Polished to soft brown, fine straight grain. Used as veneer by the 18thC French *ébénistes.*
Coromandel See **Ebony.**
Crabwood From Brazil. Red-brown, straight-grained with ribbon markings.

Used as a substitute for mahogany and often wrongly called 'Brazilian mahogany'.
Curl Feathery markings, usually the result of cutting across junction of stem and branch. Typically **mahogany**.
Cypress Grows in southern Europe and Asia Minor. Red-brown, close-grained, very durable, aromatic and repellant to moths. Used in Ancient Egypt for mummy cases, valued as a rare wood in the Middle Ages, but in general use for chests in the 16thC, especially in Italy. Shakespeare mentions 'cypress chests' in *The Taming of the Shrew.*
Deal Generic term for coniferous woods. In 1803, Sheraton wrote 'fir or pine timber cut into thin portions are called deals.'

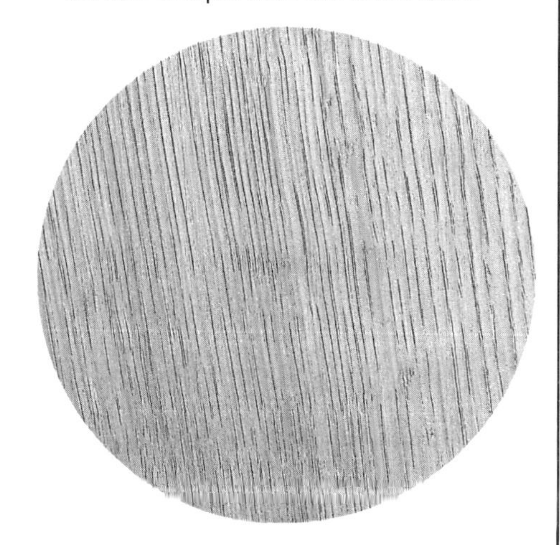

Oak, freshly sawn.

Dogwood Small tree providing red-yellow heart surrounded by yellow sapwood, used for turnings and, in the 16th/17thC, inlay.
Ebony Black variety from Madagascar and Mauritius used in the Ancient World and in Europe from the 17thC in both solid and veneer forms. Figured ebony with light brown or grey stripes (**Calamander** or **Coromandel**) from Ceylon used mainly as veneer, late-18thC. **Macassar** ebony from Celibes, with black stripes, used in Art Deco pieces.
Elm Pale yellow, fairly hard, broad grain. Much used for country furniture, typically in chair seats, table tops. **Wych Elm** has knotty growths. See also **Yoke Elm**.
Eucalyptus See **Jarrah.**

Fig Used for furniture by Ancient Egyptians and, like most other fruitwoods, by country craftsmen in Spain, Greece, when an old tree is past its prime.
Gonçalo Alves Often mistaken for **rosewood** (its importers could not tell the difference) and so used in the 19thC as if it was rosewood, though it has finer pores. Used in the solid for chairs; veneers for cabinets, tables.
Harewood See **Maple**. True harewood is known as concha satinwood from San Domingo.
Hickory North American. Tough, pliant, varies from white to yellow-brown or pale red. Much used in New England for chair spindles and bent work.

Oak from the 1620s, wax polish and age forming genuine patination.

Holly Widely grown. Very white with small speckles, used mainly for inlay.
Hornbeam Widely grown, yellow-white, very strong. Used for turning utensils and shaping agricultural implements, but occasionally for parts of furniture. Sometimes stained black to imitate ebony.
Jacaranda Brazilian rosewood much used in Portugal. Brown with darker stripes.
Jarrah From western Australia. A variety of eucalyptus. Reddish brown, darkens with age to resemble mahogany.
Juniper A variety of cedar, widely grown. Rich brown, usually small girth suitable for 'small carvings and images' (J. Evelyn, 1679) but occasionally made into larger pieces. See also Cedar.
Kingwood Known as **Princewood** or **Bois**

Violet when first imported from Brazil in the 17thC. Deep, rich purple-brown, straight line markings. Fades to pale yellow-brown. Much used in the 18thC for crossbanding, especially in France. Often confused with rosewood, to which it is related botanically.

Laburnum Yellow with brown streaks. Used from 17thC mainly as 'oyster pieces', veneers obtained by cutting across grain of saplings or small branches to reveal the annual rings. Looks like a dish of oysters when pieces are assembled.

Lacewood See **Plane**.

Lignum vitae Very hard, heavier than water. Dark brown heartwood. Sapwood light yellow. Very distinctive. Sometimes used in veneer form on furniture, but mainly for turning, especially apothecaries' mortars. Believed to have medicinal properties when first imported from Cuba and West Indies in the 17thC.

Lime Widely distributed. White, soft, almost no cross grain, mellows to light brown. Favoured by carvers, especially in Germany and by the school of Grinling Gibbons in England. The American variety – **Basswood** or **American Whitewood** – has a slightly green tinge in raw state.

Mahogany 'Spanish' mahogany came, not from Spain but from Spanish colonies in Central America and the West Indies. It arrived in Europe in the 16thC and was used in Spain soon after, but (with rare exceptions) not in England and North America until about 1725 and in France about 1780. Jamaican merchants supplied Europe with indigenous timber and with imports from Cuba and Honduras, thus leading to confusion as to origin. *Jamaican* mahogany is hard, heavy, durable, light red when cut; usually close, straight grain, sometimes figured. *Cuban* is light red in raw state, and darkens on exposure to air but no further after polishing. Hard and heavy, sometimes with curls in grain providing finely figured veneers, for example 'fiddleback'. Imported into England in large quantities from 1750. *San Domingo*: hard, dark red becoming darker on exposure; smooth, takes high polish; mostly straight-grained but sometimes has beautiful figure. *Honduras*: softer than Cuban, red-brown, becomes pale on exposure. Usually lacks figure. Sheraton described it as having 'black or grey spots . . . and of a spongy appearance.'

W. African ('Gambia'): imported into Europe after about 1825. Usually lacking in interest, but durable and more easily worked than 'Spanish'.

Maple Many varieties, widely grown. *Sugar maple*: From North America. Yellow-brown with dark lines and decorative figure. Much used for Early American furniture. 'Bird's eye' effect, much prized for veneers, caused by buds that cannot emerge through bark and cause small whorls in grain. *Sycamore*: Mainland Europe, British Isles. White, close-grained, durable. Used from Middle Ages onwards by turners and joiners – mentioned in Chaucer's *House of Fame*, about 1380. Many British country tables – especially Welsh – have sycamore tops. *Harewood*: sycamore cut into veneers and dyed grey-green, used in association with satinwood, late-18thC.

Oak Many varieties, widely grown. Most are pale yellow-white to light brown, turning very dark in smoky atmosphere, bleached to silvery colour if left outdoors – 'weathered oak' – not to be confused with the 'silver grain' of riven oak – split into segments vertically at right angles to expose the medullary rays. This creates an effect of silvery, diagonal flecks – beautiful in themselves but, as they shrink less than the surrounding timber, they eventually stand slightly proud of the surface – enough to cause veneer laid over them to crack. Oak was the principal timber for

*Grand marquetry furniture can display dozens of different woods, but this 18thC chinoiserie cabinet on a stand (whole piece illustrated **opposite**) is remarkable in employing different woods as show pieces in their own right. Each of the hundred-odd drawers (there are additional drawers obscured by doors in the left and right 'wings') is veneered with a different wood, or with woods cut for differing effects. The cabinet well illustrates the problems facing amateurs in recognizing woods, for even experts find it impossible to positively identify all the woods in the piece. As an exercise in getting to know woods, try – with the help of a dealer or restorer, and the verbal descriptions on these pages – to put a name to some of the drawers shown **left**. The cabinet, presented to the Lady Lever Art Gallery, Port Sunlight, Liverpool, by Lord Leverhume, was in the collection of Percy Dean sold in 1909. Its earlier history, and maker, are unknown.*

furniture in northern Europe until about 1700 and long continued as the staple material in rural areas.

Olive Southern Europe. Greenish-yellow with black markings – appearance resembles horn. Used mainly as veneers, and late-17th/early-18thC oyster pieces, especially when tree has been **Pollarded**.

Padouk Burma. Introduced into Europe early-18thC. Hard, heavy, often confused with rosewood which it resembles, but has silkier texture. Used in veneers and in the solid, especially for chairs, mid-18thC.

Palisander See **Purpleheart.**

Palm See **Cane**.

Partridge From Venezuela. Often wrongly called 'brown ebony'. Heavy, hard timber, the straight grain marked with brown and red streaks giving a game-bird appearance. Used for inlay, parquetry and veneering in late-17th and late-18thC.

Pear Pressed into service for furniture-making, especially in rural areas, typically tops for French farmhouse tables, chairs in England, south of Yorkshire. Also cut into veneers and stained black as substitute for ebony, used on clock cases, but naturally pale.

Pigeon See Zebra.

Pine Very widely grown. The term is often applied indiscriminately to other coniferous woods – fir, larch, some kinds of cedar. In Britain, Scotch (or Scots) pine – soft, white and straight-grained – is used for construction, especially drawer-sides, backs of carcases; as foundation for veneers; and for gilding or for 'carvers' pieces', for instance ornate mirrors, console tables. In Alpine regions and Scandinavia, pine was the usual wood for vernacular furniture, often painted. In North America, pitch pine – very resinous, yellow with light brown grain; large trees provided tops for New England tables.

Plane A variety of maple, originally from eastern Europe. Yellow-white when taken from a young tree, brown from older growth. Close-grained. When cut into quartered veneers it exhibits a lacy figure and is known as **Lacewood**, popular with Art Deco designers. In the late 18thC, plane was used in the solid as a substitute for beech in painted chairs and frames of folding tables.

Plum Hard, heavy, varying from yellow to brown, some-times taking on a purple hue with age and regular polishing. Mainly used in country work in the 17th to 19thC, often with other fruitwoods.

Pollard Wood taken from stumps left when crown of tree has been cut back, causing abnormalities that produce curious veneers. 'Pollard oak' is usually a misnomer.

Poplar Widely grown, especially in France and eastern Europe. Soft, creamy-yellow, sometimes with grey tint. Often used for drawer linings in France; as principal wood and veneers in Russia; for inlay in Britain.

Purpleheart From Brazil. Open grain, purple in raw state going darker on exposure. Used for banding, 18thC.

Rosewood Many varieties. Those used in European furniture mainly from Brazil, some from East Indies. Varies from light brown with dark markings to near-black. Widely used as veneer and – especially in Portugal where Brazilian variety was known as **Jacaranda** – in the solid. No connection with roses, other than the scent emitted when worked.

Rosewood veneer, unpolished.

Sabicu Mainly from Cuba and sometimes known as Cuban rosewood. It looks very like mahogany. Very hard, and so durable that, when used for stairs in the Great Exhibition (London, 1851), it showed little sign of wear after six months of constant public use. Used occasionally in 18thC furniture as a substitute for mahogany. Sometimes known as horseflesh wood.

Sandalwood India, Pacific Islands. Pale yellow-brown darkening to red-brown.

Aromatic. Used mainly for small pieces, for example boxes, jewel cabinets.

Sapele ('Sapele mahogany' or 'Gold Coast Cedar') West Africa. Light red-brown, hard but easily worked. Much used in later 20thC in both solid and veneer forms.

Sapwood Soft, whitish wood found between bark and heart of any tree. Very prone to attack by **Woodworm**.

Satin Birch See **Birch**.

Satin Walnut Red gumtree, southern states of North America. Red-brown with darker stripes, used late-19th/early-20thC for cheaper furniture, especially bedroom suites.

Satinwood East and West Indies. Varies from pale golden colour with beautifully

Rosewood veneer with its original 1830s polish.

rippled figure to orange-yellow reminiscent of marmalade. West Indian satinwood had the better figure. Widely used as veneers in late-18thC, especially in Britain with marquetry decoration, in Holland in association with lacquer panels. San Domingo variety is silver grey when fully seasoned, sometimes used as, and called 'harewood' (see **Maple**).

Snakewood From Brazil. Pale yellow with serrated mark ings, used in 18thC for marquetry and banding.

Stinkwood South Africa. Figure resembling walnut, but belongs to laurel family. Brown to black, close-grained, smooth. Used for building and furniture since Dutch Colonial days. Has a bad smell when first felled.

Strawberrywood Southern Europe and south-west Ireland. A variety of *arbutus* that has berries resembling strawberries. Light yellow-brown with distinctive dark flecks. Used in Killarney area, mid-19thC, for marquetry on table tops and trays.

Sycamore See **Maple**.

Teak Two distinct types, Indian and African, both reddish brown, greasy-looking when planed, pungent odour in raw state. Very durable, weather-resistant, used in West for garden furniture, ships' fittings.

Thuja (thuya) African and American varieties, mainly African used for furniture, in form of veneered panels. Golden brown when polished, with small bird's eye figure, which looks like a **burr** figure.

Tulip From Brazil. Name derives from appearance – vivid pink-yellow-brown. Fades to light yellow-brown, pinky-red stripes. Used as veneer, mainly for bandings.

Yew Hard, close-grained, pliable; pink-heartwood, white sapwood fading to golden yellow-brown. Pleasing figure with small, distinctive knots. Used for country furniture (typically Windsor chairs in England) and as a veneer (burr form) in the 18thC for sophisticated pieces.

Walnut Two main kinds used for furniture: *European*: golden brown, sometimes close-grained and, when used in the solid, unspectacular; sometimes boldly marked with dark and light irregular stripes. Much more evident and attractive when, from the 17thC onwards, it was cut into veneers (especially prized when **Burred**) *American black walnut* (Virginian): dark and mostly straight-grained, imported into England in the early-18thC when a severe winter destroyed thousands of European trees (see also **Butternut**).

Willow Widely grown, mainly for **Pollarding** to harvest young shoots for basket work. Willow pegs used in Early English oak and country furniture. The trunk was sometimes hollowed and made into dug-out chairs.

Yoke Elm See **Hornbeam**.

Zebrano (zingana) West Africa. Golden yellow, dark brown markings similar to figured ebony. Used in veneer form, 19th-20thC.

Zebra (tigerwood, pigeonwood) Red-brown, dark stripes. Used 18th-19thC in veneer form, sometimes over large surfaces but mainly for banding.

INTRODUCTION

FINISHES

Typical finishes are mentioned throughout the book for every type of furniture. The following explains the background and the meaning of the terms used.

Varnish: Until the 17thC, oil varnish was made by dissolving a resin – for example, copal – in boiled oil of linseed, poppy, walnut or juniper. From then on, seed-lac, or shell-lac (shellac), dissolved in sprits of wine, largely, but not entirely, replaced oil varnish. In the 18thC, the quality of varnishes improved, the finest being *vernis Martin*, patented by the Martin brothers and made in various colours.

Wax polish: Wood primed with linseed oil and polished with beeswax dissolved in turpentine,often after varnishing. Before the invention of sandpaper and glasspaper, excessive wax was removed with brick dust sieved through a stocking.

French polish: Introduced in France in the late-18thC, but not widely employed elsewhere until the early-19thC. An 1830 recipe specifies one pint of spirits of wine, a quarter-ounce each of gum-copal and gum-arabic, and an ounce of shellac, applied with a 'rubber' made of cotton waste, after filling the grain with varnish or, later, whiting (which shows through with the passage of time). Successive coats were sanded down to a hard finish.

Stains: Vegetable stains, mostly oil-based, to darken or colour wood, have been used at least since the 17thC, often to 'counterfeit and deceive the unwary' (John Evelyn, 1664). Beech was stained to simulate walnut with juice from the green husks of walnuts; pear-wood was ebonised with a stain made from logwood (*Haematoxylon campechianum*). Alkanet root, used in the 18thC to redden mahogany and to imitate it, was replaced in the early-19thC, first by potassium bichromate, later by potassium permanganate. (The latter resulted in a purple tint.) Sycamore was stained with oxide of iron to produce the grey-green of harewood.

Paint: Painting in bright colours was widely practised from the Middle Ages onwards, using opaque colours bound with a medium such as honey and water. Oil-bound paints were used from the 17thC onwards.

Japanning: In the 17thC, oriental lacquer derived from the sap of the lac-tree (*Rhus vernicifera*) was imitated with coloured varnishes made from gum-lac, seed-lac or shellac; all were resins deposited on trees by an insect, *Coccus lacca*.

Gilding: Water gilding more usual because it could be burnished or left matt. It was also more expensive than oil gilding which could not be burnished. The ground for gilding was prepared with several coats of gesso (plaster mixed with size), coated with coloured mordant (blue, red or yellow) and, in the case of water gilding, wetted before an application of gold leaf over very small areas at a time. A cheap substitute for gilding was 'Dutch gold', using copper in place of gold leaf.

THREATS TO WOOD

Woodworm The common name for several wood-boring beetles that lay eggs in crevices of woodwork. The eggs hatch out as larvae that tunnel their way through the wood. The adults emerge as beetles through 'wormholes' on the surface, and lay eggs so that the life cycle is repeated unless checked. *Treatment:* Proprietory products are effective if used repeatedly until no fresh holes or tell-tale powder is seen. Some timbers, for example pine, walnut, elm and beech, and most sapwoods, are more vulnerable than others. Mahogany and teak are virtually immune. In general, it is best to avoid pieces that are badly riddled, but it is difficult to furnish a home with antiques – or even with modern furniture – without incurring the risk to some extent. Keeping furniture clean and well-polished helps to remove the eggs.

Central heating Furniture, especially if veneered, suffers from lack of moisture in the air. To avoid splits, cracks and the lifting of veneers, provide adequate and consistent humidification. Simple humidifiers hung on panel radiators provide excellent protection.

Sunlight, especially through south- or west-facing windows and glass doors will fade, dry out, warp, twist or crack solid or veneered furniture. Drop-leaf tables (pembroke and sofa) are particularly vulnerable, also tripod and tea tables.

Glass tops have a tendency to attract moisture. Veneers beneath glass can lift.

ENGLISH

GUIDE TO PERIODS AND STYLES: ENGLISH

English furniture styles developed in ways broadly in line with those of mainland Europe, but were interpreted in a distinctive fashion. There were also many regional variations within the British Isles – a term that once encompassed England, Wales, Scotland and Ireland.

In England itself, regional accents are marked by the differences between, say, North Country chairs and those of the West Country; Salisbury and Norwich were noted centres of production at an early date.

Wales retained the dresser and the press cupboard as status symbols long after they had ceased to be fashionable in England, and further distinctions are to be drawn between those of North and South Wales.

In late-18thC Scotland, Edinburgh was producing sophisticated furniture, some of it with distinctive differences from that of London.

In the mid-18thC, Irish furniture was so extravagant in its use of richly carved mahogany – especially for side tables on cabriole legs – that a whole class is described as 'Irish Chippendale'.

The following summary concentrates, in common with the rest of the book, on the mainstream.

If you are a 'mainland' European (or an American) you will find it useful to understand the broad relationships between British and mainland European styles; and of course vice-versa. This is the purpose of these summaries, and of those on p. 188-197 and on p. 272-275.

***Right**, oak dresser from south Wales, about 1800.*

Christie's

***Left**, oak armchair, south Lancashire or north Cheshire, about 1680.*

Christie's

MEDIEVAL

Romanesque Imported to Britain by the Normans following the conquest in 1066. Rounded arches – a typical Romanesque feature – occur on chests as late as the 17thC, but the few examples still in existence which date from earlier than 1300 are simply constructed and mostly carved with roundels bearing little relation to Romanesque architecture.

Gothic About 1300 to 1550. The change from Romanesque was gradual. Panelled construction from about 1480, the panels often carved with linenfold. The coronation chair at Westminster Abbey has a back with a pointed arch; made in 1296 by Master Walter of Durham, it was the first English piece firmly attributable to a named maker. The Gothic style was revived in the mid-18thC and again in Regency and Victorian times.

ELIZABETHAN

Renaissance When Elizabeth I came to the throne in 1558, most furniture was functional and plain. After 1570, a version of Renaissance style owing more to France and the Netherlands than to Italy found expression in fat turnings surmounted by Ionic capitals, solid inlay, carved caryatids, strapwork, split baluster turnings.

JACOBEAN

Strictly speaking, the reign of James I, 1603-25 but also used to cover that of Charles I (1625-49). Geometric mouldings, split balusters, bobbin-turnings; popular until about 1720.

Christie's

Carved and panelled oak coffer, about 1650.

CROMWELLIAN OR COMMONWEALTH

Plain mid-17thC furniture said to be made for Puritans. Square-backed chairs on turned legs, with leather upholstery fixed with large-headed nails; so-called 'refectory' tables on turned legs. Wood is generally oak, but solid walnut occurs.

RESTORATION

Sometimes known as Carolean, in reference to Charles II, restored to the throne in 1660. Also covers the reign of James II, 1685-9. Dominant style is **baroque** but more Franco-Dutch than Italian. Twist legs, carved scrolls, caned seats, veneering, floral marquetry, japanning. Skilled French workers sought refuge in Britain when Louis XIV of France ceased to protect Protestants, 1685.

Japanned 'oriental' cabinet on gilded stand, about 1670-1680.

Bonhams

WILLIAM AND MARY

More foreign craftsmen (Dutch and French) arrived in Britain following the accession of William of Orange and his wife Mary, the daughter of James II, in 1689. Fine cabinet-

William & Mary walnut bureau on stand, about 1690.

Sotheby's

making, walnut and ebony veneers, floral and 'seaweed' marquetry. Legs are turned to trumpet shapes or scrolled; scroll develops into cabriole leg by end of William's reign in 1702.

QUEEN ANNE

During her reign, 1702-14, the cabriole leg dominated; surfaces were veneered with walnut, but marquetry became less evident. English craftsmen, having acquired foreign skills, adapted these to their own style.

Queen Anne walnut tallboy, 1710-1720.

Sotheby's

EARLY GEROGIAN

George I and early years of George II until about 1730; mainly a continuation of the Queen Anne style, but rather heavier. Claw-and-ball feet became the fashionable termination of the cabriole leg. Architect William Kent designed Italianate baroque furniture as a dramatic contrast to cool Palladian interiors.

Sotheby's

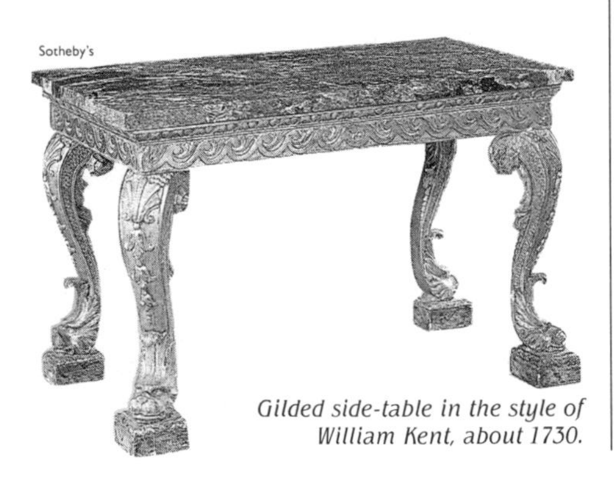

Gilded side-table in the style of William Kent, about 1730.

MID-GEORGIAN

George II, 1730-60 and the first years of George III. Mahogany replaced walnut as the fashionable wood. In 1754, Chippendale's designs appear; Ince and Mayhew's, 1759-62. Ribbon-back chairs, ornate gilt mirrors and console tables expressed the English interpretation of rococo. Some designs closely followed French (Louis XV) fashions. Chinoiseries popular. Gothic style revived.

Mid-Georgian Chippendale-style mahogany chair, about 1750.

Sotheby's

LATE GEORGIAN

The George III period lasted from 1765 to 1800, but the term is sometimes extended back to 1730. First came the neo-classical style led by Adam – vertical lines, ovals, circles, columns, urns, disciplined carving, gilding and painting related to the Louis XVI style. Designs by Hepplewhite appear 1788, those of Sheraton 1791-4, providing a domestic, middle-class version of neo-classicism.

Late-Georgian Hepplewhite-style mahogany chair, about 1780.

Sotheby's

REGENCY AND GEORGE IV

About 1800-30. Sometimes included with Late Georgian. Furniture has much in common with French Empire style. Greek, Roman and Egyptian models used – sabre legs on chairs, lion monopodia, sphinx mounts. Thomas Hope and George Smith head the list of designers, some featuring a second Gothic revival; also Chinese and Indian styles.

Sotheby's

Regency rosewood secretaire, in French Empire style, about 1820.

WILLIAM IV AND EARLY VICTORIAN

Much furniture made 1830-50 was still neo-classical, but heavier than Regency; some affinity with Charles X (French Restauration), Biedermeier in Austria and Germany. Parallel with this are the Gothic revival led by Pugin and the rococo revival by commercial manufacturers making balloon-back chairs, asymmetrical *chaises longues* on cabriole legs. Increasing use of machines.

MID-VICTORIAN

The Great Exhibition at Crystal Palace, 1851, brought Continental exhibitors to London, stimulating an eclectic taste for revivals of almost all historic styles, and imitated in poorer quality, mass-produced furniture. Massive dining and bedroom suites; but parlour pieces more elegant, with some sofas and chairs fringed and deep-buttoned in Napoleon III style. There were serious attempts at reviving medieval craftsmanship by reformers, such as Morris, Burgess, Talbert. Godwin experimented with Japanese concepts.

Sotheby's

Mid-Victorian rococo-style mahogany extending table, about 1860.

LATE VICTORIAN, ART NOUVEAU AND EDWARDIAN

Heavy Victorian styles persisted until about 1910, along with reproductions of English, French and Italian historic types, but the Arts and Crafts Movement, led by Mackintosh, Ashbee, Baillie Scott and Voysey introduced new ideas in sympathy with some aspects of European art nouveau, to which are often married commercial products that are partly an offshoot of the Edwardian revival of Sheraton styles in mahogany with inlaid decoration.

Christie's

Oak buffet by M.H. Baillie Scott, about 1897.

MODERNIST AND ART DECO

The period between the two world wars, marked by genuine desire for greater simplicity and honest, economically made furniture of the type produced by Heal and Russell, but in competition with mass-produced junk on the one hand and finely made but expensive products on the other. The term Art Deco – like most stylistic labels – was unknown at the time the furniture was being made. It derives from the 1925 *Arts Décoratifs* exhibition in Paris, and only came to be applied to the style in the 1960s.

BEDS, TESTER

About

1500-1690

Christie's

Right, very grand late-16th/early-17thC bed with some later restorations.

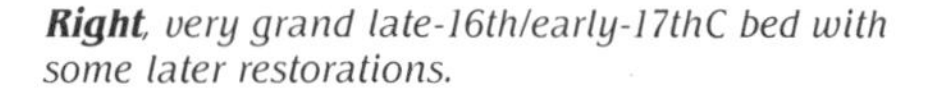

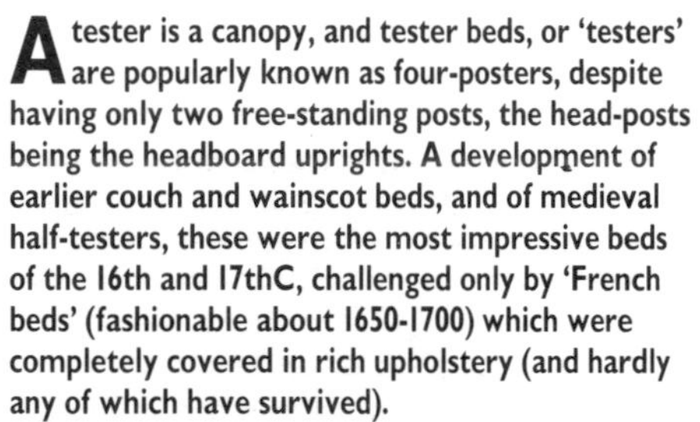

A tester is a canopy, and tester beds, or 'testers' are popularly known as four-posters, despite having only two free-standing posts, the head-posts being the headboard uprights. A development of earlier couch and wainscot beds, and of medieval half-testers, these were the most impressive beds of the 16th and 17thC, challenged only by 'French beds' (fashionable about 1650-1700) which were completely covered in rich upholstery (and hardly any of which have survived).

Testers themselves are exceptionally rare in their original form; many were remodelled or reduced in size when 'Jacobean' furniture was fashionable in the 19thC.

Below, a fully upholstered 'French' bed.

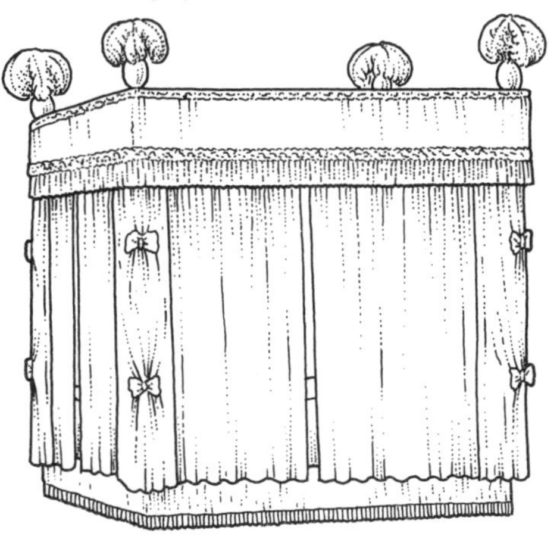

STYLE AND APPEARANCE

A standard, genuine tester-bed comprises: **1** Headboard, divided horizontally into two panelled sections and a deep frieze, the lower section (hidden by bedding) plain, and the upper section and frieze elaborately carved. **2** Panelled tester (or canopy) carved with repeated designs and bordered by a cornice and carved frieze. **3** Bedstock, with interlaced ropes to support the bedding. **4** Two foot-posts, the lower parts in square section and the upper turned with columns above distinctive cup-and-cover mouldings. Cups were

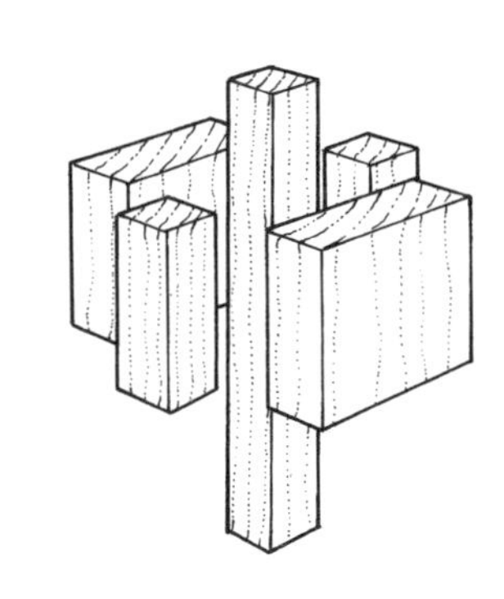

*Cup-and-cover leg: **above** the start; **opposite**, the finished leg.*

broadest on Elizabethan beds, more vase-shaped on later examples.

As time went on, testers became increasingly 'architectural'. Carved linenfold and Gothic architectural motifs were gradually replaced during the 16thC by Renaissance designs which commonly featured arcading, pilasters (sometimes in the form of terminal figures), strapwork, lozenges, scrolls and full and half roundels.

MATERIALS

Surviving examples are mainly oak. Occasionally walnut. Holly, box, bog-oak, poplar and sycamore used for inlay, joined around 1600 by imported ebony, ivory and mother-of-pearl.

CONSTRUCTION

Framed and panelled with pegged mortise-and-tenon joints. Rails pierced and grooved horizontally for bed cords. Side rails occasionally pierced vertically to hold wooden staves to secure bedding. Iron curtain rings on rods on inner side of tester frieze.

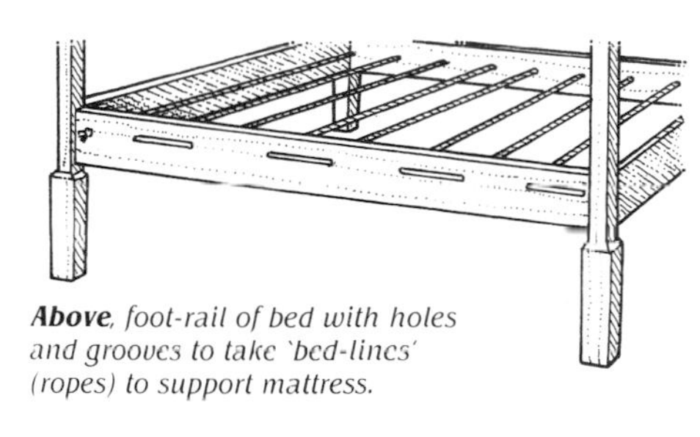

Above, *foot-rail of bed with holes and grooves to take 'bed-lines' (ropes) to support mattress.*

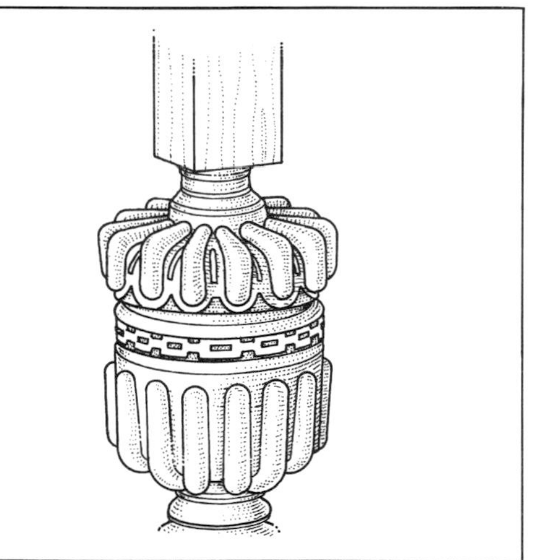

Late-16th/early-17thC tester bed with fine marquetry decoration.

Christie's

DECORATION

Mostly carving, at its n[illegible]uberant on Elizabethan pieces. From around 1600, occasionally inlay of simple floral patterns, and traces of painted or gilt decoration.

FINISH

Originally varnish, later wax polish. Paint or pigment rare. Either wax polish or thick, dark stain on Victorian reproductions.

RELATIVE VALUES

Late Victorian reproductions are relatively cheap. Near-intact Elizabethan originals are very expensive. Later alteration need not affect value to a great extent.

BEDS THROUGH THE CENTURIES

From the Middle Ages until the mid-19thC, the beds of prosperous households were valuable items, symbols of their owner's status. Although the wooden framework became a feature, the rich fabrics suspended from their canopies were the tester's chief glory. Once these had deteriorated, the frames were generally replaced.

Most surviving beds from this period are of this grand type. (The majority slept on simpler versions, or on plain box or low-post 'stump' beds.) During the first half of the 19thC countless wooden beds were destroyed in favour of metal in an attempt to exterminate the ubiquitous bed-bugs.

BEDS, FOUR-POST

About

1700-1800

In the early 18thC, up to about 1730, the grandest beds were the immensely tall and richly upholstered four-post and half-tester type introduced from the European mainland, a few of which have survived in stately homes. From around 1730, these went out of fashion, and the standard bed in households of substance was the four-poster. The richer the owner, the more lavish their decoration and hangings.

Many 18thC bed posts were later made into standard lamps and plant and candle stands.

***Right**, a 'state' bed, about 1695, very similar to contemporary designs by Marot.*

STYLE AND APPEARANCE

1700-1750: Full height panelled headboard with minimal carving. Sometimes a show-wood foot rail. Panelled tester gradually replaced by inner fabric covering or drapes. Generally a shallow frieze carved with classical ornament below straight cornice, often surmounted by bold gadrooning. High (sometimes 8-ft) posts divided into three sections – a column (often fluted) above a vase (popularly with acanthus carving) above initially a square foot, later, a cabriole leg with lion's paw or claw-and-ball feet.

1750-1765: Gradual reduction in height. Fashion for Gothic, rococo and chinoiserie designs brought elaborate gilded carving for headboard and cornice. Low, shaped headboard (separate from posts) backed by and sometimes covered in drapery. Fabric tester with shaped, usually serpentine, cornice, often elaborately scrolled. Frieze frequently absent. A popular design for posts was Gothic cluster columns above acanthus-carved vase and cabriole feet.

1765-1800: Generally no headboard, only drapery. Cornices simpler, but often still serpentine, or arched with corner vase finials. Shallow carved frieze. Domed canopies fashionable. Popularly fluted posts, generally more slender and tapering, above vases or urns on square feet. All parts painted or carved with neo-classical motifs such as anthemions, husks, paterae, or ribbons and garlands of flowers.

Rococo-style bed, posts concealed by hangings.

MATERIALS

Mostly mahogany (walnut until about 1730) joined after 1770 by satinwood. Generally beech, or rarely, oak, for parts concealed by upholstery, gilding, and so on.

George III mahogany four-post bed, about 1790.

CONSTRUCTION

Posts generally form continuous uprights from floor to cornice, with rails tenoned into them; sometimes secured by metal bolts rather than pegs, the holes concealed where necessary by decorative rosettes or suchlike. Bedding still mostly supported on ropes; wooden slats, running from side to side, were introduced around 1750.

DECORATION

Principally carving. Figuring of mahogany a decorative feature on panelled headboards. Japanned decoration for chinoiserie pieces around 1750-1765. Painted decoration fashionable after about 1775 on a painted or polished wood background.

FINISH

Wax polish; japanning, gilding, paint.

RELATIVE VALUES

Plain mahogany relatively cheap in four figures; up to five figures for later, painted and satinwood beds.

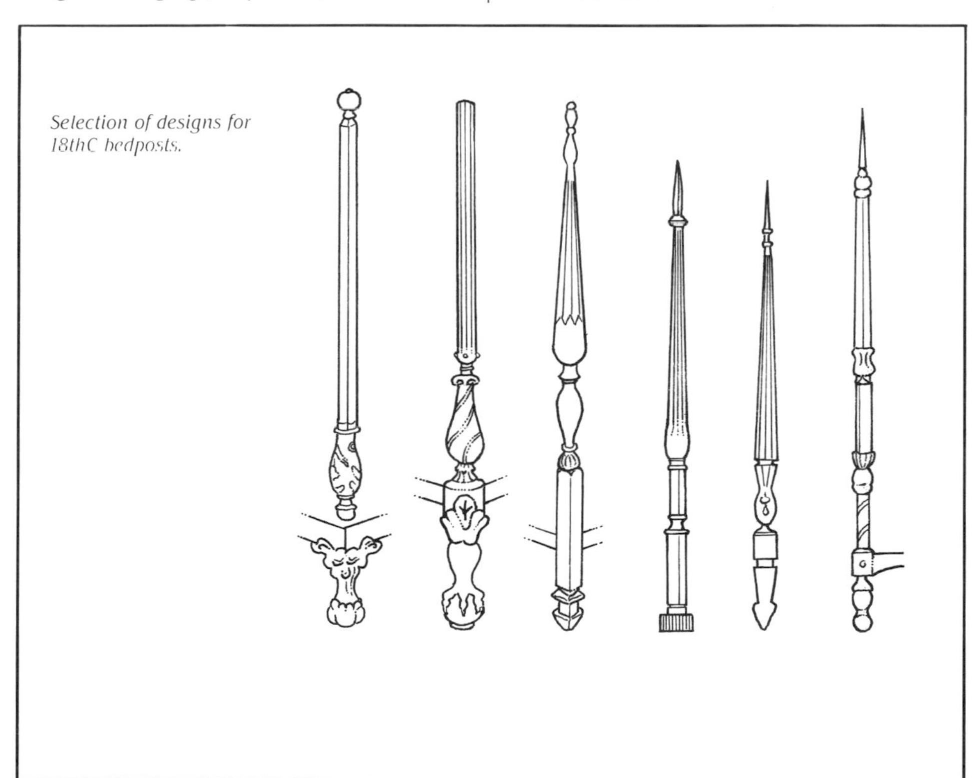

Selection of designs for 18thC bedposts.

BEDS, 19thC

Four-post frame with wagon-tilt canopy.

An enormous variety of beds were made in the 19thC. Concern for hygiene brought metal beds (see p. 28) and eventually the end of hangings. Single and twin beds arrived in the 1890s. There are fine 20thC reproductions.

STYLE AND APPEARANCE

Four main types:

Four-post, 1800-1860: Continuing classical designs but heavier. Bun feet, reeding and lotus flower vases common on posts. Decorative shaped head and footboards around 1850 (previously plain headboards only). Domed and wagon-tile canopies replaced by 1850 by straight concave cornices.

French beds (modern term *lit en bateau*), 1800-1840: In the Grecian style popular for all Regency and Empire furniture. Like a double-ended sofa; two scroll ends of equal height with deep, usually curved, show-wood sides. Placed side-on to wall, hangings suspended from pole or wooden canopy attached above. Many discarded when unfashionable, or converted into sofas. Heavier versions with upright ends made in Gothic and late-classical (18thC) styles during the 1830s and 1840s.

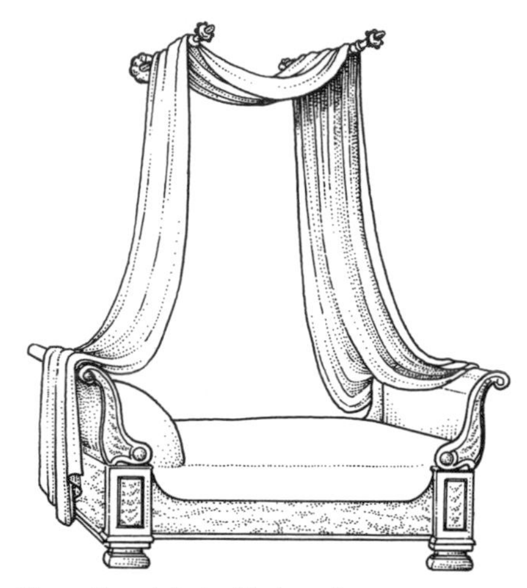
***Above**, French bed with draped canopy.*

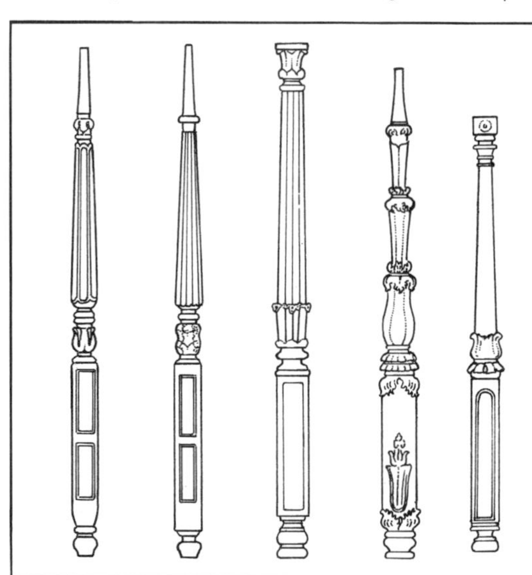
Selection of designs for 19thC bedposts.

Walnut half-tester with plain moulded cornice, about 1860.

Elizabethan-style carved bed, about 1840.

Half-testers, 1840-1880: Wooden D-shaped canopies, mostly with moulded cornice and plain concave frieze; occasionally carved ornament above. Tall, decorative panelled footboard only, many also D-shaped with turned, sometimes semi-free-standing posts and finials. Scrolling rococo revival ornament common until 1870s; after, more complex neo-classical carving pilasters, urns. Similar, but double-ended beds without canopy made after about 1875.

'Modern' designs, 1890-1915: Show arts and crafts influence. Double-ended, head usually higher than foot. Often square-sectioned horizontal and vertical members. Slatted ends of flat panels of veneer. Usually a metal mattress frame.

MATERIALS

Mahogany, with rosewood until 1840, walnut after. Oak for both Gothic and for later modern designs.

CONSTRUCTION

Screwed mortise-and-tenon joints, holes filled with decorative rosettes or, more commonly, wooden discs. French beds veneered. Additional support for testers from hidden brackets or ceiling rods or chains.

Mattress supports; stretched canvas, wooden slats. Wire mesh and springs on 'modern' beds which had metal rails dovetailing on to projecting metal brackets screwed to uprights.

DECORATION

Regency: metal mounts.

Victorian: Applied split mouldings and carving; figured veneer; inlay of contrasting woods, ivory, ebony or mother-of-pearl.

FINISH

Oil or wax polish; French polish on large areas; later oak pieces generally stained.

RELATIVE VALUES

Often large and cumbersome objects and never very popular, so prices generally low; almost always near the bottom of the four-figure range.

BEDS, BRASS AND IRON

About

1825-1900

First made during the 1820s, but not generally popular until about 1850. Considered a hygienic alternative to wood, used by all classes. Price was largely dictated by the amount of brass in the construction, the cheapest being all-iron or iron with brass knobs and end-rails, the most expensive all brass. The best (and largest number of) manufacturers werein Birmingham, most notably Peyton & Harlow and R.W. Winfield.

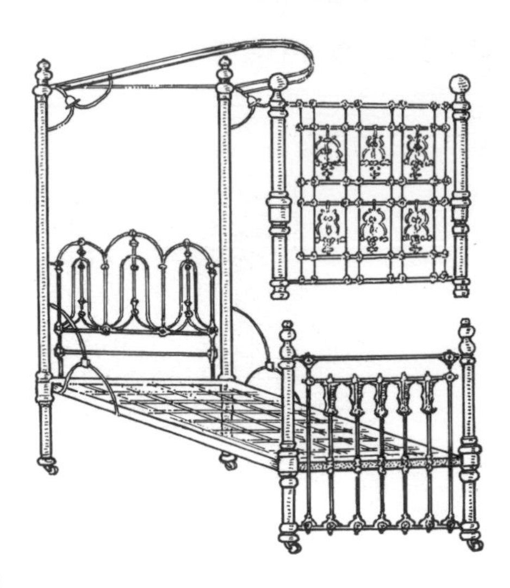

Half-tester with decorative ends.

STYLE AND APPEARANCE

Some four-post beds were made, but most were half-tester or had curtains hung from side wings. Straightforward double-ended beds without drapery were increasingly common after 1875.

Designs were variable, generally *not* following contemporary fashions. Most had a strong vertical and horizontal emphasis; some had fancy scrollwork. Cast decorative cornices were a rare bonus.

MATERIALS

Cast- and wrought-iron and taper brass tubing; after about 1860, brass-plated steel. Knobs and other ornament sometimes solid cast brass.

Standard double-ended bed showing metal strap frame for mattress.

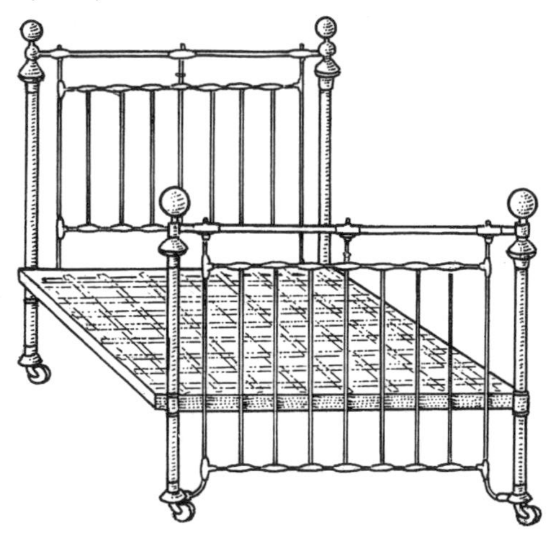

CONSTRUCTION

Parts slotted together, held in place by tension or by bolts, their ends concealed by screw-on decorative knobs or the like. Ornament sometimes welded on.

Mattress-frames were initially interwoven flat metal straps bolted to angled side rails; but by 1900 various wire mesh and spring arrangements were being hooked to the rails through small holes. Entire frame usually dovetailed on to uprights.

Legs invariably fitted with castors.

DECORATION

Iron parts originally japanned to simulate wood; later lacquered plain black.

FINISH

Brass polished; iron painted or lacquered.

RELATIVE VALUES

Perennially popular and increasingly scarce, though only immensely valuable if all-brass and of complex design.

TWENTIETH-CENTURY BRASS

Modern brass beds are usually lacquered and therefore need no polishing. But they lack the deep glow and slightly worn look of the real thing.

BED-STEPS

About

1790-1900

Christie's

George III bed-steps, Brussels carpet on treads.

People of consequence had many layers of mattresses on their beds; sometimes the bedding was so high that steps were needed. For a long time bed-steps were crudely made and hidden beneath the bed; but from about 1790 they doubled as commodes and became more significant and decorative pieces of furniture.

Many are now sold as 'library steps', their innards removed and the carpet originally covering their treads replaced with leather.

STYLE AND APPEARANCE

Two phases:

1790-1830: Generally three steps, the lowest a platform base and the upper step or steps formed a receptacle for a chamber pot with hinged lid or lids. Sometimes a bidet was fitted in the remaining step; very occasionally, this had a front-opening cupboard. Commode drawer slid forward to provide a seat. Steps mostly straight-fronted, occasionally curved. Some with raised sides. Legs were short, either square sectioned and tapering, splayed, sabre or turned.

William IV mahogany bed-steps with shaped sides.

Sotheby's

1830-1900: Generally two steps only. Most were a rectangular box form with broad, stumpy turned legs and feet, the front ones moving forward, pulling lower step from underneath a hinged top commode.

Christie's

George III bed-steps enclosing a bidet.

MATERIALS

Usually mahogany; occasionally satinwood. Oak for Victorian Gothic.

CONSTRUCTION

Early and better quality pieces were veneered, otherwise solid. Commode drawer could pull forward on system of counter-balanced weights, otherwise on runners.

DECORATION

Simple boxwood or ebony stringing lines on Regency pieces. Carving on more elaborate Gothic examples.

FINISH

Wax polish.

RELATIVE VALUES

Prices very variable, falling rapidly from thousands (for Regency) into hundreds (for Victorian). Fine timber – particularly satinwood – a great advantage.

CLOSE STOOLS, NIGHT COMMODES, BEDSIDE TABLES, POT CUPBOARDS

About

1700-1890s

Mahogany tray-top night commode with dummy drawer, about 1770.

Despite the existence of outside privies, chamber pots were generally used at night and various pieces of furniture were devised in the 18thC to conceal them. These 'conveniences' mostly became redundant when flushing water closets were perfected in the late 19thC. Many have subsequently had their innards removed.

STYLE AND APPEARANCE

The most common types seen today are:

Close, necessary or **night-stools**. Made until about 1780. Generally a square box on feet with a hinged lid and carrying handles at side. Before 1700, often upholstered; alternatively oak with bun feet and iron handles. After 1700, walnut (and later mahogany) with brass handles and bracket feet. Dummy drawers on front.

Night table or **'commode'**, about 1740-1810. A squarish box raised on straight, square legs with a cupboard for the pot or a cupboard above a commode seat sliding forward on hidden castors. The front legs split to allow movement and the pot was hidden by a deep front-rail or apron masquerading as one or two drawers. Generally a tray top, often with handles pierced in the raised sides. Tambour-front doors common around 1790.

Bedside tables, about 1780 onwards. A small, simple cupboard on tall, narrow, legs, usually turned though sometimes tapering. They had a raised gallery on three sides and small knob handle. Usually mahogany, sometimes satinwood. Often in pairs. Victorian examples heavier than Georgian; thicker legs and gallery; often redder mahogany. This type popular for late Victorian/Edwardian revival styles.

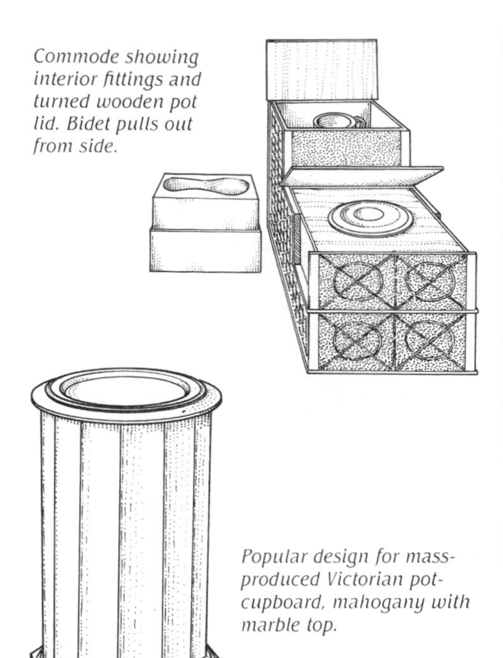

Commode showing interior fittings and turned wooden pot lid. Bidet pulls out from side.

Popular design for mass-produced Victorian pot-cupboard, mahogany with marble top.

MATERIALS

Commonly mahogany; at various times oak, walnut and satinwood.

CONSTRUCTION

Standard practices employed. Sliding seats generally moved on bearers. Mostly solid wood used; only occasionally veneer.

A, tray-top night commode with tambour-fronted cupboard, about 1770; B, a mahogany tray-top bedside table, about 1760; C, a Sheraton inlaid mahogany bedside table, about 1800 and D, a Victorian burr walnut bedside cabinet, about 1870.

Bonhams: A, D; Sotheby's: B; Christie's: C

VICTORIAN POT CUPBOARDS

Commonly tall and narrow, on plinth base with single panelled door with wooden knob. Usually square-sectioned, sometimes circular. Latter often had inset marble top, occasionally scalloped sides. Sometimes low with hinged top and double doors revealing seat. Mahogany or walnut. After about 1870, more decorative, with carved door panel, shaped feet and gallery at back.

Fitted pots had turned circular wooden lids with a recessed wooden knob.

DECORATION

18thC: Minimal carving, rare. Brass handles according to prevailing fashions. Later small brass knobs.

19thC: Regency period, sometimes restrained inlay. After about 1870 only, panels of carved decoration in prevailing Gothic, Renaissance and 18thC revival styles. Sometimes additional carving on uprights, friezes and galleries. Small knobs until about 1820, thereafter larger wooden knobs universal. Metal drop handles after about 1870.

FINISH

Wax polish.

RELATIVE VALUES

Conventional bedside tables may be priced in thousands, but 'night tables' and commodes usually less, even when 18thC. Original commode fittings nowadays a bonus. Pairs command much higher prices.

COMMODE CONVERSIONS

Commode chairs, which looked like other chairs of their day, but had deep, shaped aprons around the seat to conceal the pot, were made in large numbers in both sophisticated and country styles. Because they sell better as standard chairs, many have had their seats replaced and their aprons removed. Similarly 'commode chests', made to look like small chests of drawers, have been turned into standard chests of drawers, their small size making them particularly valuable. On any smaller-than-average chests therefore, check the interior carefully for signs of alteration.

WASH-STANDS

About

1740 to 1915

Sotheby's

Mahogany wash-stand with bowl and soap-ball, about 1770-1790.

First introduced during the 1740s when hygiene was recognized as a matter of importance. By 1780 'bason' stands were present in every fashionable bedroom. They were utilitarian and discreet, rather then showy. Late-19thC washstands were generally made *en suite* with other bedroom furniture.

STYLE AND APPEARANCE

Designed to provide storage space for tooth brushes and shaving accessories as well as support for a basin and ewer of water, 18thC wash-stands were of three basic types:

Tripod stand: Introduced about 1740. Often inaccurately called a 'wig stand'. Open ring at top, scrolled uprights and legs, two triangular drawers. Lower platform, usually dished to hold ewer. Spherical wooden box for the wash ball (ball of soap) above the drawers, usually slotting on to a fixed wooden peg. (These are very often missing today.)

Christie's

Fold-over wash-stand with rising mirror and bidet drawer.

Enclosed wash-stand, box form: About 1750 onwards, with cupboard and drawer(s), one real, other(s) dummy. Hinged top opening to the back forming a splash-back, or two flaps opening to either side. Straight, square-sectioned legs. Holes for the bowl, soap and sponge dishes cut in inner top. Often a rising mirror at back. Tambour front to cupboard fashionable around 1790. Usually small, about 14 inches/35 cm square, but for a while (1780-1810) slightly larger and more complex. Could be combined with a night commode (see **p. 14**) or have dummy drawer at front concealing bidet actually pulling out from side. Bidet drawer supported on two thin legs joined by stretcher hinged to lower drawer edge and folding up when the drawer was pushed in.

Corner wash-stand: About 1785 onwards. Delicate-looking objects with thin legs, front two splayed. Usually an open shelf at base with raised ring to hold the ewer; either a drawer with a cupboard above or sometimes a separate drawer set some distance below an open shelf with a shallow, shaped apron. Curved splash-back, commonly fixed, but sometimes composed of two quadrants, one hinged to the other and the whole hinged to one side, both folding down to conceal the basin when not in use.

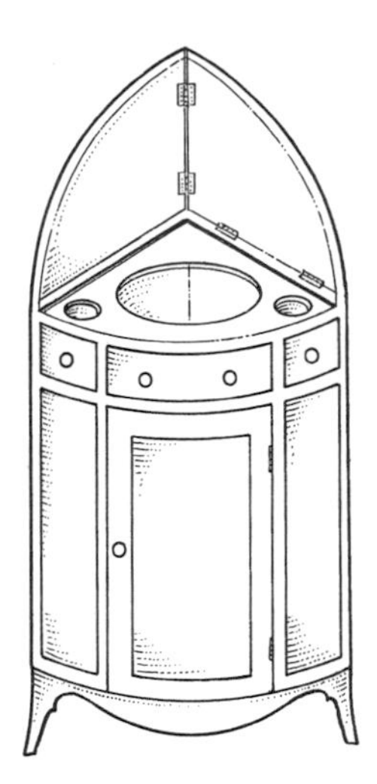

Corner enclosed basin stand.

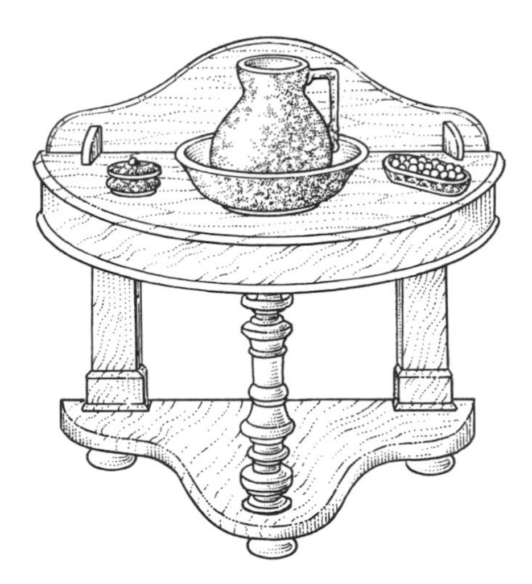

Victorian wash-stand with marble top.

Wash-stands proliferated in the 19thC, although the basic theme was a table form with a single frieze of drawers, a marble top and a fixed splash-back. Ceramic jug and basin sets with matching dishes, shaving and tooth mugs were openly displayed on top. Tiled splash-backs were introduced around 1870, fixed towel rails around 1890. Cupboards – to conceal chamber pots – were another late feature.

Sotheby's

A common early 19thC mahogany wash-stand.

MATERIALS

Principally mahogany; occasionally satinwood. Also walnut, birch and deal during Victoria's reign. Oak for progressive 1890s pieces.

CONSTRUCTION

Veneer on some 18thC pieces. Rising mirrors hung on counter-balanced weights.

DECORATION

Very little in 18thC apart from cross-banding and other decorative veneers. Restrained inlay occasionally present about 1790-1820, followed by similarly restrained carving until about 1840.

Marble tops – universal from about 1830 – decorative in themselves. Commonly blue-veined white marble; best quality pieces had more striking colours and figuration. Splash-back tiles frequently multi coloured and variously patterned; the cheapest were plain leaf green.

Handles followed prevailing fashions (for details, see **p. 15**)

FINISH

Polish; green, brown or 'natural' wood stain on Victorian deal followed by paint during the 1890s, popularly green, sometimes white.

RELATIVE VALUES

Early basin stands, low four figures;corner and fold-over top, three to four figures. Victorian (plain mahogany or walnut with marble top) three figures; pine with tiled splash-back (stripped of original finish), low three figures.

CLOTHES (OR TOWEL) HORSES

About

1750 onwards

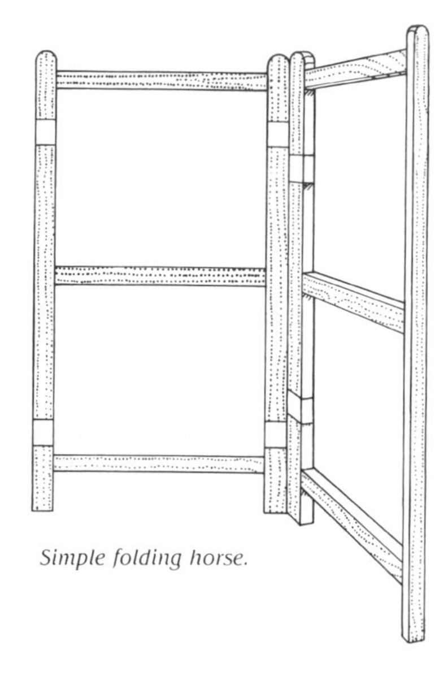

Simple folding horse.

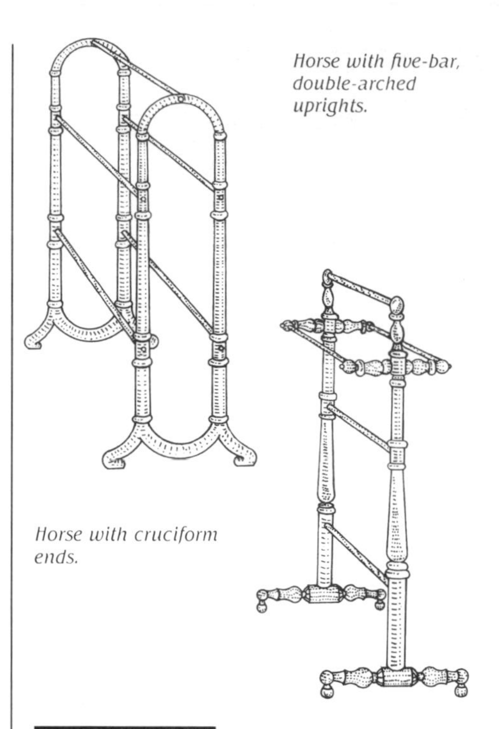

Horse with five-bar, double-arched uprights.

Horse with cruciform ends.

A light wooden framework over which clothes or towels could be spread to dry. Seldom seen before the late 18thC, but common in the 19thC, when it often formed part of a bedroom suite.

STYLE AND APPEARANCE

In the 18thC could be simply two or three narrow horizontal bars tenoned into two straight uprights supported on shaped feet (commonly ogee or claw); or with two leaves hinged together and feet one side of each leaf only.

In the 19thC, bars and uprights were usually turned with three, four or five horizontals. Folding types became less common. A four-bar type had uprights branching at top to support parallel bars. Five-bar type had double uprights joined by arched top, single bar at highest point and two pairs of parallel bars below. Ends could also be of cruciform shape.

MATERIALS

Mahogany, beech or deal.

CONSTRUCTION

Horizontals glued into holes bored in uprights or set right through and screwed from outside. Screw-heads covered with small knob.

DECORATION

Very little. Sometimes fancy turning and occasionally carved feet and ends.

FINISH

Polish on mahogany; typically stain and paint on beech, pine. A few may now be stripped.

RELATIVE VALUES

Genuine antique clothes horses unusual, but nevertheless not of great value.

VICTORIAN REPRODUCTIONS

The popularity of clothes horses has revived in recent years and Victorian reproductions abound. These can usually be identified by a generally more robust look, thicker and straighter horizontal bars – those on originals have often warped – and by their natural (waxed or varnished) finish, and lack of traces of former paint or stain around the joints.

BOOKCASES, BREAKFRONT AND LIBRARY

About

1730 onwards

George III mahogany breakfront bookcase with broken pediment.

Christie's

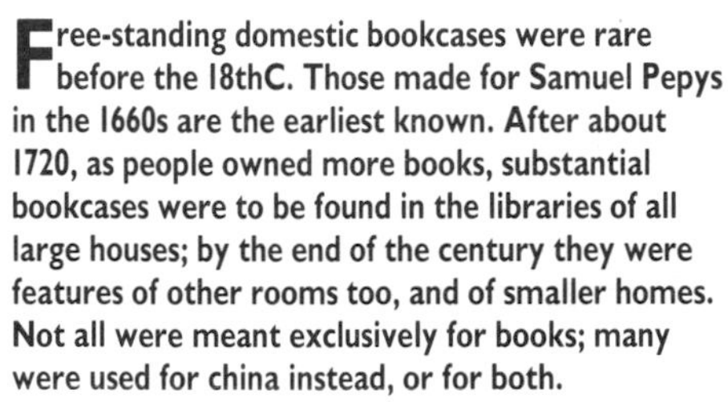

Free-standing domestic bookcases were rare before the 18thC. Those made for Samuel Pepys in the 1660s are the earliest known. After about 1720, as people owned more books, substantial bookcases were to be found in the libraries of all large houses; by the end of the century they were features of other rooms too, and of smaller homes. Not all were meant exclusively for books; many were used for china instead, or for both.

18thC bookcases were predominantly architectural in character and sometimes of monumental size. After 1740 many were made in breakfront form: a large central section projecting forwards beyond two flanking wings. Straight-fronted bookcases are today generally distinguished from breakfronts by the term 'library bookcase'.

STYLE AND APPEARANCE

Six categories; but they share basically the same form. An upper, generally glazed, section for books, with a carved and moulded cornice, sometimes surmounted by a pediment, sits above a deeper and shorter lower section comprising cupboards (and sometimes drawers too) for storage of maps, prints and other papers. Occasionally, a secretaire drawer is also present. Pediments were often broken, their centre (with or without a raised plinth) holding a bust, carved eagle, urn or other work of art.

The six categories are:

Kentian, about 1710-1740 (rare today): Bold classical architectural features: broken pediments, deep cornices, pilasters faced with pendants of fruit and flowers. Central doors often arched. Upper section with large rectangular panels of glass set in broad, moulded bars, or blind of mirror panelling. Base with panelled doors, sometimes shaped and fielded, supported on a plinth.

Chippendale period, about 1740-1765: Still with classical features, but more restrained. Cornices narrower and plainer. Fashionable pieces had a central pediment with pierced carving, wings surmounted by fretwork gallery. Pediment could be swan-neck. Availability of mahogany meant thinner and lighter glazing bars, often carved in rococo, chinoiserie and Gothic patterns (rococo occasionally gilded) or astragals (see **p. 329**) arranged in geometric patterns. Today, a large number of panes in an individual pattern (say 13 or 15) is considered to be a sign of quality. Base still panelled, with decorative carved edging or applied blind fret mouldings. Plinths often replaced by bracket feet.

Neo-classical, about 1770-1790: Neat and formal over-all. Simple pediments, often with urns in centre and at corners. Cornices carved with repetitive classical ornament; astragals in geometric patterns. Lower doors with simple mouldings applied in square, circular or oval shapes, often with paterae at corners. Stands on a plinth base.

Sheraton-style, about 1790-1810: Often narrower than before, lower section taller. Pediments scroll- or lunette-shaped. Upper doors sometimes with brass wire trellis and pleated silk rather than astragals. Astragals could be painted or gilt lead. Lower doors with decorative veneers. Large central ovals common. Splay feet fashionable, occasionally turned feet after 1800.

Regency/early Victorian, about 1810-1850: Large bookcases less common at first than small. Could have Egyptian or Grecian ornament (see **DWARF BOOKCASES, p. 32**). Antefizae on corners. Lunette-shaped pediments, if any. Fluting interspersed with paterae popular feature on cornices. Late Regency plain. Straight moulded cornices, scrolled or acanthus carved supports typical of day.

Victorian, about 1840-1900: Often very plain, even best quality relying only on veneers for decorative effects. A large number almost style-less. Arched doors with plain glass echoed by applied arched mouldings on lower doors. Sometimes rococo/naturalistic mouldings below. Lower part could also be glazed. Cornices deep and heavily moulded, sometimes with rounded corners. Simple bracket supports sometimes present.

Could also be reformist Gothic; characteristic features: chamfered edges, diagonal boarded panelling on lower doors; or, Renaissance style: heavily carved all over. (See under **DECORATION**)

18thC styles were revived at end of the 19thC. Sheraton-style particularly popular during Edwardian period, but often a poor imitation. Considerable reduction in size. Brightly contrasting cross-banding and inlay of shells, fans, combined with dentil-moulded cornice common. Often yellowish mahogany with poor, treacly-looking finish.

MATERIALS

Walnut in the Queen Anne period; sometimes painted and gessoed pine. Mahogany from about 1730, joined by satinwood around 1790. Rosewood only rarely, during Regency. Both walnut and mahogany during Victoria's reign; oak for reformist Gothic and (less common) Renaissance style.

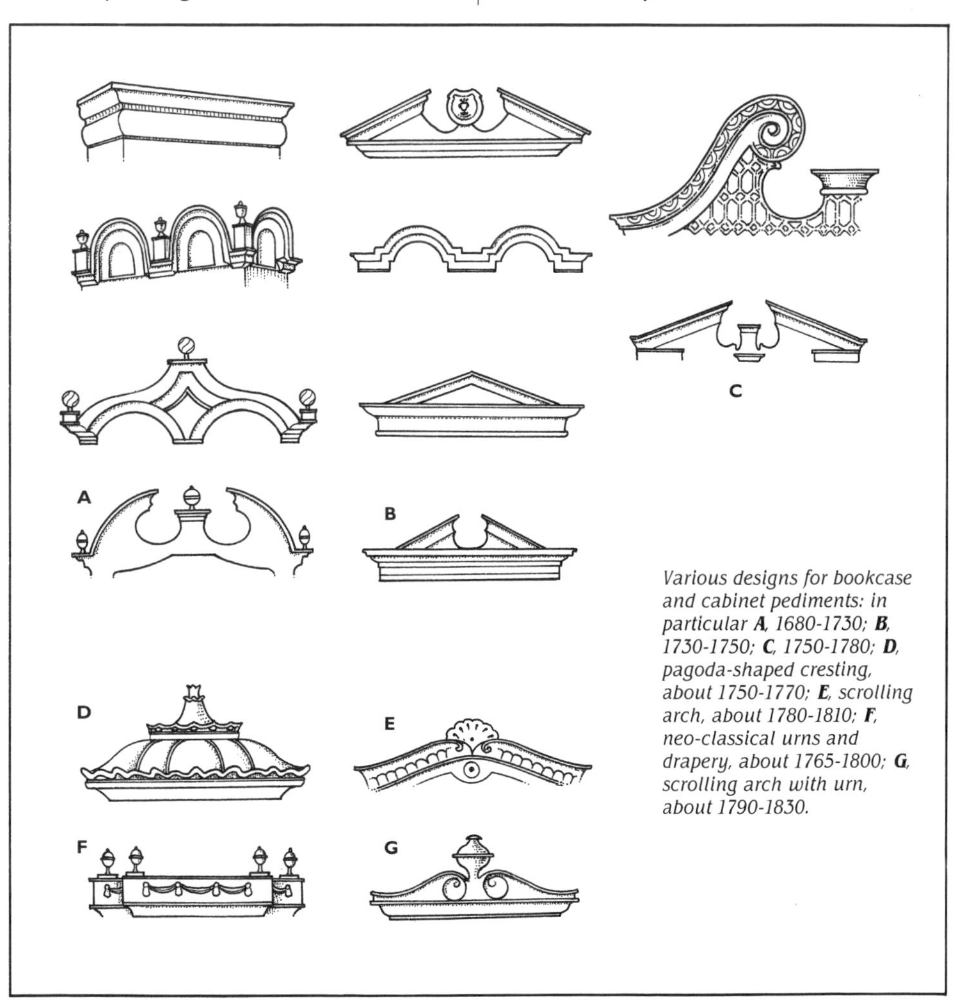

*Various designs for bookcase and cabinet pediments: in particular **A**, 1680-1730; **B**, 1730-1750; **C**, 1750-1780; **D**, pagoda-shaped cresting, about 1750-1770; **E**, scrolling arch, about 1780-1810; **F**, neo-classical urns and drapery, about 1765-1800; **G**, scrolling arch with urn, about 1790-1830.*

CONSTRUCTION

Standard practices employed. Sometimes revealed mortise-and-tenon construction on reformist Gothic. Many convincing reproductions of 18thC bookcases were made by the Victorians and at a glance look right, so look for indications of age, such as:

Shelf supports: Early 18thC pieces have shelves slotted between narrow strips of wood glued to the sides at regular intervals. From about 1730, shelves were more usually rebated into grooves cut in the sides. After 1800: supported on wood or metal pegs plugged into pairs of evenly spaced holes.

If the shelf supports continue right up to the top of each side, the bookcase has almost certainly been cut down. They should finish a book's height below the cornice.

Glazing bars: Before 1800 bars were usually rebated into stiles and rails, therefore flush with surface. After 1800: more commonly tenoned, therefore slightly recessed.

***Left**, glazing bar rebated into style; **right**, astragal glazing bars.*

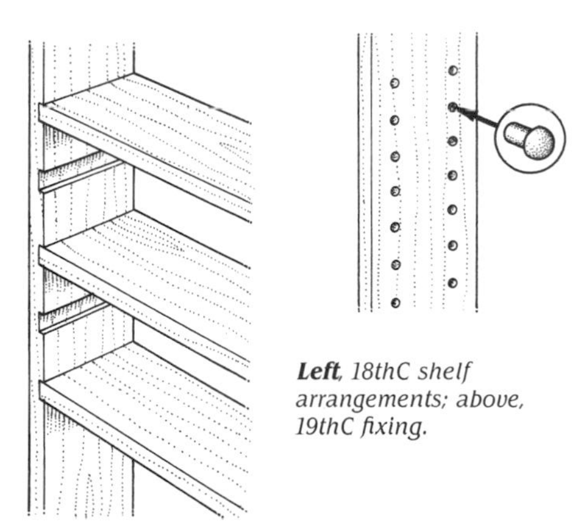

***Left**, 18thC shelf arrangements; above, 19thC fixing.*

Other points of interest: Cases originally intended for china may have grooves at the back of the shelves for the support of plates.

Original glass will not be completely flat and clear. The putty holding it in place will be very hard and dark and will have accumulated a good deal of dirt.

If there was once a pediment there will be obvious marks where it once sat. Its absence does not necessarily affect value. Try and get up there to take a look.

DECORATION

Principally carved ornament, mostly on cornices. In 18th and early 19thC, classical style. Could be Vitruvian scrolls, egg-and-dart, tongue-and-dart, dentil moulding, acanthus, Gothic fret, fluting interspersed with paterae, swags.

Blind fret carving on lower doors and cornices, in mid-18thC sometimes open fret on pediments.

Figuring of veneer always a main feature. Decorative use of veneers in the forms of ovals, cross-banding on Sheraton and Sheraton revival pieces, occasionally restrained inlay in addition.

Incised decoration sometimes present on reformist Gothic pieces; occasionally inlay of ebony, ivory too, in small repetitive geometric patterns. Bold carving of lion's masks, foliage, geometric mouldings, cartouches, on Renaissance revival pieces.

Handles: When present, they follow prevailing patterns (see **p. 93**).

FINISH

Polish. Stain on 19thC oak; light, often yellowish, for Gothic, dark for Renaissance.

RELATIVE VALUES

Quality 18thC bookcases in original condition are valuable items, many fetching well into five figures. Pediments, secretaire drawers, a pre-1750 date and, most important, breakfronts, will increase value. Similar library versions are generally cheaper as are small Sheraton-style pieces with decorative veneers. Late Regency/William IV mahogany, Victorian/Edwardian mahogany reproductions of 18thC pieces, Victorian oak and walnut are all variable.

BOOKCASES, DWARF

About
1800 onwards

The burgeoning popularity of reading at the turn of the 19thC, particularly among women, created demand for small, readily accessible bookshelves of only table height, where books of relatively small value could be stored openly in rooms used in an informal way. Especially popular during the Regency period when they were made in pairs to stand at either end of a room, or as moveable 'bookstands'.

__Right__, Regency rosewood chiffonier with brass gallery and shelf supports.

Christie's

Sotheby's

__Above__, simple Regency bookcase with open shelves.

Christie's

__Above__, fine Regency bookcase with pilasters in Egyptian style. The brass grilles were originally backed by pleated silk.

STYLE AND APPEARANCE

Three standard types evolved:

Chiffonier: A cupboard fitted with two open shelves above; usually a frieze drawer too. (Also popularly used by the Victorians as a form of sideboard in the dining-room – see **SIDEBOARDS p. 120**). Door panels fashionably fitted with brass wire grilles backed by pleated silk. Substantial pilasters or columns at either side, fashionably in Egyptian style. Low turned, or lion's paw, feet. Plinth base increasingly common after 1810. Similarly, marble tops. Upper shelves at back supported on slender turned columns (sometimes brass). Occasionally mirrored rather than wooden backboard. Victorian versions of similar form, but plainer: wooden door panels and tops. Turned spindles supporting shelves.

Could also be of breakfront form, without superstructure and with additional open or

Sotheby's

Above, *simple free-standing mahogany bookcase.*

enclosed shelves at sides. (See also **CUPBOARDS p. 43**) Occasionally all sections had open shelves.

Tiered set of two, three or four open shelves, shallowest at top. Continuous uprights forming sides, shaped on front edge. Generally two drawers below, occasionally small cupboard instead. Four short turned legs or stump feet. Top bordered by sides and backboard or by low, brass or wood, gallery.

Bookstand (or 'moving library'): Similar to above, but arranged as two sets placed back-to-back. Sometimes legs as two columns supported on splayed feet linked by stretcher as seen on contemporary sofa tables – see **TABLES: SOFA, p. 181**). Feet fitted with castors. Occasionally sides of brass wire trellis.

Below, *double-sided mahogany bookcase.*

Sotheby's

MATERIALS

Most commonly rosewood, satinwood, mahogany, and, later, walnut. Sometimes painted beech. Highly figured exotic veneers used during Regency for cross-banding.

CONSTRUCTION

Standard practices employed. Many plain Victorian chiffoniers have now become 'Regency' following replacement of their door panels with brass wire trellis and pleated silk, and their wooden tops and superstructure with a marble slab. Look for signs of fresh saw marks and staining on the relevant sections.

DECORATION

Much use of Grecian and Egyptian ornament during Regency. Brass inlay and applied gilt brass ornament in the form of sunbursts, paterae, anthemions, sphinxes and other Egyptian heads, feet etc. Lion handles on larger frieze drawers, otherwise turned knobs.

Sotheby's

Above, *ormolu-mounted Regency bookcase showing French Empire influence.*

FINISH

Polish, occasionally paint, partial gilding.

RELATIVE VALUES

All types are sought after and expensive, Regency especially so. Pairs always at a premium.

BOOKCASES, HANGING SHELVES

About
1750 onwards

Chinese Chippendale style shelves with fretwork sides and galleries.

A small set of open shelves for books and china which hung on the wall above table height, often called a 'hanging chiffonier' in the 19thC. Usually designed for ladies' rooms, hence generally rather light and pretty objects.

STYLE AND APPEARANCE

Could have two, three or four shelves, either tiered or of equal depth, and sometimes one or a pair of shallow drawers below. Totally open at front and back, partially at sides.

Mid-18thC examples had fret-cut sides – fashionably in Gothic or Chinese style – extending in a curved outline above the top and below the bottom shelf.

Popular **Regency** design: Plain shelves with brass pillar supports and brass cross-bars at sides. Sometimes brass gallery too. Victorian: Scroll or turned baluster supports and scrolling back-board above.

Bookstand, 1850-1875, with diminishing shelves and scrolled ends.

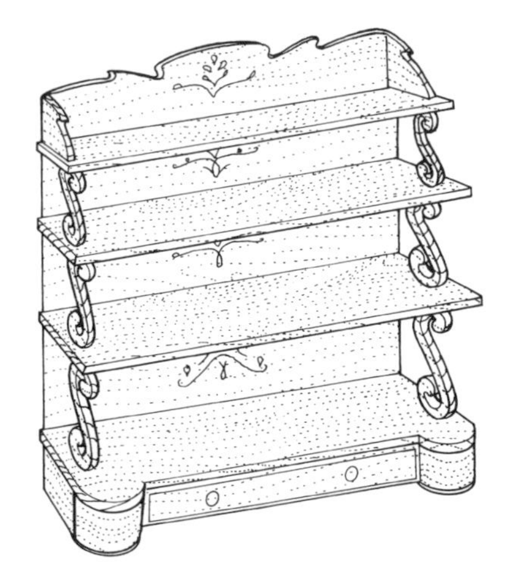

Top shelf occasionally galleried; sometimes backed by shaped board. Size variable, but mostly small, the average width about 24 inches/60 cm.

MATERIALS

Mostly mahogany, occasionally satinwood or rosewood. Victorian: Mahogany, walnut, oak or deal.

CONSTRUCTION

Shelves rebating into sides. Post-1800 uprights generally dowelled into shelves, set-in slightly from corners.

DECORATION

Fret carving. Small knob handles on drawers.

FINISH

Polish, stain, occasionally paint.

RELATIVE VALUES

A huge range: 18thC examples may be affordable; 19thC a cheaper alternative. Into five figures for a really good mid-18thC Chippendale-style piece.

BOOKCASES, REVOLVING

About

1790 to 1915

Regency four-tier revolving bookcase, with splayed legs.

Christie's

A smallish open-shelved bookcase revolving on a central pillar. A patent for a bookcase with individually rotating shelves was granted to Benjamin Crosby in 1808, but many pre-date this. Especially popular during Regency and, in a different form, during the Edwardian period.

STYLE AND APPEARANCE

Usually circular. Could have been two and six tiers, slightly diminishing in diameter towards the top. Central pillar turned at base – usually in baluster form – with three (occasionally four) legs. These could be scrolling with narrow pad feet, or splayed (and popularly reeded) ending in brass box castors.

Shelves with wedge-shaped dividers, usually fronted by dummy book spines. Top could have a wooden, or more commonly a brass gallery.

Edwardian examples are generally square with only two tiers, each side having either a

Bonhams

Edwardian model with slatted sides and inlay.

solid panel or row of wooden slats forming end support of adjoining shelf.

Bottom shelf bordered by deep skirting; slightly projecting moulded cornice at top. The structure rotates on the column rising from flat platform cross-bars with semi-concealed castors.

Top occasionally has hinged book stand supported on ratchet system.

MATERIALS

Mahogany, occasionally rosewood. Edwardian sometimes oak.

CONSTRUCTION

Shelves rotate around central pillar rising from base. Standard methods employed for pedestal support (see **TABLES, TRIPOD, p. 175**).

DECORATION

Edwardian: Oak usually carved with scrolling and/or floral ornament in Renaissance style. Sheraton-style indicated on some pieces by simple inlay of shells, fans, stringing lines.

FINISH

Polish; stain.

RELATIVE VALUES

Very desirable objects; the best Regency examples fetch five figure sums. Edwardian examples do not compare.

COURT CUPBOARDS WITH OPEN SHELVES (BUFFETS)

About

1570-1680

Christie's

Court cupboard with carved cup-and-cover supports.

A piece of furniture derived from medieval prototypes, comprising a set of three open shelves, which in grand houses was draped with fabric or carpet and used to display plate, but in lesser homes could be used as a side-table. The names buffet, court cupboard, sideboard and dresser were seemingly inter-changeable.

STYLE AND APPEARANCE

Three shelves of equal size, each with a deep frieze; the top and middle shelf frieze are generally deeper than the lowest and often contain a drawer. Turned front supports, either continuous from top to bottom, form the corner framing, or are dowelled into separate framed shelves. Continuous rect-angular stiles at the back, sometimes with simple carved mouldings. Feet formed as the square base of the continuous uprights or as the stiles of the lowest shelf framing; can be concealed by mitred base moulding. Some-times panelled cupboard with central door and angled sides in the upper half

Decoration of the shelf friezes seldom matches; the turnings of the supports may or may not be identical on the different layers.

MATERIALS

Principally oak; sometimes walnut, elm, beech etc. (though survivals rare). Holly, bog oak, boxwood, bone and imported ebony and ivory used for inlay.

CONSTRUCTION

Framed, with pegged mortise-and-tenon joints. Drawers (where present) rebated and nailed; grain running mostly back to front; run on side bearers. Supports may dowel into shelves above and below. Mouldings are usually carved out of solid wood, though on late examples may be glued on. Many buffets were originally made without a cornice moulding, with a planked top merely nailed to the frieze; cornice mouldings are often there-fore a later 'improvement'.

DECORATION

Principally carving; often elaborate, with guil-loche, strapwork, gadrooning, S-scrolls and other repetitive motifs. Occasionally grotes-que figures and heraldic emblems. Heavy bul-bous cup-and-cover turnings on supports, sometimes fantastic animals.

Some have additional inlay, particularly on cupboard doors, of floral designs (sometimes with birds) and black and white chequer pat-terns. The latter are common on bottom-shelf friezes.

FINISH

Originally varnish and/or wax polish. Should now have good patination (see **p. 8**).

RELATIVE VALUES

Early examples in original condition rare; fine, extensive carving and presence of inlay may push price into five figures; certainly in four.

VICTORIAN ALTERATIONS

Watch for Victorian carve-ups, which are quite common. Look for dark all-over stain (particularly seepage around joints), regular saw marks (made by machine saw), regularly shaped machine-cut pegs (or no pegs at all), the presence of round-headed nails or screws, and discrepancies in quality and execution of carving between the various parts.

COURT CUPBOARDS WITH ENCLOSED SHELVES

About

1610-1800

A prestigious item in the 17thC, much less so in the 18thC, when it was only country-made. Used for displaying and storing food and plates, cups, in the hall (later in the parlour) where meals were taken. Originally made without locks, therefore not intended to contain valuable items. Earliest surviving examples date mostly from about 1650.

In Wales, called a *deuddarn*; a *tridarn* when a third stage is present.

STYLE AND APPEARANCE

Generally in two cupboarded sections, the upper cupboard shallower than the lower (providing a display shelf), with a projecting cornice and frieze. Until about 1630-1640 this was linked to the base by turned baluster supports (until approximately 1610 bulbous and carved, then plain and elongated); thereafter replaced by small pendant turnings. Frieze carved and sometimes surmounted by shallow moulding (often a later addition).

Upper section with two cupboards, typically enclosing a decorative central panel, behind which may be a secret shelved compartment. Lower section with ornamental frieze above variously panelled doors and, in the 18thC, a frieze of two (or three) short drawers. Plain panels at sides. Stile feet.

In the 17thC stiles, rails and muntins usually moulded; in the 18thC plain, with fielded and sometimes arched panels.

Christie's

A 17thC oak court cupboard with carved panels and turned pendant finials.

Sotheby's

18thC Welsh oak tridarn with arched and fielded panels.

MATERIALS

Principally oak, sometimes walnut, elm, beech etc. (though survivals are rare). Holly, bog oak, boxwood, bone used for inlay; sometimes ebony and ivory.

OTHER CUPBOARDS

Various other joined and decoratively carved cupboards were made for similar purposes. Some have areas of pierced carving to allow air to circulate inside. Often-mentioned types include: aumbries, hutches, livery, game or bacon cupboards. Conformation and value vary considerably. Check construction, finishes and use of timbers to determine authenticity and date.

CONSTRUCTION

Framed and panelled with pegged mortise-and-tenon joints. Chamfered edges to panels. Turned supports and pendant dowelled into place. Backboards and top nailed on. Applied mouldings glued. Drawers on 18thC pieces dovetailed; linings rebated and running on bearers. Inner shelves approximately ½ inch/1 cm thick.

Watch out for Victorian 'carve-ups' and for marriages of lower and upper halves (further details, see **p. 89**).

DECORATION

Carving, principally on friezes and upper panels (these are often arcaded), but can be more extensive. Generally greater geometric emphasis than on open-shelved type. Occasionally applied mitred mouldings and split turnings (see **CHESTS OF DRAWERS, EARLY PANELLED OAK, p. 84**). Inlay of geometric and floral patterns (sometimes with birds) or chequer inlay of bone (or ivory) and ebony quite common.

Handles and hinges: Turned wooded knobs and generally exterior flat iron hinges in 17thC; brass knobs or handles and interior brass hinges in 18thC.

FINISH

Varnish or oil polish, followed by wax polish.

RELATIVE VALUES

Much more common than open-shelved variety, but still fetch four-figure sums; only very late examples in three figures.

Late medieval oak livery cupboard.

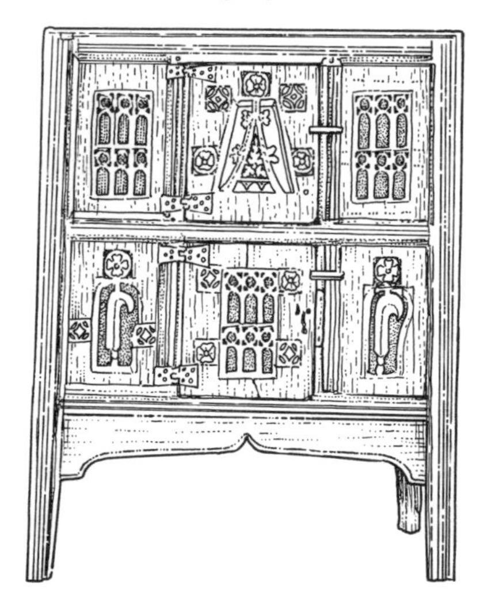

CABINETS: SIDE AND DISPLAY

About

1580-1915

A very variable piece of furniture made in numerous forms and for many purposes throughout the 18th and 19thC. Preceded by the prestigious cabinet on stand.

Bonhams

Sotherby's

***Above right**, 1930s burr-veneered cocktail cabinet. **Above left**, Victorian mahogany chiffonier, about 1855-1865.*

DISPLAY CABINETS ON STANDS

In the late 16thC and the 17thC the richest people kept their curios in cabinets containing numerous small drawers. Many of these cabinets were imported from the Continent – particularly from Italy and Southern Germany – and were valuable and decorative objects in themselves, being made from exotic materials such as ebony, ivory and tortoiseshell with plaques of inlaid marbles or precious gemstones. Chinese and Japanese lacquer cabinets were especially prized – particularly after about 1670 – as were those of fine Dutch marquetry after about 1680.

Most were mounted on English-made stands – sometimes with a matching cresting; these could be quite simple, with turned supports linked by turned or shaped stretchers (see **CHESTS ON STANDS, p. 88**) or very elaborate with bold, gilded carving.

DISPLAY CABINETS

The practice of storing and displaying precious objects in glazed cabinets dates from the first half of the 18thC when wealthy people began collecting fine porcelain and books on a large scale. Few pieces were designed solely for display (although designs were published in popular pattern books), but usually formed the upper part of a chest, cupboard, bureau or secretaire. (For details of the glazed sections of these see **BOOKCASES p. 37** and **DESKS p. 100**.)

During the second half of the 19thC free-standing glazed display cabinets were made in revived 18thC styles, some of Chinese Chippendale type, others rather loose interpretations of Sheraton designs. The majority are in mahogany and glazed on three sides, raised from the floor on tall, narrow, straight legs. 'Chippendale' pieces are sometimes highly carved, while those in Sheraton style are delicate and often inlaid with stringing, fans and shells. Sometimes a panelled or cupboard area beneath the shelves is painted with flowers or landscape scenes. The glazing bars on these are invariably applied to a single sheet of glass; they do not enclose a number of small panels cut to shape as they would on an 18thC piece.

Christie's

Left *Victorian 'Chippendale' display cabinet; right, Edwardian 'Sheraton' display cabinet.*

STYLE AND APPEARANCE

Range from simple breakfront or one or two-door cupboards, with flat tops and plinth bases, to more complex pieces with various shelves, drawers, cupboards and turned or straight feet. Most distinctive types are chiffoniers (see **DWARF BOOKCASES, p. 38**) and ebonised 'aesthetic' or 'Art Furniture' cabinets (from 1870 onwards). These were composed of numerous shelves, small cupboards, niches, spindled galleries, bevelled mirrors and panels of embossed 'leather' paper or gilding. These were followed by similar cabinets of 'architectural Queen Anne' style, with mirrored and pedimented superstructure.

Victorian walnut bookcase.

Sotheby's

Doors can be wood-panelled or glazed, or have brass grilles backed by pleated silk. Can have shaped and mirrored superstructure.

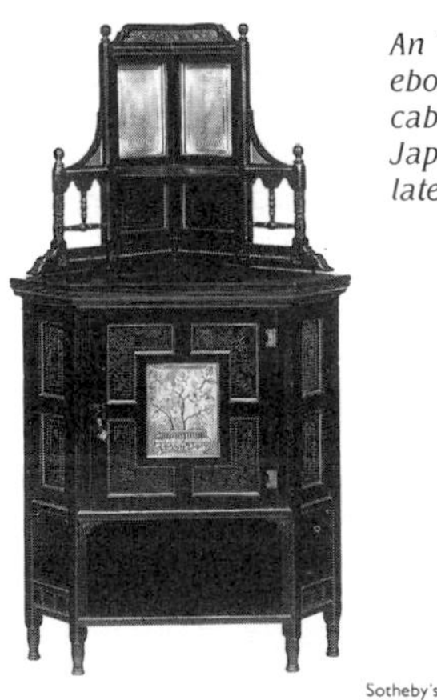

An 'Art Furniture' ebonised corner cabinet with stylized Japanese decoration, late-1870s.

Sotheby's

Victorian burr walnut sideboard cabinet, about 1865.

Sotheby's

MATERIALS

Rosewood, satinwood, mahogany, oak, walnut, and other decorative veneers. Various woods; ebony, ivory, and so on, used for inlay. Sometimes marble for tops (usually grey/white for cheaper peices; other colours for better quality). Pine or cheap Honduras mahogany for carcases.

CONSTRUCTION

Standard methods were employed. Many veneered; after about 1830 finer (about 1/16th inch/1.5 mm) machine-cut veneers were used. They are relatively easy to detect.

Many simple Victorian cabinets converted to Regency by removal of their superstructure, addition of a marble top, and replacement of their wooden door panels with brass grilles and pleated silk. Check construction of the grilles; Victorian and later grilles have soldered and studded joints; earlier ones were simply notched together.

DECORATION

Brass inlay during Regency. Some carving and turning. Gilt metal mounts (and sometimes porcelain plaques) on some pieces from about 1860. Painted and gilded panels (often of Japanese design) and embossed 'leather' paper used for decorative effect on aesthetic pieces after 1870.

FINISH

Wax polish. French polish after about 1820. Ebonised (i.e. black-stained) finish especially popular after 1870.

RELATIVE VALUES

Straightforward side cabinets (and chiffoniers) are often expensive because of their small and useful size as well as their simple and usually elegant appearance. Rosewood rather than mahogany, brass inlay and lattice grille doors (if originally intended) are all indicators that a higher price may have to be paid. All but the cheapest quality Victorian pieces are priced in three figures, even if they are 'converted' Regency.

Music and other small Victorian cabinets may fetch least; so also elaborate ebonised 'aesthetic' cabinets – despite high quality – because ebonised furniture has never been popular.

CREDENZAS

About

1850 to 1880s

Victorian ebonised credenza, about 1870.

Although their name means sideboard in Italian, in Britain, credenzas were drawing-room rather than dining-room pieces, distinguished from chiffoniers and simpler side cabinets by their extensive decoration and their shaped (usually curving) outline. The best show strong French or Italian influence.

STYLE AND APPEARANCE

Generally a central, straight-fronted section with one or two panelled doors, flanked by curved end sections containing display shelves, either open, or enclosed by glazed doors. Inner shelves polished or covered in velvet. Can be more complex serpentine shape, or straightforward breakfront form. Central door panels may be fully veneered or fretted, mirrored or glazed (and have often been altered at a later date). Plinth base (plain or with decorative aprons) or plinth supported on small turned feet. Uprights flanking central cupboard often faced with carved columns.

Rococo walnut side cabinet, about 1865.

Sotheby's

Polished (occasionally marble) top above decorated frieze; cheapest versions with dullish-grey/white marble, but other colours on best quality.

MATERIALS

Mostly highly figured (often burr) walnut or satinwood; less commonly rosewood; simplest in mahogany. Tulipwood, kingwood, box and many other woods for inlay and marquetry; brass and tortoiseshell for boulle. Pine or cheap Honduras mahogany for carcases.

CONSTRUCTION

Standard methods employed. Always veneered on dovetailed carcase. Generally too decorative to reproduce economically; most likely alteration is the replacement of the wooden top with marble. Originally these had no fixings (i.e. the marble just sat on top); signs of fixings on the carcase therefore indicate change.

DECORATION

Inlay: Single or double stringing defining the outline of various sections is common.
Marquetry: Mostly confined to friezes and centre of door panels. Floral until about 1865; thereafter neo-classical.

Some doors have porcelain plaques set in the centre with gilt metal surround; occasionally *pietre dura* (polished marble/stone mosaic) usually in floral pattern.

Overall patterns of **boulle** marquetry of brass and tortoiseshell, usually of Louis XIV inspiration.

Occasionally patterns of carved **fretwork**.

Many pieces have applied **ormolu** or gilt brass mounts (in French taste) at top and/or base of uprights; occasionally smaller mounts on frieze.

FINISH

Usually French polish. Sometimes ebonised (i.e. black stain).

RELATIVE VALUES

Tremendous variation in price depending on quality and extent of decoration. Boulle or fine marquetry at a premium; ebonised pieces never much liked. Almost all in four figures, the best edging into five.

CORNER CUPBOARDS

About

1690-1800

Mahogany corner cabinet with swan-neck cresting, chamfered sides and typical brass H-hinges.

Bonhams

Thought to have been introduced from Holland, coinciding with the fashion for painted pine-panelled rooms, corner cupboards were used to store and display fine china, silver or other valuables in the drawing-room. Some could be hanging, above dado level, others are of double height. They generally disappeared from main reception rooms around 1750 (when the fashion for wallpaper replaced panelling) but were still made for other rooms and for country parlours until the end of the century, and have been popular reproduction pieces ever since.

STYLE AND APPEARANCE

Considerable variation throughout the century. Can be:

Simple mahogany bow-fronted corner cupboard.

Christie's

Hanging, with bow front: Mostly in japanned pine or walnut veneer. A pair of doors, their curve continuing on the side framing. Simple moulding above and below. Doors generally rebate together (to form continuous smooth curve) but sometimes narrow moulding conceals join.

Hanging, with flat front: Usually a single panelled door with chamfered framing at sides (this sometimes decorated with fluting or carved columns). Simple base, but bolder cor-

Right, 18thC pine corner cupboard; ***left****, reproduction Georgian-style mahogany corner cupboard.*

Christie's; Bonhams

nice; moulding, sometimes with frieze below. Occasionally a broken pediment. Door can have a shaped, and on country versions, fielded, panel, sometimes glazed, with or without glazing bars. Earliest versions evidently had a panel of mirror glass, seldom still in place.

Double-height: Mainly straight-fronted; occasionally bow-fronted. Initially made to match (and sometimes actually fitted into) wall panelling, with a join at dado level. Many therefore made of pine (once painted, now often stripped and waxed) with two panelled doors below, and two glazed or even open shelves above. The most desirable have a rounded barrel back, the half-domed top occasionally carved as a shell. The grandest have architectural mouldings (often with doors forming an arch bordered by broad carved pilasters). Continuous plinth or bracket feet; the plainest (oak) country versions have plinth or stile feet.

Later veneered versions have bracket or, after 1780, 'swept' feet, below plain, panelled base door(s). Upper door(s) panelled or glazed, the latter with decorative arrangements of glazing bars. Bolder, deeper moulded cornice than hanging types, sometimes frieze too. (If seen on a single hanging cupboard, this probably indicates there was once a base.)

On all types, interior shelves are nearly always curved and shaped. Both they and the backboards were fashionably painted, mostly blue or green, sometimes red or yellow.

LATER REPRODUCTIONS

This type of corner cabinet was popularly reproduced by the Edwardians, often with a dentil frieze (a feature of only some 18thC examples) on top of a glazed cabinet, and rather bright, yellow inlay or green-stained stringing, fans and conch shells. Also widely reproduced today – often veneered in yew or cheap mahogany – but frequently too narrow overall, with a tall, lower cupboard.

MATERIALS

Walnut and mahogany veneer on a pine (occasionally oak) base. Pine if painted or japanned. Country versions mostly in solid oak.

CONSTRUCTION

Framed construction with glued mortise-and-tenon joints. Mitred joints and veneer on better quality. Many veneered all over. Tops rough, but under-side of hanging cabinets finished. Always locks, but generally no (or very simple wooden) catches. Invariably backed with unfinished planking.

Curved doors on bow fronts coopered (i.e. large number of verticals cut at slight angle and glued (or grooved and glued) together before being planed to a smooth surface. Cornice and base mouldings similarly constructed.

Watch for marriages on double-height pieces; check for matching colour and grain of timber (both back and front); also for shape of interior shelves and matching lockplates and escutcheons. Blind doors may now be glued.

DECORATION

Principally figuring of timber. Occasionally simple inlay and stringing in late 18thC (and on Edwardian reproductions). Mahogany cross-banding and occasionally inlay (often star shapes) on country-made oak pieces.

Japanning popular for early pieces, with chinoiserie decoration on a mainly black ground.

Hinges: Exterior H- or butterfly hinges until about 1760 (later on country versions). Decorative lock escutcheons.

FINISH

Varnish, followed by wax polish. Japanning, paint (many now stripped and waxed).

RELATIVE VALUES

Popular, but seldom immensely valuable, items. Many hanging cupboards (especially country versions) priced in three figures. Good walnut veneer, a broken pediment or fine inlay will increase value considerably.

Japanned examples – even when early – may seem surprisingly cheap unless in red, blue or yellow (cream) rather than the normal black. These are rare and may fetch five-figures.

Double-height cupboards are approximately double the value, but much more if early and architectural with a barrel back.

CANTERBURIES

About

1790-1900

Christie's

***Above**, typical early Regency mahogany canterbury.*

In 1803 Thomas Sheraton used the term 'Canterbury' to describe two different items: a small stand with partitions to hold music which could slide under the piano when not in use; and a small trolley for transporting cutlery, condiments and so forth for an informal supper. Although the term is popularly thought to derive from the latter (a lazy archbishop was supposed to have ordered one in order to save himself the trouble of rising to eat) virtually all canterburies made after 1800 were for music. Today they are generally used as magazine racks.

STYLE AND APPEARANCE

Canterburies were made throughout the 19thC in huge numbers and in varying qualities. Regardless of date, the majority consisted of a rectangular framework with single drawer below three or four partitions, open at top (and sometimes at sides also). Four, short supporting legs on castors. Two knobs (occasionally one) on drawer.

Georgian/Regency: Legs usually continuous with uprights. Could be ring-turned baluster columns topped by finials, or straight, square-sectioned finishing flush with top rails. Rows of slats or turned balusters forming dividers, generally vertical. Central divider on four-partition type often had raised centre with pierced carrying handle. Top rails of dividers sometimes dished.

For Regency variations see illustrations. Lyres sometimes have brass strings.

Bonhams

***Above**, later Regency rosewood canterbury with wreath and X-frame partitions.*

Victorian: Turned legs – often shorter and broader than previously – generally attached underneath drawer.

Drawer sometimes without knobs, opened instead by pulling groove cut under and behind drawer front.

Partitions fashionably formed of fret carving. Corners often finished with turned finials.

Variations include: elliptical and kidney shapes; table canterburies – with upper shelf on tall, turned uprights; fretwork gallery around top; occasionally lift-top forming writing/reading-slope.

Victorian walnut canterbury with fret-cut dividers.

Bonhams

Early Victorian rosewood canterbury.

MATERIALS

Until about 1840 mahogany or rosewood. Figured walnut for most Victorian pieces, occasionally papier mâché or bamboo. Ebonised mahogany or beech for Art Furniture pieces of the seventies or eighties.

Victorian walnut canterbury doubling as an occasional table.

CONSTRUCTION

Some convincing reproductions of Georgian and Regency canterburies made in the early-20thC may now be very hard to tell from originals. Look for a build-up of dirt around the joints and general signs of wear. The elaborate carving of many Victorian canterburies is too expensive to reproduce so this is a sign of originality. Repairs though, are likely, particularly to fretwork and projecting finials.

DECORATION

Occasionally brass inlay or applied brass ornaments on Regency pieces. Fret carving in scrolling and naturalistic patterns on Victorian. Occasionally inlay of light coloured woods and mother-of-pearl. Typically, papier mâché decoration (see **p. 330**); Japanese lacquer on bamboo (see **p. 330**). Small, turned wooden knob(s) on drawers.

Early Victorian rosewood canterbury.

FINISH

Polish. Ebonised surfaces on some.

RELATIVE VALUES

Highly decorative Victorian examples often fetch more than more elegant earlier ones. Value may seem disproportionate to quality and extent of workmanship.

VICTORIAN REPRODUCTIONS

Early canterburies of Georgian form were still made during the 1850s, so may be later than they look. Generally – though not always – they are slightly heavier than their predecessors.

CHAIRS, WAINSCOT OR 'JOINED'

About

1550-1660,

but still made in country areas, particularly the North, until about 1750.

17thC wainscot chair with carved cresting, ear-pieces and panelled back.

Before 1600 chairs were used only by the master and mistress of the house, everyone else sitting on stools, benches or settles. Although increasingly used by lesser mortals too during the 17thC, the presence of arms and the extent and elaboration of carving found on wainscot chairs indicate their high status. Originally they would have had a loose, upholstered seat cushion.

Most show distinctive regional characteristics too numerous to describe. For further information, see *Oak Furniture* by Victor Chinnery (Antique Collectors' Club).

STYLE AND APPEARANCE

Flat wooden seats with moulded edge projecting slightly beyond deepish, moulded or carved seat rail. Turned legs at front, straight at back, joined by four straight and low stretchers. Gently scrolling arms with scrolled ends on turned supports; supports usually continuous with legs. Moderately tall panelled back with decorative carving and occasionally inlay. Uprights and rails often carved too; top rail extending beyond sides with supporting 'ears' and arched cresting.

Detail of scrolled arm and turned supports.

MATERIALS

Oak, with holly, bog oak; fruitwoods and the like for inlay.

CONSTRUCTION

Tongue-and-groove panelling; pegged mortise-and-tenon joints.

DECORATION

Carving: Extremely variable, with many regional characteristics. Mostly stylized flowers and vines, occasionally birds. Sometimes geometric. From the late-16thC some Renaissance classical ornament such as guilloche.

Inlay or marquetry: Usually floral, occasionally geometric borders.

FINISH

Polish. Should have good patina.

RELATIVE VALUES

The most expensive (into five figures) will show all the most desirable features – a fine cresting, 'ear pieces', inlay or marquetry, good patina and plentiful and vigorous carving.

VICTORIAN WAINSCOT CHAIRS

Wainscot chairs were sometimes reproduced by the Victorians, but these lack patina, are generally too dark in colour and have shallow carving, restricted in extent. If these features are not obvious, look for genuine signs of wear, particularly on the front stretcher or the under-sides of the feet; and for 'rubbed' areas on the ends of the arms. Be suspicious if all four stretchers are equally 'damaged'.

CHAIRS: BACK-STOOLS, FARTHINGALES, CANED AND OTHER 17THC SEATS

About

1615-1700

Typical upholstered farthingale chair.

The 17thC saw the widespread introduction of the single chair, referred to at the time as a 'back-stool', literally a stool with a back. Fixed upholstery sometimes replaced loose cushions and after 1660 woven canework – introduced from the East Indies – was fashionably seen on the seats, and often the backs too, of most chairs.

Chairs were increasingly made in sets, comprising both arm and single chairs.

Continental (and particularly Dutch) influence was strong on all furniture. Under William and Mary, chair design was greatly influenced by the Huguenot designer Daniel Marot (p. 200).

STYLE AND APPEARANCE

Three most common types were:

Farthingales: Fashionable about 1615-1660. The name refers to the gap between the seat and back which presumably allowed women wearing hooped farthingale skirts to sit in relative comfort. These were probably the earliest type of back-stool. At first, they had four matching turned legs joined by four straight and low stretchers. Upholstered seat; low, upholstered rectangular back with uprights covered in same material. Before long, the front legs only were turned back, the back legs being plain, square-sectioned, and slightly splayed. Back raked. Baluster turning replaced about 1650 by bobbin and twist.

Oak dining-chairs: About 1650-1700, many of 'country' appearance, but not necessarily of provincial manufacture. Considerable regional variations though, the most distinctive being the 'Yorkshire and Derbyshire' chair. Despite its name, made in other areas too. Generally square seats, rimmed around the edge. Back with vertical or horizontal slats, sometimes carved. Often a shaped or scrolling top rail. Turned legs at front. After 1660, a new stretcher arrangement became apparent. The plain back, and turned or carved front stretchers, were set higher than before with two stretchers at either side. This type was quickly superseded in fashionable London (and soon elsewhere) by:

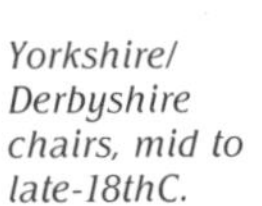

Yorkshire/ Derbyshire chairs, mid to late-18thC.

Christie's

Bonhams

Oak dining-chair, common from about 1660-1680.

Canework chairs: First introduced to Britain about 1665. Inexpensive and common, made in large numbers for all types of houses. At first, a squarish seat and back with large gap between. Widely spaced canework. All uprights and stretchers fashionably twist, occa-

Sotheby's

Late-17thC chair with canework seat and back, and scrolled front legs.

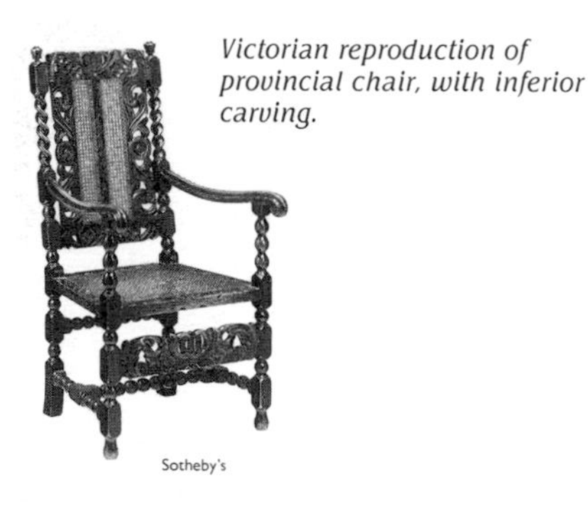

Victorian reproduction of provincial chair, with inferior carving.

Sotheby's

sionally bobbin, turned. Back uprights ending in finials. Flat arms, slightly shaped. 'H' stretchers introduced with additional and higher stretcher at front and back.

In 1670, the height of the back increased. The back top rail was formed as carved cresting, complemented by deep, carved front stretcher. Framing of the back also carved. Swept arms, scrolling over the uprights, which were still continuous with the legs. S-scrolls sometimes appeared in the design of front legs and increasingly on the front stretcher and framing of the canework on the back. This could be one or two rectangular panels, occasionally an oval.

After 1685, backs grew taller and narrower, with turned column uprights, sometimes fluted. Mesh of canework finer. Cresting sat on, rather than between, the uprights and sometimes matched the front stretcher. Seats smaller, supported on S scroll and baluster turned legs, fashionably ending in an inward-scrolling 'Braganza' foot, a Spanish feature. Front stretcher often of Dutch bow form.

During the 1690s, caning on back was often replaced by openwork carving and an upholstered seat. Sometimes a serpentine X-frame stretcher, close to the ground and supported on bun feet with tapered legs above and inverted cup knees. Alternatively, the carved front stretcher was set back several inches and tenoned into side stretchers. Legs sometimes formed as broad S-scrolls. Cabriole legs began to appear around 1700.

Bonhams

1690s walnut chair of Marot type, with inverted cup knees and Dutch bow stretcher.

DUTCH IMPORTS

Many almost identical caned chairs were imported from Holland in this period and usually can be identified by thicker and shallower twist turning than English pieces; and by the absence or low position of the rear stretcher (level with the 'H' stretchers). More than one type of turning may be present within a single chair.

MATERIALS

Oak, walnut. Cheaper beech sometimes used for painted or japanned chairs.

CONSTRUCTION

Tenoned joints until about 1685. Thereafter, cresting dowelled on to up-rights and seat dowelled on to legs at front. Chairs of this type made in walnut or beech may be structurally weak. Check for signs of repair.

DECORATION

Turning: Bobbin and twist more fashionable until about 1685, then baluster, but all types used at all times.

Carving: Mostly scrolls, flowers and foliage. By 1685 often pierced. Amorini supporting the crown (signifying the restoration of the monarchy) a popular motif for cresting, even during the William and Mary period. Found as late as 1700.

FINISH

Generally polish. Grandest painted or gilt. Sometimes ebonised. During Restoration period fashionably japanned. Sometimes beech 'grained' (painted) to simulate more expensive walnut.

RELATIVE VALUES

Singles cheaper than armchairs. Those showing strong Dutch influence, with elaborate carving and swept arms fetch the largest sums, especially the Marot types, with upholstered seats, pierced backs. Generally increasing in value as they get later and more elaborate.

CHAIRS: QUEEN ANNE

About

1700-1730

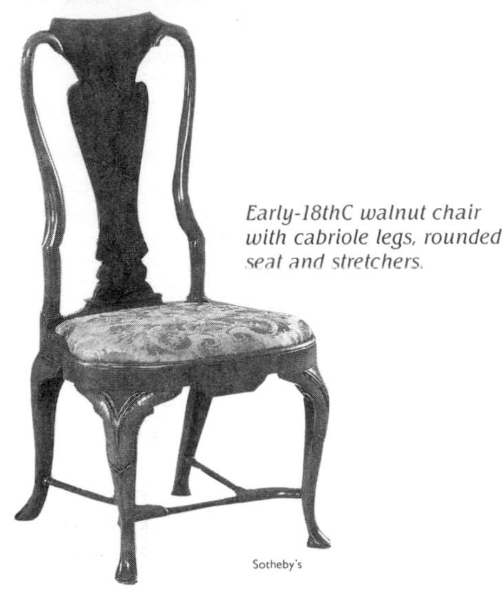
Early-18thC walnut chair with cabriole legs, rounded seat and stretchers.

Sotheby's

A highly distinctive style, actually extending well beyond Queen Anne's reign.

STYLE AND APPEARANCE

Backs have a curving outline, with elongated S-scrolls flowing into dipped top rail. Broad vase-shaped splats, after about 1710 slotting into a 'shoe' (**p. 59**). Cabriole legs and drop-in seats. All these are classic features.

Early, taller, 'bended back' versions were curved in section to fit the sitter's back. Seat rails were shallow, cabriole legs slender and ending in hoof or pad feet. They had simple turned stretchers with one additional stretcher at the back.

Spindly Victorian reproductions.

Christie's

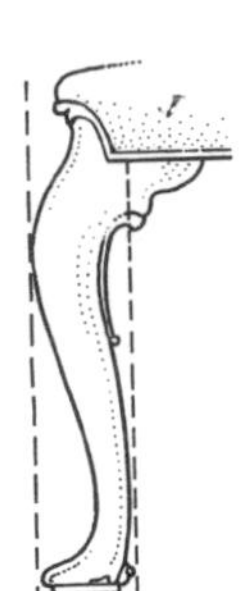
Cabriole leg, carved from one piece of timber, with additional 'ear-piece' at the knee.

Later versions had lower backs, sometimes broader and occasionally rounder seats, with deeper, often shaped, rails, no stretchers and bolder, squatter cabrioles, sometimes ending in claw-and-ball feet. Strengthening 'ears' or 'shoulder pieces' were added either side of the knee. Legs could be decorated with fine C-scrolls and/or scallop shells carved on the knee. The back uprights were flat-fronted, a feature which subsequently became standard on chairs of most types.

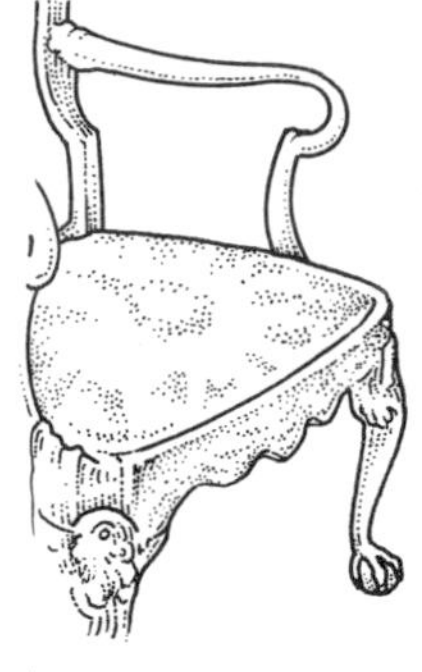
Queen Anne armchair with distinctive shepherd's crook arms.

Armchairs had their arms set back several inches from the front rail – they were no longer continuous with the front legs. Some had distinctive 'shepherd's crook' arms.

A few chairs had upholstered seats and backs, with no gap between them. These could be tall, with straight sides and top, or lower and 'spoon-backed'.

Later Queen Anne chair with square seat and without stretchers.

MATERIALS

Walnut. Very occasionally mahogany around 1730. From this date onwards beech was used for the frames of upholstered seats. Because it is very susceptible to woodworm, these have often been replaced. Frequent re-upholstery may also hasten their demise.

CONSTRUCTION

During this period methods evolved which set the standards for virtually all chairs made until the present day. (For details, see **CHIPPENDALE, p. 56**).

One feature relating specifically to chairs of this period was the veneering of flat surfaces: the splat, the front faces of the uprights, and the facings of the seat rails.

DECORATION

Restrained carving on knees, popularly a scallop shell (on the best pieces 'hipped' into the seat rail), but could be foliage, cartouches, or husks. Sometimes a single ornament present in centre of front seat rail. Limited decoration – mostly small scrolls – began to appear on the back towards 1730.

Some very grand pieces were decorated with silver or gilt gesso (museum pieces today). A few had marquetry decoration on veneered surfaces.

FINISH

Polish.

RELATIVE VALUES

Top quality later versions with all the best features have the highest values. Pairs may be about three times the value of a single; a set would be exceptional. Armchairs too are rare, and very expensive.

REPRODUCTIONS

Victorian (and later) craftsmen loved to reproduce Queen Anne chairs, but often in mahogany – generally an instant giveaway – and too thin in the legs. The backs were often too high and the seat rails too shallow. They tend to look rather mean, reflecting the economic use of timber. Construction of the seat frame (**p. 68**) should indicate its origin.

CHAIRS: PRE-CHIPPENDALE

About

1725-1750

Robust chair of the 1740s reflecting the ponderous architectural style of William Kent.

Sotheby's

A transitional phase, its most significant feature being the introduction of mahogany – hard, richly coloured and ideal for carving – following the destruction of the European walnut crop in the exceptionally hard winter of 1709. The grandest furniture of this time was made in the ponderous classical style of the architect William Kent; regular household furniture retained the simple, elegant lines of the Queen Anne period, and combined them with some of the 'new features' now thought of as 'Chippendale'.

STYLE AND APPEARANCE

Solid and substantial, with broad seats and squatter and broader cabrioles than before, typically with claw-and-ball, sometimes 'hairy paw' feet. Winged serpentine rail characteristic of Chippendale chairs now started to appear but it was less elegant, with protruding, scrolling corners, or shoulders were rounded, dipping sharply into centre of crest rail. Splats were pierced, often ribbed and splaying out towards the top. Carving on the knees was often hipped into the seat rail. Drop-in or stuff-over seats, sometimes with show-wood rails.

MATERIALS

Mainly mahogany, but still some made from walnut (as stocks lasted), even for 'mahogany-style' chairs.

CONSTRUCTION

No longer part-veneered, but constructed from solid timber throughout (see **CHIPPENDALE CHAIRS, opposite**).

DECORATION

Carving on knees and crest rail. Acanthus and foliate designs replaced former shells and small C-scrolls. Grandest chairs could be 'parcel-gilt', meaning small areas of gilded decoration.

FINISH

Polish.

RELATIVE VALUES

The scarcity of quality, well-proportioned chairs in this transitional style pushes their price up well into the thousands. A fine pair may fetch three or even four times as much as a standard quality pair. Country or provincial versions will usually be less than half the price.

Transitional chair with Queen Anne legs and stretchers, but serpentine rail and pierced splat.

Sotheby's

PROVINCIAL DESIGNS

Because of poor communications, makers outside London did not have full access to new designs. Thus provincial designs of this time may still retain stretchers, even when made in mahogany with the 'new' pierced splats and winged crestings. Similarly, Queen Anne splats are still found on mid-18thC chairs with straight, Chippendale-style legs.

The time-lag between the evolution of a new style in fashionable London and its adoption by makers elsewhere gradually diminished as communications improved, but even so, in some areas local preferences remained strong and individual types and designs of chair persisted for several decades.

CHAIRS: CHIPPENDALE

About

1750-1780

Sotheby's

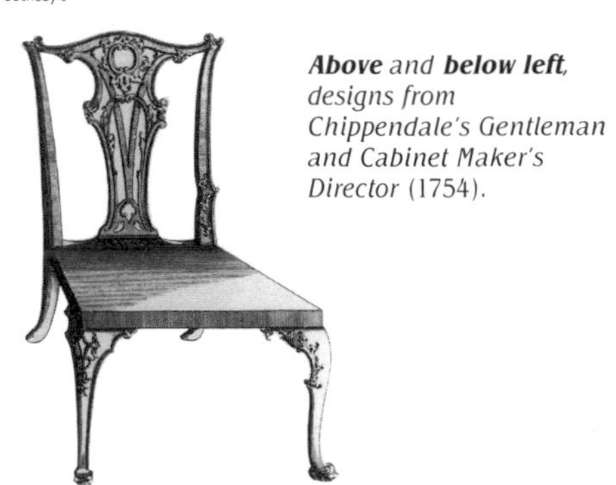

***Above** and **below left**, designs from Chippendale's Gentleman and Cabinet Maker's Director (1754).*

Thomas Chippendale's *Gentleman and Cabinet Maker's Director*, published in three editions (1754, 1755 and 1762) had a historic influence on mid-18thC chair design. In it, Chippendale applied popular rococo, chinoiserie and Gothic design motifs to already fashionable shapes for both grand and simple household furniture. Few designs were copied precisely. Chair makers at all levels – London, provincial and country – adapted and modified their designs to suit their own capabilities, and their clients' tastes and pockets.

STYLE AND APPEARANCE

Lower backs than previously, with serpentine crest rails, generally ending in outward-curving scrolls. (Rounded shoulders rare.) Carved and pierced splats of varied design including rococo C-scrolls, ribbons ('ribband-back' in 18thC terminology), Gothic arches, tracery and quatrefoils, scrolls and many other interlacing patterns. 'Chinese' chairs with Chinese fretwork instead of a splat with a pagoda-shaped cresting. Space under arms sometimes similarly filled with fretwork. (Because of their fragility and because chinoiserie was often confined to bedrooms, not many of these chairs survive.)

Side uprights were flat and either plain or fluted. Carving not unknown, but unless of high quality and obviously by the same hand as the crest rail, be suspicious.

A design often seen today, but not illustrated in Chippendale's *Director*, was the ladder-back, in which the pierced and carved horizontals echo the crest rail in shape and design. Thought to date from the 1760s onwards.

Seats were flat and straight (dished seats not introduced for dining chairs until about 1750). Square corners with straight legs, rounded with cabrioles, the latter usually indicating an early date. Stuff-over (occasionally with show-wood rail) or drop-in seats; stuff-over seats correctly finished with close brass nails, not gimp (a 19thC method).

Comfortably shaped arms with supports rising two thirds from back.

Front legs could be cabriole, with foliate carving on knees and claw-and-ball feet, or, more commonly, straight, either plain or with simple mouldings. Sometimes chamfered inner edges. Blind fret-carving or legs composed of carved Gothic cluster columns occasionally seen on highest quality chairs. On both types, rear legs raked backwards. As a very general rule, the steeper the angle, the poorer the quality.

H-stretcher arrangement, the cross stretcher closer to the front than previously, with an additional higher back stretcher.

Corner brackets sometimes present at top of legs. Could be Chinese fret-work.

MATERIALS

Mahogany was the fashionable wood, with beech for stuff-over seat rails (see **CONSTRUCTION**). Oak, walnut, elm, ash and beech were used too by country makers.

COUNTRY VERSIONS

Instantly identifiable when made in woods other than mahogany. Often less well-proportioned and slighter overall. Can have a top-heavy look. Simpler, less confident design of splats with very little, or no, carving. Legs often completely plain; cabrioles end in pad feet. Crudest versions may have wooden seat with side-to-side planking nailed to seat frame.

VICTORIAN REPRODUCTIONS

Either rather clumsy with too much, too ornate carving and bandy and too thin cabrioles ending in heavy claw-and-ball feet; **or** mean and spindly-looking with flat, shaped splats and no carving at all. Frequently ill-proportioned with narrow seats, tallish backs and thin, shallow seat rails. Shoe-piece is often formed as part of seat rail. Rear legs seldom raked far back. On claw-and-ball feet, claw tends to perch on, rather than clutch, the ball.

More reproductions have been made of mid-18thC chairs than of any other period, but a distinction should be made between those 'in the style of' (as above) and genuine copies, whether intended to deceive or not. It was, and still is not uncommon for a good set of chairs to be enlarged. If this was done some time ago, it may be virtually impossible to identify the later chairs. However, as they were made from different timber, there will probably be a difference in weight.

Long sets were often numbered with incised Roman numerals on the seat rail. If these are present and are not consecutive, the set is obviously incomplete.

Occasionally, arms have been added to one or more single chairs in a run to make a more saleable set. Identify these by comparing the width of the seats – a true armchair is a few inches wider than a single.

CONSTRUCTION

The methods employed by London makers of the mid-18thC set the standards for virtually all wooden chair manufacturers until the present day. **Principal features:** With one exception, mortise-and-tenon **joints** through-

MODERN REPRODUCTIONS

These have a particular tendency to be smaller and narrower than originals, a necessity for many of today's smaller dining rooms. If you are thinking of buying a set of old chairs to fit around a modern reproduction table – or vice versa – it may well be worth marking out the floor to ensure that they all fit comfortably.

A *Typical Chippendale chair with cabriole legs and claw-and-ball feet;* ***B*** *fine quality armchair with pierced legs and stretchers;* ***C*** *mahogany armchair with 'Gothic' splat;* ***D*** *'Chinese' chair with pagoda cresting;* ***E*** *ladder-back;* ***F*** *simple provincial chair with wooden seat;* ***G*** *Victorian Chippendale reproductions.*

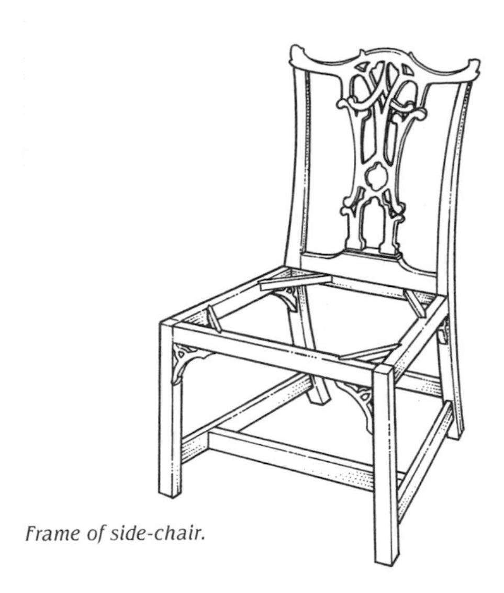
Frame of side-chair.

out; stretcher joints usually dove-tailed. Until about 1715, all joints pegged, but after that date those on backs and leg/stretcher joints only glued. Pegging on all joints appears on country-made furniture until much later.

Arms screwed to side seat rail and back uprights, the screws countersunk in a circular groove, their heads concealed by pegs or dowels. Pointed machine-made screws did not appear until about 1850 so earlier screws can be identified by their irregularities and blunt ends. If a hand-made or lathe-turned screw has been undisturbed since the 18thC, the wood around the head will probably be noticeably stained with rust.

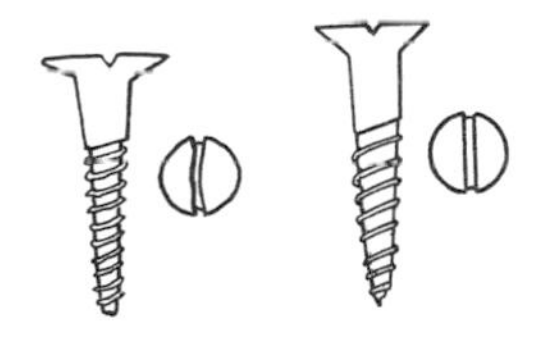
***Left**, hand-cut screw; **right**, machine-cut screw.*

The **back splat** tenons into the crest rail and into the shoe below, but is glued only at the top to allow some movement of the wood. The shoe is a separate piece of wood from seat rail. Sometimes the splat passes right through the shoe, tenoning into the rail below. On stuff-over seats, the shoe is removable to allow fabric to pass beneath and simply nailed on. A re-upholstered chair will therefore have more than one set of nail holes.

The **crest rail** over-rides the side uprights when curving outwards, but is set between them on a chair with rounded shoulders. In this case, each upright is in two pieces.

Backs of chairs were un-decorated. In the 18thC they were designed to stand against the wall when not in use and in theory the backs were only seen by servants. This practice persisted even when chairs were more often left around a central table – about 1830 onwards.

Drop-in seats were rebated and the frame strengthened by small, close-fitting triangular blocks glued into the corners.

Stuff-over seats with rails of beech or other softwood (beech being a softer and easier wood to hammer tacks into) were strengthened at front – and just occasionally at back too – with corner braces, strips of ½ inch/1.75 cm square sectioned wood about 4-6 inches/9-15 cm long which rebated into grooves cut in the rails. These have often been replaced at a later date with triangular blocks with a curving outer edge, screwed to all four corners. This was a post-1840 practice and will indicate either a later date or a later repair. If the latter, the grooves cut for the original braces will be clearly visible.

A stuff-over seat with a show-wood rail was also usually made of beech, the show-wood being either a strip of veneer or a carved (or gadrooned) moulding, glued and tacked on.

Fretwork **brackets** and railing of 'Chinese' (and some other) chairs were sometimes cut from laminated wood (a process normally associated with the 20thC). Layers of veneer were glued together, the grain of alternate sheets running in opposite directions.

Ear pieces added to either side of cabriole knees were simply glued on, therefore often missing or replaced. These were separate pieces of wood because cabrioles were cut from a single piece of wood and extra width at the top would have meant more wastage. Replacements are usually identified by slight difference in colour and grain of wood and by carving obviously by a different hand.

Straight **legs** are always united by stretchers, cabrioles never at this date.

DECORATION

Carving, principally on splats and top rails and knees of cabrioles.

FINISH

Polish. 19thC chairs may be stained in parts to disguise the use of different batches of timber.

CHAIRS: HEPPLEWHITE

About

1775-1790

Chair designs from George Hepplewhite's Guide (1788).

Light and elegant chairs, greatly influenced by the designs of the architect Robert Adam who advocated the use of neo-classical decorative motifs, light coloured woods and upholstery, and painted or inlaid decoration. Chairs of this date are popularly called Hepplewhite because so many furniture craftsmen followed George Hepplewhite's *Cabinet Maker & Upholsterer's Guide*. Published in 1788, this was the standard guide to style for a wide range of simple domestic furniture in the neo-classical fashion.

STYLE AND APPEARANCE

The most distinctive feature was the shape of the back. This could be oval, hoop, heart or shield. Facings usually moulded; splats delicate and less centralized, with emphasis on continuous verticals rather than curves and scrolls. Popular filler designs include wheatsheaf and neo-classical urns, drapery, swags, anthemions and lyres. Hepplewhite is credited with the first use of the most common motif, Prince of Wales feathers. A slightly concave back – to fit the sitter's back comfortably – is often a sign of quality and authenticity.

Seats were drop-in or stuff-over. Both may have serpentine front rail; latter a deep serpentine apron.

Sides often curve inwards towards the back. Dished seats introduced about 1780. Canework seats on painted or japanned chairs, with loose, flat squab cushions.

RELATIVE VALUES

Value always depends on a combination of factors – well-proportioned correct design and quality of craftsmanship being the most obvious reasons for a high price. Repairs – even when skilfully made – will detract from the value of the piece, especially if there are replacement parts.

The price of a good single chair of this period is often into four figures and in exceptional cases close to five. As a very general guide, a pair of chairs of any date is worth about three times as much as a single, a set of four six times, and a set of six or more at least ten times as much. Until fairly recently six was thought to be a desirable number for a set, but this has now increased to eight. Examine long sets carefully for 'enlargements'.

A chair with arms will invariably be worth more than a similar chair without, though not as much as a pair of singles.

The value of sets of good Victorian or Edwardian reproductions of 18thC chairs has increased substantially in recent years. The price of each one may equal that of a single original chair, though the set as a whole will be considerably less valuable than an original set of equal size.

The price of provincial and country versions is less predictable because of considerable variation in design, but such pieces seldom fetch more than the value of their more sophisticated counterparts.

WEAR

If construction does not provide you with sufficient indication of date, look for genuine signs of wear.

The front stretcher and outer edges of the front legs will always show more signs of knocks than any other part. The undersides of the feet will be rubbed and the corners may be rough from constant knocks. The crest rail and uprights may show signs of repair where the chair has been damaged by incorrect handling.

It is, incidentally, always better to lift a chair by its seat, not its back or arms. Dirt and grease deposited by hands constantly lifting the chair will have stained the underside of the front seat and crest rails and will also have accumulated in the crevices of carving and around the joints. The undersides of seat rails on 19thC copies were often stained to simulate dirt, but the handled areas will probably look lighter where the stain has rubbed off.

Hepplewhite-style mahogany shield-back chair with carved wheat-ears, about 1780-1790.

Sotheby's

Changes in dress fashion allowed narrower seats and arm supports rising almost from the front corners in a concave curve to meet the rests about half way back.

Legs were straight and tapering, tapering on the *inside* edge only, and mostly slender, ending in delicate spade feet. Can be plain, moulded, reeded or fluted, with or without stretchers.

MATERIALS

Mahogany; satinwood for finest quality pieces. Beech or birch for painted and japanned chairs. Oak, elm, beech, birch and local woods still used by country makers. (For details on gilded and upholstered-back Adam-style chairs see **p. 71**.)

CONSTRUCTION

Mostly standard methods employed (see **p. 59**). The shoe was dispensed with for shield, heart and oval backs; instead, rear legs were extended and waisted to join back several inches above seat. Joint secured by screws concealed with dowels. Rounded lower part of shields and ovals made in mitred parts; mouldings help to conceal joins.

DECORATION

Low-relief carving. Painted decoration of flowers, ribbons, some neo-classical urns, garlands, garrya husks on satinwood; on black-japanned or pastel-coloured, painted ground.

FINISH

Polish. Paint, japanning.

RELATIVE VALUES

Prices for quality singles mostly in four figures, provincial and country versions only three. Pairs and sets: multiply as for Chippendale (details, see **p. 60**).

Good points: shield-shaped backs, Prince of Wales feathers, elegantly tapering legs *without* stretchers.

Sotheby's

Edwardian interpretation of Hepplewhite designs.

PROVINCIAL DESIGNS

Provincial and country versions were often plain – no mouldings on legs and back. Most had stretchers, unadventurous splat (no carving). Camel-backs with humped crest-rail (reminiscent of Chippendale) quite common.

Hepplewhite has been much reproduced. These imitations are often identifiable by faulty proportions (for example, shield too wide); flat rather than concave backs; legs tapering on *both* edges.

Late-18thC mahogany hoop-back chair.

Sotheby's

CHAIRS: SHERATON

About

1780-1810

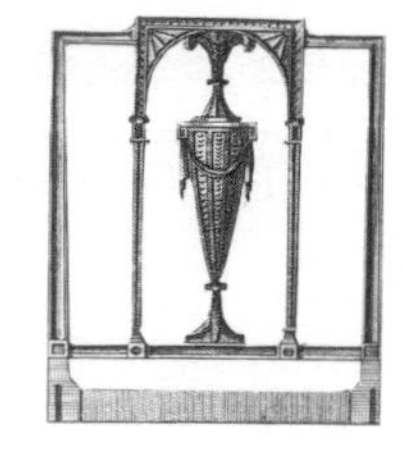
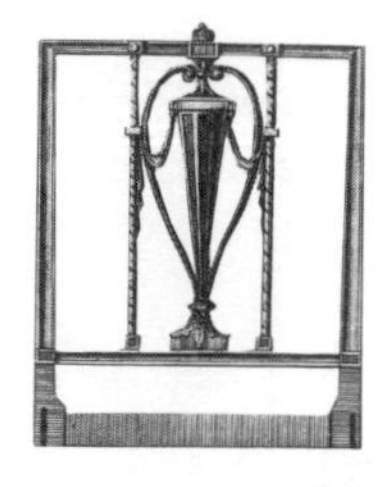

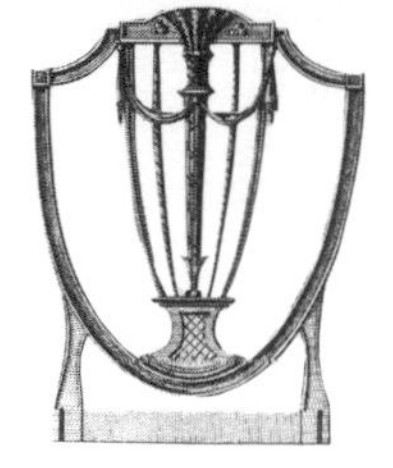
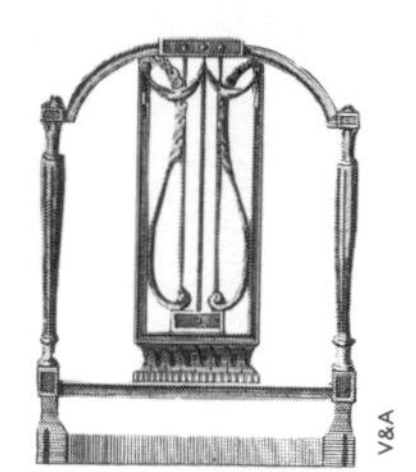

Designs for chair backs from Thomas Sheraton's Drawing Book (1792).

V&A

Although contemporary with Hepplewhite and sharing many features, the designs of Thomas Sheraton (published between 1791 and 1803), exerted a broader and longer-lasting influence. A designer, not a practising cabinet maker, Sheraton illustrated both English and French styles, many of them anticipating the Regency style. Some were highly imaginative and technically ingenious, and probably were never executed.

STYLE AND APPEARANCE

Lighter designs than Hepplewhite's; lower, square backs with strong horizontal and vertical emphasis. Typically a narrow cross-rail several inches above seat with an increasingly broad crest rail. Space between filled with delicately carved and moulded vertical or diagonal bars in a variety of geometric, lattice-work and popular patterns. Fewer curving lines than previously. Sometimes filler design over-rides crest rail in centre (see illus.).

Designs of armchairs were particularly successful: arm rests sweeping down from a point close to crest rail, either to meet vertical supports set slightly back from seat front, or, continuing into a second curve meeting short supports, or even extensions of front legs.

Pair of Sheraton-style mahogany chairs, about 1790-1800.

Bonhams

Very simple Sheraton-style side-chair, 1800.

Sotheby's

Side uprights, arms and legs occasionally turned and sometimes fluted (this more common after 1800). Legs end in spade feet.

Seats were drop-in or stuff-over. May be gently curved at back and sides. Canework and squab cushions on painted and japanned chairs. Not uncommon for these to be over-stuffed at a later date; removal of upholstery will reveal canework holes in frame. (These may have small panel of canework incorporated in the design of the back.)

Narrow, straight, tapering legs, moulded, reeded or fluted, sometimes with spade feet. With or without stretchers.

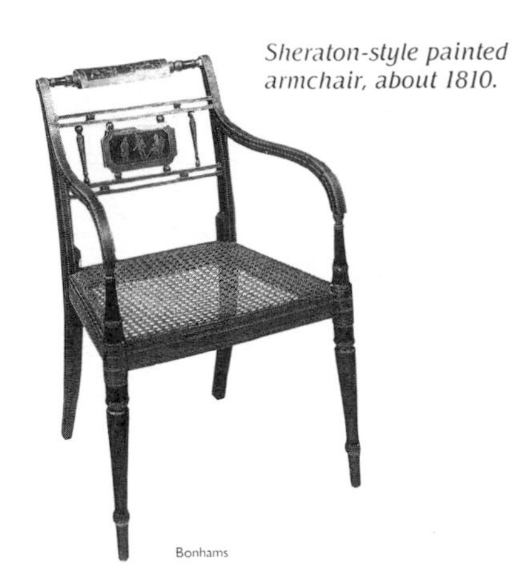

Sheraton-style painted armchair, about 1810.

Bonhams

CHAIRS: REGENCY

About

1800-1840

(extending several years either side of the Regency itself, 1811-1820). Chairs made between about 1825 and 1840 are often referred to as 'late Regency' or 'late classical'; those of the 1830s occasionally still 'William IV').

Regency 'Trafalgar' chair with rope back, sabre legs and drop-in seat.

Sotheby's

Usually very elegant chairs, some based on previous Sheraton types, but many inspired by Ancient Greek *klismos* chairs, with their distinctive sabre legs. Nelson's naval victories resulted in the inclusion of many naval emblems in furniture design after 1803, and in chairs is apparent in back supports carved as twisted rope. This has earned all sabre-leg chairs of Regency date the popular name 'Trafalgars', though correctly this only refers to those with rope designs.

MATERIALS

Mahogany; satinwood; beech and birch when painted or japanned. Beech and sometimes ash for underframes. Oak, beech, elm and local woods for country versions.

CONSTRUCTION

Standard practices employed (see **p. 59**); crest rail set between uprights, not overriding them.

DECORATION

Delicate, often restrained, low-relief carving on splats. Sometimes fine inlay on crest rails, mostly in form of stringing lines. Painted decoration of flowers. See **HEPPLEWHITE, p. 60**.

FINISH

Polish, paint, japanning.

RELATIVE VALUES

Not dissimilar to Hepplewhite (**p. 60**). Even sets of eight seldom more than four figures. The more delicate the design (without losing structural strength), the more desirable will be the chair.

PROVINCIAL AND COUNTRY INTERPRETATIONS

Very plain surfaces, little or no moulding, carving or turning. Straight tapering legs, usually retaining stretchers. Backs were composed of simple vertical and horizontal bars.

STYLE AND APPEARANCE

Sabre-leg chairs: Flush-sided (will lie completely flat when on side), with two horizontal rails forming back supports set between side uprights. Uprights with neatly scrolled ends forming continuous curving lines with side seat rails *and* legs. Sometimes continuous reeding present on front/upper surface. Front legs of sabre form (see illus.), rear legs also outward-curving, but less pronounced. No stretchers. Crest rail may be deep and flat, often with restrained carved or inlaid decoration. Lower support usually carved and pierced (in a great variety of designs). Either rail can be of twisted rope form, sometimes bordering section of other shape.

Sotheby's

Cane-seated armchair similar to 'Trafalgar' chair on previous page, with typically scrolled arms.

Shallow, removable, upholstered seat (sometimes canework with squab cushion instead) contained within side rails and flush with rail at front and back. Armchairs with bold scroll arms curving down from lower part of crest rail several inches from front, but sometimes resting directly on it. Small rosette may conceal counter-sunk screw or pin on outer side of knee, strengthening seat rail joint. May not be original, but added later to disguise a mend.

Deep, broad crest rails over-riding side uprights introduced about 1820, though most post-1830. Later examples undecorated and may be curved in section for greater comfort. Actually a more correct interpretation of *klismos* chair-back than previous form and known at the time as 'Grecian'.

Many chairs made with similar backs but stuff-over seats and **straight, tapering legs**. These could be ring-turned or reeded or, after 1820, fluted, becoming thicker and clumsier with time.

William IV chair with broad crest-rail and straight legs.

Bonhams

Arms were of the previous Sheraton type, by about 1830 always curving straight down into the front legs.

Country versions with straight tapering legs of square section, still joined by stretchers, and planked, dished seats. Popular design for lower back support a double rail enclosing wooden balls. Some rope turning will occasionally be found.

After 1835 designs became noticeably fussier, with shaped and carved crest rails, heavy legs and deep, moulded show-wood seat rails. Sometimes drop-in seats of sabre-leg chair type were incorporated.

Regency chair retaining elegant rope back but with straight turned legs.

Bonhams

MATERIALS

Predominantly rosewood and mahogany. Elm, oak and fruitwoods for country chairs; beech

'SCRAMBLING'

Because of their relatively simple structure and design, a set of straight-legged chairs of this date is easy to enlarge by 'scrambling' – taking all the chairs apart, removing one or two members from each one – sufficient to make up a number of 'new' chairs – and by replacing the missing parts with new timber. The resulting set does not include a single totally new chair, but a large number of 'repaired' ones. This practice can be very difficult to detect without examining every member and comparing it with corresponding members in the rest of the set for colour, grain, finish, knocks, and so on. If openly done, and within reason, and reflected in the price, scrambling is not always unacceptable.

and pine for painted pieces. Brass and ebony used for inlay.

CONSTRUCTION

Sabre-leg chairs: Back and seat rails tenoned into sides. Flat crest rails sometimes veneered. Legs and side rails cut from single piece of timber, the wood sawn across the grain, thereby creating structural weakness, particularly below the knees. Check there for signs of repair. (Because of this design flaw and the technical difficulties involved in the cutting, country makers appear to have avoided sabre legs altogether.)

Drop-in seats sit on pegs rising from centre of front and back rails. Stuff-over seats rare and probably indicate provincial manufacture.

Straight-leg chairs. Standard seat frame construction was employed.

On both types, the over-riding top rail is rebated into front of uprights and screwed from behind. Holes filled with dowels.

DECORATION

Ebony stringing and inlay on crest rails from about 1805-1815, thereafter brass. Alternatively, shallow carving flush with surface. Most popular motif for both types, the anthemion. Palm leaves also popular.

Gilt decoration on ebonised (black-painted) surfaces, mostly as simple lines and small rosettes.

Some sabre-legs painted and grained to simulate more valuable rosewood.

FINISH

Polish, paint.

RELATIVE VALUES

Always popular, so, despite sets being relatively common, prices are level with those of earlier Hepplewhite and Sheraton chairs.

Desirable features which raise the price include solid rosewood and brass inlay.

Grained beech (of which sets abound) cost considerably less than rosewood.

Late Regency/William IV, with over-riding crest rails, used to be a cheaper option, but they have become more popular.

Sotheby's

Regency beech chair turned to simulate bamboo.

MOCK-BAMBOO

The exotic furnishings of the Prince of Wales's Brighton Pavilion encouraged a fashion for simulated bamboo chairs made in beech and pine and painted in cream, brown or pastel colours. All members are turned, with double collars representing the nodes of the cane. With caned seats, simple arrangements of verticals and horizontals forming the backs, and tapering legs splaying outwards towards the foot, these delicate little chairs were intended for occasional or bedroom use, not for dining. Crudely gilded modern versions have been made since the thirties for use by the hotel and catering trades.

CHAIRS: VICTORIAN BALLOON-BACKS

about

1840-1885

Typical delicate mid-Victorian parlour chair.

The most familiar Victorian chair, made in various forms and for a variety of rooms, long after its rococo or 'Old French' style was generally unfashionable. The rounded seat and waisted back reflected contemporary dress fashion.

STYLE AND APPEARANCE

The majority with slender cabriole legs flowing down from serpentine seat rails and ending in neat, slightly pointed French-type, or scroll feet, the scroll formed almost as a ball. Continuous narrow moulding running along edge of seat rail – just visible beneath upholstery – and down legs. D-shaped seat with serpentine front and deeply padded upholstery. Backs waisted, base of sides being continuous with back legs or formed as carved scroll.

Most with round, literally 'balloon-shaped' backs with carved and sometimes pierced cross-rail, but there are several variations:

- Dipped top (an early feature).
- Shouldered top.
- Circular or oval back, the lower curve taking the place of the cross-rail.
- Upholstered Louis XV back.
- Angular 'Gothic' shape (this was a later feature).

Dining versions with straight turned legs, become thicker and more bulbous with time. Early versions may have Regency-type drop-in seat, later a deep, sometimes moulded, show-wood seat rail. Later backs often considerably

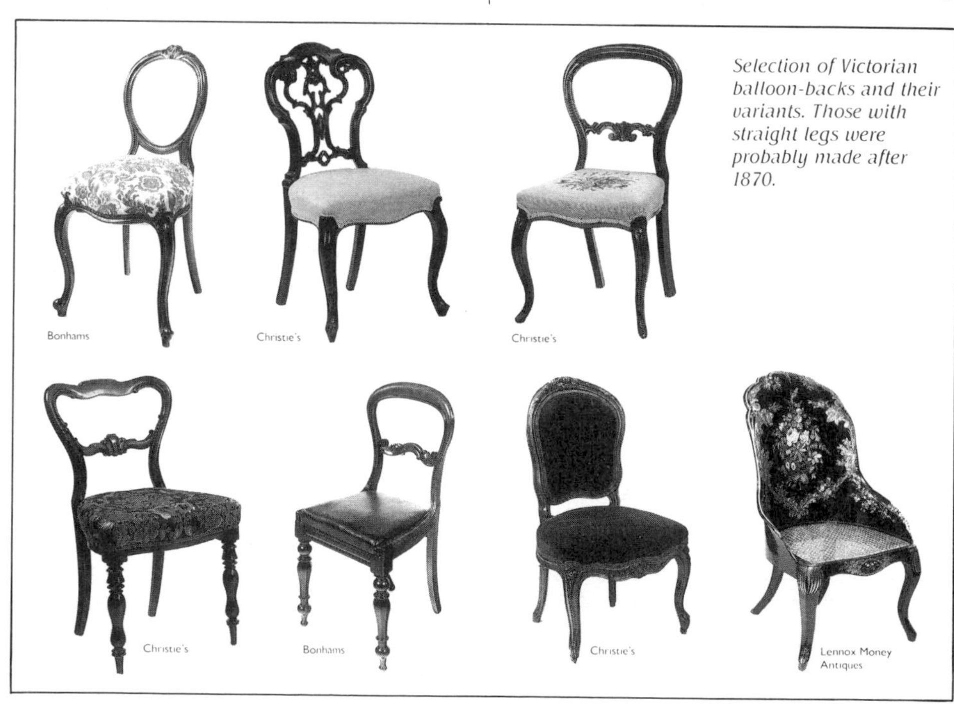

Selection of Victorian balloon-backs and their variants. Those with straight legs were probably made after 1870.

heavier, occasionally with a vertical splat.

Lighter 'fancy' versions were made for bedrooms, in beech with thin, turned legs splayed at the foot and joined by stretchers, canework seats, and often painted or japanned surfaces. Similar, but stained, cheap beech types mass-manufactured for country use.

MATERIALS

Solid rosewood, walnut and mahogany. Sometimes beech, grained to simulate rosewood; or painted or japanned. Beech and birch for under-frames. Occasionally papier mâché (or purporting to be so, but actually of wood with typical papier mâché decoration).

CONSTRUCTION

Standard methods generally employed, but dowels instead of mortise-and-tenon joints became increasingly common after 1850. These *may*, but not necessarily, be detected by the presence of a small, *single* cutting gauge mark at the side of joints. Two marks will indicate a mortise-and-tenon.

Because of their fragile construction it is not advisable to use cabriole leg versions for dining; they will not tolerate heavy use. Indeed, marriages of front and back legs are not uncommon. Check for matching timber.

DECORATION

Limited carving on backs, sometimes pierced; occasionally on knees too. Incised machine-carved dot-dash carving on later (often Gothic-style) versions.

Papier mâché with mother-of-pearl, painted and gilt decoration on a black ground, mostly flowers and scrolls.

FINISH

Polish, japanning, paint. Stain for cheapest.

RELATIVE VALUES

Great variations in price. Most valuable – whether sets or singles – are rosewood, followed by walnut, then mahogany. Stained beech considerably cheaper. Fine carving and cabriole legs add to value. Price of singles now into three figures, sets of any quality into four.

Papier mâché is very collectable. Price of one of these can be equivalent to a set of six others of low quality.

CHAIRS: OTHER 19THC AND EARLY 20THC TYPES

About

1840-1915

Typically late-Victorian, yet in no easily identifiable style.

Bonhams

More varied in style and quality than any time before or since, traditional hand-craftsmanship having to compete with cheaper mass-manufacture aided by machinery. Numerous (variously-interpreted) pastiches of historic styles (plus later reproductions) and new arts and crafts, aesthetic and progressive or art nouveau styles appeared at various times.

Sets of (usually six) side-chairs were often purchased *en suite* with sofa (or *chaise longue*) and pair of easy chairs.

STYLE AND APPEARANCE

Styles are too varied to describe in detail, but the broad categories are:

Rococo (sometimes described in the 19thC as 'Old French' or 'Louis Quatorze'); about 1840-1885: See **CHAIRS: VICTORIAN BALLOON-BACKS, p. 66**.

Post-1870 chair in a vaguely Renaissance style.

Gothic (i) about 1830-1870: Fashionable for halls, libraries. Dark oak. Ornate carving of decorative motifs derived from Gothic architecture. Tall backs typically with pinnacles. Square seats; straight, carved legs with or without stretchers.

Gothic (ii) 'Reformed Gothic', about 1830-1870: Light oak. Very simple frames of architectural form, sometimes buttressed underframes (after Pugin, see ***p. 228***). Chamfered edges on straight members. Legs turned or square. Square seats, leather upholstery. Some geometric inlay in dark colours.

Gothic (iii) 'Commercial Gothic', about 1860-1890: Often inferior quality manufacture. Inlay or shallow-carved dot-dash decoration with shallow-carved quatrefoils on non-Gothic forms (see **Nameless Victorian styles** opposite).

Elizabethan (or **'Jacobean'**), about 1830-1865: Popular for dining-rooms. Often confused use of decorative motifs and forms. Many chairs actually of Restoration type with tall backs (rectangular panels of upholstery rather than canework), spiral turned uprights, ornate carved crestings, turned and carved legs and stretchers. (See also **CHAIRS: UPHOLSTERED** for the prie dieu, a popular 'Elizabethan' type.)

Renaissance, about 1870-1915: Also popular for dining-rooms. Dark stained wood. Ornate carving all over of strapwork, cartouches, and other Renaissance motifs. Leather or rexine (imitation leather) upholstery on square seats and rectangular central back panels.

Arts and Crafts, about 1865-1895: See **CHAIRS: WINDSORS, COUNTRY** for Morris & Co. rush-seated chairs and ladder-backs.

Art Furniture (or Aesthetic), about 1870-1890: Ebonised finish with shallow incised carving, mostly of straight lines. Strong vertical and horizontal emphasis. Turned uprights with many spindles. Straight close-ring-turned legs. Square seats.

Some similar art furniture chairs in Anglo-Japanese form. Generally a lighter feel overall with thinner, plainer members. Not always ebonised. Sometimes the back included a painted and gilded panel.

Art nouveau (or 'Quaint' or 'Old English'), about 1890-1915: Tall narrow backs, sometimes tapering inwards towards top. Straight, often spindly legs. Plain vertical splats, often pierced or carved with hearts, stylized flowers, trailing vines.

Variations include Liberty's heavy oak chairs.

Reproductions of 18thC styles, about 1865-1915: (See **p. 57**.)

MATERIALS

Mahogany, rosewood, walnut, oak. Some satinwood. Beech and birch for ebonised and cheaper stained or painted chairs.

CONSTRUCTION

Machine-cut dowels used extensively instead of mortise-and-tenon. (Pegged mortise-and-tenon used on some reformed Gothic chairs, but not many of these around.) Seat frames strengthened with triangular blocks at each

Underframe showing screwed-on corner blocks.

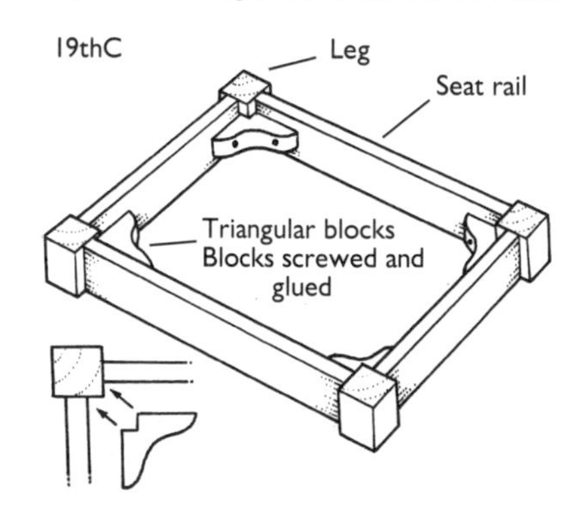

corner with outer edge waved to take screws. Screws machine-made and pointed. Machinery also widely used for cutting and carving. Many pieces stamped underneath with registration number of design.

DECORATION

Virtually all chairs with some carving, much done by machine and therefore shallow and often lacking in character. Often flush with surface. Grooving and dot-dash ornament very common after 1870. (Sometimes picked out in gold on fashionably ebonised surfaces.)

Some inlay, particularly of ebony or boxwood on Gothic pieces.

Some papier mâché pieces typically japanned, with painted, gilt and mother-of-pearl decoration.

FINISH

Polish for better quality pieces. Cheaper pieces frequently stained and varnished. Ebonised finish especially popular between about 1870 and 1890.

RELATIVE VALUES

Extremely variable, according to quality. In general, the same rules apply for sets versus singles as for chairs of other dates, but prices often start at a lower base, definitely in two rather than three figures. A reputable maker's stamp (say Gillow's or Shoolbred's) or a verified design by a noted aesthetic or arts and crafts designer will certainly add to the value.

NAMELESS VICTORIAN STYLES

From around 1870 many chairs which are instantly recognizable today as Victorian were made in nameless styles. Really squared-up versions of balloon-backs, they tend to have low, squarish backs, D-shaped or square seats with shallow moulded seat rails, narrow carved splats of cross-rails, and straight turned legs with or without stretchers. Shallow machine-carved decoration often runs around the back.

Many distinctive chairs were also made in new materials such as bamboo and wicker (many for gardens and conservatories). Cast iron was used only for garden chairs. Papier mâché was used for a variety of styles, mostly providing only the surface decoration.

CHAIRS: UPHOLSTERED, WING (OR EASY)

About

1700 onwards

Mid-18thC wing chair with straight legs and stretchers.

Christie's

Deriving from adjustable-back French sleeping chairs of the 1670s and made in virtually standard 18thC form at various times until the present day, wing chairs were for relaxation, not formal use. The wings protected the sitter from draughts.

STYLE AND APPEARANCE

About 1700-1750: Cabriole legs, either plain with pad feet and turned stretchers, or with carved knees, claw-and-ball feet and (usually) no stretchers. Rear square legs raked backwards. Until about 1730, a marked divide between back and wings, with high curved back, and wings curving sharply down to top of bold, outward-scrolling arms. After 1730, wings and back seem to follow one continuous curve. Two types of scroll arm. Plump upholstery with deep, loose seat cushion.

About 1750-1780: Legs, straight, plain and square, sometimes moulded, linked by stretchers. Occasionally with blind fret carving of Chinese or Gothic nature. Back straight or waved. Wings of equal height to back. Outward roll of arms less pronounced. Padding and seat cushion less fat.

About 1780-1810: Straight, plain, tapering legs without stretchers. Sometimes on castors. Narrower look overall, with flat top and comparatively straight wings and arms.

Victorian: Various simple curving outlines and stumpy turned bun feet on castors. Reproduction Queen Anne with thin cabrioles around the end of the century.

MATERIALS

Walnut and mahogany for legs. Beech and other softwoods for under frame. Legs (and stretchers) were the only visible wooden parts, otherwise fully upholstered.

CONSTRUCTION

Standard methods employed. Carving on knees sometimes hipped into seat.

Repairs likely, particularly to wings. Check for loose joints. Marriages of old legs to new frames not uncommon. At least part of the underframe should be visible for inspection. Upholstery unlikely to be original.

DECORATION

Some carving on knees, legs and feet until about 1770.

FINISH

Polish. Fashionable upholstery fabrics included silk, silk velvet, needlework, leather, silk damask. Early examples were edged with braid; after about 1750 with close brass-nailing. Gimp or tasselled fringes in Queen Victoria's reign.

RELATIVE VALUES

18thC chairs certainly in four figures, some early ones almost into five, but decreasing towards three according to date and simplicity of design. Original, usable upholstery is a considerable bonus.

INADEQUATE REPRODUCTIONS

Many, many 20thC reproductions. Apart from some exaggerated Queen Anne versions produced before and between the wars, most lack robust quality of originals. Their appearance is not helped by insubstantial synthetic upholstery materials.

CHAIRS: UPHOLSTERED

About

1720-1840

Queen Anne side-chair, about 1730.

Sotheby's

Surviving upholstered chairs made for drawing-room use date mostly from after 1720 and, although originally made in sets, are more often found today in pairs, or even singles.

Many resemble contemporary dining-chairs in the design of legs and stretchers and the general shape of arms, but have fully upholstered seats (sometimes with a show-wood rail), fully or partly upholstered backs and mostly open arms with padded rests. Some (particularly those with cabriole legs) will have shaped and carved rear legs – a sign of high quality.

STYLE AND APPEARANCE

Most common types:

Side-chairs (without arms), about 1720-

Mid-18thC side-chair with fine pierced stretchers.

Sotheby's

***Left**, mahogany 'Gainsborough' armchair, about 1760-1770.*

***Right**, neo-classical gilded drawing-room chairs in the style of Robert Adam.*

1770: Straight, flat, upholstered backs, often with slightly rounded corners. Occasionally serpentine top around 1750.

Spoon-back or 'Compass-seated' chairs, about 1720-1740: Shepherd's crook arms, cabriole legs, waisted 'spoon' backs.

Chippendale style, about 1750-1775: Low, square backs and broad, square seats. **Either** 'French' with undulating seat rails, scrolled arms, cabriole legs (the grandest are highly carved – and sometimes gilded – with separate 'escutcheon' back) **or** 'Gainsborough' with straight legs and stretchers, arm supports sweeping down from rest to front of seat. May have Gothic or chinoiserie carved detail.

Neo-classical Adam-type, about 1770-1800: Often highly carved and painted or gilded. Oval backs, arms usually sweeping down to meet turned and fluted or reeded legs; curved and shaped seats. Seat rails were also often reeded, interspersed with paterae and so on.

'French Hepplewhite', about 1775 to 1800: Delicate version of French rococo armchairs, often with a shaped back separate from the seat.

Regency forms, about 1800-1830: French Empire type with continuous rounded backs forming arms and sabre legs. Or, distinctive continuous U-shaped seat and arms with plain, low, rectangular back.

Armchair in 'French Hepplewhite' style.

Sotheby's

Sotheby's

MATERIALS

Walnut, mahogany; rosewood during Regency. Beech when painted or gilded (mostly from 1770 onwards) and for underframes.

CONSTRUCTION

Standard methods employed. See full details on **p. 57-59**.

Upholstery is unlikely to be original throughout. The number of empty tack holes in the frame may indicate the extent of former upholstery. Remember that correctly shaped padding and authentic reproductions of textiles and trimmings of the right date will greatly enhance a chair's appearance (and maybe increase its value). Perfectionists would advocate the use of traditional upholstery techniques and materials, too.

DECORATION

As for side-chairs, but often more elaborate and extensive carving.

FINISH

Polish, paint, gilding.

RELATIVE VALUES

Mostly in the lower half of four-figure sums, decreasing with younger age. The grandest, highly carved and gilded chairs with good provenance, are at a premium. Period upholstery – if in usable condition (particularly needlework and tapestry) -will add considerably to the value.

CHAIRS: VICTORIAN UPHOLSTERED

About

1840-1900

Typical mid-Victorian lady's drawing-room chair.

Christie's

The introduction of the coiled spring for upholstery in the late 1820s brought greater comfort and a more rounded appearance to padding. A great variety of upholstered furniture became available, often sold in suites comprising a sofa, or *chaise longue*, a pair of easy chairs (one gentleman's, with arms; one lady's, without) and six side-chairs.

STYLE AND APPEARANCE

The majority were in a curvaceous rococo style, with moulded show-wood frames, rounded and waisted 'spoon' backs and short

***Left**, a late-Victorian gentleman's chair with scrolled arms, rounded back, straight legs.*

Armchair with continuous curves from arm to foot.

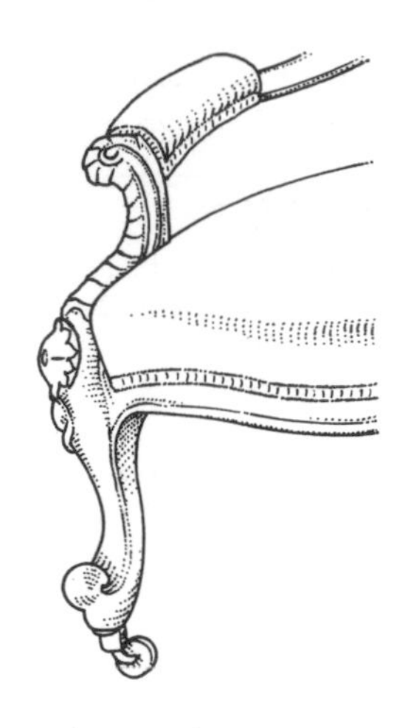

scrolling cabriole legs. Arms, when present, formed as one continuous scroll with front leg, bulging over the knee and ending in ball-like 'French' scroll feet. Low seats; deep naturalistic carving on knees and centre of top and front seat rails. Always on castors, sometimes of white or brown porcelain (a post-1850 feature). Distinctive convex curve evolved for slightly outward-splaying back legs.

Later spoon-backs (post 1870) may have straight, turned legs.

Occasionally a separate padded oval back supported on carved, inward-curving extensions of back legs.

Squared-up versions with straight, turned legs and arched backs appeared around 1860, becoming increasingly heavy with carving of classical rather naturalistic nature. Deep mouldings replaced by incised lines.

Variations abounded after 1880, their only common features being straighter contours,

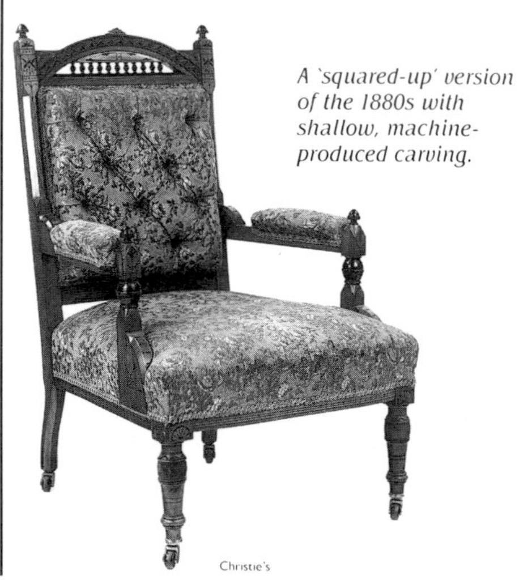

A 'squared-up' version of the 1880s with shallow, machine-produced carving.

Christie's

turned legs and arm supports (the latter sometimes as a row of spindles).

MATERIALS

Mahogany, walnut, occasionally rosewood. Stained beech and birch on later cheaper versions and for underframes. Sometimes frame of cast iron.

CONSTRUCTION

Standard methods employed (see **VICTORIAN BALLOON-BACKS, p. 66**, and **OTHER 19THC AND EARLY 20THC TYPES, p. 67**). Legs structurally weak, so look for signs of new staining around repaired joints. Almost inevitably re-upholstered, not always correctly. Should have *plain* seat, padded armrests and deep buttoning on the back and inside of arms only. Note that the back buttoning starts *above* the waistline.

DECORATION

Carving: Occasionally floral or classical inlay on crest rails of squared-up versions.

FINISH

French polish.

RELATIVE VALUES

Only the best quality, most curvaceous examples fetch more than three figures. Very many examples of all types are within the average buyer's reach. Always take the cost of re-upholstering *and* fabric and trimmings into account when negotiating.

Watch out for the new wood that characterizes increasing numbers of reproductions. These may look impressive at a glance but they lack patination and will probably have insubstantial foam upholstery.

> **PRIE DIEU**
>
> A very popular occasional drawing-room chair, ostensibly designed for prayer. Tall, narrow, straight back with flat top and T-shaped upholstery. Sometimes bordered by (fashionably twist) turned columns. Generally cabriole legs on castors but later versions with straight, turned legs. Often covered with Berlin woolwork, a form of needlework popular with Victorian ladies.

CHAIRS: CORNER

About

1710-1770

and about

1890-1915

Early-18thC corner chair.

Sotheby's

Peculiar to the 18thC, and to the late Victorian/ Edwardian period, corner chairs are thought by some to have been designed as gentlemen's writing chairs. Nearly always single, only rarely seen in pairs. Despite their awkward and uncomfortable appearance, surprisingly numerous today. Country versions abound. Often made as commode chairs.

STYLE AND APPEARANCE

Incorporating many features of standard chairs of their day – vase-shaped splats, cabriole legs, turned stretchers and so on; during Queen Anne period, straight legs and stretchers and pierced splats for Chippendale period, but they exhibit specific features of their own too.

Most have **stretchers**; there can be four of equal height, one on each side, or they can be arranged on a cross.

The **back**, which extends around two sides, has two splats between three identical and always turned uprights, supporting a curved, flat, horizontal rail which broadens out slightly as it extends beyond the side uprights to form arm supports. The centre of the rail rises up a few inches to form a back support. A few of these chairs have a much taller, shaped back support, in which case they are called 'barber's chairs'. Virtually all have drop-in seats.

Mid-18thC corner chair.

On early versions, the **front leg** only may be cabriole, the other three being turned to match the uprights above.

As with all country-made chairs of the 18thC, **design motifs** may be mixed – Queen Anne splats for example, might be used with later straight legs.

Edwardian 'revival' versions were sometimes made of dark mahogany in Chippendale style (see **p. 56**) with straight legs, but more often in light mahogany with spindly, turned legs, stretchers and delicate pierced splats. Some had raised, ornamental cresting. The seat could be drop-in; or fixed, with flattish upholstery set in one or two inches from the edge. Some country versions were made in oak with rushseats.

MATERIALS
Walnut, mahogany and oak.

CONSTRUCTION
Standard practices employed. Uprights dowelled into 'arms' of the top rail.

DECORATION
Restrained carving on the best examples.

FINISH
Polish.

RELATIVE VALUES
Walnut Queen Anne cabriole leg versions are the most sought after.

CHAIRS: READING, WRITING, DESK AND LIBRARY

About

1700-1900

Early-18thC 'horseman's' or 'cockfighting' chair.

Various gentlemen's reading and writing chairs evolved during the 18thC for use in libraries and studies and, in the 19thC, in clubs.

STYLE AND APPEARANCE
'Cockfighting', 'horseman's' and later, 'conversation' chairs, about 1700-1800: Fully upholstered pear-shaped seat, padded back with narrow base rising into flat curved section. Cabriole legs, at first with substantial stretchers. The sitter sat astride the chair and leant forward on the crest rail. Sometimes the back is fitted with a book-rest and/or candlestands or holders. Mid-century onwards more often wooden splat with flattened wooden crest rail, sometimes dished for candlesticks.

Regency 'bergère' armchairs, about

Below, *Regency bergère armchair with book-rest and candle-stands.*

Sotheby's

Above, *a late Regency/William IV reading chair anticipating the popular Victorian Eaton Hall type.*

Sotheby's

1800-1830: Wooden frame and back, sides and seat filled with cane work. Loose leather back and seat cushions and fixed padded armrests. Often adjustable bookrest or candleholders fixed to arm(s). Straight, turned front legs continuous with column arm supports. Back legs raked. Rectangular, flat-topped back can be shaped for comfort. All legs were mounted on castors.

'Eaton Hall' chairs (particularly popular for clubs), about 1830-1900: A development of earlier corner chairs (see **p. 73**) and 'horseman's' chairs (above), but for conventional use. Circular seats with semi-circular flat wooden or deeply padded crest rail following same line, joined by broad pierced splat or, more commonly, ten turned spindles. Turned front and raked back legs on castors. Crest rail can have raised centre. In general, the heavier and more bulbous the turnings, the later the chair was made.

MATERIALS

Walnut, mahogany; occasionally oak in the 19thC. Nearly always leather upholstery.

CONSTRUCTION

Standard methods employed. Bookrests adjustable on ratchet system.

DECORATION

Generally none, other than turnings on legs, spindles and arm supports.

FINISH

Polish. French polish in 19thC. Ebonised finish occasionally from about 1870-1890.

RELATIVE VALUES

The rarity of horseman's chairs and elegance of bérgères usually push their prices into four figures. Pairs of the latter are especially sought after and often more than the normal three times the price of a single.

Victorian desk and club chairs vary according to quality, but most are somewhere in the low hundreds.

New leather upholstery on all types should be valued at cost.

CHAIRS: HALL AND PORTER'S

About

1740-1850

Distinctive 18thC mahogany hall chair with a carved shell back.

Designed to stand in the hall (also corridors and landings) of large houses. Used by servants and visitors of low standing while waiting to be called in attendance. Consequently they have hard wooden seats, always *without* cushions. Usually made in large sets, often of a dozen or more.

STYLE AND APPEARANCE

Distinctive waisted backs, the sides of the lower part inward-curving or scrolled. Generally solid back with carved decoration, but can be partly pierced (usually on cresting or lower part). Often a central panel containing the carved or painted crest or emblem of the owner (a device intended to impress visitors on entering the house). Shape variable. Popular designs include: shells, shields, crescents, ovals and vases. Heavily carved Gothic architectural forms such as arches, pinnacles, crockets popular around 1830.

Regency hall chair with sabre legs.

Solid wooden **seats**, often of curvaceous outline and sometimes with circular dish turned in centre (to stop the sitter sliding off the shiny surface).

Legs followed prevailing patterns set by early versions: cabriole legs with pad feet, followed after about 1765 by turned or square-sectioned tapering legs. Sabre legs common during Regency followed by straight turned legs again, becoming heavier after about 1825. A few based on Italian Renaissance *scabello*; could be (correctly) heavily carved, or completely lacking decoration.

MATERIALS

Nearly always mahogany, but occasionally oak. Rosewood or walnut only rarely.

CONSTRUCTION

Standard methods employed for legs and seat frame. The wooden seat simply rests on top of the underframe.

DECORATION

Mostly carving. Monograms were painted on. Additional partial gilding was not uncommon after about 1800.

FINISH

Polish. If the piece is completely painted beech or pine it is probably not a hall chair. Very similar chairs – often with a 'shell' back – were made for use in gardens and garden buildings.

RELATIVE VALUES

Very often found in pairs today, seldom in long sets. Not very popular, due mostly to their total lack of comfort. Best quality long sets of pairs fetch four-figure sums.

PORTER'S CHAIRS

Large porter's chairs, hooded to exclude draughts, were common in very large houses, but are rare today. Most were totally covered with leather upholstery edged with brass nails. Without exposing at least part of the underframe it is difficult to distinguish these from modern reproductions when re-upholstered. Solid wood panelled versions are not unknown, but are seldom for sale. Wicker examples (possibly the most common) are similarly rare and are in such poor condition as to render them valueless other than in terms of historical interest.

Fully upholstered hall or porter's chair.

CHAIRS: COUNTRY LADDER- AND SPINDLE-BACKS

About

1700-1939

Yorkshire ladder-back chair, made from about 1730 onwards.

Bonhams

Traditional ladder-back, spindle and other turned chairs were made in all parts of Britain throughout the 18th and 19thC. Although regional variations exist in the shape of turnings and so on, most follow the same basic patterns. Some arts and crafts designers were influenced by the tradition, and from the 1860s onwards the style appeared in more sophisticated interiors than previously. Between the wars many authentic reproductions were made of both spindle- and ladder-backs; if well worn these are difficult to identify and many are sold with an earlier date.

STYLE AND APPEARANCE

Ladder-backs originated in 17thC Holland. Between four and seven horizontal, usually waved, slats, sometimes curved to fit the sitter's back; with or without a turned or shaped top-rail, sitting on rather than between the uprights. Turned front legs (on armchairs con-

Christie's

Left, *Two spindle-back chairs, made from 1750.*

Christie's

Cotswold school ladder-back armchairs, about 1890-1910.

tinuous with arm supports) and decoratively turned front stretcher. Often modified version of pad foot. Always two plain side stretchers and one or two at back. Arms flat and slightly curved for comfort.

Spindle-backs, principally from Cheshire, Lancashire and Northern England, were similar, but with square-sectioned horizontal cross rails in back enclosing arrangements of small turned spindles. Over-riding waved crest rail. On armchairs generally three rows, on singles only two.

Both types commonly had rush seats, but some had wooden seats with a raised and moulded edge.

Common arts and crafts-inspired types include the Morris & Co. 'Sussex' chairs (about 1865 onwards) and versions plagiarised by other firms; also various, sometimes spindly, ladder-backs based on designs revived by Ernest Gimson (about 1880 onwards) and his later bobbin-turned version of a spindle-back.

A Morris & Co. 'Sussex' chair, made from 1865.

Haslam & Whiteway Ltd

MATERIALS

Oak, elm, fruit and other local woods. Occasionally mahogany in the 18thC; beech and birch common in 19th.

CONSTRUCTION

Dowelled or tenoned joints. Seat rails under rush often crude; machine-made versions smoother and more evenly shaped. Edges of rush seats (particularly on late-19th and early-20thC versions) were sometimes concealed by flat strips of wood tacked on to the rails beneath.

DECORATION

None other than regionally different turning.

FINISH

Polish: Black or green stain for arts and crafts type chairs in late-19thC, popularised by Morris & Co.'s Sussex chairs. Stain devised for them by the artist Ford Madox Brown.

RELATIVE VALUES

Single ladder- and spindle-backs are still in three figures but sets of eight are well into four. Same applies to 19thC adaptations, and even later reproductions.

Despite their arts and crafts appeal, single Sussex chairs are often still in two; sets cost more, but are still relatively affordable, mostly because they were made in large numbers. Distinctive, one-off designer example will be considerably more expensive.

CHAIRS: COUNTRY WINDSOR

About

1700

to the present day

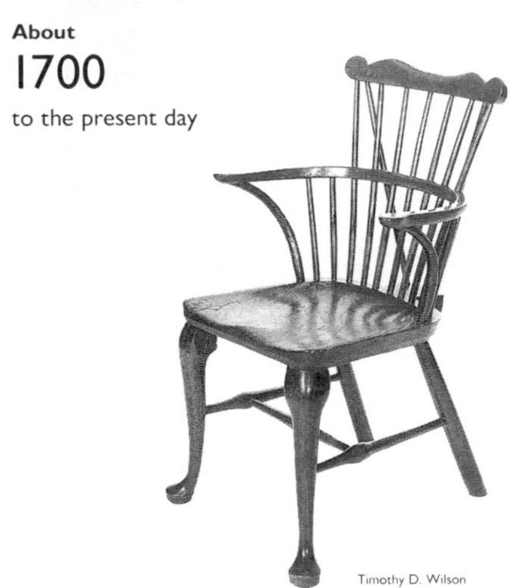

Late-18thC yew comb-back Windsor chair.

Made from the early-18thC onwards by wood turners or 'bodgers' setting up temporary workshops in woodland areas. Although made in many parts of the country – hence enormous regional differences in detail – High Wycombe in Buckinghamshire became, and has remained, the centre of the industry. Since the late-19thC, Windsors and their variants have been mass-produced there by machine.

They have many uses – particularly in gardens, coffee-houses and sometimes in halls (18thC) and in kitchens, farmhouses and institutions in the 19th and 20thC.

STYLE AND APPEARANCE

Early **'stick-back'** versions were simple, with taper-turned sticks (turned with tapering ends) rising from a saddle seat through a horizontal yew-wood hoop forming back and arm supports and dowelling into a shaped crest rail. The most distinctive of these have a comb shape – hence the term 'comb back'. Splayed, turned legs, at first without stretchers, but soon with either turned H or curved crinoline (or cow's horn) stretchers.

Hooped backs (with a continuous hoop rising from the back support to replace the horizontal crest rail): Shaped and pierced central splats (at first sometimes set below the back support only); and cabriole legs all appeared around 1750.

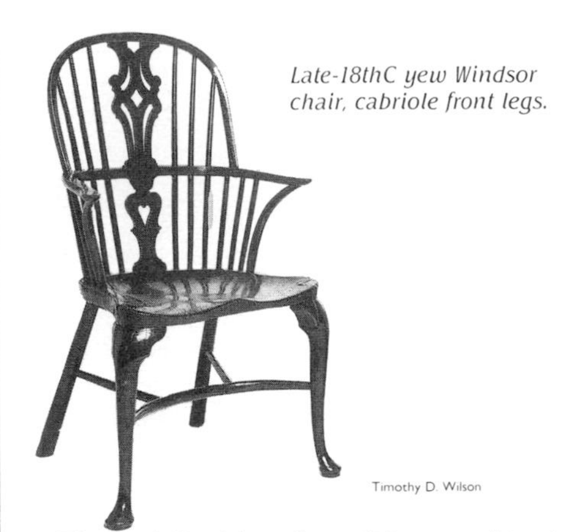

Late-18thC yew Windsor chair, cabriole front legs.

Pierced Gothic splats: Often combined with pointed arch backs and cabriole legs, were introduced about 1760. The familiar wheel-back splat and diagonal struts rising from a 'bobtail' extension of the seat – both common features on machine-made Windsors – first appeared around 1775.

'Gothic' Windsor armchair.

With the exception of cabrioles, front and back were turned and identical (from the late-19thC usually machine-turned with double or triple collars.

Saddle seats were common to all and arm supports either turned or (mostly before 1810) curved.

For popular variants – including the 'Mendlesham' chair (early-19thC onwards) and the collectable 'smoker's cow' – see illustrations.

MATERIALS

Various combinations of elm, ash, yew, beech, birch and fruit woods. Occasionally mahogany. Elm used almost invariably for seats; beech common for legs and, until the 19thC nearly always yew for hoops.

Selection of 19thC chairs: ***A****, Mendlesham;* ***B****, smoker's bow;* ***C****, farmhouse kitchen;* ***D****, child's Windsor highchair;* ***E****, rope-back kitchen chair.*

CONSTRUCTION

All parts dowelled. Legs and back uprights always separate (legs never continuous with uprights above). Seats split, not sawn (saw marks indicate a later date). Sticks taper-turned on a pole lathe, hence of irregular thickness. (Machine-cut stocks have an even shape and are *not* tapered.) Hoops steam-bent into shape. On single chairs, the hoop passes through seat and is split and wedged underneath. On machine-made versions this does not occur – sometimes the hoop does not pierce all the way through the seat.

DECORATION

Carving and piercing on splats. Turning on legs and some arm supports.

FINISH

Paint common in 18thC, most fashionably green, sometimes black (japanned). Otherwise polish; some left unfinished for outdoor use. Stain and varnish used in 19thC.

RELATIVE VALUES

Plenty of variation. Good early and hoop back Windsors are expensive, few selling for less than four figures. 19thC versions correspondingly less. Harlequin sets of all ages are common and, if matched well, no less expensive than an identical set. Few post-1900 sets fetch less than four figures.

Yew, crinoline stretcher, cabriole legs, comb back, Gothic splat and arched back all enhance the value.

CHESTS OR COFFERS

About

1200-1800

Typical 17thC three-panel carved oak chest. Christie's

Known as blanket chests in the 18thC, these were used for the storage of clothing and linen and, in the Middle Ages, other valuables too (hence their often elaborate, sometimes multiple locks). Originally placed at the end of the bed they sometimes doubled up as a seat or table. They were largely superseded in the mid-17thC by the more sophisticated chests of drawers. Surviving examples available for sale date mostly from the late-16thC onwards; earlier examples are rare except in churches or public collections.

STYLE AND APPEARANCE

Medieval forms included the dug-out, ark and clamp-fronted chests but most of those now available are:

Plank or 'boarded': Comprising six pieces of timber simply nailed together. Sides extend to the ground with V shape cut out to form feet. Usually carved decoration on front (and sometimes sides), simply carved border on sides of lid and vertical edges of front. Normally exterior plain, with square-plated iron lock with hinged hasp fastening. Although largely replaced around 1550 by panelled chests, boarded chests were still made in country areas in 18thC.

Joined/panelled: Made from about 1550, though panelled construction had been used in building since the previous century. Rectangular, with two, three (occasionally four) panels at front and back, one or two at sides. Lid flat, or panelled in line with base. Plain or moulded edges. Side stiles continue down to form legs. Nearly always carved decoration on front (often sides too), varying in extent; never carving on lid. Rails, stiles and muntins often moulded; sometimes chamfered around panels. Interior sometimes fitted with small, lidded, incorrectly named 'candle box', probably to contain sweet-scented herbs.

On both types the underside of the lid was sometimes cross-battened.

MATERIALS

Predominantly oak. Less durable woods such as elm, ash, chestnut and other local varieties also used, but few examples have survived. From about 1650 much 'wainscot oak' imported from Scandinavia (favoured for its fine, even grain) was used.

Cypress and (in the early-18thC) cedar occasionally used for their moth-repelling qualities.

CONSTRUCTION

Boarded: Front and back overlapping sides and pinned with iron nails. Timber split rather than sawn, hence no saw marks. Grain of sides runs top to bottom, other boards side to side. Should be some shrinkage along grain, probably some 'bowing' of lid. Rust stains on wood around nails. Lid fixed with large strap or small wire loop hinges (early chests often had pin hinges). The lockplate would also have been fixed with iron nails.

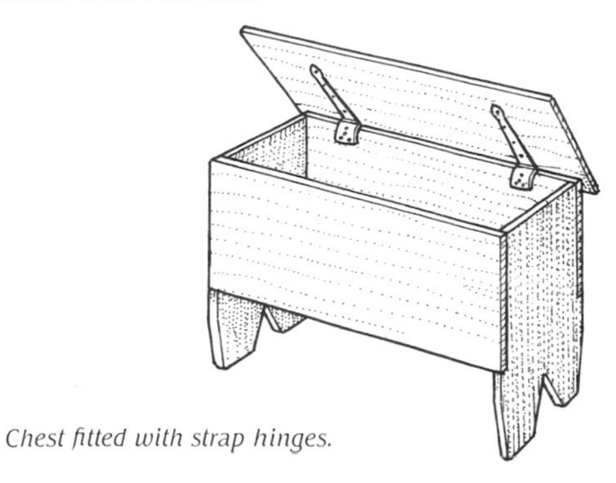

Chest fitted with strap hinges.

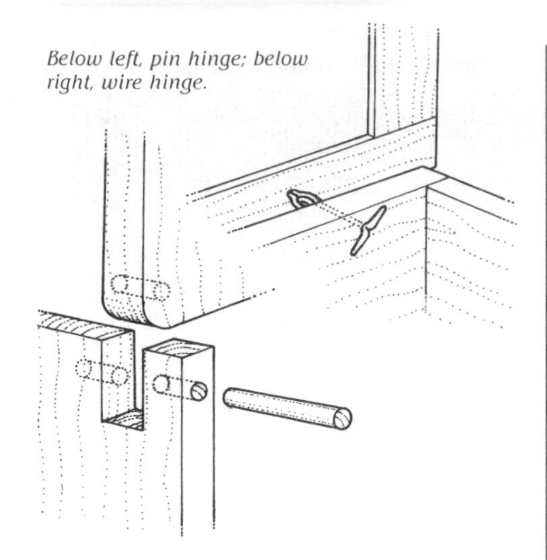

Below left, pin hinge; below right, wire hinge.

Panelled: Joined frame and panel construction; pegged mortise-and-tenon joints. Pegs of green willow (unlikely to split or shrink). Should be of irregular shape and size and protrude slightly above surface where surrounding wood has shrunk. Two rather than one peg per joint the norm in 17thC.

Dry panel construction (i.e. no glue) allows for shrinkage and movement of timber; panels therefore now slightly loose. Panels usually thinly cut, sometimes with chamfered edges to fit into grooves of frame.

Stiles always continue to top, the rails tenoning into their sides and muntins into rails.

The timber was either split or sawn: irregular saw marks therefore may be visible on under-sides.

On both types the interior should be 'dust-dry', i.e. with a smooth but not shiny surface. Recently sawn wood will have a slightly rough, splintery surface. There should be good patination from constant handling around the lock and front under-side of the lid. The under-sides of the feet will be worn and slightly ragged. Signs of repair to hinges and lock are not unusual.

DECORATION

Carving: Of many qualities; much simple chip-carving. Common motifs include Gothic tracery, roundels, arches, columns, Renaissance strapwork, guilloches, lunettes, lozenges, stylized foliage and flowers and arcading (the latter particularly on panels).

Some shallow **'punched decoration'** – punched on with a mallet and specially shaped metal tool – especially on boarded chests. Motifs include stars, crescents, crosses, dots.

Sometimes **inlay** during 16thC and early 17thC, mostly of floral or geometric patterns.

NONESUCH CHESTS

The best known and most elaborately inlaid of these are Nonesuch (sometimes spelt Nonsuch) chests, believed to have been made by immigrant craftsmen working in Southwark. All depict views of Henry VIII's Nonesuch Palace in Surrey which was demolished in 1670. Although intriguing and beautifully made, they are small in number, seldom for sale, and not typical of other chests of their day.

FINISH

Originally stained and wax polished. Subsequent dry-rubbing has generally produced a good patina, i.e. a rich, dark colour, with a deep shine. Occasionally traces of paint are seen (especially on boarded chests). Although it is known that some early oak was painted – probably all over in plain colours rather than finely decorated – the extent and exact procedure is yet to be fully researched.

RELATIVE VALUES

Plenty of variation; generally only boarded, simply chip-carved and completely plain panelled chests fail to reach the thousand mark. Plus points are: extensive vigorous carving (chip carving and punched decoration are at the bottom of the scale), no signs of repair or replacement parts, original locks and hinges, good, deep colour and patina.

Beware of large numbers of Continental chests imported for the 'decorator's' market. Look at decoration and for any difference from standard methods of construction.

VICTORIAN ALTERATIONS

Some chests had additional carving executed in the 19thC when 'Jacobean' furniture was popular. Others were made up from old fragments of carving and discarded wall panelling. Check the construction; look for later and now discoloured staining intended to disguise new joints, and check all carving for inappropriate ornament, execution by different hands, and 'mechanical' appearance.

CHESTS: MULE, DOWER OR COUNTER CHESTS

About

1630-1800

Bonhams

Late-17thC oak mule chest.

A lidded chest with one or two drawers added below. A transitional piece in the 17thC, marking the change from simple chest to full chest of drawers; a country piece in the 18thC.

Thought by some to have been used by tradesmen; many have a small till or partitioned area in the drawer(s), suitable for coins. Early inventories sometimes refer to the drawers themselves as 'tilles'.

THE DOWER CHEST

The term 'dower' is self-explanatory, but is also used to describe the 18thC chest of trunk form mounted on a low frame, with a flat or domed top, heavy brass carrying handles, a shaped and/or carved apron or frieze, and cabriole, bracket or straight feet according to date. Imported Oriental lacquer trunks were often displayed in this way (on English-made stands) in the 18thC and 19thC.

Christie's

Late-17th/early-18thC leather trunk mounted on a stand.

STYLE AND APPEARANCE

Three, sometimes two, panels, with one long or two (occasionally three) short drawers below. In 17thC often made in two sections, a projecting mitred moulding – echoing that on base – concealing the join. Can be very simple, resembling plain panelled coffers, or more sophisticated, with applied and/or inlaid decoration. 18thC versions have fielded, and sometimes shaped, panels. Stile, bun or bracket feet according to date.

MATERIALS

Oak, walnut, occasionally mahogany; elm, chestnut and other local woods (though few examples survive).

CONSTRUCTION

Framed and panelled; earliest with pegged, but most with glued, mortise and tenon joints. Early drawers rebated and nailed; later dovetailed and glued (see **CHESTS OF DRAWERS: EARLY PANELLED OAK, p. 84**).

DECORATION AND HANDLES

Carving, inlay, applied mouldings in 17thC. Turned wooden knobs replaced by brass ball handles after 1700.

FINISH

Stain; wax polish.

RELATIVE VALUES

Earliest and most decorative invariably in four figures; plain 18thC in three. Prices considerably reduced if stand is wrong.

For further details of all points see **CHESTS OF DRAWERS: EARLY PANELLED OAK, p. 84** and **CHESTS OF DRAWERS, VENEERED, p.86**.

CHESTS OF DRAWERS: EARLY PANELLED OAK

About

1650-1730

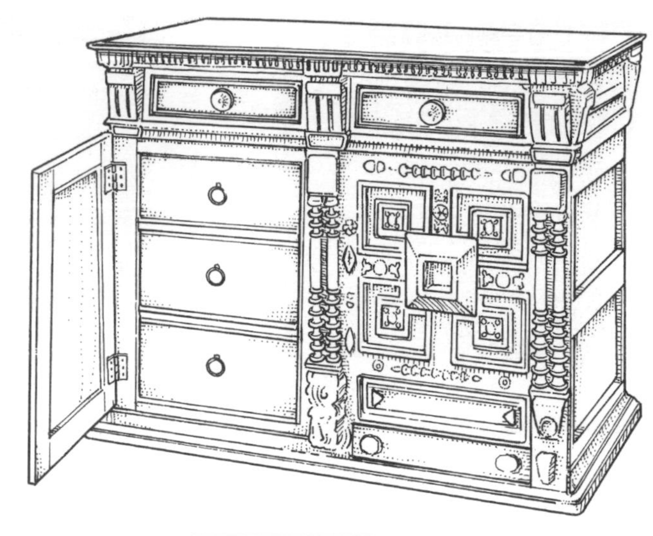

Oak chest of about 1680, with applied, mitred and geometrical mouldings.

Distinctive, often ornamental, pieces of furniture made by traditional methods. Still produced by provincial and country makers long after more sophisticated walnut-veneered chests were introduced from the Continent in about 1670.

STYLE AND APPEARANCE

Various combinations of single and double depth drawers, cupboard doors enclosing drawers, and chest with hinged lid (latter early type). Four-drawer version became the norm in about 1680.

Sometimes two separate sections, join concealed by projecting mitred moulding. Shallower mouldings are found between all drawers (or cupboard).

Two small, or one long, drawer(s) at top above three long, inside seldom reaching right to back of carcase. Separate overhanging top with moulding below (thumb-nail moulding from about 1700). Similar inverted moulding at base. All parts of front (and sometimes side frieze) decorated with mitred mouldings, and often split turnings too, sometimes combined with inlay. Drawer fronts divided decoratively into two panels. Stile feet (i.e. the stiles of the carcase extend below the base moulding) until about 1690 when bun feet appeared.

MATERIALS

Oak (mostly imported Scandinavian 'wainscot' oak). Elm, yew and other local woods used, but few examples survive.

Ebony, ivory, bone and mother-of-pearl for inlaid decoration.

CONSTRUCTION

Framed and panelled with glued (i.e. no longer pegged) joints.

Early drawers with thick sides (about ¾ inch/2 cm) rebated and nailed. Thick groove in middle of side cut to run on bearers nailed to inside of carcase. Two or three crude through-dovetails (see illustration), their ends concealed on the front by mouldings, introduced about 1680, sometimes nailed for extra strength. By 1690-1700 dovetails lapped (i.e. no longer passed right through to the front) (see illustration). Linings now rebated and glued. Grain of drawers runs front to back.

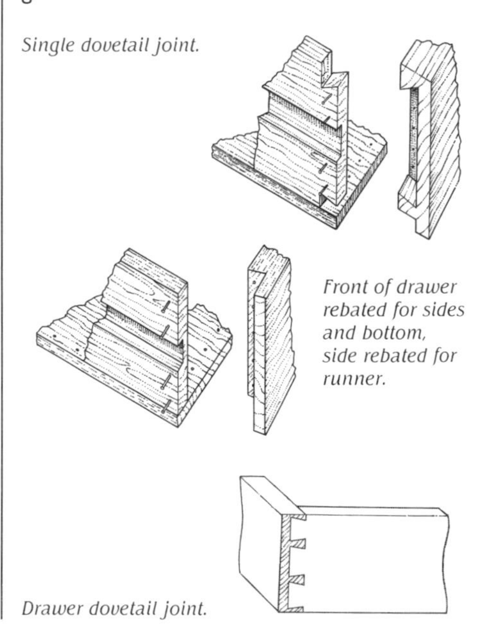

Single dovetail joint.

Front of drawer rebated for sides and bottom, side rebated for runner.

Drawer dovetail joint.

Oak chest of drawers, about 1680. Bonhams

Alternative drawer supports introduced about 1660 (but not universally adopted) whereby bottom runner fixed to under side of drawer edge ran on bearer fixed at appropriate height. Drawer sides correspondingly thinner, about ½ inch/1 cm. Dustboards (i.e. solid shelves between the drawers) often replaced or combined with bearers after 1680.

All moulded and turned decoration glued on. Nailed rough, planked oak backboards. Bun feet dowelled in holes drilled in underside of carcase base (visible inside). Handles attached by split-pin (or tang) method.

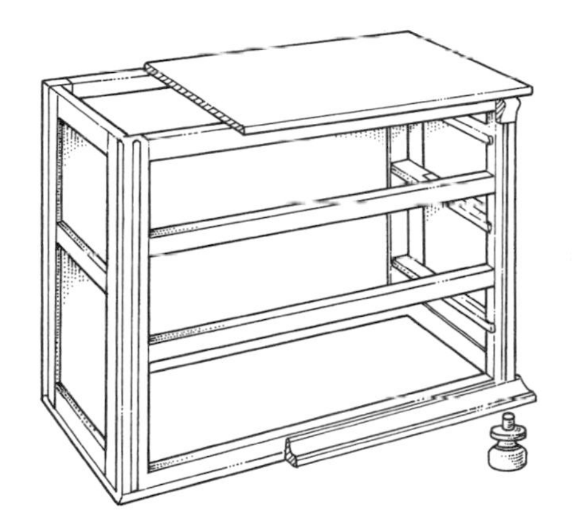

Carcase of framed oak chest with panelled ends.

For authenticity, look for signs of genuine wear – especially on drawers and runners – and natural movement of the wood with slight warping and shrinkage along the grain. Underside of feet will be slightly frayed and the drawer fronts will have light indentations from constant knocking of pendant handles.

DECORATION

Applied mitred architectural mouldings on drawer fronts; on the simplest, around the edge only, on many, all over. Split turnings arranged in pairs common on stiles, until about 1680 sometimes combined with inlay of ebony, ivory, bone and mother-of-pearl in patterns of Spanish/Moorish origin (fashion introduced from Holland).

Handles: Earliest versions have exterior turned wooden knobs, interior iron loop handles. Later, iron (or brass towards 1700) drop handles, pear-shaped with decorative rosettes. Also, centrally placed decorative escutcheons.

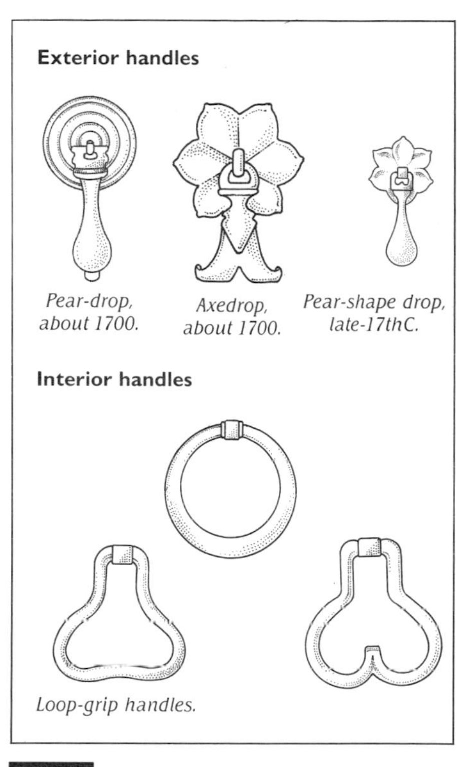

Loop-grip handles.

FINISH

Often stained with oils coloured with various plant substances; then polished with beeswax softened with spirit.

RELATIVE VALUES

In the past, of limited appeal; more recently popular with decorators for 'bold' interiors.

Those with inlay and plenty of moulded and split-turned decoration four or five times as much as those with only edge mouldings to drawers. Only the latter still in three figures.

CHESTS OF DRAWERS: VENEERED

About

1680-1740

Bonhams

Walnut veneered chest of about 1690.

The art of veneering was introduced to England by Dutch and Flemish craftsmen working in and around London during the Restoration period.

STYLE AND APPEARANCE

Generally three long drawers below two short. Most with over-hanging **top**, formed at first by a cornice, later ovolo or thumb moulding. Later pieces occasionally with caddy top (i.e. inset with narrow moulding all round). Tops often quarter-veneered (i.e. veneer laid in four identical pieces) until about 1710; thereafter one piece, usually with broad, cross-banded border.

Bun feet with simple plinth moulding until about 1710, then bracket. (Many have had their bun feet replaced with brackets at a later date. The original holes will still be visible in the carcase base.)

Drawer fronts flat, fashions for edge decoration and finish varying, some running concurrently:

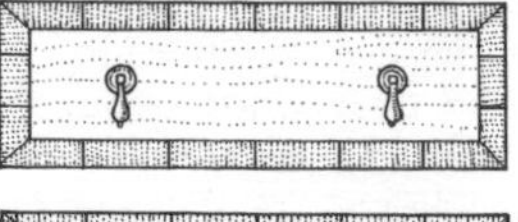

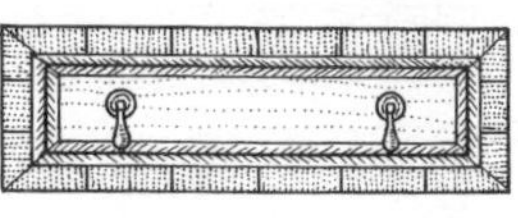

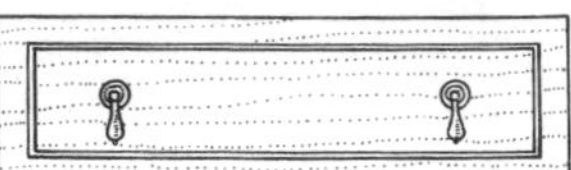

***Right**, simple cross-banding, late 17thC; **centre**, feather cross-banding, early 18thC and **below**, all-over veneer with inset stringing, late 17thC.*

About 1680-1710: Simple cross-banding.

About 1690-1720: Feather (or herring-bone) cross-banding.

About 1690-1710: All-over veneer with inset stringing.

With these types, front of carcase between and around the drawers has a single or double half-round moulding.

About 1710-1720: Rebated ovolo lip moulding extending beyond edge of drawer, concealing gap between drawers and carcase.

About 1730 until late-19thC: Cockbead (i.e. a narrow and slightly projecting moulding rebated around drawer but not extending beyond edge).

With these types, drawer dividers plain.

THE BACHELOR'S CHEST

A popular variant, dating from about 1710-1740, and mostly made in walnut, though occasionally mahogany, is the bachelor's chest. This is much shallower than average and characterized by a folding top, hinging down from the front and supported on lopers to provide a writing slide. Unusual and desirable, so fakes are not uncommon. Check that the drawer runners stop short of the back; if not, it is almost certainly made up from a cut-down standard chest.

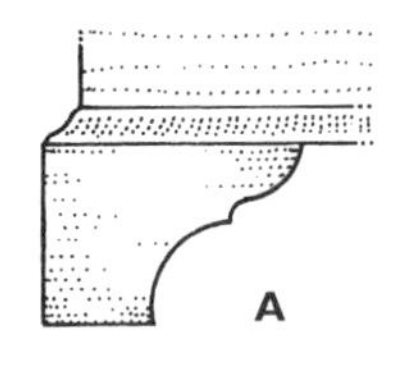

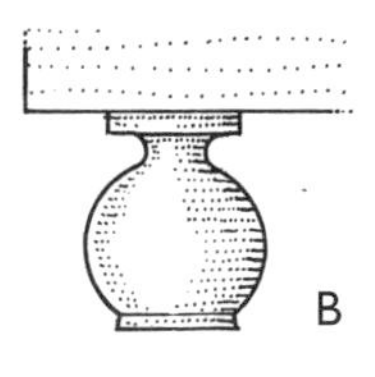

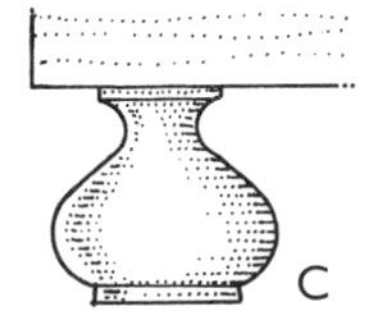

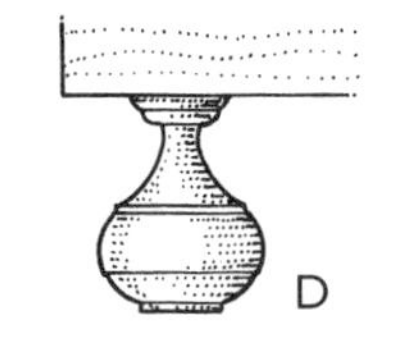

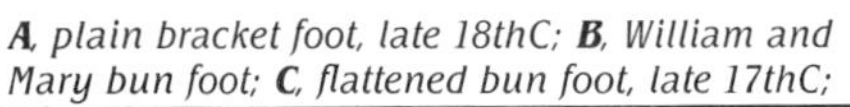

***A**, plain bracket foot, late 18thC; **B**, William and Mary bun foot; **C**, flattened bun foot, late 17thC; **D**, turnip foot, early 18thC.*

MATERIALS

Veneer: Predominantly walnut; occasionally mahogany after about 1720. Also yew, mulberry, sycamore and many other burr and figured woods. Laburnum, lignum vitae, kingwood, olive-wood and others used for oyster veneers (i.e. veneers cut across the grain from small branches). Boxwood, holly, ebony, and other woods for inlay and marquetry, also occasionally bone.

Carcases: Pine for all veneered surfaces; oak for drawer linings (except the drawer front. On these a strip of oak often concealed the pine top edge). Oak or deal carcase when japanned.

CONSTRUCTION

Hand-cut veneers, at first thick (about 1/8 inch/3 mm), cut across the grain. Early through-dovetails on all parts originally covered by veneer; lapped dovetails from about 1690-1700. Sides of drawers narrower.

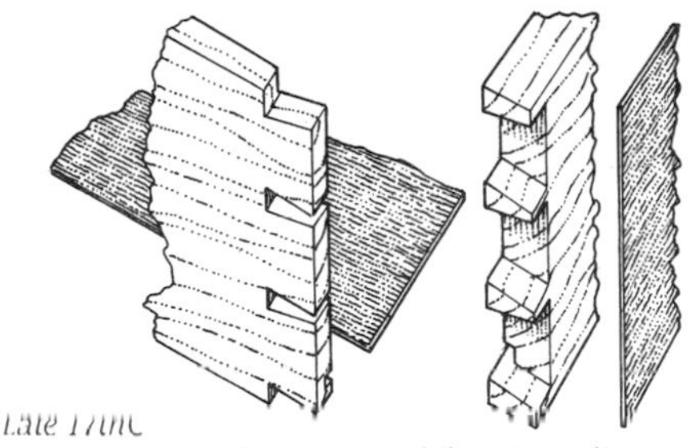

Late 17thC drawer construction, veneer hiding dovetails.

Drawer linings rebated and glued into sides. Grain running front to back except on very large drawers, when side to side. Drawers with runners on underside, supported on bearers, often with solid dustboards too.

Drop handles attached by split-pin (or tang) method. Plate handles with bolts and circular nuts (fixed with special tool). Pine, sometimes oak, backboards nailed on.

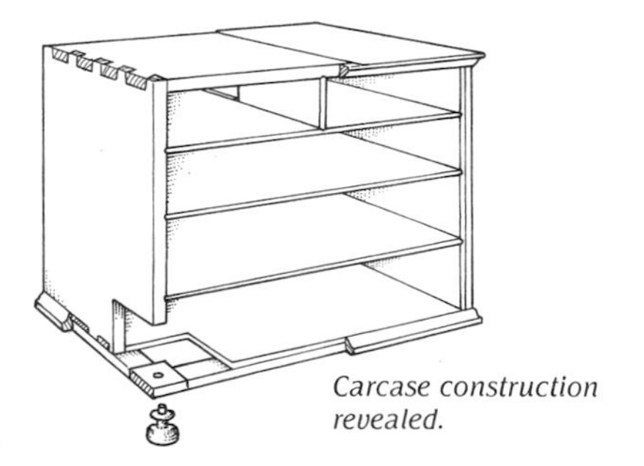

Carcase construction revealed.

REPLACED HANDLES

It has been estimated that approximately 90 per cent of all chests of drawers have had their handles replaced at least once. This will be obvious from the number and position of holes visible on the inside and probably from filled holes on the outside. On veneered drawers, if the holes on front and back do not tie up, the piece has certainly been re-veneered, or even veneered for the first time (see below).

DECORATION

Principally geometric patterns of figured veneer. Inlay (often as stringing or circles or ovals), cross-banding. Much use of symmetrically arranged burr and oyster veneers.

Floral marquetry, about 1690-1720; usually contained within panels, not all over as on contemporary Dutch chests.

After about 1680 occasionally chinoiserie japanned decoration on black ground (survivals rare).

Handles: Iron (towards 1700 brass) drop handles. C-scroll bail handles with backplates from about 1700. Early backplates solid and shaped, with bevelled edges; sometimes incised. From about 1720 more often pierced.

Largish centrally placed decorative lock escutcheons.

FINISH

Varnish (diluted glue applied in layers and sanded down between applications) to fill the grain and produce a smooth surface, followed by wax polish.

Unfortunately many 'antiques' were French polished by the Victorians and have subsequently had to be re-polished, thereby losing their original finish and the mellow colours produced by patination.

RELATIVE VALUES

Prices invariably in four figures, many in five. Being particularly valuable – and rarely in totally original condition – false versions are not uncommon. Watch out for all-oak or all-pine construction. In both cases the chest probably started life without veneer; the first in the 17thC or 18thC, the latter in the late 19thC (although it could possibly be an imported Continental version). Look carefully at the construction of the drawers.

CHESTS ON STANDS

About

1680-1730

Many fashionable chests of drawers of this period were raised about 2 feet/60 cm from the ground on turned stands. By 1730 these seem to have been replaced by the more capacious tallboy. The information below relates to the stands only; for details of the chest sections see under CHESTS OF DRAWERS: PANELLED OAK p.84 and CHESTS OF DRAWERS: VENEERED, p.86.

Late-17thC chest on stand of William & Mary type.

STYLE AND APPEARANCE

Pre-Queen Anne stands have one long (or after 1690 three short) drawer(s) supported on six turned legs joined by a platform, or turned stretchers with bun feet below. Cabriole legs with pad or hoof feet and without stretchers introduced about 1700. On both types, there is sometimes a shaped apron below the drawer(s). On three-drawer types, the central drawer is shallower than the side ones. Inverted projecting moulding at top of stand (into which chest slots) echoes similar moulded cornice at top of chest.

Early-18thC type with base in form of a lowboy or side-table.

MATERIALS

Oak; solid walnut for legs; walnut veneer on pine for drawer sections and platform stretchers; oak for drawer linings (except for the drawer fronts).

CONSTRUCTION

Glued mortise-and-tenon joints. Turned legs dowelled into frame. Cabriole legs extend upwards to form corner stiles of framing.

Structural weakness and the partiality of wood-beetles for walnut have often contributed to the disappearance of the stand. The remaining chest section can easily be converted into a standard chest of drawers by the addition of a polished top – the original top being rough and concealed by the cornice – and bun feet. These can often be identified by the presence of three rather than two small drawers at the top.

DECORATION

Drawers and drawer frieze as for chests, otherwise very plain.

FINISH

Wax polish after varnish. Occasionally japanned. Spiral turnings occasionally ebonised (i.e. stained black).

RELATIVE VALUES

It is unusual to find a chest on stand without at least replacement feet, if not legs too. Even so, prices are well into the thousands. Replacement legs and stretchers, even if the drawer section is right, may reduce the value by as much as 40 per cent. Fine and extensive marquetry is a huge bonus, possibly raising the price to a five-figure sum.

TALLBOYS OR CHESTS ON CHESTS

About

1710-1820

Chippendale-style mahogany tallboy, about 1765-1780.

Christie's

Christie's

Sotheby's

***Left**, Sheraton mahogany tallboy, about 1800; **right**, late-18thC mahogany secretaire tallboy.*

A development of the chest on stand, used in bedrooms to store clothing. Especially popular during the second half of the 18thC – from when most date – despite being too high to use fully without standing on a chair.

STYLE AND APPEARANCE

Formed as two chests of drawers, the upper one slightly narrower than the lower. Nearly all straight-fronted, with bracket (often ogee) feet, though some around 1760 are serpentine, and later, from about 1780, bow-fronted, with splayed 'swept' feet.

Upper part has two or three short drawers above three feet long. A projecting moulded cornice is common; occasionally a broken pediment. Some have a frieze too; on early examples, occasionally, a cushion frieze conceals a drawer.

Fashionably, corners canted; carved as columns or pilasters, in the mid-century, shallow Gothic or Chinese fret, or simple reeding or fluting.

Lower chest has three long drawers; mouldings around base and top into which upper chest slots. Occasionally a cavetto moulding (semi-circular concave niche) decorated with marquetry sunburst pattern, on bottom drawer of walnut examples. Occasionally a brushing slide at top; sometimes a secretaire drawer (see **DESKS, p. 111**).

Drawers usually – not always – of diminishing depth within each chest. Handles sometimes aligned.

MATERIALS

Walnut veneer; mahogany (solid or veneer). Occasionally rosewood, amboyna and other highly figured woods during Regency. Sometimes country versions in oak. Oak and pine for carcases.

CONSTRUCTION

As for **CHESTS OF DRAWERS** (see p. 87). The separate projecting cornice slots over blocks glued at corners of top.

DECORATION

As for **CHESTS OF DRAWERS** (see ***p. 87***). Occasionally low relief carving on frieze.

FINISH

Polish; (rarely) japanning.

RELATIVE VALUES

Even the plainest tallboy will now fetch a four-figure sum and the best quality easily five. An early date, a cavetto moulding, a secretaire drawer, and, to a lesser extent, a brushing slide, and well figured and coloured veneers, will push the price up.

MARRIAGES

In the past tallboys were less fashionable than today and many were split up and sold as two separate chests of drawers. The reverse process is now common, so watch for marriages. Look for: correct conformation of drawers; matching timber on all sides, including backboards; identical construction of all drawers; rough, unfinished surface on tops of both parts (neither would have been visible); canted corners on top and bottom, or top only.

CHESTS: DRAWING-ROOM COMMODES

About

1750-1800

Fine quality drawing-room commode in French style, about 1775.

Sotheby's

Valuable and prestigious objects made for the main rooms of fine houses. Probably seldom used in a practical sense; principally valued for their fine decoration. Usually made in pairs to stand at either end of a room or against the window piers. Gradually replaced by simpler cabinets during the Regency period.

STYLE AND APPEARANCE

Differently proportioned to bedroom chests; usually longer in relation to height.

Two, three or four drawers, sometimes enclosed by doors (occasionally interior shelves instead). At first in French rococo style, or bomb shape (i.e. with swelling serpentine sides), keeled corners and splayed feet with ormolu (gilt bronze) or gilt brass mounts with matched handles. Marble or wooden tops.

Ormolu, mounted on keeled front edges of serpentine commode.

Ousted from fashion about 1770 by straight-sided semi-circular shape with straight, tapering, later turned, legs.

MATERIALS

Fine quality woods, particularly mahogany, satinwood. Tulipwood, kingwood, harewood (green-stained sycamore), chestnut, fruit and many other woods used for marquetry and inlay. Oak when japanned. Oak and pine for carcases. Marble or scagliola (a plaster-based material imitating rare marbles) was sometimes used for tops. The latter can be plain or patterned.

CONSTRUCTION

Generally standard methods were employed. Mostly veneered. Bombé sections coopered or laminated beneath veneer. On mid-century examples dustboards between drawers (not a feature of French commodes until late in the century).

DECORATION

Many have variously arranged mahogany veneers; often geometric patterns. Before about 1770 the finest have marquetry of floral patterns, musical instruments, trophies, birds. Neo-classical inlay from about 1770 onwards of urns, shells, husks, bell flowers, acanthus leaves, sometimes shaded with scorching or overlaid with pen and ink. Oval and fan shapes were popular.

Painted decoration (*not* all over) included ovals containing classical figures, borders of flowers, ribbons, garlands etc. Occasionally low-relief Wedgwood plaques incorporated, with gilt brass framing.

Chinoiserie decoration (especially for bedrooms and dressing-rooms) sometimes japanned, occasionally partly composed of genuine Oriental lacquer taken from broken-up imported screens.

FINISH

Polish, japanning, paint.

RELATIVE VALUES

A specialist market, prices in four, five or even six figures. Not objects to be purchased without expert advice.

CHESTS: MILITARY CHESTS

About
1810-1915

Teak military chest with removable bun feet.

Regulation campaign furniture for British army officers, dating originally from the Napoleonic Wars and still available in virtually identical form from the Army & Navy Stores in London as late as 1915. Originally transported in green-painted pine packing-cases.

STYLE AND APPEARANCE

Made in two parts for easy transportation, with screw-on feet, usually of bun type, but on early Regency examples could be carved paw; some just have rectangular block, occasionally fitted with small castors. Most, but not all, have heavy brass or iron carrying-handles at sides. Corners generally protected by flush-fitting brass caps. Brass locks, escutcheons, hinges etc. Various drawer arrangements – most common, two small and one long in top, two long below, all of equal depth. Back solid and polished.

Variations include:

Central fall-front secretaire at top with square drawer either side.

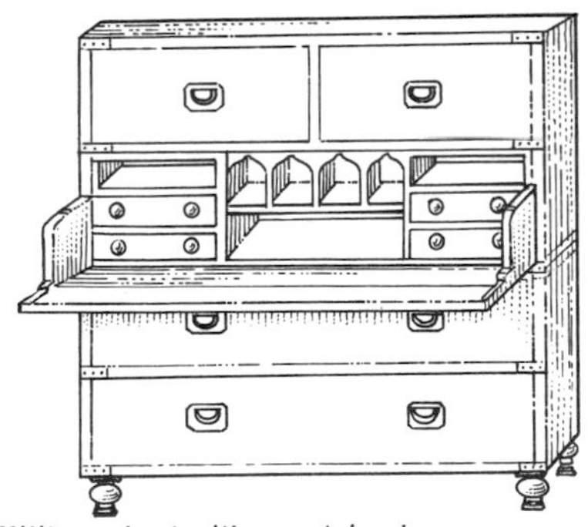

Military chest with secretaire drawer.

Full width secretaire drawer.

Fall-front section as above but containing dressing accessories.

Six or eight shallow drawers in lower half (like a plan chest) for storage of trousers.

MATERIALS

Durable, inexpensive woods – cheap mahogany, cedar, camphor, padouk, oak. Drawer-linings of oak, pine, sometimes camphor (to repel moths). Far Eastern and Indian versions made also in teak. Modern reproductions in pine or various veneers, popularly yew.

CONSTRUCTION

Solid wood, only rarely veneered (some early examples with amboyna, a type of padouk). Glued dovetail construction. Indian and Far Eastern versions often crudely cut and ill-fitting (hence easily identifiable).

DECORATION

Generally undecorated. Occasionally brass stringing and restrained inlay found on Regency pieces.

Always countersunk brass handles, mostly of rectangular shape, attached with countersunk brass screws.

FINISH

Stain and/or wax polish on early examples. French polish on many Victorian pieces.

RELATIVE VALUES

Disproportionately expensive to their simple appearance and straightforward construction. A secretaire drawer and a Regency date will push the price well into the thousands. Only the later, plain versions still in the hundreds.

CHESTS OF DRAWERS: MAHOGANY

About

1730-1830

Mostly simple, undecorated pieces based on classical proportions and varying more in shape than detail or construction.

Mahogany serpentine chest of drawers, about 1760, with bracket feet.

STYLE AND APPEARANCE

Many straight-fronted, others serpentine (often with canted corners) from about 1750-1800, or bow-fronted, about 1780 onwards. Three or four **drawers** of graduated depth.

Hepplewhite-style inlaid serpentine chest, about 1800, with 'swept' feet.

After 1800 a pair of drawers replacing the top long drawer re-introduced. All drawers fitted with interior locks; plain escutcheons flush with surface. Cockbeading on **edges** until around 1790 when sometimes replaced with light-coloured stringing (occasionally combined with narrow contrasting cross-banding); ebony stringing after 1810.

Straight, lip or thumb-moulded over-hanging **tops**. Sometimes edge reeded after 1800. Can have pull-out brushing-slide below (actually for writing, not, as once thought, for brushing clothes).

Occasionally cabriole **legs** around 1750, but much more commonly bracket feet, fashionably plain before 1750, ogee from about 1750-1800. After about 1780 splayed 'French' or 'swept' feet popular (extension of the sides and front), remaining so until about 1830. A few post-1810 chests have turned legs.

Early-18thC onwards bracket foot.

Ogee bracket foot, mid-18thC.

Splayed bracket foot, late-18thC.

Variations (highly sought after now) include those with a secretaire drawer (see **DESKS; SECRETAIRE BOOKCASES, p. 111**) or those with the top drawer fitted with dressing accessories. These normally have a number of open and/or lidded compartments and a central lift-up mirror which adjusts on a ratchet system.

A gentleman's dressing chest of about 1780.

MATERIALS

Mahogany (imported mostly from the West Indies and South America).

Pine used for all surfaces to be veneered; oak (occasionally cedar) for drawer linings (pine of drawer front concealed by strip of oak). Pine also used for backboards, sometimes replaced towards 1800 by oak or low-grade mahogany.

Country versions can be all oak with mahogany cross-bandings on drawers. Some similar and very fine quality chests made around 1780-1810 in satinwood.

CONSTRUCTION

Dove-tailed carcase (joins concealed by mouldings when solid timber employed). Lapped drawer dovetails, more numerous (about five or six) and finer than previously. Drawer linings thinner, about ¼ inch/6 mm (though ½ inch/1 cm still on country versions). Grain of linings front to back until about 1770; thereafter side to side. (NB This is not a golden rule and should not be used as conclusive evidence of age.) Large drawers with a central strengthening batten (or muntin) between two panels from about 1790. Drawer fronts flat with cockbeading (simple, slightly protruding moulding) rebated around edge.

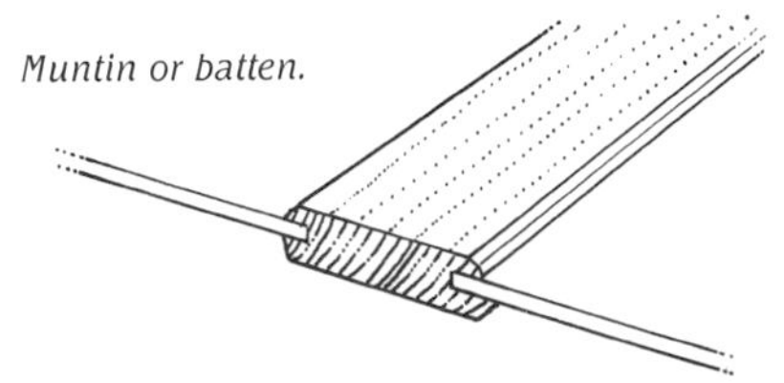

Muntin or batten.

Top beading may extend over entire top of drawer front (taking place of former oak strip to conceal pine). Drawers running on bearers fixed between front and back cross rails, with or without separate dustboards.

By 1750, the top is a separate item, screwed on from underneath. Sometimes there is an additional solid under-top (formed by top of carcase); alternatively cross rails with large fixed corner brackets (see illustration).

Backboards planked or panelled (but still rough); nailed on. On best quality pieces from about 1780 sometimes fixed with screws.

Bracket feet not structural, but glued to blocks. (These are very prone to damage and have often been replaced.)

CONVERSIONS

Watch out for chests which once formed part of a tallboy. These may be identified by features such as three drawers at the top, a deep carved frieze, and a rebated rather than over-hanging top. (Although some chests were made correctly in this way, with a 'caddy' top, the surrounding moulding was much finer than it would have to be for a converted tallboy.)

DECORATION

Figuring of veneer often most important feature, particularly Cuban 'curl' or 'flame' mahogany.

Carving rare, occasionally low relief Gothic or chinoiserie patterns around 1750, later quarter columns, reeding or fluting on canted corners.

Handles: All types in brass; attached with bolts and circular nuts (fitted with a special tool) until about 1770; thereafter square.

Some early pieces still with bail handles with pierced backplates, but generally after 1740 simple swan-neck designs common, with two separate circular and variously decorated roses. About 1780, oval or circular stamped (or pressed) brass handles, the loops following lower line of plate.

Brushing slides first with small loops, later small turned brass knobs (about 1765 onwards).

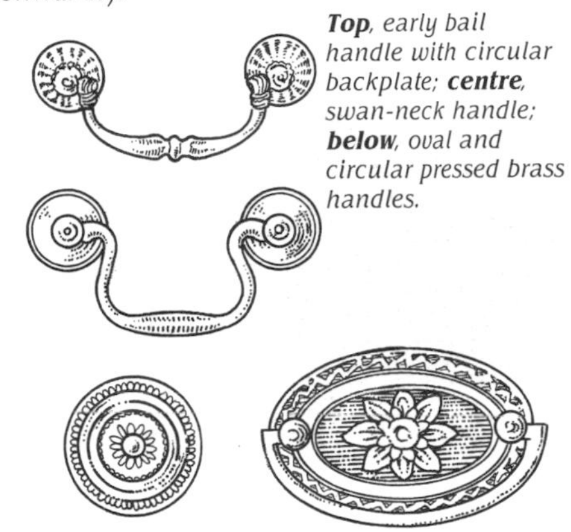

***Top**, early bail handle with circular backplate; **centre**, swan-neck handle; **below**, oval and circular pressed brass handles.*

FINISH

Polish: Oil and/or wax combined with varnish. Great variation according to maker's preference and variety of timber.

Varnish: Applied in several layers and rubbed down between each application; used to fill grain and produce smooth surface.

Lesser quality Honduras mahogany – which had a duller surface – either rubbed with oil, or polished with mixture of linseed oil and brick dust. Fine Spanish and Cuban mahogany sometimes lightly stained with oil prepared with crushed alkanet root for reddish finish.

Deep glossy shine subsequently retained by frequent domestic dry-rubbing or polishing with beeswax softened with spirit.

French polish: Although it produces a high sheen, it is not long-lasting.

RELATIVE VALUES

All but the simplest in four figures, the very best in five. Considerable sums paid for dressing chests and (rare) matching pairs.

CHESTS OF DRAWERS: VICTORIAN AND EDWARDIAN

About

1840-1915

Huge numbers of very simple chests were produced, in a wide range of qualities; a few followed fashionable styles in their decoration. After about 1860 they often formed part of a suite – chest, wash-stand, wardrobe and chair.

Bonhams

Early-Victorian bow-fronted chest of drawers, still of Hepplewhite type, but with coarse-grained veneers and large wooden knob handles.

STYLE AND APPEARANCE

Usually two short drawers above three long, but can be taller, with five or six drawers. Bow-fronted were most popular until about 1860, thereafter straight fronts were more common. The majority have turned bun feet – longer and less spherical than previously – otherwise bracket feet, or a continuous plinth.

Overhanging top; curved or flat-edged when veneered, moulded when solid (usually thumb or ovolo). Drawers flush with carcase, with almost flat cockbeading around edge. Until end of century all drawers fitted with locks (usually Bramah after 1846).

Around 1800, chests were sometimes combined with wash-stand or with dressing-table.

MATERIALS

Predominantly mahogany followed by walnut; occasionally satinwood, rosewood, maple, ash, oak. Sometimes solid, mostly veneered on pine or, on better quality pieces, cheap Honduras mahogany. Pine when stained to resemble other woods, or when painted.

CONSTRUCTION

Use of machinery widespread by this period, seen in even saw marks on timber, very thin veneers (about 1/16th inch/1.5 mm) and regularly shaped and cut dovetails. On best pieces dovetails are fine, almost pointed.

Base of larger drawers comprises two panels with central batten (or muntin) supported at sides on runners and held down with narrow quarter mouldings (this feature replaced rebates around 1830). On best quality examples, back of drawer is sometimes fixed to base with three countersunk screws in gouged-out slots. Drawer linings are occasionally lightly polished.

Knobs fixed in ½ inch/1 cm diameter holes with screw-turned dowel, or shank glued into threaded hole. Sometimes just dowelled and glued, others fixed with metal bolt.

Many very poor quality chests were mass-produced in East End of London using cheap, knotty, improperly seasoned woods and poor quality glues, resulting in lifting of veneers.

DECORATION

Some restrained carving or inlay when in a specific style, otherwise plain, relying only on figured (often burr) veneers.

Handles: Large turned wood knobs from about 1825; white porcelain knobs on painted chests from about 1870. Brass handles re-introduced where style demanded.

FINISH

French polish; sometimes stained to produce a reddish colour beforehand. Stain and varnish used to simulate quality timbers, particularly on cheap servants' furniture. Paint popular towards 1900: typically white or green.

RELATIVE VALUES

Prices very variable, closely related to quality of construction and choice of veneers. The majority still in three figures, the best in four. Pine still the cheapest buy.

WELLINGTON CHESTS

About

1810-1900

The origin of these tall, narrow chests is unknown, but their association by name with the Duke of Wellington, their simple appearance and the quick and easy method of locking the drawers, have been thought to imply use on military campaigns. Definitely a 'masculine' piece of furniture, probably intended as a specimen chest or just for the storage of small valuables and papers. Often seen in Victorian libraries.

Common type of mid-Victorian Wellington chest.

STYLE AND APPEARANCE

Usually seven narrow drawers of diminishing depth. Average height about 5 feet/1.5 m, width 18 inches/45 cm. Drawers completely plain and flush with carcase, held closed by narrow, lockable, hinged flap (matching plain fixed upright on opposite side) ending in simple carved capital or scroll. Flat-edged or simply moulded overhanging top, sometimes with plain frieze below. Mitred plinth base. Interior drawers sometimes compartmented and lined with velvet or other fabric.

Wellington chest with secretaire drawer.

Occasionally one or more dummy drawers conceal a fall-front secretaire. Squatter, miniature versions sometimes found for desk use. A few very similar chests without the lockable flap also made – not strictly, therefore, Wellington chests, but otherwise identical.

MATERIALS

Mahogany, rosewood, walnut, oak, satinwood, occasionally maple. Usually solid but sometimes veneered on pine or baywood (cheap mahogany) carcase.

CONSTRUCTION

Standard methods employed.

DECORATION

Seldom any other than figuring of timber. Occasionally stringing lines, restrained inlay. Small, turned wooden knobs; brass or bone knobs on some miniature versions.

FINISH

Wax or French polish. Cheap, later versions sometimes stained.

RELATIVE VALUES

Not immensely valuable items; the best make it into four figures, the majority don't.

COTS, CRADLES AND CRIBS

About
1500-1915

Today the term 'cradle' describes a baby's bed which rocks, either standing at floor level on two curved rockers, or suspended between two uprights. A cot or crib (the latter now an American term) implies the high-sided bed on legs, with sides of equal height, which was first devised for toddlers around 1800. In the 18thC and 19thC though, the term 'cot' distinguished the swing-type cradle from its more common rocking counterpart.

STYLE AND APPEARANCE

Cradles: Always panelled. Before 1600 the head-end just had raised sides; thereafter fully hooded. In the 17thC hoods were generally flat; in the 18thC arched, often ogee form. Large knob finials (used to rock the cradle) present on some uprights. Could be on four outer corners, or on one end only, or both ends and front of hood too. Small storage cupboard sometimes present at back of hood.

Swing cots: Fashionable from about 1750. Main body and hood panelled. Panels could be wood, but were more often of woven canework. Supported on trestle base on which the

Mahogany swing cot, about 1810.

Early-18thC oak cradle.

turning varied. At first vase-shaped, sometimes decorated with foliate carving; after 1790 more often straight-edged columns on splayed and reeded legs.

An alternative type, after 1800, had a rectangular body (without a fixed wooden hood), the sides formed of turned spindles. Similar trestle base to the above. The hood was formed by drapery, either hanging from a pole projecting from the wall above, or more often

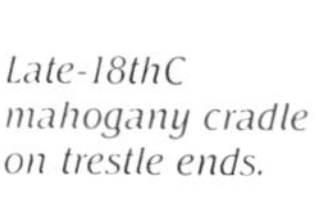

Late-18thC mahogany cradle on trestle ends.

suspended from a horizontal metal rail attached to an extended head-post.

Some Regency designers devised swing cots in elegant Greek, Roman or Egyptian style with many classical motifs, ormolu mounts and elaborate drapery. Few of these were made, fewer still survive.

Very large numbers were made during

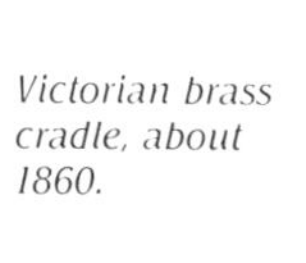

Victorian brass cradle, about 1860.

Queen Victoria's reign in cast iron or brass or combinations of the two. Generally an iron base (for stability) and brass decorative parts. On all-iron pieces the body was covered with drapery and was therefore purely functional, usually simply ribbed or latticed.

Modern-style cribs or cots: First appeared during Regency. Initially in rectangular box form with turned spindles and straight, square-sectioned uprights continuous with legs. Victorian examples marked by cast-iron construction with variously patterned mesh sides; sometimes raised around one end. Could have half-tester canopy (see **p. 22**). By 1900, generally plain slatted or turned wooden verticals, usually painted in plain colours. Height was adjustable on one side and on the base of wire mesh.

Victorian brass and iron swing cot.

MATERIALS

Oak, sometimes elm or other indigenous woods, for rocking cradles; mahogany, sometimes rosewood, for the swing type. Cast iron and brass tubing in the 19thC. Victorian reproductions often made in beech or pine, painted and grained to simulate oak.

Until about 1800, the majority of cradles were evidently made in wicker (with wooden rockers), but survivals in Britain in unknown.

Late Victorian/Edwardian metal child's bed.

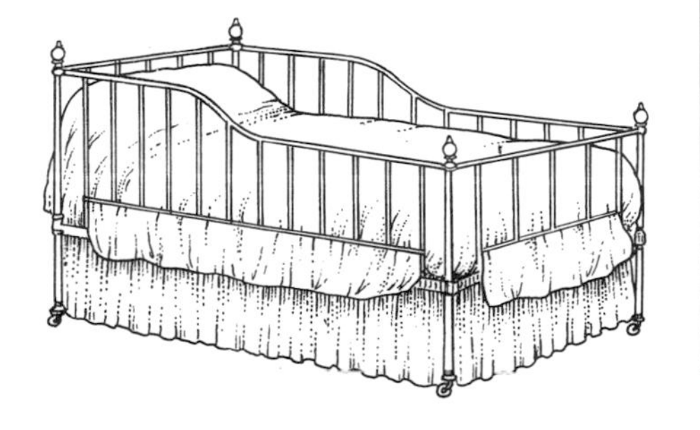

In grand houses, cradles, like beds, were an indication of status and could be elaborate. State cradles were made in beech and completely covered with upholstery.

CONSTRUCTION

Cradles: Panelled. In early 18thC fielded panels were fashionable. Rockers usually cut and pegged into base of corner uprights, but could be attached via short turned supports dowelling into rockers and underside of frame. Hood occasionally hinged at back to allow easy access to baby. Sometimes holes, large wooden pins, or metal loops present at top of sides to take ropes to hold baby in place. Bottom usually had similar holes for bedlines (see ***p. 23***). Alternatively could have fixed laths or a solid base, the planks removable for easy cleaning.

Swing cots: Straightforward panelled construction. Alternative type with spindles dowelled into upper and lower framework. For brass and iron, see **p. 28**.

DECORATION

Humblest cradles could have simple chip-carving with lozenges, or more complex designs (see CHESTS, **P. 82**). Occasionally simple inlay of flowers or geometric borders. Grandest had additional painted or gilt decoration of which traces may still be visible. Many were carved with initials and a date. This could be details of a birth, but sometimes the initials of the reigning monarch. Not a reliable method of dating as cradles were usually family heirlooms and the date could refer to a later occupant. Many spurious dates were added in the 19thC to fake authenticity.

FINISH

Polish. Japanning on cast iron, often to simulate wood or bronze. Paint began to be a feature of cots around 1900.

RELATIVE VALUES

Despite their age and charm, not very valuable objects, the majority (of all types) being priced in three figures, many at the lower end of the scale. While their usefulness for their intended purpose may be short-lived, they make very good jardinieres.

DESKS: BUREAUX AND BUREAUX CABINETS

About
1690-1740

Walnut veneered two-part bureau, about 1700.

A combination of the bureau on stand and the escritoire, having an upper desk section with a fitted interior mounted on a chest of drawers; can have a cabinet above with further interior fittings for ledgers, papers.

STYLE AND APPEARANCE

Initially made in two sections with applied 'waist' moulding around join. (Moulding sometimes retained for decorative effect, even when made in one piece.)

Base: Until about 1725, square (oak) lopers at top, thereafter rectangular. May have single or pair of drawer(s) between, above two or three long drawers of graduated size, or blank space fronting a well with sliding top accessible from desk interior. A well suggests a slightly earlier date.

Usually narrow moulding at base. Bun feet until about 1710, then bracket. (Many buns replaced with brackets at later date; modern trend is to revert to type.)

A few have full-width writing-slide at top, usually with corresponding book-rest moulding on fall.

For details of drawer fronts, etc. see CHESTS OF DRAWERS, p. 86.

Desk: Sloping fall; generally flush with surrounding framework. Sometimes ovolo lip moulding around 1710-1720, matching drawers below. Narrow cock-beading introduced about 1730. Top always flush with sides; never overhanging.

Interior fittings: Plenty of variation, but always symmetrically arranged and set back from front edge. Simplest with open pigeon holes (often with arched top and aprons) and maybe two or three shallow drawers below, frequently of undulating outline. Early interiors generally stepped (later on country versions), with drawers of convex or concave section. Best have central cupboard flanked by pilasters (the grandest with ormolu or gilt brass capitals). Secret compartment usually concealed behind; reached by removal of shelf, drawer or other fittings.

Upper cabinet: Sits within applied moulding. Two, occasionally one door(s). Fashionable early pieces panelled with mirror glass (with bevelled edges), but can be wooden, finished both inside and out, as doors were often left open to show off elaborate interior. This has further drawers and pigeon-holes etc. all flush with front. Some partitions tall and narrow for ledgers, folios.

Moulded cornice above may be:

- straight
- domed (single arch)
- broken dome
- double dome (most highly prized in its day)
- broken architectural (i.e. straight-edged) pediment (found after 1725 and on mahogany only)

All with finial(s) at centre and/or sides.

Mirrored cabinets may have pair of candle slides at base (so that light could be reflected in glass). Both features went out of fashion around 1740.

MATERIALS

Principally walnut veneer on pine carcase (with oak for drawer linings). Occasionally other figured veneers of mulberry, yew etc. Mahogany after about 1725.

Oak for some country and provincial pieces;

sometimes elm, ash or other indigenous woods.

Oak and walnut for interior fittings, sometimes with inlay of box, holly, bone.

CONSTRUCTION

Standard methods employed (see **CHESTS OF DRAWERS** for details, **p. 87**). Basically veneer on dovetailed carcase; through dovetails increasingly replaced by lapped after 1700. Double-lapped on bureau top.

Figured veneers were often used only on top and front (i.e. the most visible surfaces) with vertically-running, straight-grained veneer on the sides.

Hinged fall cleated for stability (to prevent warping). Expect signs of damage to hinges and around lock due to faulty handling.

Usually – but not invariably – cabinet cornice integral with carcase until about 1725; thereafter more commonly separate piece, merely sitting on top with glued corner blocks to carcase to maintain position.

FAKE BUREAUX

Because of their very high value, fakes and marriages of early walnut bureaux and bureaux cabinets are not uncommon. Check for matching grain and colour of all timbers, and for matching interior and base drawer construction. The top of the bureau section should be rough, dry and untouched, with no signs of new timber, if a cabinet was originally present.

Newly-veneered – but originally plain and solid – oak bureaux may also be encountered, not infrequently veneered with *old* timber taken from a less valuable piece. So even though the veneer itself may look right (i.e. hand-cut and of irregular thickness, about 1/8 inch/3 mm) the all-oak carcase will indicate this practice. The interior fittings will either be too plain for the outer casing, or will also have been veneered, or even replaced. Check for signs of new wood and see if the drawer construction matches that of the large drawers below. See also if signs of former handles inside the drawers correspond with filled holes outside.

DECORATION

Principally figuring of timber, especially burr veneers. Additional effects achieved by cross-banding, feather banding, quartering. Occasionally fine marquetry; mostly floral, preferably seaweed, patterns.

Handles: Typical for day (for details see **page 87**.) Earliest with brass drop handles (smaller inside than out; seldom matching). Thereafter brass bails with solid backplates outside, smaller ring handles with circular backplates inside. Interior fittings more commonly have small bone, ivory or brass knobs. Fan-shaped pulls common on lopers until about 1725, then brass knobs.

All drawers and fall fitted with locks and surface-mounted escutcheons.

Generally large brass carrying handles at sides; usually on both parts of two-piece base; only occasionally matching those on drawers.

FINISH

Oak: Stain (applied in oil).

Walnut: Varnish (to fill grain).

Mahogany: Varnish or oil stain.

All followed by wax polish (for further details see **CHESTS OF DRAWERS, p. 82**).

RELATIVE VALUES

Early walnut pieces extremely valuable, especially those with cabinets; prices can be counted in tens of thousands. Original handles and bun feet – although both unlikely – an advantage; so too interesting veneer, intricately shaped and stepped interior fittings.

Walnut bureau cabinet, about 1700.

Sotheby's

DESKS: BUREAUX AND BUREAUX CABINETS

About
1740 onwards

Now made in one piece, with or without an additional upper cabinet or bookcase. A piece of furniture which changed very little over the following 150 years and which has been widely reproduced for a further century.

Country-made oak bureau with mahogany cross-banding on drawers, 1760-1770.

OAK BUREAUX

Oak bureaux were made in large numbers by provincial and country makers throughout the 18th and well into the 19thC. Unlike much other oak country furniture, many of these are of considerable quality and sophisticated design and construction, and as such, command high prices.

STYLE AND APPEARANCE

Base: Rectangular (oak) lopers at top with single or pair of drawer(s) between, above two or three long drawers of graduated depth. Sometimes three deep drawers only after 1800. Mostly cock-beaded edges. Sometimes mahogany cross-banding on oak. From about 1780 drawers occasionally replaced by two-door cupboard (but only when cabinet above). Bracket feet with straight apron; ogee brackets fashionable between 1730 and 1775. Occasionally swept feet after 1780.

Desk: Flap mostly cock-beaded around edge (matching drawers below); sometimes ovolo lip moulding on solid mahogany after 1780.

Interior fittings: Symmetrically arranged and set back from front edge. Less frequently stepped; straight-fronted drawers increasingly common. Almost invariably central cupboard flanked by pilasters; usually secret compartment behind.

Upper cabinets: Majority glazed by 1750 with interior shelves for display of books, china etc. Decorative patterns of glazing bars,

Mahogany bureau bookcase, about 1770.

***Below**, alternative designs for glazing bars.*

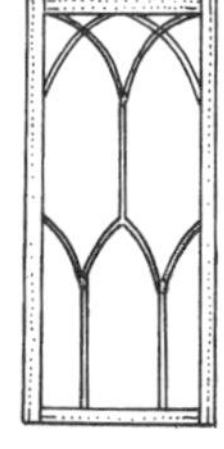
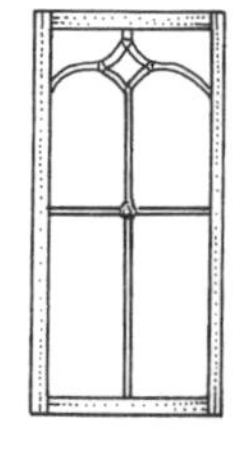
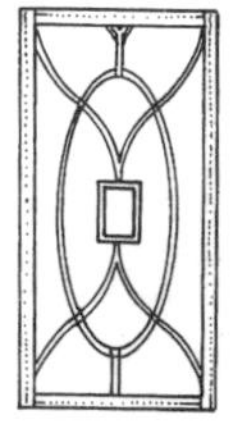

Christie's

Hepplewhite mahogany bureau, about 1780-1800.

astragals etc. (see **BOOKCASES, p. 37**). Otherwise wood-panelled (also with shelves rather than fitments inside) often of shaped outline.

Cornice can be:

1725-1800 broken architectural pediment with central vase or bust.

1760-1810 swan-neck pediment, pierced or solid, also central vase or bust.

1780-1810 straight, with dentil or other moulding.

1800-1830 straight with central and side antefixae or carved and scrolled, frequently with central anthemion.

All can have decorative frieze carved with prevailing fashionable design. Chinese and Gothic motifs fashionable to about 1780; thereafter, fluting interspersed with paterae was most common.

Tendency for whole piece to become wider and taller around 1760, but smaller again towards 1800.

REPRODUCTIONS

18thC bureaux a popular subject for Victorian and Edwardian reproductions (and pastiches), particularly after 1870. Some reasonably authentic, many definitely not. Even those of standard form often given away by inappropriate feet or vulgarly matched veneers. Most popular today are those in Edwardian 'Sheraton' style with bold satinwood cross-banding and single inlaid shell in centre of fall.

Out of the mainstream of design, but surprisingly numerous today, are rather tall, angular oak bureaux, with a number of open shelves and small cupboards flanking the desk section, which were made in progressive style from 1900.

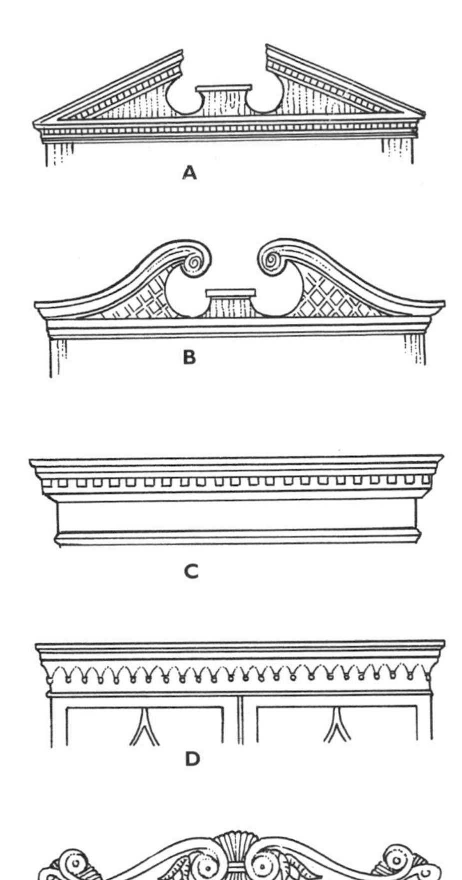

*Various pediments: **A** broken, about 1730-1830; **B** swan-neck, 1760-1810; **C** plain dentil, 1725-1800; **D** moulded dentil; **E** Regency scroll, 1800-1830.*

MATERIALS

Majority in mahogany (either solid or veneered); closely followed by oak. Sometimes elm (or combination of oak and elm), ash and other indigenous woods.

Pine (with oak for drawer linings) for carcases and backboards, also cheap Honduras mahogany around 1760. Pine or beech when japanned.

Oak or mahogany for interior fittings. Sometimes with inlay of box, holly, bone; later harewood, kingwood, satinwood too. Satinwood facings to mahogany drawers common in late 18thC.

CONSTRUCTION

Standard methods employed (see **CHESTS OF DRAWERS, p. 87**). Veneered on carcases with lapped dovetails. Double-lapped (in order to conceal construction) on top of solid mahogany pieces.

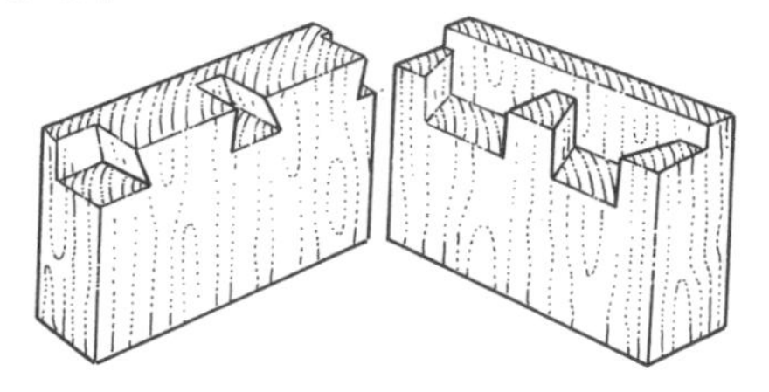

Hidden or lapped dovetails.

Flaps clamped to prevent warping.

Upper cabinets held in place with screws fixed through bottom shelf.

Sometimes figured veneers used for front (i.e. most visible) parts with straight-grained veneer on sides.

Marriages even more common than previously; check carefully (see ***p. 89***).

Bonhams

Edwardian 'Sheraton' bureau bookcase.

Christie's

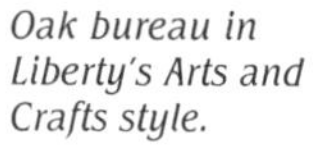

Oak bureau in Liberty's Arts and Crafts style.

DECORATION

Principally figuring of veneers. Some restrained carving on upper cabinets. Simple mahogany cross-banding on some oak pieces. Some inlay on drawers after 1780; mostly simple stringing lines, sometimes shells, fans and so on.

Japanning; mostly in black, but can be red or green with gilt and coloured chinoiserie patterns. Original examples of these are rare today; many are 20thC reproductions. Decoration alone usually gives these away, being more convincingly Oriental and covering a greater surface area than before, with plenty of gilding, especially in the borders. Flat, engraved hinges, escutcheons and handle backplates identical if modern, irregular if old.

Note: a small amount of English-made furniture was shipped to China in the 18thC to be decorated by Chinese craftsmen, a procedure which can lead to confusion over origin. Examples are however extremely rare and unlikely to be encountered outside the top salerooms. Lacquer is a specialist subject; it's always best to seek expert advice if considering a purchase.

Handles: Typical for day (for details see **page 87**). Mostly swan-neck and other bails. Interior fittings with small bone, ivory or brass knobs.

All drawers and flap fitted with locks and escutcheons. Latter nearly always surface-mounted on flap, skeleton on drawers after 1750. Inlaid diamond (often bone or ivory) became common around flap keyhole after about 1780.

FINISH

Oak: stain (applied with oil).

Mahogany: stain or varnish.

Both followed by wax polish. French polish almost universal after 1820. Many earlier pieces re-polished in this way at later date.

RELATIVE VALUES

Plenty of choice so price very variable. Small size (less than 2.5 feet/75 cm) will add to value considerably, as will a fine interior and attractively glazed and pedimented cabinet.

Usually, good country-made oak bureaux are generally worth more than reasonable quality 19thC mahogany examples.

Prices for virtually all standard bureaux (excluding pastiches) are in four figures, and frequently in five.

DESKS: DAVENPORT

About

1795-1885

Christie's

Regency rosewood Davenport with swivel top.

A small free-standing writing-desk made in large numbers and with many variations through the 19thC. The name derives from an entry in the 1790s cost books of Gillow in Lancaster – *'For Capt. Davenport, a desk'* – alongside a design for a box-like desk with drawers opening to one side and a writing-slope above. Although presumably as a space-saving design for use on board ship, its small size and lower-than-average height ensured its popularity with women and children.

STYLE AND APPEARANCE

Regency examples had a simple slope-top box which could either slide forward or sideways on runners to provide knee-space, or swivel to one side on a stout peg. Some had a brushing and/candle slide at one side (see ***p. 329***). The flat surface above the slope was generally bordered by a brass gallery. Many had a long, narrow drawer fitted with small compartments for ink and writing implements which pulled out from one side. This was usually released by removal of a long pin inside the desk, its head masquerading as the knob of a small dummy drawer. Most were supported on bun feet, some on short, turned legs on castors.

During the 1820s the front was often faced with pilasters, but more commonly a fixed slope, supported on pillars rising from a plinth, replaced the sliding top. The lower drawers became correspondingly narrower. Galleries were constructed from wood, and bun feet were flattened or replaced by semi-concealed castors.

By the mid 1850s elaborately carved rococo cabriole (or triple C-scroll) supports were fashionable, their curves often echoed by a serpentine front to the slope above. Gal-

Sotheby's

Rosewood, with ring-turned column supports, about 1880.

Black walnut Davenport with inlaid stringing and ebony bandings, about 1860.

Sotheby's

Mid-Victorian walnut Davenport with 'rococo' scroll supports.

leries grew ornate, often fret-carved in naturalistic patterns.

After 1860 'piano lid' tops were popular, with pull-out writing-slides.

Pillars gradually retreated under a cantilevered top and by the 1870s were more decorative than functional, in some cases being replaced by brackets.

During the 1880s fashionable 'Art Furniture' Davenports had short ring-turned legs and panels of gilded and painted decoration.

The greatest variation in Victorian Davenports occurred in the position and conformation of the stationery compartments which could be quite varied:

- Simply inside the desk (as in a bureau, see ***p. 100***);
- The early-type pull-out drawer, hinged to lie flat against the side of the desk when fully extended;
- A raised and lidded box on the flat shelf above the slope, or a lidded compartment set beneath it;
- In a large 'secret' compartment rising up at the back of the desk when released by a lever, button or sliding panel hidden somewhere inside. Sometimes they moved in conjunction with a pull-out writing-slide. Pieces with these rising 'harlequin' superstructures are generally referred to as 'harlequin Davenports';
- Later examples sometimes had a small two-door cupboard above the slope.

Design for Davenport of around 1880.

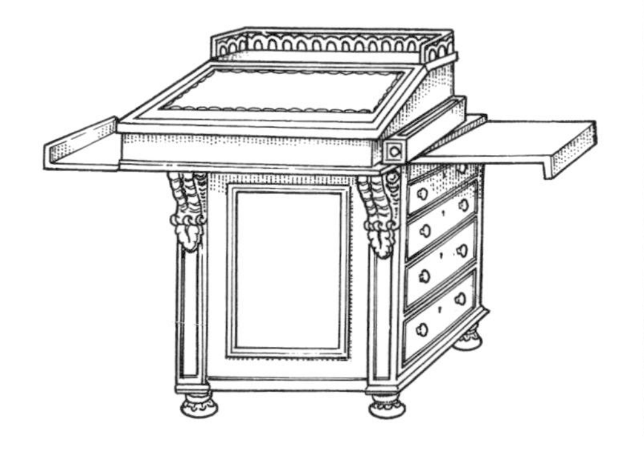

***Right**, Victorian walnut Davenport, with piano front and harlequin writing superstructure.*

Very late mahogany example.

Features common to all types include:

- Symmetry of design. Drawers matched by dummy drawers on opposite side. Similarly, a panelled door enclosing drawers matched by panelling.
- Finished on all sides. The back panelling usually complements the front.
- Matched colour and grain of timber on top and bottom sections. (Failure to do so may indicate a later 'marriage'.)
- Locks on desk, stationery compartment and all drawers (or enclosing door). Commonly Bramah locks (see **p. 94)**, but sometimes skeleton escutcheons).

CONSTRUCTION

Standard practices for the day employed. Harlequin rising superstructures generally work on a spring mechanism, but occasionally on counter-balanced weights.

MATERIALS

Solid mahogany, rosewood and walnut, and veneers of the same on an oak or deal base. Occasionally satinwood. Other highly figured veneers such as amboyna or burr walnut were greatly favoured by the Victorians. Cheaper versions were made in solid oak, elm or poor quality mahogany or imported walnut.

Brass, ebony, mother-of-pearl, boxwood and many other timbers used for inlaid decoration.

Writing-surfaces fitted with inset leather panels, with tooled and often gilded borders.

DECORATION

Restrained inlay and stringing lines of brass or ebony on some pre-Victorian examples.

In the early Victorian period (up to the mid-1860s) decoration was largely supplied by ornate carving on the supports, applied split mouldings on flat surfaces and pierced galleries around the top. Until about 1870 highly figured veneers were considered a decorative feature in their own right.

During the 1860s inlaid panels of stylized or naturalistic flowers popularly adorned the front panel and occasionally the sides too.

Handles: Small, turned wooden knobs on all drawers. Metal handles only correctly seen on very late examples.

FINISH

In most cases, wax polish. Very cheap Victorian versions were heavily stained and usually finished with a glossy French polish (see **p. 16**). During the 1880s many were fashionably ebonised with gilt incised decoration.

RELATIVE VALUES

Totally plain Victorian pieces are within the average buyer's reach. Highly decorative, burr veneer, harlequin examples can fetch sums in high four figures. The majority are in the low four figures. Surprisingly, fussy Victorian Davenports sell better today than more elegant Georgian ones.

DESKS: KNEEHOLE

About

1700-1780s

Mahogany kneehole desk with bracket feet, about 1760-1770.

A small and attractive piece, originally devised as a dressing-table, not a desk, but in appearance like a chest of drawers with a central recessed kneehole space backed by a cupboard. Occasionally a hinged top, lifting to reveal fitments for dressing accessories; rarely, a secretaire drawer.

STYLE AND APPEARANCE

One long drawer above two tiers of three small drawers of graduated depth. Generally a shaped apron fronting recess between. Overhanging top with moulded edge. Base moulding above either four or six bracket feet (ogee after about 1750). Maybe a brushing (or writing) slide immediately below top.

Door of recessed cupboard often panelled; sometimes flush, with cock-beaded edge to match drawer fronts.

Straight or serpentine front; sometimes with canted corners; these either plain, or carved, sometimes with half-columns, pilasters. (See **CHESTS OF DRAWERS, p. 92**).

MATERIALS

Walnut, mahogany; occasionally other indigenous hardwoods. Pine (with oak for drawer linings) for carcase when veneered. Sometimes also mahogany around 1760.

CONVERSIONS

Conversions from chests of drawers were common, particularly in early 20thC. Despite the high costs involved most ended up as four-feet type (to save creating two new ones).

Dovetails and suitable timber for drawer linings, as well as the new recessed door and inner sides, have to be well-matched in colour and grain to be convincing. Check the edges of the drawers for equal wear on both sides and for similar wear from the movement of drawers within the carcase. New locks will have been fitted and handles possibly repositioned.

CONSTRUCTION

Standard methods employed, as for chests of drawers.

DECORATION

Both decoration and handles as for chests of drawers (see **p. 93**). Decorative veneers and/or marquetry on walnut; sometimes restrained carving on mahogany.

FINISH

Varnish on walnut; stain on mahogany. Both followed by wax polish.

RELATIVE VALUES

These are valuable pieces when right, especially if walnut or with secretaire or dressing drawer. Prices invariably well into four figures; be suspicious if not.

Edwardian 'Sheraton' kneehole desk.

Christie's

DESKS: PEDESTAL

About

1750 onwards

Bonhams

Mahogany pedestal desk, early-19thC.

A substantial piece of writing furniture deriving from the type of pedestal 'library' or 'writing-table' made and illustrated by Thomas Chippendale and other high quality London-based cabinet makers in the mid-18thC. Subsequently made in a wide range of sizes, the largest being the double-sided partners' desk, the smallest the half-pedestal devised around 1900. Particularly popular during the 19th and 20thC for office use.

STYLE AND APPEARANCE

Early library tables with two pedestals of four drawers with a plain top with frieze below and carved and shaped apron fronting kneehole recess. Sometimes panelled cupboard doors enclosing pedestal drawers.

From about 1765 standard form evolved. Made in three parts: two pedestal bases, each containing a flight of three drawers of graduated depth. Sides generally flat when veneered, panelled when solid. Top with three frieze drawers, outer two of equal width to drawers below. Continuous plinth around bases (in late 19thC sometimes fitted with concealed castors). Occasionally bracket feet; short turned legs after 1790. Overhanging top with lip or thumb-nail moulding; narrow moulding around lower edge of top section. Writing- surface with tooled (sometimes gilt) border. Later 19thC cloth imitation common. Can be laid in three sections. One pedestal sometimes has a cupboard, fronted by dummy drawers.

__Above__, late-Victorian mahogany pedestal desk, about 1880-1890; ***below****, kidney-shaped mahogany pedestal desk, about 1800-1820.*

Christie's

By far the majority were rectangular; a few kidney- or D-shaped between about 1790 and 1820. Being free-standing, all visible surfaces were finished (i.e. back and inner sides of pedestals). Occasionally there was a solid back to the recess. (This feature was often found on simple provincial and country-made versions; used in smaller rooms of smaller houses, against the wall – i.e. not free-standing.)

Second half of 19thC saw continuous production of the standard model, but also an attempt to apply the prevailing historic revival and other styles such as:

Reformed Gothic: Chamfered edges, panels of diagonal planking, incised line decoration, carved trefoils.

Elizabethan: Heavily carved, dark-stained oak, carved wood, lion's mask, pull handles.

Sheraton: Principally inlay, some marquetry, in contrasting coloured satinwood. Crossbanding too.

Variations included:

Partners' desks (from about 1770): As a standard pedestal but double-sized and double-sided. Sometimes there are drawers one side and cupboards the others, but usually the configuration was identical.

Half-pedestals (about 1900 onwards): Made in one piece with apron below single drawer and simple legs replacing missing side.

Simple office desks (about 1900 onwards):With two four-drawer pedestals and plain top (i.e. without drawers). Curved apron fronting recess.

Late versions of standard pedestals may have bracket feet or short, turned or tapering legs ending in cup of box socket castors, considerably altering overall proportion, generally looking too insubstantial to support significant weight above.

From 1900 solid backs to recesses of office desks (for purposes of modesty) much more common. Some pieces with additional floor-level foot-rail.

MATERIALS

Mostly mahogany. Commonly oak in 19thC, or pine, originally stained to simulate mahogany, but now usually sold stripped and waxed. Occasionally rosewood during Regency; burr walnut, yew and other figured woods in Victorian times. Sometimes satinwood for decorative panels of veneer.

CONSTRUCTION

Standard methods employed (see **CHESTS OF DRAWERS, p. 93**). Top framework with mortise-and-tenon joints. Top slots over blocks were glued to top of base.

Structural alterations not common, but occasionally marriage of bases to different top, or the superstructure (feature sometimes found on late 19thC pieces) removed and top re-veneered or replaced with new. Occasionally plain oak versions were veneered later to up price; look for all-oak carcase.

MOCK-GEORGIAN DESKS

Very many Victorian and early 20thC desks refurbished with new leather and period-style brass handles and sold as 'Georgian'. Check construction of drawers carefully; watch particularly for plywood linings (an inter-war feature). The holes left by former handles may give a clue to the date. The horizontal wooden pulls common from about 1900 will show two screw holes (both inside and out) further apart than you would expect on a standard handle; the semi-elliptical metal handles popular between the wars will leave three small screw or pin holes on the outside only, arranged as the three points of a triangle; Victorian wooden knobs will leave a ½ inch/1 cm diameter hole on both sides.

DECORATION

Very little decoration. Some carving on verticals and friezes of early writing-tables. Inlay, mostly in the form of stringing lines, and occasionally marquetry of neo-classical inspiration, on drawers from about 1780; revived again in late 19thC (though this tends to be heavier, executed in strongly contrasting yellow satinwood). Sometimes narrow cross-banded veneer rather than inlay.

Some use of burr or highly figured veneers throughout 19thC.

Bonhams

Lion's mask handles on 19thC pedestal desk.

Handles: Generally very simple brass swan-neck in 18thC, turned wooden knobs in 19th, joined by a variety of metal ring, bail or drop handles around 1870, and horizontal wooden pulls around 1900.

Generally skeleton escutcheons; sometimes surface-mounted in late 19thC.

FINISH

Stain or varnish followed by wax polish. French polish from about 1820. Dark – almost black – stain on 'Elizabethan' oak. Various brown stains and varnishes to simulate mahogany used on cheap quality pine.

RELATIVE VALUES

Very few genuine 18thC pedestal desks about; those that are fetch enormous sums. Any example pre-dating 1900 invariably in four figures; only the cheapest type of post-1900 examples can be found for less. On pieces of all dates, any decorative feature – even the use of a wood other than oak or mahogany – may seem to raise the price disproportionately.

Note: Original leather is rare; replacement (if done properly) does not affect value.

DESKS: BONHEURS DU JOURS AND CHEVERETS

About

1770-1915

A satinwood bonheur du jour with simple inlaid decoration.

Sotheby's

Sometimes simply described as writing cabinets on stands, these are small lady's writing-tables, with a superstructure of drawers, pigeonholes and cupboards. Those with a long bookshelf above drawers and a lifting handle at the back are called cheverets (sometimes spelt sheverets). Both types were introduced from France (as their name suggests).

Another popular subject for Edwardian reproductions. Manufacture restricted at all times to high quality makers.

STYLE AND APPEARANCE

The base was a small rectangular-topped table with one, sometimes two, shallow frieze drawer(s), occasionally opening to the side. Narrow, tapering legs (in 18thC tapering on inside edge only), usually ending in spade feet, sometimes with applied ankle mouldings; not infrequently in socket castors. Turned legs not unknown, but rare. Sometimes top folds out to form larger writing-surface, supported on small lopers in frieze, or occasionally on (opened) drawer.

Conformation of superstructure varies

considerably. Most pieces bordered by low brass or wood gallery.

Can have tray shelf below, with shaped front to accommodate feet. Sometimes narrow stretchers on back and sides, or of X-plan.

Some burr walnut pieces in so-called 'Louis' style with cabriole legs, ormolu mounts etc. made from about 1860.

MATERIALS

Principally satinwood; also mahogany and rosewood. Occasionally walnut from 1860 onwards.
Pine or mahogany for carcases (with oak or mahogany for drawer linings). Kingwood, harewood, tulipwood etc. for inlay and for small panels of contrasting veneer.

CONSTRUCTION

Standard methods employed.

Many good reproductions about: check drawer construction carefully for indications of date (see **CHESTS OF DRAWERS, p. 103**). Look particularly for 19thC machine-cut dovetails and quarter mouldings around inside edges. Being good quality, inner surfaces may be lightly polished.

DECORATION

Principally figuring and arrangement of veneers; often inlay, mostly of stringing lines and simple ovals.

Some pieces painted with neo-classical motifs and/or flowers, wreaths etc. particularly from 1860 onwards. Late decoration tends to be less delicate than previously and covers greater surface area. Panels of classical figures also popular.

Occasionally Wedgewood plaques or imitation Sèvres porcelain panels set in doors.

Handles: Standard for day (for details see **page 93**).

FINISH

Principally varnish, sometimes stain, followed by wax polish. French polish after 1820.

RELATIVE VALUES

Even 19th/early 20thC reproductions command substantial sums; in fact there isn't always a lot between them and the originals. Prices well into the thousands. Inlay a bonus.

DESKS: CARLTON HOUSE

About

1785-1915

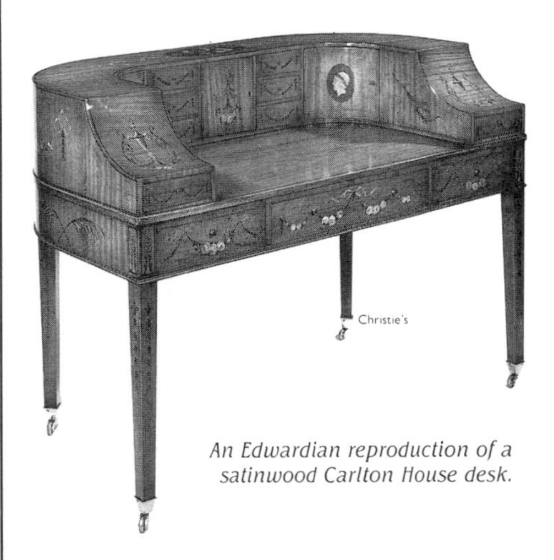

An Edwardian reproduction of a satinwood Carlton House desk.

Associated by name with the Prince Regent's London house, and mostly dating from the Regency period, these were first mentioned as such in the 1796 cost books of Gillows of Lancaster. Described in contemporary pattern books as a 'lady's writing-table'. Made throughout the 19thC; very fine 'Sheraton' reproductions made by the Edwardians. Still reproduced today.

STYLE AND APPEARANCE

Carlton House desks are distinguished from other writing-tables by their large size (width usually more than 5 feet/1.5 m) and their low superstructure extending around the curves of their D-shaped top.

Made in two parts, the lower with two or three shallow frieze drawers; sometimes with an additional shallow lower drawer on each side. Generally tapering legs with spade feet (correctly tapering on inner edge only), extending up to form corners of framing and standing slightly proud of vertical rails. Alternatively, turned legs with occasional ring mouldings (from about 1800) set underneath rectangular top, often with rounded (but no D) corners. Slightly overhanging top with moulded edge; inset leather writing-surface bordered by cross-banded veneer.

Early superstructures comprised a small central cupboard flanked by tiers of drawers, they in turn flanked by concave-fronted cupboards and concave-lidded compartments with single or dummy drawer below. Continuous flat top generally bordered by brass – occasionally wood – gallery. Later superstructures more varied, often lacking concave-sectioned parts.

MATERIALS

Principally satinwood and mahogany, with inlay of box, holly, harewood, kingwood etc. Occasionally rosewood. Sometimes amboyna and other figured woods. Bird's-eye maple used for some Victorian pieces.

Pine or mahogany for carcases (with oak or mahogany for drawer linings). Pine throughout used for late reproductions.

CONSTRUCTION

Standard methods employed. Glued mortise-and-tenon joints with fine, lapped dovetails on drawers (machine-cut in later 19thC). All outer surfaces (except turned legs) veneered.

FINISH

Stain or varnish, followed by wax polish.

DECORATION

Chiefly figuring of veneer with inlaid stringing lines and neo-classical motifs such as shells, drapery, scrolls etc. Sometimes similar painted decoration (these often Edwardian reproductions).

Handles: Can be simple bails with circular backplates on lower drawers; small brass knobs above. Occasionally lion's mask ring handles below. Often small ring handles – matching on all drawers – with plain or decorative (but basically circular) backplates.

RELATIVE VALUES

Original, early and finely veneered and inlaid examples are immensely valuable. Even good Edwardian reproductions may reach five figures. The least desirable are mid- to late-Victorian rectangular versions – particularly those with a raised centre to the superstructure – but even so, prices can still rise to four figures.

DESKS: CYLINDER AND TAMBOUR

About
1780 onwards

George III satinwood tambour desk with pedimented bookcase above.

Both terms are used to describe any desk with a superstructure enclosed by a half- or quarter-round sliding lid which disappears into the structure when lifted. A cylinder top has a continuous smooth surface; a tambour is slatted. This type of desk originated in France a little earlier.

STYLE AND APPEARANCE

Early examples (about 1780-1830) mostly with a base as a lady's writing-table (see **BONHEURS DU JOURS, p. 108**), but often larger and sometimes with extra lower drawer on each side. Frequently an upper cabinet or bookcase above. Super-structure fitted with small drawers, pigeonholes. Sometimes the inner writing-surface pulls forward as top lifts. If quarter-round (most common type) the flat shelf at the top bordered by a brass gallery.

Pedestal versions (mostly tambour) about 1870 onwards. Similar interior fittings; inset leather (later 'imitation') writing-surface. Flat top above bordered by low wooden gallery. Tambour sometimes serpentine instead of quarter-round.

At all times lid on both types lifted by two (occasionally one) knob(s) or handle(s) fitted at its base.

MATERIALS

Mahogany, occasionally satinwood in 18th/ early 19thC. Commonly mahogany or oak in Victorian, Edwardian and inter-war periods. Mahogany or pine for carcases when veneered, with mahogany or oak for drawer linings. Matching timber usually used for interior fittings, but popularly 'satin walnut' from about 1870.

CONSTRUCTION

Standard methods employed.

Tambour: Constructed of large number of horizontal laths or narrow mouldings, laid close together, their flat sides glued to a piece of stiff fabric.

Note: These are often damaged – especially if the fabric and glue have dried out – and are difficult and expensive to repair. Do inspect the tambour carefully and open and close it several times to make sure it functions well.

Cylinder: Always veneered; on base composed of many long and narrow, angled or grooved, pieces of timber, planed on the outer edge to provide a smooth surface.

Both types slide in grooves cut in sides of superstructure.

DECORATION

Some restrained inlay on early writing- table types; more pronounced inlay, occasionally painted decoration, on Edwardian Sheraton revival versions. Seldom any decoration – not even interesting figured woods – on pedestal.

Handles: Standard for dates. Brass bail or ring on table type; wooden knobs, joined by various metal handles around 1870, in 19thC. Horizontal wooden pulls after 1900.

FINISH

Stain followed by polish. French polish from about 1820.

Victorian and later oak more often stained a light honey colour rather than the usual dark, treacly, brown.

Early-19thC mahogany tambour desk.

RELATIVE VALUES

Very large numbers of these desks were mass-produced for office use beween the wars (though some would date them pre-1914). Characteristic features are horizontal wooden pull handles on lower drawers, rectangular metal label frames (either with integral pull or separate small turned knob) on inner drawers, panelled back to recess and simple curved apron at front. Plywood drawer linings will be an instant giveaway.

Early writing-tables rare and correspondingly expensive: even Edwardian reproductions fetch four-figure sums. Victorian pedestals relatively less; only the meanest half-pedestal or coarsely-made inter-war pieces found for three-figure sums.

Late-19thC mahogany tambour pedestal desk, much more common in oak with wooden pull handles.

DESKS: ESCRITOIRES

Approximately

1680-1720

William & Mary mulberry wood fall-front escritoire.

Originally known as a scrutoire or scriptor, this was a valuable piece of furniture in its day, its flat fall-front providing a good surface for decorative veneers. The earliest versions are small and mounted on a stand, but the majority of survivals are large and sit on a chest of drawers. Rare objects today.

STYLE AND APPEARANCE

In two sections, the upper part slightly taller and narrower than the lower. Join concealed by applied 'waist' moulding, matching one around base. Usually a pair of drawers above two deeper drawers in base. Originally bun feet (usually replaced later with brackets).

Upper part with single fall-front writing-surface (usually with velvet or coarser cloth base), supported first on brass chains, later on elbow hinges. There is a convex-fronted 'cushion' drawer in frieze, below a projecting moulded cornice.

Interior fittings: Flush with front and reaching full height. Vary in conformation; usually lockable central cupboard above deep recess, open pigeon-holes at top, all surrounded by differently-sized drawers. May be secret drawers concealed behind.

MATERIALS

Mostly walnut (often burr); occasionally mulberry, yew or other highly figured woods. All veneered on pine carcase, with oak for drawer linings. Box, holly, harewood, various fruitwoods, occasionally ebony for marquetry.

Note: An *all*-pine carcase will indicate Continental manufacture.

CONSTRUCTION

Standard methods employed (see **CHESTS OF DRAWERS, p. 84**). Hand-cut veneers about 1/8 inch/3 mm thick. Banding cross-cut with mitred corners. Often burr veneers on front; vertically-running, straight-grained veneer on sides. Fall-front cleated to prevent warping.

DECORATION

Mostly figuring of veneers, sometimes with cross- or feather banding. Occasionally oyster patterns. Sometimes seaweed or floral marquetry is seen.

Handles: Typical for day (for details see **page 85**). Brass drop handles, smaller inside than out, seldom matching. Thereafter brass bails with solid backplates outside; smaller ring handles with circular backplates inside. Large, surface-mounted, decorative brass escutcheons.

FINISH

Varnish (to fill grain) followed by wax polish.

RELATIVE VALUES

Being rare, very highly priced, invariably in five figures. Even marriages (of top originally on stand to chest of drawers), if done convincingly, of considerable value. Fine marquetry, or any attractively figured alternative to walnut, a price advantage.

DESKS: BUREAUX ON STANDS

About
1670-1760

Late-17thC oak bureau on stand.

A development of the medieval slope-top box which in the late 17thC was increasingly mounted on a stand, either fixed or as a separate entity. Its hinged flap slopes when closed, forming a flat writing-surface with a knee space below when open. The interior is fitted with small drawers and pigeon-holes for storing writing accessories, papers, and so on.

Largely superseded by the bureau proper (with the base as a chest of drawers) around 1690.

STYLE AND APPEARANCE

Oak, to about 1690: Separate box with fall supported on square lopers when opened, pulling out from frieze of table-like stand. Sometimes frieze drawer between lopers. Legs of stand turned, with turned or straight horizontal stretchers close to ground. Box slightly overhanging stand.

Early walnut, about 1680-1700: Usually as one piece, with one or two layers of drawers below. Sometimes a shaped apron. Square lopers, either with drawer between, or a blank, fronting 'well' accessible from inside by sliding back rear portion of flat interior surface. Sometimes there is an exterior book-rest moulding on fall. Supported on turned tapering legs, often with inverted cup knees; bun feet. Flat and scrolling X-stretchers with central turned finial.

Walnut, about 1700-1715: Usually separate stand with desk sitting within border moulding. Often shaped apron; cabriole legs with pad feet. A type much used as a basis for 'Queen Anne' reproductions after 1900, though these have deeper (and sometimes more numerous) drawers. Rare.

Mahogany, about 1725-1760: Separate desk and stand as above. Cabriole legs with pad, later claw and ball, feet. Occasionally straight legs after 1750. Lopers rectangular, of equal height to drawer(s) between. Rare.

All have plain flat top flush with sides, *never* overlapping. Generally a piece of velvet or coarser cloth is glued to a portion of the writing-surface.

MATERIALS

Oak, walnut, mahogany. Pine for carcases when veneered, with oak for drawer linings.

CONSTRUCTION

Mostly veneered on carcase with through-dovetails. Lapped dovetails after 1700 if solid timber employed; double-lapped at top to disguise join. Mortise-and-tenon joints on framing of stand. Mouldings glued. For drawer construction see **CHESTS OF DRAWERS, *p. 84***.

DECORATION

Decorative veneers and cross-banding on walnut. Occasionally seaweed or floral marquetry. Sometimes carving on frieze and legs of stand when mahogany

Handles: Drop on oak; small brass knobs, later bails, on walnut. Bails on mahogany.

Decorative surface-mounted escutcheons are seen on all parts until about 1750, replaced on drawers only by skeleton escutcheons around 1750.

FINISH

Sometimes stain on oak and mahogany; varnish on walnut (to fill grain); both followed by wax polish.

RELATIVE VALUES

No common objects; prices always high, at least in four figures, but reduced by about 60 per cent if stand is wrong. Marquetry, particularly seaweed, definitely a bonus.

DESKS: SECRETAIRES AND SECRETAIRE BOOKCASES

About
1710-1830

Mahogany secretaire bookcase, about 1810-1820.

Christie's

Known in the 18thC as a secretary, this piece of furniture appears as a chest of drawers with a full-width, deep, top drawer fitted like a bureau with small drawers, pigeon-holes and cupboards. The drawer pulls half out and its front drops down to form a writing-surface.

Frequently a single bookcase/display cabinet above. From about 1790, sometimes a two-door cupboard instead of drawers below, generally with glazed cabinet above. Secretaire drawer also found in tallboys and breakfront and library bookcases (see p. 35 and p. 89).

Particularly popular between about 1790 and 1810. Survivals date mostly from 1750 onwards.

STYLE AND APPEARANCE

Almost exactly as a chest of drawers or tallboy (see **p. 89** and **p. 92**) but slightly taller, allowing for greater depth of single top drawer. Interior fittings as for bureaux (see **p. 100**) though often less ornate. Upper glazed cabinet as for bookcases (see **p. 37**), set back several inches from front of chest. The drawer itself usually has shaped side linings.

MATERIALS

Nearly always mahogany; occasionally satinwood after 1780. Earliest versions in walnut; some rosewood during Regency. Only rarely found as country-made oak. Pine or mahogany for carcases (with oak or mahogany for drawer linings).

CONSTRUCTION

Standard methods employed (see relevant sections already listed).

Upper cabinets held in place with screws fixed through bottom shelf.

Fall-front to drawer fitted with elbow hinges released by push-button mechanism.

DECORATION

As for chests of drawers (**p. 93**). Figuring and arrangement of veneers on early pieces; some carving on mahogany; arrangements of veneers plus some neo-classical inlay in late 18thC (particularly quartered veneers and ovals on cupboard doors).

FINISH

Varnish or stain, followed by wax polish.

RELATIVE VALUES

More a gentleman's than a drawing-room piece and always less popular than bureaux, so relatively less valuable. Prices still in four figures though, five if very high quality with a bookcase above. Small size an advantage.

***Below**, Hepplewhite-style secretaire bookcase, 1780-1790; **right**, Chippendale-style, 1760-5.*

Sotheby's

DRES[cut off]

About
1650-191[cut off]

Late-17thC dresser wi[cut off] applied geometric mo[cut off]ngs.

At all times a respected piece of furniture in rural homes – good enough for use as a sideboard in the parlours of large farmhouses and manor houses, but found only in the kitchens of more sophisticated town and city dwellers.

Tremendous regional variation; as a *very* general rule, an open base and open shelves above are southern characteristics, and backboards on the rack and solid drawers and cupboards below, northern features.

Welsh dresser has become a popular term for all types of dresser, regardless of their place of manufacture.

STYLE AND APPEARANCE

Until the late 17thC generally a base only was present. This could be in the form of a **long table** with a single frieze of two, three or more (often deep) drawers supported on turned (commonly baluster) front legs, occasionally joined by stretchers, sometimes by a 'pot board' (a deep platform shelf to hold large vessels). Rear legs always straight and square in section. Top usually bordered by an applied moulding, matched by a moulding beneath the drawers; or made as a **solid piece** with a frieze of drawers with cupboards below, with or without top and base mouldings, and with stile feet.

Sotheby's

Mid 18thC cupboard base dresser, rack with spice drawers above.

Sotheby's

Mid-18thC dresser with arched and fielded panels.

After 1700 a shaped apron, and occasionally cabriole legs, were introduced on the first type, and **after 1710**, bracket feet on the second. Fielded and shaped panels were common on doors; occasionally a shaped plinth, or bun feet.

Bonhams

Early-18thC dresser.

A rack (or superstructure of shelves) was introduced about 1690; until about 1750 this was seldom attached, merely sitting on top of the base or being fixed to wall above. Usually two or three shelves (sometimes of graduated depth); most have grooves or stays (narrow strips of moulding) to support plates. Sides can be shaped or straight. Projecting moulded cornice may have shaped and/or pierced apron below. Some racks have small (often square-fronted) spice drawers in, or just above the base. Some have backboards, but many are later additions (see CONSTRUCTION).

Variations include: an open **'dog kennel'** in centre of base; a **clock** in centre of upper part of rack (a Yorkshire characteristic); **glazed doors** on rack of fitted kitchen dressers (from about 1870).

A simple kitchen dresser from Loudon's Encyclopaedia (1833).

Edwardian stained oak dresser in 'Jacobean' style.

Christie's

The popularity of dressers of sideboard type for use in the dining-rooms of town houses towards the end of the 19thC resulted in some ornate machine-carved examples with turned supports and stretchers made in Renaissance or 'Jacobean' style. A few were made in Arts and Crafts and progressive styles.

MATERIALS

Predominately oak; elm, fruitwoods, occasionally ash and other local woods. Mahogany, sometimes walnut, for decorative cross-banding. Pine for some genuinely Welsh dressers from 18thC onwards, and for most Victorian and Edwardian kitchen pieces.

CONSTRUCTION

Frame and panel construction with pegged (in later 19thC, glued) mortise-and-tenon joints. Drawer rebated and nailed, with coarse dovetails. Applied and mitred mouldings on drawer fronts until about 1710-1720, when sometimes replaced by ovolo lip mouldings (covering gap between carcase and drawer. Sometimes simple cockbead after about 1730, or groove.

Shelves of rack tenoned and pegged through side uprights.

Marriages of racks to older bases common. Check for matching colour and grain of timber. Look for regular machine saw marks on underside of shelvesindicating 19thC (or later) date.

Backboards often later addition (particularly on once-fitted pine kitchen dressers). Can usually be identified by regular width. Decorative friezes and aprons may also be added to increase value. Look again for regular machine-cut saw marks on their back.

As functional pieces of furniture in everyday use, old dressers should show signs of considerable wear, especially on the top, shelves and drawer linings. As they are mostly used in kitchens, expect to see build-up of dirt and grease around handles, in plate grooves and around all exterior joints. The insides of drawers will be scratched and dented.

DECORATION

Seldom any decoration. Occasionally mahogany or walnut cross-banding on drawers and cupboards doors.

Handles: Typical for their day (for details see **page 87**). Iron or brass drop handles in 17thC, brass bails in 18thC, and wooden knobs after about 1825.

FINISH

Polish. Stain or paint on 19thC pine. (Many of these are sold incorrectly stripped and waxed today. Ironically they may be worth more in their changed condition than with their original, but usually less attractive, finish.)

RELATIVE VALUES

If 'right' (though allowing for minor repairs), price undoubtedly in the thousands; the best and earliest in five figures. Late, pine kitchen dressers not far behind, even when originally fitted.

A firm regional attribution or inclusion of a dog kennel, or clock, price advantage.

Marriages, if done convincingly, may not affect value greatly.

DUMB WAITERS

About

1750-1830

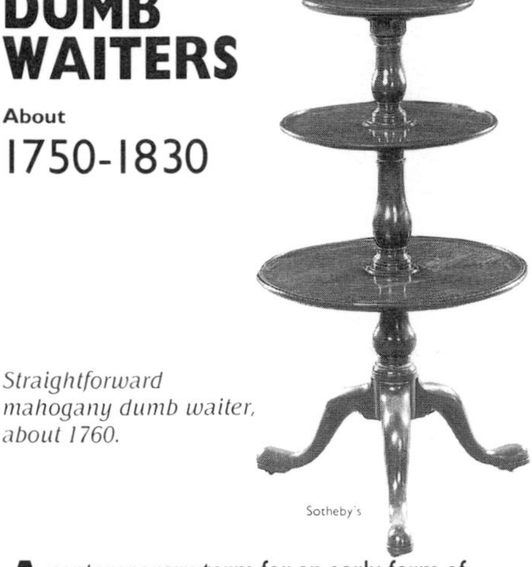

Straightforward mahogany dumb waiter, about 1760.

A contemporary term for an early form of supper trolley for use when servants were not in attendance. Designed to stand within easy reach of the table to hold condiments, plates and other dining accessories.

STYLE AND APPEARANCE

A central turned column on a tripod (or occasionally four-legged) base, with feet mounted on castors and two or three open circular shelves of graduating size with moulded rims. Rare examples have four tiers.

In mid-18thC pieces the tripod base is similar to tripod tables (see **p.175**), but with castors. Cabriole legs, pad feet and central column formed as vase-shaped baluster. Occasionally claw-and-ball feet. Knees, feet (or entire leg) and central column sometimes carved with foliate decoration.

Regency columns straight-edged, slightly tapering, with moulded collars at widely spaced intervals.

Post-1790, reeded and splayed legs on box castors. 'Kneed' legs indicate a post-1810 date. Castors can be of lion's paw or claw feet form.

In best pieces turnings between trays are of diminishing diameter.

Rims to trays usually formed as simple mouldings but occasionally scalloped or carved with leaf or other patterns. Sometimes a fret-carved gallery, on early examples of Gothic or Chinese design. Sometimes shallow recesses turned in surface to prevent dishes from sliding about.

Variations include:

- **Flat trays** with hinged, folding flaps, the flaps supported by a swivelling bar.
- **Trays of equal diameter** supported on thin brass columns fixed around the edge rather than the central column.
- A relatively complex **Sheraton-style** with drawers below, plate racks on shelves, and so on.
- Base formed as **wine cooler** with column rising from centre.

MATERIALS

Nearly always mahogany; just occasionally rosewood during Regency.

CONSTRUCTION

Trays turned on a lathe, the best quality from one piece of timber, though occasionally two, fixed together with tongue-and-groove joints. Can be very thin.

Top tray usually supported on column with wooden flange although sometimes the top section of the column projects right through and ends in a finial.

Until 1790 castors attached to separate block with grain running in opposite direction.

Column made in sections which screw together and hold the intervening trays in place.

DECORATION

Carving on some pieces around the rims and on the base. Not uncommon for carving to be added at a later date to enhance value. Original carving will stand proud of the surface; later additions flush with it.

FINISH

Polish.

RELATIVE VALUES

Yet another item invariably priced in four figures nowadays (assuming it is right). Be very suspicious if less.

CONVERSIONS

Not very popular items in the past; many converted to more valuable and popular tripod tables (usually given away by filling of the central hole). More collectable today though.

Check that borders of trays and turnings of column match exactly; if not, suspect a marriage. Check also that all the trays are level and that none have warped.

.REENS

.bout

1700-1900

Although made from Tudor times, survivals mostly date from the 18thC onwards, the majority from after 1750. A few were intended to block draughts or, in the bedroom, to protect modesty, but by far the majority were designed as fire-screens – particularly important for women, whose make-up was often wax-based. At all times these were principally decorative objects.

A good vehicle for carving. Needlework was always fashionable for the screen panel, but prints, paintings, imported Chinese wallpapers, embroidery, filigree paper, Berlin woolwork, bead and other handiwork are also found (frequently executed by ladies of the house). Around 1750 panels often contained fabric matching the upholstery, wall hangings. and so on.

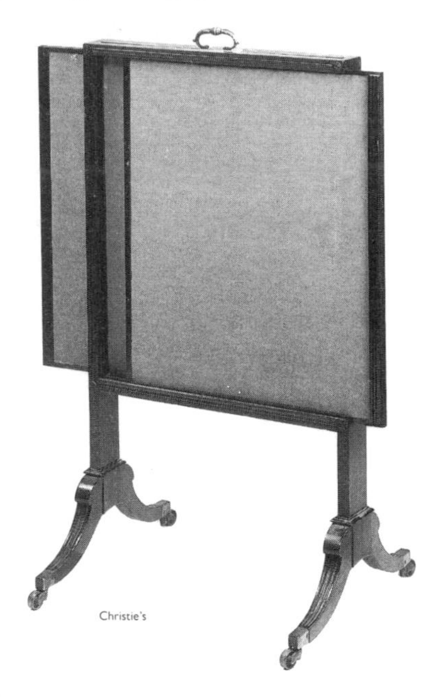

Cheval screen with sliding panel, about 1810.

STYLE AND APPEARANCE

Three main types:

Cheval, (called a 'horse' screen until about 1815): A panel set between two uprights (or standards), supported on feet projecting to the front and back. Sometimes a stretcher below. Cresting often rounded or shaped. Panel occasionally adjustable in height, moving through grooves in standards.

Generally design followed fashionable styles and showed exuberant scrolling carving (particularly on crestings and stretchers) around 1700, rather less bold carving during Queen Anne's reign, followed by curvaceous and often asymetrical rococo designs during the Chippendale period, finally becoming straighter and squarer towards 1770. Overall size was gradually reduced. Screens in neo-classical style were far simpler, often with panels of oval or shield shape, straight and simple uprights, and small carved neo-classical details. Uprights often ended in vase finials.

Considerably less popular in 19thC, but available in many revival styles – rococo, Queen Anne, 'Sheraton', Gothic, even Elizabethan. Ornament often excessive. Many made in papier mch, usually of scrolling outline. Gilded screens also fashionable, with carving of scrolling and naturalistic design, sometimes with double panels of glass enclosing stuffed birds, butterflies and so on.

Pole screens: First made around 1700, but few have survived from before 1750. Also gradually reduced in size. Originally made in pairs to stand either side of fireplace. Designed specifically to protect the face from heat. Standard pattern was tripod base with turned pillar supporting pole to which a small adjustable screen was attached. Pole topped by finial, often ivory.

Tripod base similar in design to occasional tables (see **p. 175**) but generally lighter. Shape of panel rectangular in mid-century, more varied after – circles, shields or ovals common, often with shaped edges.

Particularly popular during Regency, though by 1820 bases were clumsier and detail fussier. 'Banner' screens introduced in which screen was replaced by similarly attached tasselled fabric banner hung from a wood or metal cross-bar.

Folding 'panel' screens: Relatively seldom seen today. In the 17thC and 18thC mostly a feature of very large houses. Could have simple frame completely covered with decorative leather or painted cloth, fixed around the edges with decorative nails. Imported Oriental lacquer screens, which could have up to twelve panels, were highly prized.

Some small and simple wood-framed two-leaf screens made around 1750, generally with straight legs, their principal feature being the fabric or print contained within them.

Early Victorian pole screens.

George III mahogany pole screen, about 1770.

Two-leaf mahogany screen containing Chinese wallpapers, about 1765.

Victorian mahogany cheval screen containing needlework picture.

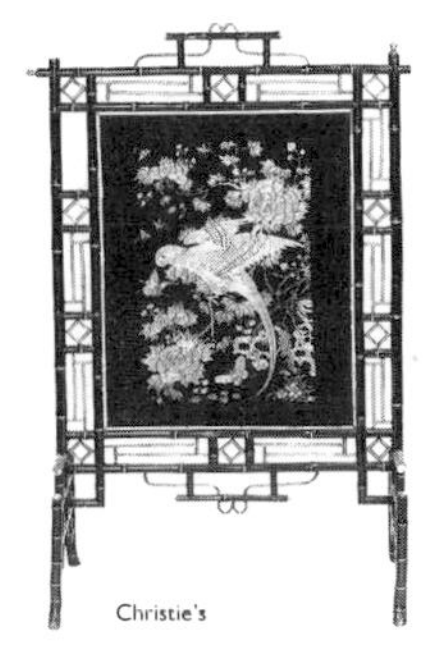

Late-Victorian 'Japanese bamboo' and lacquer screen.

19thC painted leather folding screen.

Large three- or four-leaf folding screens with straight or arched tops popular during Victorian times, covered with leather or cloth, sometimes pasted with ephemera.

MATERIALS

Typical woods of their day; beech (when painted, gilded or japanned), walnut, mahogany, rosewood, satinwood, papier mâché, bamboo and wicker. Occasionally cast iron used for the bases.

CONSTRUCTION

Standard methods employed. Height of pole and banner screens adjusted by tightening the brass ring attached to the back of the panel with a wing screw. Sheraton introduced a new mechanism with a hollow pole and counter-balanced weights adjusted on a pulley and cord system. The lower weight was hidden within a tassel below.

DECORATION

Carving of fashionable details according to date. Typical papier mâché decoration, often enclosing popular views.

Victorian screens decorated with ephemera are very collectable today. Though often damaged, relatively easy to repair as reproduction ephemera is widely available.

FINISH

Polish, gilding, japanning, paint (sometimes simulating bronze or gold).

RELATIVE VALUES

For both cheval and pole screens, an 18th rather than 19thC date makes all the difference to value; four figures for the first, seldom more than three for the latter, though an exceptionally fine or interesting panel filler could push the price up. Folding screens really too scarce and varied to evaluate in general terms.

SIDEBOARDS

About

1770-1915

Inlaid mahogany bow-fronted sideboard, about 1780-1790.

Sotheby's

A useful piece of dining-furniture comprising a number of drawers and cupboards for the storage of cutlery, table linen, condiments and so on, which evolved during the 1770s from the very grand side-table and pedestal ensembles first designed by Robert Adam. In the late-18th/early-19thC, they often incorporated a plate-warmer, wine cooler, cistern or cellaret, hence their original name, 'cellaret sideboard'. Occasionally a pot cupboard was included, sometimes set discreetly in one side.

Usually replaced in large houses around 1825 by vast serving tables accompanied by chiffoniers.

In Victorian times, sideboards were less easily defined. They can be of dresser form, or a smaller chiffonier type; some best described simply as cabinets.

STYLE AND APPEARANCE

About 1770-1810: Standard form had a central drawer flanked either side by drawers (one shallow, one deep), and a single cupboard; or one of each. Cupboards may have dummy drawer fronts. Central recess fronted by shaped or arched apron; its back either open or solid; sometimes the cupboard set half-way back. All cupboards may be tambour-fronted. Central cutlery drawer compartmented and lined with baize.

Most were bow- or serpentine-fronted; some semi-elliptical or straight. Thick, flat, over-hanging top with flush edges. Majority on six square-sectioned, tapering legs; sometimes eight. After 1800, legs were often turned with ring mouldings; sometimes reeded or fluted. Drawers flush with carcase when inlaid (edged with stringing or cross-banding); cockbeaded when simply veneered.

Later versions with brass back-rail, **either** to support plate, **or** to suspend splashback curtain. Occasionally fitted with adjustable candleholders.

Sotheby's

Mahogany sideboard with brass back-rail, about 1800.

About 1800-1850: Previous type (with turned legs) joined by pedestal sideboards with central shallow drawer retained, but sides extending to floor to form pedestal cupboards. Either carved (often paw) feet, or continuous plinth. By 1810 pedestal could extend upwards too, joined at rear by shaped wooden splashback. Separate wine cooler (now often missing) placed in central recess.

Majority in Grecian style; early Victorian plainer.

1850 onwards: Considerable variation. Made in all revival styles – Elizabethan, Gothic, Renaissance, Chippendale, Sheraton and Queen Anne. Many highly carved; some cheaply made and poorly executed. Later examples (of all types) sometimes with mirror at back (now usually removed).

MATERIALS

Principally mahogany; occasionally satinwood. Rosewood during Regency and early Victorian periods. Occasionally walnut around 1850; birch or satin maple (to simulate satinwood) on cheaper reproductions towards 1900. Pine or mahogany for carcases; oak or mahogany for drawer linings. Satinwood and other light-coloured woods used for decorative inlay.

CONSTRUCTION

Standard methods employed; majority veneered. See **CHESTS OF DRAWERS, p. 93**, for drawer construction.

Watch out for alterations. The comonest include: **1** Removal of brass rails – look for filled holes at rear of top. **2** Reduction in depth – examine back for newly cut and stained timber, and look inside the carcase for cut-off drawer runners. If in original condition, the 'wear' will stop at least ½ inch from the back. **3** Replacement of less saleable turned legs with square-sectioned ones. If correct, the legs will extend upwards to form the stiles of the carcase and the grain of the timber will be continuous. If wrong, the new join will be concealed either by a fine line of inlay, or by an applied astragal moulding, and the grain will not match above and below.

Watch also for quality Edwardian reproductions of Sheraton types. Their design may look authentic, but the veneer will be thin, and machine-cut; the dovetails, machine-cut, will look regular; and the legs will probably look too thin. The poorest of the reproductions will be recognizable by their lack of proportion and sometimes an odd combination of features.

Sotheby's

1930s Art Moderne sideboard.

DECORATION

Restrained inlay of light-coloured woods until about 1810; mostly stringing lines; some fan shapes and oval paterae. Ebony or brass inlay of classical design in early 19thC.

Handles: Standard for their day (see **p. 93**). Bold lion's mask ring handles especially popular after 1800, and on reproductions.

FINISH

Stain or varnish followed by wax polish. French polish after about 1820. Dark stain on Victorian 'Elizabethan' and Renaissance. Art Furniture pieces ebonised.

RELATIVE VALUES

Prices for the best late-18thC inlaid sideboards in original condition are in five figures; post-1800 versions (with turned legs) about a quarter to half the price. Pedestal sideboards – never very popular – even less. Plus points are decorative inlay or carving, small size and surviving interior fittings.

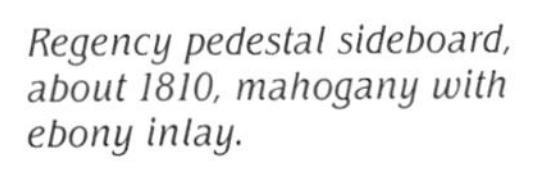

Regency pedestal sideboard, about 1810, mahogany with ebony inlay.

Bonhams

SOFAS, SETTEES, COUCHES, DAY-BEDS, *CHAISES LONGUES* AND SETTLES

About
1700-1915

Bonhams

17thC oak box settle.

Day-beds, couches and *chaises longues* were designed for lounging; sofas, settees and settles for sitting. A sofa was fully upholstered, a settee padded only on the seat, and a settle all wood with loose cushions. Today the term couch also describes a sofa, but originally meant a day-bed which, like its successor the *chaise longue*, had one end higher than the other. In the 19thC sofas and *chaises longues* were often sold *en suite* with a pair of easy chairs and six side chairs.

STYLE AND APPEARANCE

Settles were made from about 1500, but surviving examples are mostly post-1600. Still produced by country makers in the 18th and even 19thC for farmhouses, inns; otherwise unfashionable.

Like an elongated wainscot chair (**p. 51**) but usually (though not always) without the elaborate cresting and ear pieces. Panelled back, often very high to exclude draughts. 18thC panelling often fielded. Considerable regional variation in carving and turning of uprights. Holes or grooves for cords to support a mattress sometimes present in seat rails (see **BEDS p. 23**) but very often a solid wooden seat has been added above at a later date.

An alternative form has the base formed as a chest, its hinged top providing the seat; occasionally there was a pair of deep drawers instead. Some had a projecting cupboard above, in which hams were hung, hence the name 'bacon settle'.

From about 1750 'hall settles' were designed *en suite* with hall chairs but originally were a cross between a settle and a settee, with a panelled back, but more sophisticated legs and stretchers.

Interest in settles was revived in the late 19thC by some arts and crafts designers. These could be pastiches of early models – often with carved mottoes running around the top – or in progressive style, perhaps better described as high-sided armchairs than settles.

Settees, about 1710-1800: Double, triple, or even quadruple, versions of standard wooden armchairs of the day (including Windsors), with outer arms only, and extra leg(s) in between. (For details see under relevant chair headings, **p. 51-80**.)

William & Mary double wing settee, about 1690.

Sofas, made from about 1690 onwards: Pre-1750 examples, mostly in the form of a double wing chair (see **p. 69**), are rare. The following styles developed:

Chippendale: Straight, square legs (sometimes typically moulded or carved) with stretchers of modified H arrangement; tall, outward-scrolling arms and undulating backs with highest point in centre. Deep seats with loose seat cushions above the upholstery.

Hepplewhite: Turned tapering legs, no stretchers and a carved show-wood seat rail (and often back frame too). May have additional padded rests above arms.

Regency: Double scroll ends, undulating back, straight and deep front seat rail and usually Grecian (sideward-facing sabre) legs. Some were boat shaped with inward- rather than outward-scrolling arms. Late Regency types often have a more pronounced scroll on arms, back dipped in centre supporting bold

A, settle in art nouveau style, about 1900; ***B****, mahogany double-back settee, about 1745-1750;* ***C****, gilded settee in the style of Robert Adam, about 1770-1780;* ***D****, Victorian mahogany ottoman, about 1870-1880;* ***E****, Chippendale mahogany sofa, about 1760;* ***F****, early-Victorian mahogany sofa, about 1840;* ***G****, Victorian walnut sofa, about 1850-1860;* ***H****, Victorian mahogany sofa, about 1880.*

carving of anthemion or other classical motif, and heavy turned legs.

Victorian: Typical rococo designs (see **CHAIRS, UPHOLSTERED, p. 57**). Short cabriole legs, naturalistic carving on show-wood frames, deep-buttoned upholstery on back and arms. Some rather awkward, with spoon-back ends joined in centre by pierced carving. Open or closed arms. Later designs squared-up with turned legs. Some with padded arms, and sometimes backs too, supported on pierced splats or rows of turned spindles.

MATERIALS

Walnut, mahogany, satinwood; rosewood (with brass for inlay) during Regency. Oak (or elm, yew and other local woods) for settles; beech (or birch in the 19thC) when japanned, painted, gilded or stained, and for under-frames.

CONSTRUCTION

Standard methods employed, see **CHAIRS, p. 70**.

Regency 'Grecian' legs can show tell-tale

VARIATIONS ON THE SOFA THEME

Love seats, about 1720 onwards: Like an extra wide chair and probably designed originally for ladies wearing exceptionally wide skirts. Not very common.

Duchesse sofas, about 1770 onwards: Two upholstered armchairs of tub shape set face to face with an intervening matching stool of equal depth and height. Very few survive intact.

Sociables, from about 1840: Two or three upholstered chairs joined together at opposing angles.

Ottomans, about 1850 onwards: A number of upholstered units which fit together to form a continuous circular seat. Used in very large drawing-rooms and halls, and in ballrooms, picture galleries and so on.

Chesterfields, about 1860 onwards: (Forerunner of the conventional modern sofa with flat, scrolled or straight arms set lower than the back.) Continuous slightly scrolled arms and back of equal height.

Chesterfield sofa.

Short, stumpy turned feet (around 1900 sometimes square and tapering). Many made during 20thC too, more recently upholstered in leather (not previously employed). Check feet and underframes carefully for signs of age.

Knole sofas: Really a modern phenomenon, most popular between the wars, but based on an early-17thC 'couch' at Knole in Kent. Rectangular box shape, arms hinging down from the seat frame to a comfortable angle and held in position by tasselled cords tied around large, fabric-covered finials. The frame is totally concealed by upholstery. (Adjustment of the original version is by ratchet.)

Day-beds, couches and *chaises longues*, though made during the Restoration and earlier 18thC, mostly date from the 1790s when the term *chaise longue* was introduced. Basically an asymmetrical sofa with one end higher than the other and an undulating downward-curving back reaching to a point at least two-thirds along the seat, but often meeting a lower foot rail. Particularly popular during the Regency when they resembled sofas and were sometimes called *méridienne*. Always with show-wood frame. Victorian examples similarly resembled sofas and can be with or without a raised foot end.

structural weakness, their joint with the seat frame suffering considerable strain. If cut incorrectly, with, rather than across, the grain, they can split.

Until the 1830s all pieces had loose seat cushions, though these are often omitted today. Remember that their presence makes a big difference to over-all appearance. Similarly, the bolster cushions which fitted neatly into the scrolled ends of Regency pieces are integral with, and therefore essential to their design.

With any piece requiring extensive re-upholstery allow for possible repairs to the frame too: the upholstery may be holding it all together. Avoid any re-upholstered piece with even a slightly loose joint: it can only get worse.

DECORATION

As for the chairs, mostly with carving (sometimes gilded); brass inlay during Regency, wood inlay occasionally in late-19thC.

FINISH

Polish; French polish from about 1820. Sometimes japanned or gilding.

RELATIVE VALUES

Until recently prices dipped sharply for sofas and *chaises longues* later than around 1830, with only the best quality Victorian pieces making the higher grade. Now that date has moved on to about 1870.

18thC wooden-backed settees are considerably less popular than their upholstered counterparts, many equivalent in price to late Victorian versions of the latter.

Settles, despite their earlier date, cost about the same as settees, although rare bacon settles will fetch considerably more.

Original, usable upholstery considerably increases value.

STOOLS: JOINT STOOLS

Surviving examples date mostly from about

1600-1700

Sometimes incorrectly called coffin stools, these were one of the most widely used forms of seating before chairs became common. Always very popular with collectors, and reproduced and faked in large numbers at all times.

Christie's

17thC oak joint stool.

STYLE AND APPEARANCE

Four identical legs, slightly splayed to the front and back. Blocks at top and bottom of legs, with various baluster, reel and bobbin turnings between. Rectangular edge-moulded tops, with straight or shaped frieze below with moulded edge and carved with repetitive designs. Four straight and low stretchers, sometimes with a simple moulding. Could be double, i.e. wide enough to seat two, or even longer, in which case more than four – but still identical – legs.

V&A

17thC oak bench.

MATERIALS

Mostly oak, but sometimes elm, yew or other local indigenous woods.

CONSTRUCTION

Pegged mortise-and-tenon joints. Signs of authenticity:

1 Good, thick seat (at least 1 inch/2.5 cm) with grain running from side to side. No saw marks and some shrinkage along the grain. **2** Top almost always fixed to rails with six dowels, but sometimes only four (a regional peculiarity). **3** Pegs standing slightly proud of surface, due to shrinkage. **4** Hand-drilled holes cut for dowels of irregular shape. **5** Pointed ends of the pegs securing the mortise-and-tenon joints of the underframe will be visible underneath. They were only cut off if they were going to show. **6** Good, deep overhang of top showing considerable discolouration from dirt and grease deposited by constant handling. **7** Legs splayed only to front and back. This enabled several stools to be placed end-to-end to form a sort of bench. **8** Stretchers on long sides particularly showing considerable wear. **9** Under-sides of feet worn and ragged. Originally legs ended in small bun feet, but these seldom survive. Most have been worn away or their remnants cut off. Sometimes they have been replaced.

Conversely, the following are signs of Victorian reproductions:

1 Thin top, with visible saw marks. **2** Grain of top running front to back. **3** Machine-drilled dowel holes of regular shape. **4** Pegs not passing through joints. **5** Shallow machine-carved frieze, sometimes with pattern extending all round, i.e. around top of legs too.

DECORATION

Chip carving on friezes; geometric patterns, lunettes, arcading and strapwork common.

FINISH

Polish. Victorian reproductions stained.

RELATIVE VALUES

Despite their early date, joint stools are still quite numerous and if right, and with imaginative turnings and carving, their value is well into four figures. Only when wrong, or poorly executed and of little visual appeal, will it remain in three.

STOOLS: UPHOLSTERED

About
1660-1900

Ebonised stool in the style of Marot, about 1680.

Sotheby's

Once important pieces of furniture, but not so today. From the 17thC onwards both low foot-stools and stools of chair height (for sitting on) were included in suites of upholstered seat furniture.

STYLE AND APPEARANCE

As a general rule, the design of stools followed that of contemporary chairs – with the same legs, stretcher conformation, upholstery and so on – with the obvious difference that all four legs were the same and that there was no difference between front and back. For standard examples from each period see illustrations. Obvious exceptions are piano-stools and some 19thC foot-stools.

Associated with the Victorians, but first made during the Regency, **music stools** were generally circular and of adjustable height. Early examples usually had four legs, splayed for stability, while from around 1850 tripod pedestal bases with scrolling cabriole legs were more common. On these the rather

George II cabriole leg stool, about 1730.

Simple Hepplewhite stool, about 1780-1790.

Carved walnut stool, about 1745-1750.

Bonhams

Chippendale mahogany stool, about 1760.

Sotheby's

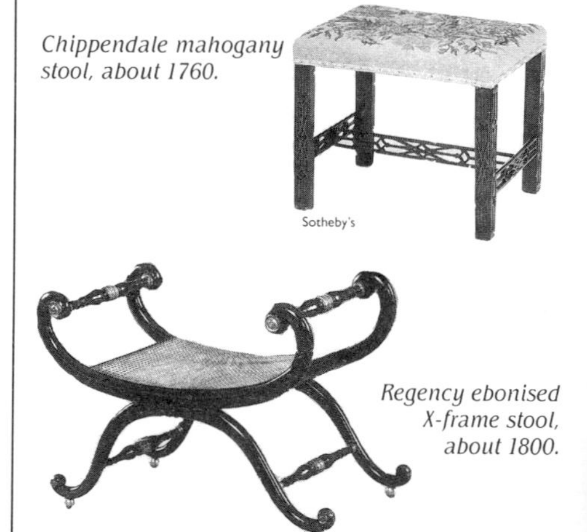

Regency ebonised X-frame stool, about 1800.

Sotheby's

clumsy-looking wooden screw mechanism which adjusted their height and which had been clearly visible underneath the earlier versions, was an extension of the base and was largely concealed by the seat. During the last quarter of the century, rectangular stools with turned rails between extended uprights forming handles, and either a drawer or hinged seat enclosing a compartment for sheet music, became more common.

Other popular Victorian stools included the circular **'hour-glass'** variety, with pleated drapes and a pinched-in waist, and the **S-scroll foot-stool**. Foot-stools in particular were made in a vast variety of shapes and sizes, many very small with tiny brass ball or wooden bun feet and were more an excuse for the display of needlework or bead-work than of any practical use.

MATERIALS

Fashionable woods of their day; oak, walnut, mahogany, rosewood; sometimes gilded beech was used.

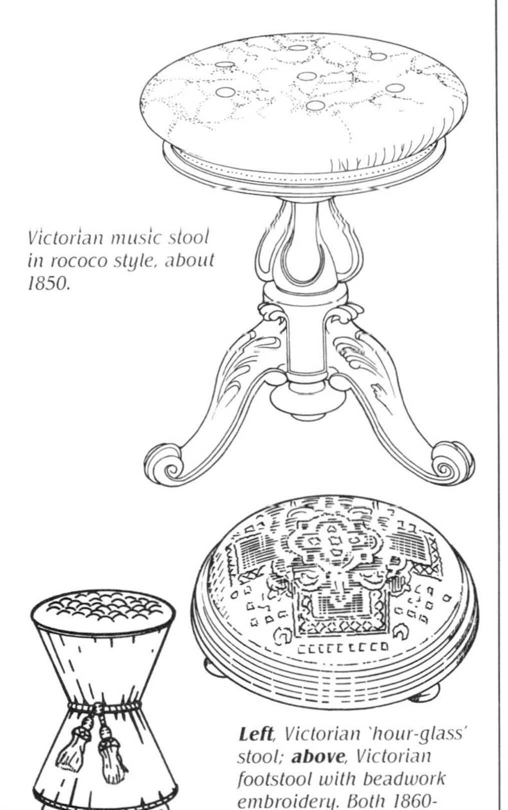

Victorian music stool in rococo style, about 1850.

***Left**, Victorian 'hour-glass' stool; **above**, Victorian footstool with beadwork embroidery. Both 1860-1870.*

***A**, adjustable music stool, about 1820-1830; **B**, Victorian walnut rococo stool; **C**, late-Regency foot or 'gout' stools; **D**, pair of simple mahogany stools about 1840.*

CONSTRUCTION

Standard construction as for chairs but always with strengthening blocks at all four corners.

DECORATION

Carving. Occasionally japanned chinoiserie motifs. Some restrained inlay after about 1780.

FINISH

Polish. Gilding, japanning, paint.

RELATIVE VALUES

Upholstered stools may seem disproportionately expensive when compared with chairs of equivalent date and quality. Only 19th and the very plainest 18thC examples generally fall in the three-figure bracket.

STOOLS: WINDOW

About

1750 onwards

Mahogany window stool in 'French Hepplewhite' style, about 1780.

Double-ended upholstered stools with raised sides designed to stand in the recesses of windows. Most popular in the 18thC when they were fashionably made *en suite* with other upholstered furniture.

STYLE AND APPEARANCE

Window stools are generally between 3 and 5 feet/90 and 150 cm long with four legs (occasionally six). The legs, seat and stretchers (when present) generally follow contemporary chair and sofa design. Ends usually scroll outwards, often continuous with seat, the upholstery extending over them.

Regency examples were sometimes larger and deeper, with vertical wooden ends.

Gilded neo-classical window seat in the style of Robert Adam.

MATERIALS

Mostly mahogany; occasionally japanned or

Regency mahogany window seat.

gilded beech. Some Victorian examples in walnut. Later versions could be beech stained to simulate mahogany.

CONSTRUCTION

As for chairs and sofas.

DECORATION

Expect some limited carving on the seat rails and the facings of arms.

FINISH

Polish; occasionally gilding or japanning.

RELATIVE VALUES

Window stools are comparatively rare and price is very variable. The best quality – tending to date from the 1780s and 1790s – are valuable items, sometimes surpassing contemporary sofas in price.

continued on page 161

FINE & INTERESTING PIECES

The furniture illustrated on the following colour pages was chosen with two objects:

- To show in colour typical examples of the principal styles illustrated in black and white elsewhere.
- To feature some selected furniture of special quality or interest. A few pieces are of museum standard, but most are collectors' items: some expensive, but not necessarily out of the private buyer's reach.

Christie's

***Above**, a large and boldly carved early 17thC oak tester bed with distinctive cup-and-cover mouldings on the foot-posts and panels of inlay, flanked by large carved ear-pieces at the head. An elaborate piece, designed to impress.*

***Left**, an oak credence table of about 1640. With a fold-over top, supported on a gate-leg when open, these tables are generally thought to have been the prototype for folding card and tea tables.*

Sotherby's

***Above**, a 17thC oak refectory table with bold carved decoration on the frieze and bulbous yet refined baluster turnings on the legs.*

Timothy D. Wilson

***Right**, an English oak coffer of about 1620 of superb quality, displaying all the most desirable features – arcaded panels, fine carving and interesting and fairly extensive inlay.*

Sotheby's

***Left**, a fine quality carved walnut armchair of about 1685 with baroque scrolls on the legs, arm supports and front stretcher. A rather grand chair – now with later needlework upholstery. Originally this would have been of silk or silk velvet, with deep fringing around the seat.*

***Below left**, a Restoration walnut dining-chair showing all the characteristic features of its date – scrolling front legs, a deep carved front stretcher, oval cane-work on the back, barley-twist turning throughout and a crest-rail carved with amorini supporting the crown.*

***Below**, a late-17thC cabinet-on-stand of a type very popular in France and Holland. The Dutch-style marquetry decoration is of superb quality; that on the inside will be much lighter and brighter where it has not been so exposed to dirt and light.*

Sotheby's

Christie's

***Left**, a very good Charles II oak gate-leg dining-table with elegant barley-twist supports.*

Sotheby's

Left, a Queen Anne dressing-mirror with its base in the form of a miniature bureau, with a front of waved outline. The chinoiserie decoration is japanned (i.e. executed in England) in imitation of oriental lacquerwork. Until the 19thC, toilet mirrors were free-standing and were placed on a separate – and usually not matching – dressing-table.

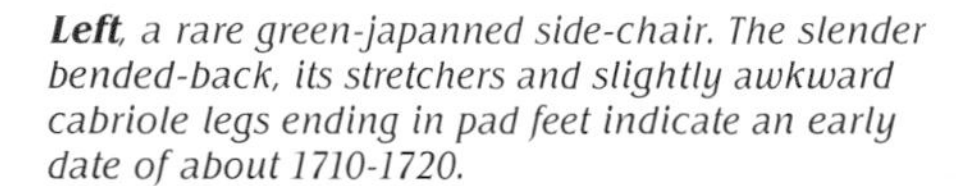

Left, a rare green-japanned side-chair. The slender bended-back, its stretchers and slightly awkward cabriole legs ending in pad feet indicate an early date of about 1710-1720.

Sotheby's

Sotheby's

Above, a walnut tallboy, or chest-on-chest, dating from about 1725. The canted corners to the top and carvetto moulding on the base are desirable features. Note the burr veneers on the front, but straight-grained veneer at the side.

Sotheby's

Right, a walnut veneered bachelor's chest of about 1730 with a fold-over top supported on small square lopers. A simple piece but nevertheless very much in demand.

__Right__, a superb quality Chippendale 'French' armchair in carved mahogany, about 1750. The rather thin and flat upholstery reflects the delicate appearance of the chair overall.

Sotheby's

__Below__, a very simple but fine quality mahogany bookcase with ogee feet to the base and a straightforward pediment cresting. The glazing bars are in Gothic style, about 1775-1780.

Sotheby's

Sotheby's

__Above__, an unusually elaborate mahogany dumb waiter with deep spindled galleries. The central upright has the twisted and jointed carved cups, seen often on tripod tables of this date, about 1750-1760.

Sotheby's

***Left**, a mahogany tripod tea table with superb quality carving on the legs and stem. The piecrust rim and birdcage support make this a very desirable piece.*

***Below**, a straightforward wing chair of about 1750, the cabriole legs only carved at the front. Shaped, rather than square-sectioned and raked rear legs are generally a sign of high quality.*

Sotheby's

Sotheby's

Left, *a satinwood demi-lune card table – for many years the most desirable type – finely inlaid with neo-classical decoration and a large fan-shape on the top.*

Sotheby's

Sotheby's

Above, *a simple and very elegant late-18thC lady's work table, the top inlaid as a games board. The pleated silk work-bag slides forward to open.*

Left, *a satinwood oval pembroke table, with fine neo-classical inlay and a large inlaid shell on the top; 1785-1800.*

Sotheby's

Left, a very elegant satinwood pole-screen in Sheraton-style with finely splayed legs. Such delicate pieces are hard to find.

Below, a serpentine-front mahogany sideboard of about 1785-90 with an unusual amount of inlaid paterae and fan shapes in bright contrasting colours.

Sotheby's

Sotheby's

Above, a gilded settee in the neo-classical style of Robert Adam. Although gilded furniture was generally found only in the grandest houses, the designs of this period could equally be made in polished wood.

Sotheby's

***Left**, a small and plain Regency rosewood chiffonier with brass supports and gallery to the superstructure, and a smart brass edging to the top. Note the pilasters reaching round the corners, balanced by one at the back.*

Sotheby's

***Above**, a Regency mahogany bergère reading chair with an adjustable book-rest. The back would have had a leather cushion, and a brass candle-holder was usually present on the other arm.*

Sotheby's

***Left**, a very grand mahogany escritoire in French Empire style, made by a French immigrant worker in 1826. The influence of immigrant craftsmen on English design was often strong.*

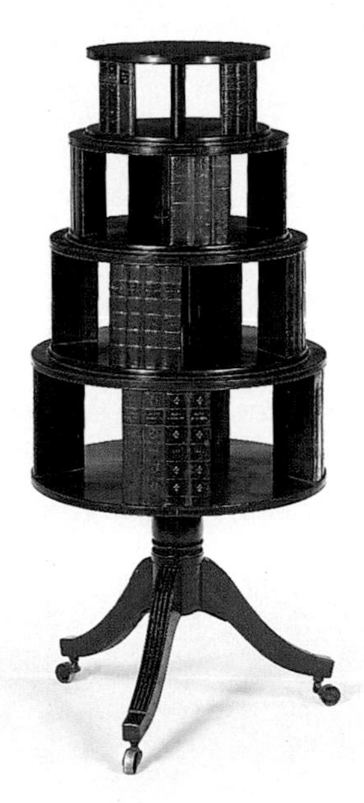

***Left**, a very smart mahogany revolving bookcase, the dummy leather books fronting wedge-shaped dividers. These bookcases are fairly rare and increasingly in demand.*

***Below**, a high quality rosewood dining-chair with brass inlaid decoration and elegant sabre legs. The canework seat would originally have supported a loose cushion.*

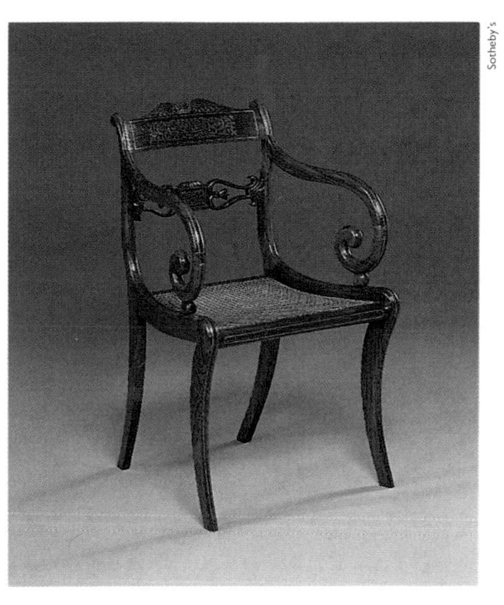

***Below**, a scroll-end sofa, grained to simulate rosewood and decorated with carving and ormolu mounts. Beginning to be somewhat heavy and elaborate; dating from the late Regency period, about 1825.*

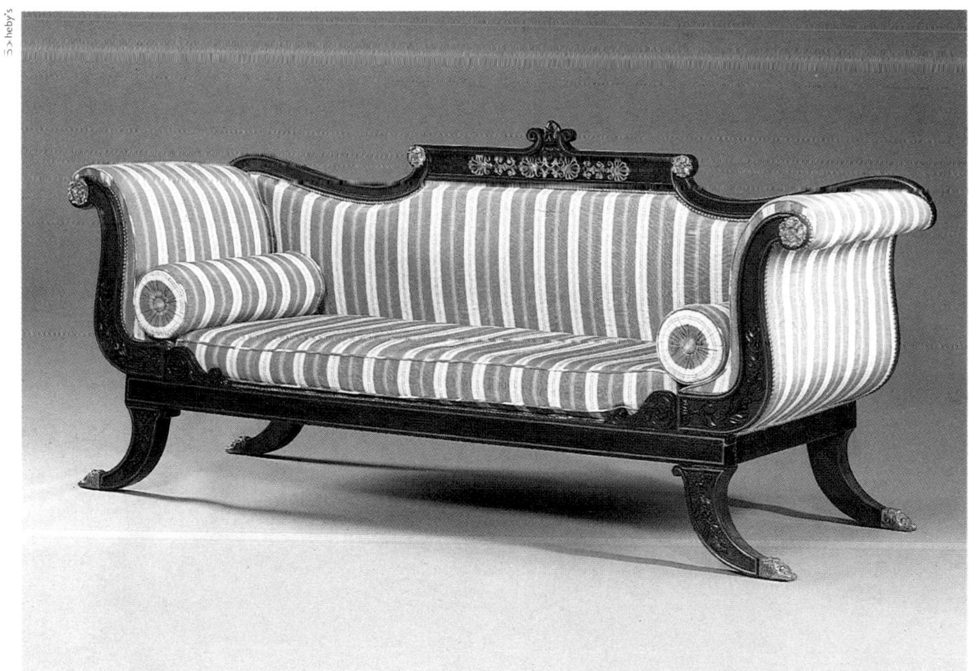

Below, *an ebonised and glazed sideboard designed by E.W. Godwin in the 1870s. Much of Godwin's furniture was inspired by Japanese design.*

Bottom right, *a mid-Victorian walnut sideboard, of massive proportions and a somewhat debased rococo-style. A solid, respectable piece designed for the prosperous middle-class.*

Below, *an inlaid satinwood secretaire cabinet made in about 1870 in the geometric Gothic style by the Leeds firm of Marsh & Jones, one of the many provincial-based makers producing furniture of superb quality.*

Haslam & Whiteway Ltd

Christie's

Sotheby's

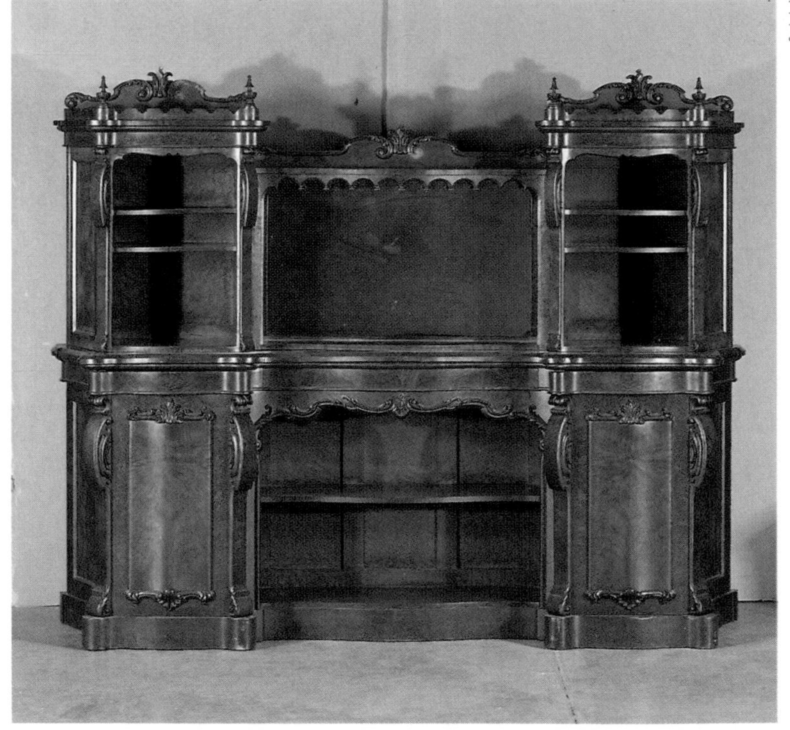

Sotheby's

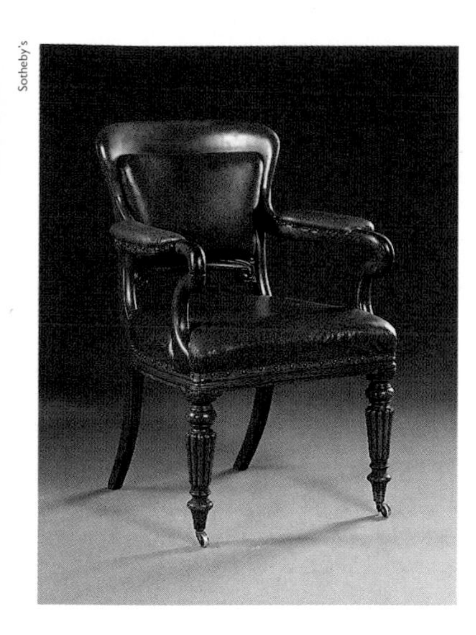

***Left**, an early Victorian mahogany chair with rather heavy fluted front legs. A strong well-built masculine chair of a type made in their thousands for clubs, libraries and offices.*

***Below**, an unusually elaborate mid-Victorian walnut and marquetry centre table with shaped outlines. A rather smart piece, probably intended more for display than for use.*

Christie's

***Below**, a selection of typical papier mâché furniture with distinctive gilded, painted and mother-of-pearl decoration. Particularly popular with the early Victorians, seldom made after about 1870.*

Sotheby's

Sotheby's

Left, *an Edwardian satinwood Carlton House desk. The Edwardians made a great deal of furniture in 'Sheraton' style. Although still neo-classical in form, its decoration tended to be fussier and was often painted, not inlaid.*

Sotheby's

Above, *an oak wardrobe by Peter Waals, a member of the Cotswold school, who designed and made very simple, yet sophisticated furniture by largely traditional methods of craftsmanship.*

Christie's

Right, *a mahogany inlaid cabinet showing the French art nouveau style as interpreted by a so-called 'commercial' (not a 'progressive') English maker.*

***Right**, a Franco-Flemish walnut armchair, of about 1685. The turned legs, carved stretchers and carved back were soon adopted in England, largely due to the published designs of Daniel Marot.*

Sotheby's

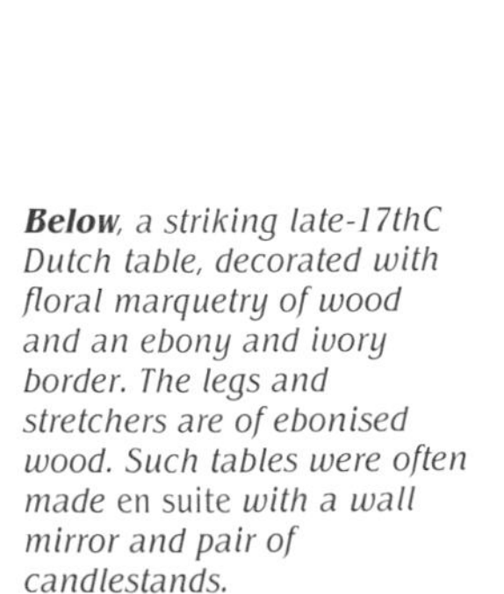

***Below**, a striking late-17thC Dutch table, decorated with floral marquetry of wood and an ebony and ivory border. The legs and stretchers are of ebonised wood. Such tables were often made* en suite *with a wall mirror and pair of candlestands.*

***Below**, a Louis XIV marquetry cabinet-on-stand attributed to the leading Parisian maker Pierre Gole, about 1670. A magnificent piece of furniture, of museum standard, very seldom available on the open market.*

Sotheby's

Sotheby's

Sotheby's

***Left**, a German walnut cabinet set with Italian* pietre dure *plaques and mounted on an ebonised stand, late-17th/early-18thC.* Pietre dure *plaques were highly prized.*

Sotheby's

***Left**, a Louis XIV* bureau Mazarin *with very fine marquetry decoration on an ebony ground. Late-17thC, but re-constructed 1800-1850.*

Christie's

***Above**, a Louis XIV ormolu-mounted brass and tortoiseshell boulle marquetry* bureau plat, *attributed to André-Charles Boulle himself.* Early-18thC bureaux plats *of this type were extensively reproduced in the 19thC.*

Sotheby's

***Right**, a Louis XIV brass and tortoiseshell boulle marquetry commode of about 1700. Another superb piece of furniture – one of a group of commodes of similar design and manufacture.*

Sotheby's

***Left**, a Louis XV writing-table decorated with geometric marquetry and small ormolu mounts. Possibly made in Strasbourg, about 1765.*

Sotheby's

***Above**, one of a pair of mid-18thC German or Dutch* encoigneures. *Chinoiserie played an important, though not universal, role in the rococo style.*

Christie's

***Above**, a late Louis XV* duchesse brisé, *about 1780, by Georges Jacob. Upholstered furniture in France was more varied and elaborate than elsewhere in Europe. Today it is fairly rare to find a sofa of this type complete.*

Sotheby's

***Left**, a mid-18thC bombé commode with lacquer decoration and very fine rococo ormolu mounts.*

EUROPEAN ROCOCO

***Below**, a Portuguese ebonised corner chair dating from the first half of the 18thC. The English influence evident in their design was due to strong economic and artistic ties dating back to Charles II's marriage to Catherine of Braganza.*

Sotheby's

Sotheby's

***Above**, a Dutch walnut side-chair of about 1740. The curving seat rail, marquetry decoration and the deep panel in the centre of the apron are characteristic features of Dutch chairs of this date.*

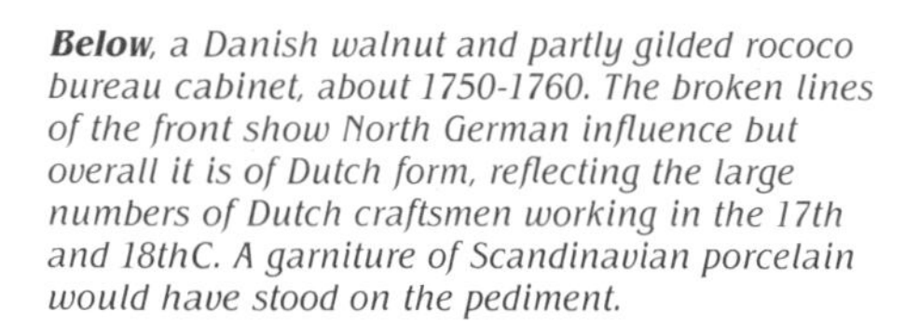

***Below**, a Danish walnut and partly gilded rococo bureau cabinet, about 1750-1760. The broken lines of the front show North German influence but overall it is of Dutch form, reflecting the large numbers of Dutch craftsmen working in the 17th and 18thC. A garniture of Scandinavian porcelain would have stood on the pediment.*

Sotheby's

***Below**, a walnut-veneered serpentine-front chest of drawers, either Dutch or German, about 1740-1750. A very ordinary piece but nevertheless desirable because of its small size.*

Sotheby's

Sotheby's

Right, *a secretaire-à-abattant dated about 1775 with panels of fine marquetry typical of this date, including vases and garlands of flowers, musical instruments and drapery.*

Below, *two Louis XVI giltwood chairs with oval backs and straight legs, spiralling at the front, about 1780.*

Sotheby's

Sotheby's

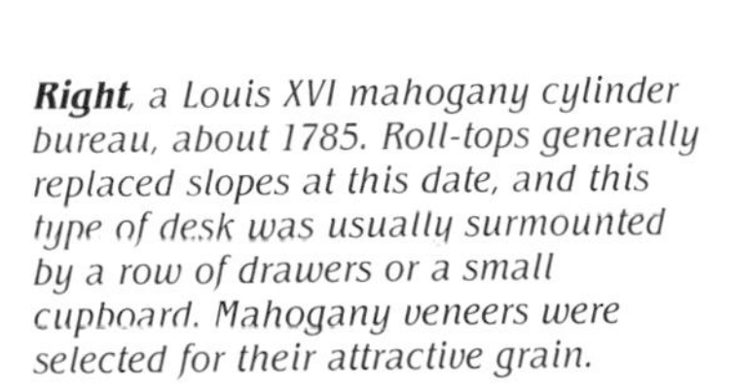

Right, *a Louis XVI mahogany cylinder bureau, about 1785. Roll-tops generally replaced slopes at this date, and this type of desk was usually surmounted by a row of drawers or a small cupboard. Mahogany veneers were selected for their attractive grain.*

Right, *a late-18thC Portuguese marquetry commode in neo-classical style with a marble top and distinctive deep apron below.*

Sotheby's

Christie's

Left, *a French mahogany cradle dated about 1830. The swan's neck is a characteristic feature of this period, often seen on the arms of seat furniture.*

Sotheby's

Above, *one of a pair of very grand Empire giltwood armchairs after a design by the influential designers Percier and Fontaine. French or Russian, about 1810.*

Sotheby's

Left, *a rosewood console table with winged chimera monopodium supports, by the leading French maker Georges-Alphonse Jacob-Desmalter, about 1830.*

Sotheby's

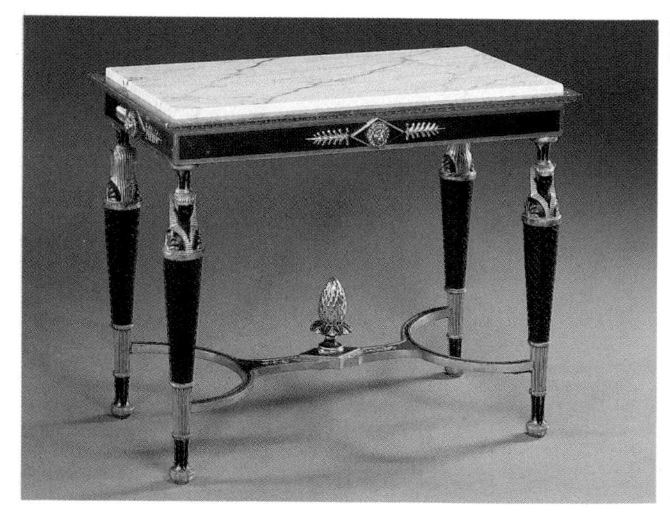

Right, *an early-19thC Swedish classical revival table with Egyptian figures on the legs. Ancient Egyptian motifs were frequently used on Empire furniture.*

Sotheby's

__Below__, a Biedermeier birchwood armchair, about 1825. While obviously of classical inspiration, a distinctive and idiosyncratic design.

Sotheby's

__Below__, a Biedermeier birchwood side-chair. Though similar in overall form to French Directoire and Empire chairs, it lacks their boldness and their grandeur.

Sotheby's

__Above centre__, a Biedermeier maplewood secretaire cabinet dated about 1820. Light-coloured, figured woods and a limited use of ebony, or ebonised, detail, were characteristic features of the Biedermeier style which flourished in Austria and Germany in the early-19thC.

__Below__, a birchwood sofa en suite with the armchair also illustrated on this page. Its scroll arms, pedimented back and platform supports are typical of the style.

Sotheby's

Sotheby's

__Below__, a marvellous quality boulle and ebony-veneered side cabinet, made in Paris in about 1855. In the second half of the 19thC, 17th and 18thC styles and techniques, in particular boulle marquetry, were widely revived and reinterpreted.

Sotheby's

***Above**, an ivory-inlaid hardstone and* pietra paesina *cabinet by Ferdinando Pogliani, a Milanese maker who showed such complex and superbly crafted pieces at international exhibitions. Definitely a collector's piece.*

***Below**, part of a giltwood Aubusson-upholstered salon suite made in about 1870 in Louis XV rococo style. The upholstery is very typical of its day; this was the fashionable 19thC covering for many 18thC chairs.*

Sotheby's

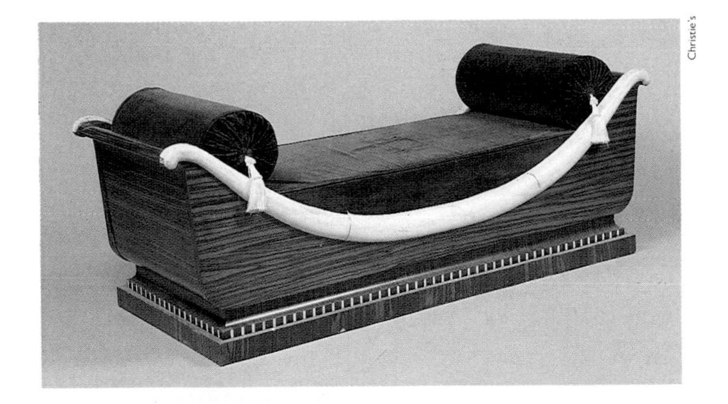

***Right**, an ebony, macassar and vellum-covered French day-bed in Art Deco style. A very chic Parisian piece of furniture, but not very practical.*

Christie's

Christie's

***Above**, two art nouveau chairs and a table by the Italian designer Valabrega, about 1900. Upholstery of art nouveau seat furniture was often of complementary design.*

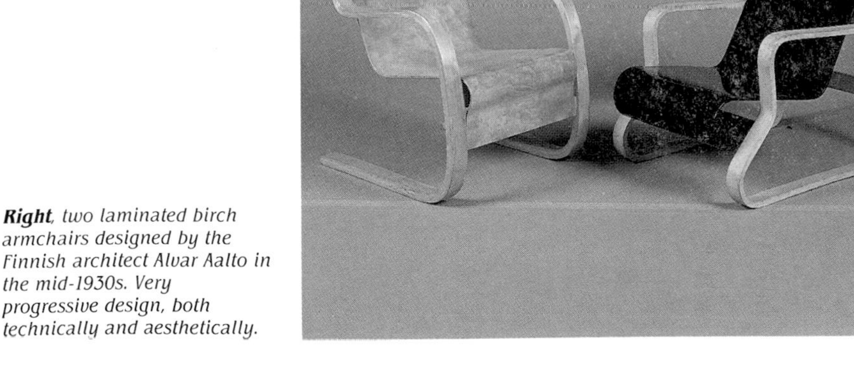

Christie's

***Right**, two laminated birch armchairs designed by the Finnish architect Alvar Aalto in the mid-1930s. Very progressive design, both technically and aesthetically.*

***Right**, a pair of beech bentwood chairs made by J. and J. Kohn to the design of Josef Hoffmann in about 1910. Hoffmann was a leading member of the Secessionist movement in Vienna and a founder of the Wiener Werkstätte.*

Christie's

***Below**, a side-chair and table by Carlo Bugatti, about 1900. Well outside the mainstream of design, but very collectable. Most of Bugatti's furniture was ebonised and inlaid in psuedo-Moorish style with pewter, bone and various woods. Some parts were vellum-covered.*

Christie's

Christie's

Christie's

__Above__, an oak chest dating from about 1680-1700. A Connecticut provenance is indicated by the presence of applied split turnings; painted decoration has replaced carving on the panelled front.

__Left__, a rare late-17thC oak and maple chamber table, painted black to simulate ebony. Painted finishes were widely used at this date to simulate more exotic timbers than were generally available.

__Below__, a black-painted maple side chair, about 1700-1740. Leather upholstery, though seldom still original, was common on early chairs in the absence of fine woven cloth.

__Near right__, a 'Cromwellian' maple and oak side-chair, based on earlier English farthingales and made in Massachusetts some time between about 1655 and 1695.

Christie's

Christie's

***Left**, a Queen Anne walnut high chest of drawers, the drawer-fronts with simple inlaid stringing. Though based on an English type, the cabriole legs are both longer and thinner. About 1730-1740.*

Christie's

***Right**, a 'Chippendale' carved maple armchair of a type associated with the maker John Gaines in Portsmouth, New Hampshire, in about 1790-1810. The Chippendale-style back is combined with a base and arms of Restoration type.*

Christie's

***Above**, a Chippendale mahogany chest of drawers, about 1765-1785. Its sophisticated bombé or 'kettle' shape, which required some skill to construct, suggests it was made in either Salem or Boston, both flourishing seaports which maintained close links with Europe.*

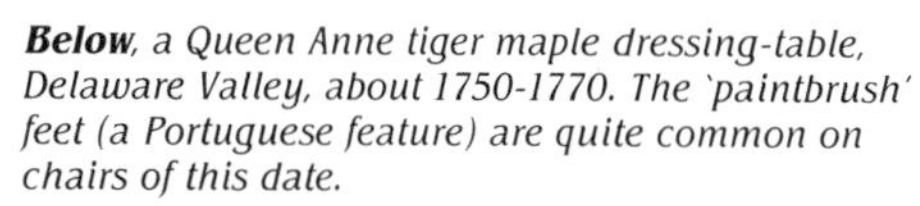

***Below**, a Queen Anne tiger maple dressing-table, Delaware Valley, about 1750-1770. The 'paintbrush' feet (a Portuguese feature) are quite common on chairs of this date.*

Christie's

***Right**, a mahogany highboy in Chippendale style by Thomas Tufft, Philadelphia, about 1779. The influence of Chippendale's* Director *was generally stronger in Philadelphia than elsewhere.*

***Below**, a very simple, but superb quality, mahogany Pembroke table, attributed to John Townsend, Newport, Rhode Island, about 1760-1790. Note the delicate fretwork on the stretchers and corner brackets.*

***Bottom**, a highly sophisticated four-post mahogany bed with claw-and-ball feet and elaborate shaped and upholstered tester. Massachusetts, about 1760-1780.*

Christie's

Christie's

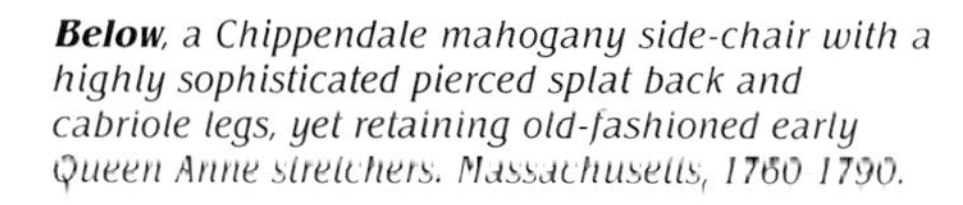

***Below**, a Chippendale mahogany side-chair with a highly sophisticated pierced splat back and cabriole legs, yet retaining old-fashioned early Queen Anne stretchers. Massachusetts, 1760-1790.*

Christie's

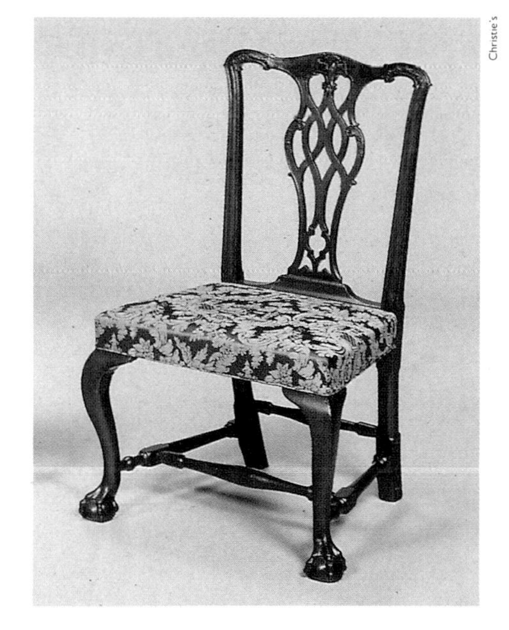

Christie's

NEW WORLD CHIPPENDALE

Christie's

Above, *a mahogany kneehole desk, about 1770-1780. Its block-front combined with carved shell decoration is characteristic of the Goddard and Townsend families of cabinet makers working in Newport R.I. in the second half of the 18thC.*

Below left, *a fine mahogany pier table, made in Chippendale style, by Thomas Tufft for Richard Edwards in New Jersey, about 1775-6.*

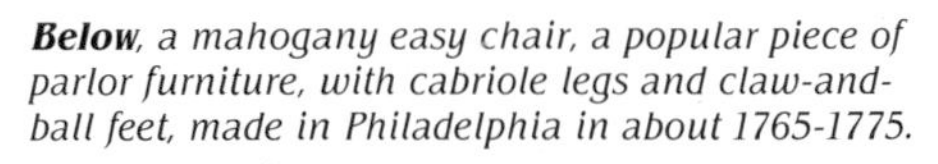

Below, *a mahogany easy chair, a popular piece of parlor furniture, with cabriole legs and claw-and-ball feet, made in Philadelphia in about 1765-1775.*

Christie's

Christie's

Christie's

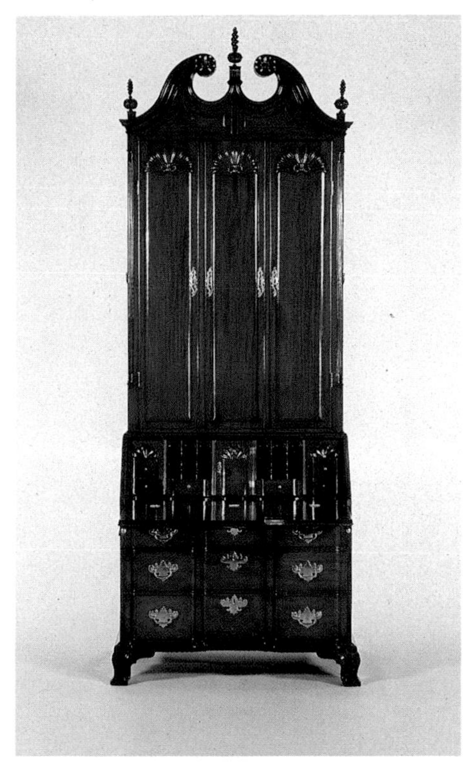

Christie's

***Above**, a very fine quality chest-on-chest attributed to Thomas Townsend, Newport, Rhode Island, about 1760-1780. Though derived from an English type, note how the bonnet-top is integral with the chest, not separated by a moulding.*

***Above**, a magnificent block-front mahogany secretary-bookcase by John Goddard, Newport, Rhode Island, about 1760-1770. Note the unusually tall bookcase section, its three panels reflecting the block-front desk below.*

***Below**, a detail of the mahogany block-front secretary-bookcase illustrated **above**, showing the exceptionally high quality of craftsmanship and its distinctive carved shell decoration.*

Christie's

__Right__, two Federal mahogany side-chairs in the Sheraton style with the Prince of Wales feathers, carved urns and drapery incorporated in the back. The pattern books of Hepplewhite and Sheraton were widely copied during this period.

Christie's

__Below__, a very simple and elegant Federal sofa, about 1800-1815. Mahogany with decorative veneer of birds-eye maple.

Sotheby's

The American Museum

__Above__, a Federal mahogany 'Martha Washington' chair, with finely turned and fluted legs and small panels of birch inlay. New Hampshire, about 1800-1810. An adaptation of earlier Chippendale-style lolling chairs.

__Right__, a Federal mahogany and birch-veneered lady's writing-desk, Massachusetts, about 1790-1810. Contrasting veneers were a characteristic feature of this popular form of Federal furniture.

Christie's

__Left__, a highly decorative and partly ebonised birds-eye maple work table, Massachusetts, about 1815-1825. A transitional piece, heavier and bolder than most Federal tables, but not yet 'classical'.

__Below__, French Empire influence is obvious in this partly ebonised and gilt-stencilled mahogany dressing bureau, made in New York, 1820-1830.

Christie's

Christie's

__Above__, a most unusual pair of classical gilt and painted rosewood fold-over top card tables, with harp supports, New York, about 1815.

__Right__, a carved mahogany and rosewood centre table in late-classical style, the top with a painted landscape bordered by flowers. Attributed to Anthony G. Querville, Philadelphia, 1820-1830.

Christie's

Christie's

__Above__, two chairs from a suite of ebonised and partly gilt parlor furniture, probably made in New York in about 1870. Plush upholstery and fringes were as important as the wooden frame.

Christie's

__Right__, a very distinctive painted pine secretary bookcase, its decoration similar to that of papier mâché with flowers, landscape scenes, scrolling foliage. Massachusetts, about 1860.

Christie's

Above, *oak dining-table and chairs designed by Frank Lloyd Wright in about 1905. Most of Wright's very simple, undecorated furniture was designed to be made by machine in order to reduce its price and therefore reach a wide public.*

Below, *a mahogany hall bench designed by C. & H. Greene for a house in Pasadena, about 1907-09. The pegs securing the joints have been stained and used as a decorative feature.*

Christie's

***Above**, a Craftsman oak buffet designed by Gustav Stickley, in about 1905. Decoration is provided by the bold metal fittings.*

***Below**, an oak Craftsman writing-desk designed by Gustav Stickley, about 1905. The construction is revealed, the through tenons projecting forward to form a positive design feature.*

continued from page 128

TABLES: REFECTORY

About

1580-1700

(but much later in country areas)

A large rectangular dining-table found only in large and prosperous households. A descendant of the simple 'trestle'. Generally superseded by the gate-leg when dining became a more intimate affair around 1660, but made in country areas until well into the 19thC. Refectory is a 19thC term.

17th to early-18thC oak refectory table.

STYLE AND APPEARANCE

Rectangular, deeply over-hanging plank top, usually cleated (or clamped) at ends; after 1660 sometimes mitred cleating all round.

Four (sometimes six) heavy turned legs (according to size) joined at top by deep (usually carved) frieze; at bottom by square or rectangular stretchers. Small carved bracket sometimes present at top of legs.

Post-1700 country versions generally plainer; often with square legs and without stretchers and cleats.

DRAW-TABLES

Similar to the refectory, but with two additional leaves mounted on bearers which pull out to extend the top. Early examples are rare today, but late-19th and early-20thC reproductions in 'Jacobethan' style are very common. Regularity of surfaces, saw marks, screws, machine-carving and (frequently) ugly, stained finish, are instant give-aways.

MATERIALS

Principally oak; occasionally yew or walnut (though few survive). Sometimes elm for tops (with oak underframe). Various fruitwoods for small versions.

CONSTRUCTION

Widely faked and reproduced in the 19th and present century. Expect some repairs or alterations, even on prices which are substantially right. Check carefully for the following signs of authenticity:

A maximum of two planks on top. The timber was split, not sawn, so expect some shrinkage along grain and away from cleats. Look particularly underneath for roughness caused by saw marks and, even if split, for unexplained screw or nail holes.

Even **patination** on all parts and natural **stains** around under-side of top from constant handling. This should stop just short of underframe. Considerable and uneven **wear** on stretchers. **Stretchers** flush with, or very

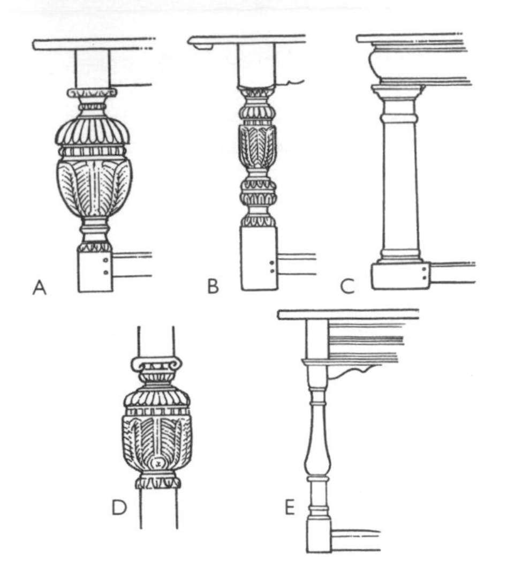

*Table legs: **A & D**, carved cup-and-cover, about 1560-1680; **B**, bulbous vase-turning, about 1700-1800; **C**, column or 'gun-barrel', about 1620-1780; **E**, baluster, about 1660-1800.*

close to, outer edge of legs. Frayed and ragged **undersides to feet**. Mortise-and-tenon **joints pegged** with hand-cut dowels of irregular size and shape. Pattern of **carving on frieze** fits precisely between ends; if cut off abruptly, it is either taken from another piece, or table has been shortened.

DECORATION

Carving on:

Legs. Cup-and-cover bolection mouldings (becoming increasingly less bulbous) from about 1560-1680; thereafter simple baluster turnings. Vase turnings in early 18thC.

Frieze. Simple chip-carved lunettes were popular, also arcading, fluting and other repetitive patterns; deeper-carved gadrooning on grander versions. Sometimes the frieze was inlaid, often with chequer or other geometric patterns.

FINISH

Original stain or varnish with dry or wax polish. Should be good, deep, even patination, resulting from accumulated dirt and subsequent polishing.

RELATIVE VALUES

If a good size and substantially original condition, prices should be into five figures; even when wrong, still well into four. The meanest-looking, badly-stained reproductions four figures or less.

Christie's

20thC reproduction of an Elizabethan draw-table; a type very popular with the Edwardians.

TABLES, DINING: GATE-LEG

About
1640 onwards

Christie's

Early oak gate-leg, with bobbin- and rim-turned legs.

Introduced in the early 17thC when private dining away from the main hall became commonplace. Before 1800 all such dining-tables were stored against the walls – sometimes actually outside the room – when not in use, hence the flaps for economical storage. Popular for provincial and rural homes well into the 18thC.

STYLE AND APPEARANCE
Great variation in size; largest (to seat 12) up to 8 feet/2.4 m long, with four gates. Smallest (to seat two) for occasional use only.

Majority with oval top; sometimes circular; less commonly rectangular or square. Central section (between hinged flaps) with rect-angular underframe, sometimes fitted with shallow frieze drawer. Four straight or turned legs, joined by straight or turned stretchers. Bun or feet on most decorative types; simplest (and many country versions) with block feet.

Small pieces may have trestle base and can be one-sided (designed to stand against wall). Flaps supported on gates, each with two straight or turned uprights joined by plain rail and plain or turned stretcher.

MATERIALS
Mainly oak, joined by walnut after 1660. Sometimes elm for top (with oak underframe). Yew and fruitwoods for smaller versions.

CONSTRUCTION
Pegged mortise-and-tenon joints. Each section of top originally a single piece of timber (though ends sometimes broken off and replaced). Until about 1700 top pegged to underframe; then alternatively glue-blocked, to about 1740; thereafter screwed.

Until 1670 flaps hinged with tongue-and-groove joints; thereafter often rule joints (to allow moulding to continue all round central section). Should be deep over-hang of flaps over gates when open. Under-sides should show circular marks caused by frequent opening of gates. Gates pivot in sockets in underframe and stretcher; these should show considerable wear. Outer upright slots into groove in strecher when folded.

No lock rail to end drawer. No runners.

> **VICTORIAN REPRODUCTIONS**
>
> Plenty of reproductions made by Victorians with regular, machine-turned legs. Check construction carefully; look particularly for the V-shaped incisions made towards the end of the century for the screws holding the top.

DECORATION
Twist, bobbin, reel, plain tapering gun-barrel, baluster or vase turning on legs, according to date. Occasionally shallow chip-carving on ends of underframe.

Handles: Simple drop, pendant or ring, with circular back-plates.

FINISH
Originally stain, followed by wax polish. Should now be good, even patination; considerable natural staining around edges of underside of top.

RELATIVE VALUES
Price principally related to size – the larger the better. If right, ten- or twelve-seaters can be well into five figures, but far more numerous six- or eight-seaters in the lower half of the four-figure range. Small, occasional verisons often only in three. Walnut, and to a lesser extent fruitwoods, a price advantage.

TABLES, DINING: DROP-LEAF

Fashionable about

1735-1770

but made later.

A more elegant table, and more comfortable to use than the gate-leg, which replaced the latter in sophisticated homes from about 1735 onwards. Country versions were made too, but with a slight time-lag.

Mahogany drop-leaf table, about 1740-1750.

Sotheby's

STYLE AND APPEARANCE

Similar to the gate-leg: central section has rectangular underframe and two large, hinged flaps, but without stretchers and without gates themselves. Two of the four legs swing on a hinge to support flaps.

Generally small in size, seating only four people. (Larger versions at a premium, see **RELATIVE VALUES**.)

Until about 1750 generally on slender cabriole legs ending in pad, sometimes claw-and-ball or hoof feet. Usually some decorative carving and scrolled ear pieces on knees. After 1750 legs straight and square; often moulded, sometimes chamfered on inner sides. On country versions often straight – but round and tapering – with blocks forming the stiles of the underframe extending well below the rails. Simple pad feet.

Tops mostly circular, with straight or thumb-moulded edge; rectangular tops increasingly popular after 1750.

Occasionally shallow drawer at one end.

MATERIALS

Nearly always mahogany; occasionally (Virginia) walnut on early pieces. Oak or pine for underframe; sometimes beech. Oak or elm (or the two combined) and fruitwoods for country versions.

CONSTRUCTION

Glued mortise-and-tenon joints with tops of legs forming stiles of underframe. Solid timber employed throughout. Best quality has each section of top made from one piece of timber (though ends often broken off and replaced later). Grain runs parallel on all three sections.

Outer edges of under-side show natural staining from constant handling; circular marks caused by movement of swing legs. Top fixed to underframe from underneath with screws fixed from rounded incision (though on country versions may be pegged from above).

The flaps were supported on brass rule hinges. Supporting legs swing out on wooden knuckle joints.

VICTORIAN VERSIONS

Very plain, rectangular-topped drop-leaf tables, with straight, square legs, were still manufactured in the 19thC. Look for poor quality, machine-cut timber, metal rather than wooden knuckle joints, and leaves reaching almost to the floor.

DECORATION

Some carving on very high quality pieces on knees of cabriole legs, of acanthus or other foliage, sometimes shells.

Handles: Small brass drop or ring handles.

FINISH

Stain or varnish followed by wax polish.

RELATIVE VALUES

Rectangular tops considerably less popular than round. Prices for all 18thC examples of the latter in four figures, more than double and often moving into five if large (i.e. seating eight or more people). Only the plainest, rectangular – or lesser quality Victorian – for three-figure sums.

DRESSING OR 'TOILET' TABLES

About

1700-1915

Inlaid Sheraton-style lady's dressing-table, about 1800.

A piece of furniture which underwent many changes over the years, but was at all times intended to support and often store a mirror and other dressing accessories. Until about 1750 very often only a straightforward side-table draped with a cloth.

In the late-19thC usually made *en suite* with a wardrobe, chest of drawers, wash-stand and occasional chair.

STYLE AND APPEARANCE

About 1700-1750: As a kneehole desk (see **p. 105**) with a separate dressing mirror. Sometimes with a dummy top drawer and hinged top lifting to reveal rising mirror and fitted compartments for brushes and bottles.

About 1750-1810: *Either* as above, but larger, *or* (more commonly) a small cabinet with a shallow box-like top divided centrally and opening to the side to reveal rising mirror and interior fittings. Various conformations of drawers, cupboards, open shelves below, most supported on tall, square, and after 1770, tapering legs, often on castors. Cupboard doors often concave-fronted; after about 1780 frequently tambour.

Typical dressing-table of the 1790s with additional writing facility.

About 1790-1840: *Either* similar to the previous hinged-top type, but wider and more complex with additional drawers, cupboards, washing and writing facilities; *or* as a table, with a single long fitted frieze drawer. Initially many were made in a French style (with serpentine shape and slender cabriole legs), but after 1800 they were more popularly a trestle type, like a sofa table without the flaps (**see p. 181**). Separate dressing mirror above.

Mid-Victorian dressing-table, about 1860.

Victorian pedestal dressing-table, about 1880.

Late-Victorian carved and inlaid dressing-table.

About 1840 onwards: Great variation. Simplest as a one-drawer table supported on turned legs, but most commonly of kneehole design. This was *either* of a pedestal type (drawers extending down to plinth base) *or* with various combinations of drawers and cupboards flanking a single central drawer, raised from the ground on square or turned tapering legs, occasionally joined by stretchers or a shaped shelf below.

All four types had a separate mirror to about 1850; thereafter it was usually fixed and flanked by small upper cupboards and nests of drawers. The shape of the mirror varied, but as a general rule, rounded outlines predominated to about 1880, thereafter straight.

Edwardians favoured dressing chests, which were chests of drawers with similar fitted upper arrangements of a mirror and small drawers.

The Duchess type, with a long mirror above a low base drawer and kneehole recess, flanked by tall pedestals of drawers at the sides, was introduced about 1900, but was not popular until the 1920s, from when most date.

MATERIALS

Walnut, mahogany, satinwood, rosewood. Sometimes oak for Victorian Gothic; pine or beech when japanned or ebonised. Pine or cheap Honduras mahogany for carcases, oak or mahogany for drawer linings. All pine on the cheapest late Victorian pieces.

CONSTRUCTION

Standard methods employed. Many veneered. Rising mirrors on counter-balanced weights or simple ratchet systems.

DECORATION

Very little before 1780 other than figuring of veneer; rarely, chinoiserie patterns if japanned. Thereafter some restrained inlay and decorative arrangements of veneers; occasionally painted neo-classical motifs and flowers. Considerable variation in the 19thC, including inlay, marquetry, carving, papier mch; gilded and incised decoration on ebonised Art Furniture.

Handles: Typical for the day. Mostly brass bails or ring handles to about 1820, then wooden knobs, rejoined by various metal types after 1870.

FINISH

Stain or varnish followed by wax polish. Can be japanned (18thC) or ebonised (1870s-1880s). Dark stain on cheap, late-19th/early-20thC pine, to simulate mahogany, or a lighter-coloured stain to simulate satinwood. Alternatively paint (from about 1890), mostly white, sometimes green.

RELATIVE VALUES

Any piece of reasonable quality made before about 1830 invariably priced in four figures if right and complete, but only the very best Victorian and Edwardian pieces make the same grade. Small size a definite advantage and, in this particular case, also a pretty and feminine appearance.

TABLES, DINING: EXTENDING, WITH LEGS

About

1750 onwards

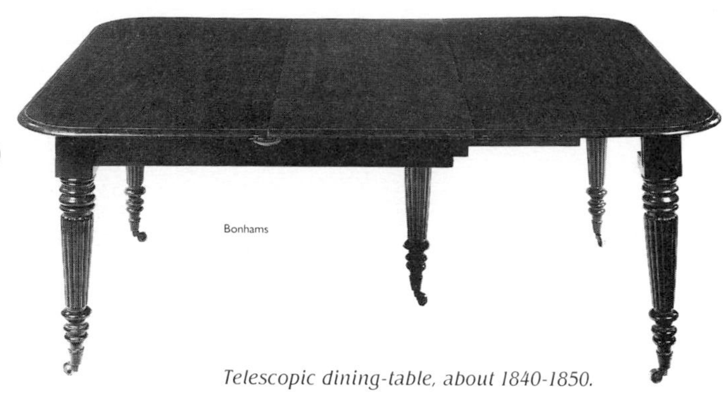

Telescopic dining-table, about 1840-1850.

During the first half of the 18thC large parties of diners had to be seated at a number of different tables, but after 1750 it became fashionable to accommodate them together around long 'extending' tables made up from three or more separate parts.

STYLE AND APPEARANCE

Made as a drop-leaf table (see **DROP-LEAF TABLES, p. 164**) with rectangular flaps and an additional pair of semi-circular or semi-elliptical tables, which all join together to form one continuous surface. Each section with four (occasionally five) legs, one or two of them swinging out to support flaps. Two end pieces may be clipped together to form smaller oval or circular tables, or to stand against the wall as pier tables when not in use. Additional rectangular leaves may also be inserted between each part (without leg supports). This is more common in 19thC. D-shaped ends (i.e. rectangular with rounded corners) common from about 1790.

Legs square and tapering before 1800, generally ending in block feet; thereafter more fashionably turned and ending in castors; increasingly bulbous after 1820.

Tops undecorated; sides plain or reeded until about 1820, then lip or thumb-moulded. Slight overhang of 18thC becoming deeper from same date.

MARRIAGES

Many large tables were broken down in the past into smaller, more saleable units, or their timber was used for other furniture. With vast increases in value today, the process has often been reversed. Always check all parts for identical construction throughout and for matching timber. Note that there may be a difference in colour though – especially on separate leaves – due to differing usage and exposure to light. Look underneath carefully for unexplained marks and holes and for uneven patination. Check the tops of legs for signs of breakage (quite common on fine 18thC pieces). While a mend – or the join of a new leg – may be disguised on the outside by a line of stringing or veneer, it will probably be visible on the inside.

MATERIALS

Mahogany (either solid or as veneer); deal or cheap Honduras mahogany for underframe if veneered. Birch or teak (a greasy wood) used for runners on telescopic tables.

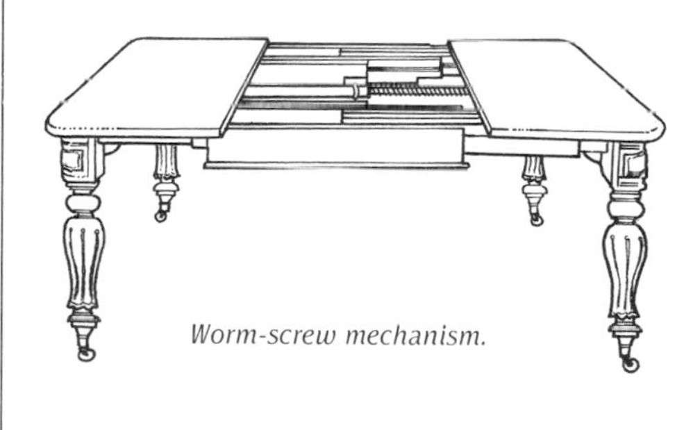

Worm-screw mechanism.

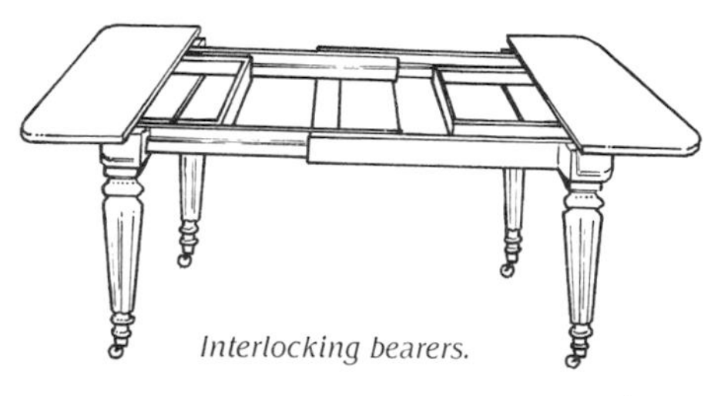

Interlocking bearers.

Mahogany D-end table with additional square flaps, about 1800.

CONSTRUCTION

Standard methods employed. Legs form stiles of underframe. Tops screwed from below in rounded incisions. Rule joints on hinged flaps. Leaves slot together with small rectangular tongues; later round pegs. Parts held in place at sides with U-shaped metal fork bolts clipping into corresponding metal straps. (These are still used today and will therefore appear on reproduction tables too.) From early 19thC onwards many tables extended on telescopic principle, via a system of interlocking bearers, with leaves sitting on top and slotting into ends (or each other) with tongues of pegs. By end of the century large worm screws, operated with a cranking handle, almost universally adopted.

DECORATION

Sometimes inlaid stringing lines on frieze and legs. Reeding and fluting from about 1780, often with paterae on stiles of underframe. Heavier reeding and (often twisted) fluting combined with bulbous turning is characteristic of Victorian legs.

FINISH

Stain or varnish followed by wax polish. French polish after 1820.

RELATIVE VALUES

Large and original 18thC examples are rare and correspondingly expensive, prices being close to, if not in, five figures. 19thC tables – even those with very bulbous legs – will be in the upper part of the four-figure range if in good condition and with well-chosen timber. Size is an important factor (many are bought as boardroom tables); anything seating more than eight people may be three or four times as much as a mere six-seater.

Mahogany table with semi-elliptical ends and removable leaves, about 1780.

TABLES, DINING: EXTENDING, WITH PEDESTALS About 1780-1840

Mahogany pedestal dining-table, about 1790.

Sotheby's

By 1780 a more comfortable form of dining table had evolved, with central supporting pedestals to each section rather than legs. The majority were made with three pedestals, but there could be only two or as many as six. Separate leaves were fitted between each part. These are popularly called pillar-and-claw tables.

STYLE AND APPEARANCE

Tops D-ended or rectangular with very slightly rounded corners. Edges plain or reeded, always corresponding with plain or reeded legs below. Can be carved (gadrooned for example) or lip- or thumb-moulded in 19thC. Always without a frieze before 1800 and only sometimes with before 1825.

Pedestals with three or four splayed legs ending in brass cast paw feet or socket castors; kneed after about 1810; later scrolling. Earliest with simple gun barrel turning on pillar; later vase; turnings more bulbous after 1800.

William IV versions may have heavy platform base, carved feet, hefty columns and frieze around top.

MATERIALS

Usually mahogany but occasionally rosewood. Top sometimes cross-banded in timber of contrasting colour. Pine or mahogany for underframe; often beech for supporting block.

CONSTRUCTION

Legs wedge-dovetailed into pillar and strengthened by metal plate screwed underneath. Join partly concealed by ring turnings immediately above. Pillar ends in square block of timber set between screwed-on bearers, chamfered towards ends to hide them from sight. Tops should be solid timber, each section cut from one piece with grain running across width. Some tops tilt. Sections and extra leaves held together with metal fork bolts slotting into corresponding metal straps.

MARRIAGES

Many tables made up (mostly with bases from damaged breakfast tables) and given new or different tops. Look underneath for unexplained marks or holes and for patination not continuing all round the edge. Watch for mismatched decoration (i.e. reeded top with plain base.) Check table and leaves have matching edges.

Beware also of large numbers of modern reproductions, most easily identified by overall lack of patination, narrow (less than 4 feet/1.2 m) tops, with semi-circular ends and thin veneer and cross-banding. 18th and 19thC tables could be as much as 6 feet/1.8 m wide.

DECORATION

Occasionally inlaid stringing lines on legs; more commonly reeding. Turning on pillars.

FINISH

Stain or varnish followed by wax polish. French polish after 1820.

RELATIVE VALUES

Costlier than equivalent tables with legs.

TABLES, BREAKFAST

About

1780-1820

The term originally applied to a small mid-18thC table with two flaps and a drawer and concave cupboard below, but now refers to the four-, six- or eight-seater single-pedestal tables used from the late 18thC onwards for informal family dining. Many, but not all, tilt, allowing the table to be stored without taking up too much space.

Christie's

Regency mahogany breakfast table, about 1805.

STYLE AND APPEARANCE

Tops oval, circular, or rectangular with rounded corners. Plain or reeded edges (corresponding with base). Simple continuous frieze, with only slightly overhanging top, a post-1800 feature only. Pedestal bases as for pillar-and-claw (see **p. 169**), but always with four legs. Narrow platform base, with splayed legs, more common than on extending tables, from about 1800.

Sotheby's

Chippendale breakfast table, about 1760-1770.

MATERIALS

Solid mahogany; sometimes rosewood during Regency. Calamander, amboyna, satinwood, ebony and other exotic timbers used for decorative veneered cross-banding and inlaid stringing.

Bonhams

Late-Regency rosewood table with platform base, about 1835.

CONSTRUCTION

Standard methods employed. Legs wedge-dovetailed into pillar, strengthened by metal plate beneath. Top of pillar tenons through square block set between bearers. Bearers chamfered towards table edges. Additional cross-bearers around block if tilt-top, with metal pivot passing through one side and metal spring catch (to hold top in horizontal position) opposite.

Common alterations to watch for:

Removal of frieze (to present an earlier date): The wood the frieze once covered will be lighter and cleaner than the rest, possibly newly stained. Holes for previous screw fixings will be visible.

Conversion of rectangular to oval top: Lack of patination around newly cut (and usually reeded) edges; natural dirt marks on underside made by frequent handling not continuing all around top.

Shaving off of Regency knees on legs to make more graceful flowing line. Early legs seem to flow down directly from the pillar, 'kneed' legs appear to come from its sides. Difficult to detect other than by lack of proportion and slightly thin look to top of legs.

DECORATION

Fine quality pieces sometimes cross-banded around edge in contrasting wood. Some inlaid stringing. Occasionally ebony or brass inlay during Regency.

FINISH

Stain followed by wax polish.

RELATIVE VALUES

Prices invariably in four figures if right, occasionally in five, especially if cross-banded. So too larger eight-seaters and early examples with plain top edges and gun barrel pillars.

TABLES, FOLDING CARD AND TEA

About

1690-1915

Mahogany card table showing candle supports and sunken dishes to hold counters, about 1730.

Common items in the drawing-room from the early 18thC onwards when card playing and tea drinking became universal pastimes for the moneyed classes.

Based on earlier ecclesiastical 'credence' tables and designed to stand against the wall when not in use, hence their folding tops. Often made in pairs – one with baize (for cards) and one without (for either purpose). A few have inlaid games boards.

STYLE AND APPEARANCE

At all times with a hinged, fold-over top, variously supported on one or two hinged rear legs (between about 1720 and 1770 moving with a concertina action – see illustration) or, after 1800, swivelling on a pivot.

Three flaps sometimes present, to provide both alternative surfaces within the one piece.

Concealed frieze drawer common (for counters or cards) common; sunken compartment, usually baize-lined, concealed in under frame of pivot type.

Simple D-shaped folding card table about 1790

About 1690-1720 (rare today): Semi-circular or rectangular top. May be small, visible frieze drawer(s); sometimes shaped apron. Generally six turned legs joined by flat, sometimes shaped, stretchers, two of them gated to swing out and provide support for top.

About 1720-1750: Rectangular top with rounded corners providing candlestands. Straight turned or cabriole legs, ending in pad or claw-and-ball feet. Often sunken dishes (for counters) turned in inner surface. Sometimes shaped apron to frieze.

About 1750-1780: Mostly rectangular, occasionally serpentine, top; straight, square (sometimes still cabriole) legs; usually some carved decoration on frieze, legs and edges of top.

About 1780-1820: Semi-circular or D-shaped top; straight, square tapering legs; usually spade feet. Turned legs after 1800. (This type popularly reproduced by the Edwardians; look for machine-made screws, thin, machine-cut veneers and rather spindly legs.)

About 1800-1850: Majority with D-shaped or rectangular top on pedestal base. Can have single or 'birdcage' (four) column supports rising from small platform, with splayed (after 1810 kneed) legs ending in castors. Alternatively semi-circular band (or arc) support. From about 1820 platform lower, broader and concave-sided, on carved scroll or paw feet. Carved and/or shaped front frieze increasingly common.

About 1850 onwards: Previous type joined by similar but curvaceous rococo version with scrolled feet and supports and sometimes serpentine top. Birdcage support with heavy turned central finial especially popular after 1870. Some have trestle support with turned stretcher.

MATERIALS

Walnut, mahogany, satinwood, rosewood; oak, elm (or both) and some fruitwoods for country versions. Pine or cheap Honduras mahogany for carcases; oak or mahogany for drawer linings.

CONSTRUCTION

Nearly always veneered. Mortise-and-tenon joints on underframe with legs forming corner stiles. Tops glue-blocked to underframe to about 1740; thereafter generally screwed from below in rounded incision. V-shaped incision introduced at end of 19thC.

Moving legs swing on knuckle joints. Concertina tables have slide beneath (with cut-out handle) moving forwards in grooves to brace joints (see illustration). Swivel-top with pivot set on cross-bar fixed approximately two-thirds along underframe.

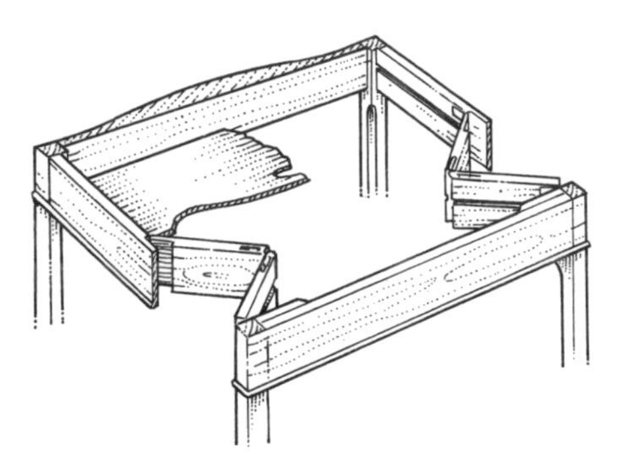

Underparts of concertina-action table.

DECORATION

Until about 1780 carving on legs, frieze and edge of top. About 1780-1810 decorative use of veneer; occasionally inlay, mostly simple stringing lines, some fans, shells, paterae.

MARRIAGES

Be wary of pairs; one of them may be a later copy. Look for identical construction and matching timber. Both should show the same degree of patination.

Baize is seldom original and is sometimes added to tea tables to make them more saleable. If the surrounding veneer is cross-cut all round, the piece started life as a card table; if it is straight-grained right across the piece, the baize has been added later.

Regency pedestal card table with swivel top.

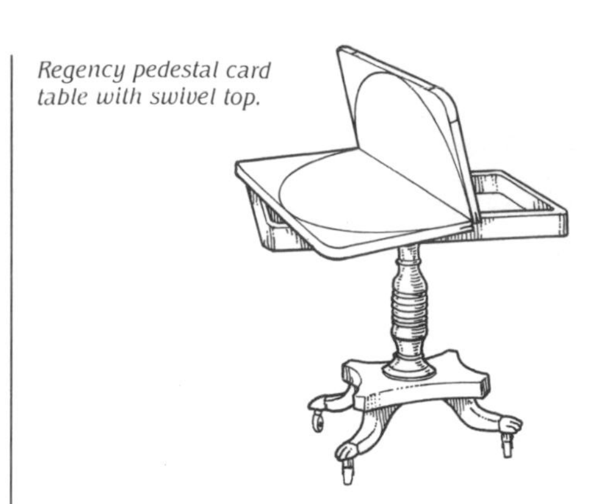

About 1810-1835 restrained classical inlay in ebony or brass. From 1850 some curvaceous, naturalistic carving of scrolls, foliage.

FINISH

Stain or varnish followed by wax polish. French polish after 1820.

RELATIVE VALUES

Only the very plainest, post-1820 versions in less than four figures; the best make it into five. Decoration is the key to high value (though demi-lune tables are also at a premium, even if plain); those with fine carving or inlay may be double the price of the same piece without. Condition is important too – particularly that of the top. This affects the value considerably. Always check the top for warping, best done with the flap closed.

Victorian scrolled 'rococo' walnut card table, about 1850.

Bonhams

TABLES, CENTRE AND LOO

About
1820 onwards

Bonhams

Typical mid-Victorian walnut centre table with 'rococo' scrolled legs.

Circular pedestal tables, with either fixed or tilting tops, were universal features of 19thC drawing-rooms and parlours. They could be used for informal meals, for writing, or for playing games. Eight-seater versions are often called 'loo' tables, after the very popular card game, which required eight participants.

STYLE AND APPEARANCE

Tops nearly always circular but occasionally oval, with slightly overhanging edge, plain, shallow frieze, and simple, narrow mouldings.

Until 1840, low triangular or quatrefoil, concave-sided, platform bases, with carved, later flattened bun, feet. Simple, often triangular-section, column supports, tapering towards the top. Tops usually plain, relying on grain or simple cross-banding and stringing for decoration.

Victorian tops often inlaid. Bases curvaceous with single or four-column (after 1870) turned supports (latter with large central finial between); carved and scrolling cabriole legs. Some with four scrolled supports, set towards outer edges of top rather than in centre.

MATERIALS

Mahogany, rosewood, walnut (solid or as veneer). Mahogany, oak or deal for carcases. Various burr veneers, tulipwood, zebrawood, satinwood, harewood and many others used for inlay, marquetry and cross-banding.

CONSTRUCTION

Standard methods employed (see **p. 170**). Marriages of tops to different bases quite common. Check that proportions look right and that timber and quality of both parts match.

DECORATION

Decorative effects often achieved only by veneers; otherwise fine marquetry and inlay in constrasting-coloured woods, mostly of stylized floral patterns. Bases deeply carved after about 1850, principally with scrolls and naturalistic foliage. As Victorian tables were covered with a cloth when placed horizontally, inlay and other decoration indicates that they were often displayed tilted.

FINISH

French polish. Underside of tilt-top sometimes stained – even grained – to present finer finish when vertical.

RELATIVE VALUES

Five-figure sums for the finest Regency, or Victorian marquetry, tables, to three-figure prices for vulgar post-1850 pieces. Exotic veneers and extensive marquetry add value.

Table of similar date to the one ***above****, the top decorated with floral marquetry.*

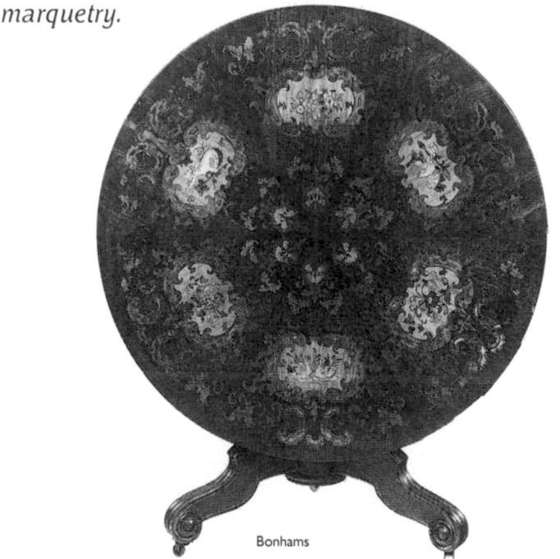
Bonhams

TABLES, SIDE (INCLUDING LOWBOYS)

About

1660-1800

Fine oak lowboy, about 1730.

Bonhams

Simple, mostly unpretentious tables designed to stand against the wall. Those with two layers of drawers called 'lowboys'. Used at various times for dressing, for serving food, or for writing. After about 1740 largely a provincial and country piece.

STYLE AND APPEARANCE

Invariably deeply overhanging, rectangular top, usually with moulded edge. Either one frieze of one (occasionally two) drawer(s), or three or four drawers, arranged as one long above two or three short, or one shallow central drawer flanked either side by one deeper drawer. Lowboys, and sometimes single frieze drawer pieces too, have shaped apron at front, and sometimes sides.

At all times four legs, design tending to follow that for contemporary chairs (see pp. **52-62**) with various turnings with straight, turned or flat and serpentine stretchers and bun feet to about 1700; thereafter cabrioles (and no stretchers) with hoof or pad feet; straight, square legs from about 1750; finer and tapering from about 1780; alternatively turned.

MATERIALS

Walnut, mahogany. Oak, elm, fruit and other local woods for country pieces. Sometimes laburnum, kingwood, olivewood, and other fine veneers were employed in the 17thC. Oak or pine for carcases with oak (occasionally mahogany) for drawer linings. Oak or pine for backboards of lowboys.

CONSTRUCTION

Majority in solid timber. Standard construction. Pegged (later glued) mortise-and-tenon joints. Tops of legs form stiles of underframe. Back rough (as intended to stand against wall); sometimes back of actual top unfinished too. Often no lock rail above drawers. Grain of timber on top runs from side to side. Should be signs of natural staining from handling on deep overhang of top. Tops pegged to underframe from above on early and many country versions. Some glue-blocked from below to 1740; after, screwed, in rounded incisions.

REPRODUCTIONS

Late-19th/early-20thC reproductions in 'Jacobean' style quite common. Watch for smaller than usual size, regular machine-cut twist or bobbin-turned legs, similarly produced applied mouldings to the drawer-fronts and underframe, and a thick, dark, lifeless stained finish.

DECORATION

Majority very plain. Sometimes applied, mitred, geometric mouldings on drawers of earliest examples; occasionally finefloral marquetry of oyster veneers on tops and drawers of Restoration pieces. Cross- or feather-banding in contrasting woods on drawer fronts after about 1710. Some restrained carving on knees of cabriole legs. Turned legs can be stained black or be of contrasting dark colour.

FINISH

Stain or varnish followed by wax polish. Dark stain on Victorian/Edwardian reproductions.

RELATIVE VALUES

The majority of examples – despite their simplicity – priced in four figures; those with Restoration marquetry or fine veneers easily reach into five.

TABLES, TRIPOD: OCCASIONAL (CHINA, TEA, SUPPER AND WINE)

About
1730 onwards

Left, mid-18thC mahogany tripod table with fretwork gallery; right, Sheraton period table, 1790-1800.

A smallish, occasional table formed as a tray on a stand; based on 17thC candle-stands and widely used in the second half of the 18thC for informal serving of tea, desserts and other refreshments. Many have a tilt-top; some – with a 'birdcage' support – also swivel. Mid-18thC examples frequently reproduced in both 19th and 20thC, not always of correct size and proportions.

STYLE AND APPEARANCE

Usually circular (but occasionally square, rectangular or octagonal) tops of varying diameter. Generally flat and plain on country versions but often with a raised rim on more sophisticated pieces (to prevent items sliding off). The rim was either carved, or turned with simple moulded or waved outline. Some scalloped; many have popular 'piecrust' rim. This is particularly popular for 20thC reproductions. Some additionally turned with eight or more dished circles (illustrated by Chippendale as 'supper tables').

Occasionally top bordered with fine, applied, spindled or fretwork gallery.

Stem turned; sometimes gun barrel (on early and country versions); more often balusters, of varying outline. Sometimes fluted (often spiralling) and/or carved.

Legs are mostly scrolling (scrolls becoming progressively less bold towards 1800), ending in pad, hoof or claw-and-ball feet. Scrolled feet seen on many Victorian versions. Some provincial pieces have flat-sided legs of rectangular section.

Both stems and knees may be carved.

Regency versions sometimes have splayed and reeded legs ending in socket castors. Tops can be circular, straight or multi-sided. From about 1830 many with low, three- or four-, concave-sided platform base on carved paw or scroll feet. May have deep frieze.

Victorian examples show great variety. Many with skimpier bases; but fussier carved decoration and small, scroll feet to pronounced cabriole legs. Edges of top often thumb-moulded; pendant finial common under base.

Note: The top of an 18thC tripod table should stand between 27 and 30 inches/67.5 and 75 cm from the floor; modern reproductions are very often lower.

MATERIALS

Principally mahogany; early (though now extremely rare) versions in 'black walnut'. Yew, elm, fruitwoods and other local woods employed in country pieces. Sometimes oak for tops (but not bases); also – with ash and beech – for junction discs and blocks (see CONSTRUCTION). Satinwood and other decorative woods were used as veneer for tops (and later bases too) in the 19thC. Japanned papier mâché (combined with deal) for some Victorian pieces.

CONSTRUCTION

Always solid wood in 18thC, never veneer. Only tops of some country versions made from more than one piece of timber. Raised decoration (except galleries) always integral with top. Under-side tapered towards edge to reduce thickness and give lighter, thinner 'dished' appearance. Galleries were constructed from plywood (three layers of cross-grained veneer laid in opposing directions). Top was either finished with veneer or with central line of stringing disguising ply. Whole rebated into the top.

Grain of stem should be continuous and running vertically. Very early versions may have stem screwing into turned junction disc (or wooden collar) fixed to underside of top. Otherwise square block set between parallel bearers. Tilt-tops pivot on wooden lugs passing through block and bearers; held in position with metal spring catch (as for **BREAKFAST TABLES, see p. 170**) but without the additional cross-bearers.

Some rotate on 'birdcage' composed of two square blocks (upper one pivoting as above) with four turned corner column supports between. Stem passes through, and rotates within, hole in lower block. Held in place with wedge or pin.

Legs wedge-dovetailed into stem, joints partly concealed by ring-turning or swelling immediately above. Strengthened by metal plate underneath.

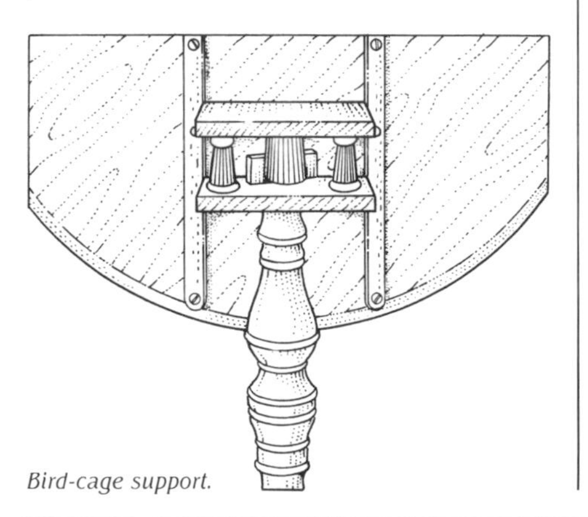

Bird-cage support.

DECORATION

Turning on stems, carving on bases and sometimes around edge of top. Shells, lion's masks, acanthus and other foliage; sometimes Gothic motifs, fashionable from about 1750. Typical papier mâché decoration (see **p. 330**) on some Victorian pieces.

FINISH

Stain or varnish followed by wax polish. French polish after 1820.

RELATIVE VALUES

Difficult to generalise because of enormous variation in date, size and quality. The very best, carved, mid-18thC tables well into five figures, but their totally plain country equivalent may still be in three (though only just). On the whole the majority of 18thC examples are priced in four figures; 19thC (unless with an interesting provenance, identifiable design, or papier mâché decoration) in three. Tilt-top – and in particular 'birdcage' tables – always preferred to those with fixed tops and correspondingly more expensive.

Sotheby's

Victorian papier-mâché table incorporating game-board, about 1840.

Watch carefully for the following:

Fakes were produced in the early years of the 20thC using 18thC turned trays mounted on bases of unfashionable pole screens or candlestands. If right, the underside of the top will show natural staining from frequent handling around the edges; if formerly a tray, dents and scratches will be visible over the entire surface.

Originally plain tables, subsequently carved on base and around top to increase value. If original, the carving will stand well proud of the surface; if not, it will be incised.

Plain tops later 'dished' to produce raised rim. Outer edges may not show characteristic taper underneath. Holes from screws fixing bearers below may be revealed above and consequently filled.

Modern reproductions with applied rims and veneered tops. Look for lack of patination on underside and base, machine-cut timber, and poor surface finish and colour.

On all tables watch for unexplained holes and marks on the under-side of the top and repairs to the legs.

TABLES: PEMBROKE

About

1770-1830

Simple mahogany Pembroke table with 'butterfly flaps', about 1790-1800.

A small, delicate occasional lady's table with two shallow, hinged flaps and one or two frieze drawers opening to the side. The first reputedly made for the Countess of Pembroke in 1750.

STYLE AND APPEARANCE

Majority with slightly overhanging oval tops; alternatively rectangular (with rounded corners) or serpentine (with butterfly wing flaps). Flaps fall approximately one-third table height. Tapering square legs (sometimes with collars) ending in socket castors; sometimes turned (and fluted or reeded) legs. Typically one real, backed by one dummy, drawer their fronts following line of top above. (An oval top with a straight-fronted drawer may indicate alteration of the top to increase value.)

MATERIALS

Mahogany, satinwood, kingwood, harewood, ebony, purplewood, rosewood and other decorative or exotic veneers used for carcases and underframe, with oak or mahogany for drawer linings. Beech or plane for fly brackets.

> **APPROXIMATIONS**
>
> Solid timber variations – mostly with straight square legs – were made by provincial and country makers from about 1780. The Victorians produced similar two-flap tables – also with straight, square legs and, generally, rectangular tops – but these are really not delicate or decorative enough to deserve the name 'Pembroke', despite following the same lines.

CONSTRUCTION

Underframes with mortise-and-tenon joints; legs forming corner stiles. Tops fixed with hand-made screws in rounded incisions. Sides of underframe recessed to accommodate brackets when closed. Under-sides of flaps could be plain-veneered; hinged with rule joints; supported on small wooden fly brackets fixed with knuckle joints. Legs taper on inner side only (if not, a replacement or more likely, an Edwardian or later reproduction).

DECORATION

Broad cross-banding, inlay and stringing in contrasting veneers on all parts. Ovals containing shells, fans, paterae common. Sometimes fine marquetry of flowers, urns, garlands etc. Occasionally painted (with similar decoration) but this may be an Edwardian addition or even reproduction.

Handles: Mostly circular ring handles with solid pressed backplates; sometimes brass knobs are seen.

FINISH

Stain or varnish, followed by wax polish. French polish after 1820.

RELATIVE VALUES

Expensive items, prices for the very best being well into five figures. Only the plainest, solid mahogany, versions less than four. Oval tops (with curved drawer fronts), fine veneers and inlay, the most desirable. Turned legs (even with oval top) always less popular than square.

TABLES: DRUM OR RENT

About

1790-1860

Small mahogany Regency drum table, about 1810.

A mostly circular table with a frieze of drawers, which traditionally stood in the hall or library of grand houses where it was used to store details of estate business and the records of rents paid by tenants (hence its name). Later it became simply a gentleman's writing-table.

STYLE AND APPEARANCE

Generally circular, though occasionally hexagonal or octagonal, tops, slightly overhanging a frieze of mostly four drawers, with either dummy drawers, false books, or open bookshelves, between. Drawers sometimes wedge-shaped inside. On true rent tables, drawers often inlaid or inscribed with initials, numbers or alphabetically arranged letters.

Tops usually inset with leather writing-surface; occasionally central lidded compartment for inkwells, pens, and so on.

Majority have central turned pillar support with three or four splayed or scrolled legs ending in castors. Legs often reeded; generally kneed after 1810. Some have square, cupboard base with plinth or carved paw feet. After about 1820, concave-sided platform bases with three, sometimes four, paw, scroll or bun feet increasingly common. Occasionally four-column support instead of single pillar.

MATERIALS

Mahogany, rosewood; oak, elm (or both together) in mid-19thC. Sometimes beech stained and grained to simulate rosewood during Regency. Pine or cheap Honduras mahogany for carcases with oak or mahogany for drawer linings.

CONSTRUCTION

Standard methods employed. Usually solid bases with veneer tops. Top rotates on large central pivot. Veneer surrounding leather cross-grained; if straight, right across, then leather late addition.

Popularly reproduced after 1945, but smaller in size. Original examples were generally large, sometimes over 6 feet/1.8 m in diameter. Check drawer construction and thickness of veneers for authenticity.

DECORATION

Little decoration on earliest examples; sometimes inlaid stringing, simple cockbeading around drawers. Gadrooning, simple fluting and reeding, and other narrow, carved mouldings common around top and lower edges of frieze after 1820; also bolder carving on bases. Heavier carving and pendant finials around top common on mid-Victorian, multi-sided, Gothic pieces (judging by their numbers available today, a popular type).

Handles: Ring handles, sometimes lion's mask, with circular backplates. Turned wood or brass knobs.

FINISH

Stain or varnish followed by wax polish. French polish after 1820. Light-coloured stain on Victorian oak.

RELATIVE VALUES

Fairly scarce, therefore expensive; a pre-1800 date and pedestal base a great advantage, putting prices into five figures. Rosewood preferred to mahogany after 1800. Victorian Gothic recently more popular than before; prices presently rising disproportionately to others.

TABLES: LIBRARY

About

1790-1900

Late Regency library table, about 1835.

Simple, free-standing, rectangular-topped tables with a single frieze of drawers. Mostly intended for gentlemen's use in the study or library.

STYLE AND APPEARANCE

Either very simple and large in size, with rectangular top and frieze drawers (usually combined with dummy drawers), supported on four, straight, tapering, generally square, but occasionally turned, legs, ending in castors. Tops of legs (forming stiles of underframe) stand proud of rails. Inset leather top.

Or (more commonly like a sofa table without the flaps (see **SOFA TABLES, p.181**). Top usually, but not invariably, with inset leather writing-surface. After about 1820, frieze drawer sometimes absent.

REPRODUCTIONS

Cheap mahogany or stained deal versions with cloth tops, machine-turned legs and wooden knobs, were mass-produced for office use in later 19thC. Finer quality 'Sheraton' reproductions were made by the Edwardians; these are usually identified by yellow cross-banding on drawer fronts.

MATERIALS

Mahogany, rosewood; oak and walnut for Victorian pieces. Sometimes stained beech or pine (simulating mahogany) for very cheap versions. Pine or cheap Honduras mahogany for carcases when veneered, with pine or mahogany for drawer linings.

CONSTRUCTION

Standard methods employed.

DECORATION

Some restrained inlay of stringing lines on earliest pieces. Carving on standards of trestle type and around top more common and increasingly bold from about 1820 onwards. Fashionable pieces have turning on columnar standards and stretchers from about 1840.

Handles: Brass ring handles with circular bookplates or turned wooden or brass knobs.

FINISH

Stain or varnish followed by wax polish. French polish after 1820. Light-coloured stain on Victorian oak.

RELATIVE VALUES

Once again prices well into four figures; the best pieces in five. Only the cheapest Victorian office tables for less.

ADDITIONAL TYPES

Also designed for gentlemen's studies and libraries were:

Large architect's tables (fashionable about 1745-1775), in which the front slides forward to provide a working surface, and the top – usually with a bookrest moulding – rises at an angle to support ledgers.

Artist's tables, like a smaller version of the above, with a hinged, rising bookrest.

Smaller reading stands, with similar bookrest tops and various slides, supported on a central pillar on three legs.

All three types often have adjustable candle slides or brass candle branches.

TABLE: WORK (INCLUDING TEA-POYS)

About

1775-1880

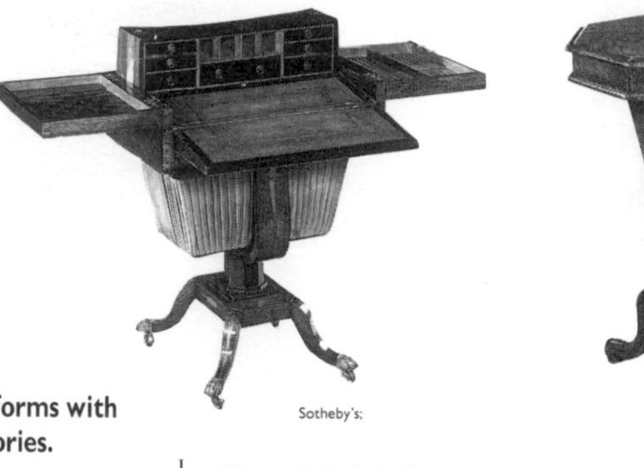

Sotheby's;

Bonhams

***Above left**, late-Regency rosewood work-cum-writing table; **above right**, distinctive Victorian cone-shaped work table, about 1870.*

Popular pieces made in a variety of forms with interior fitments for sewing accessories. Sometimes double as games tables.

STYLE AND APPEARANCE

Majority have square or rectangular tops, with small, real or dummy drawers below. Sometimes bag of pleated or gathered silk, sliding forwards on a frame for access. Earliest supported on square, tapering legs with narrow stretchers; followed after 1800 by either turned legs (without stretchers), trestle supports with lyre or scroll ends, or single pedestal with splayed legs. Lower, concave-sided plinth base with scroll, paw or bun feet, from about 1820, soon joined by turned column end standards after 1830. Short, scrolling legs and supports increasingly common after 1850; also distinctive cone-shaped table with circular top and short cabriole legs.

Can also have:

- **side flaps** supported on fly brackets
- **slide(s)** inlaid with games board(s)
- **hinged top** supported on ratchet system providing bookrest
- **double top** (as a card table) swivelling to provide games surface
- **extra wings** at side (during Regency) with brass galleries.

Christie's

Victorian walnut work table, about 1850.

MATERIALS

Satinwood, rosewood, mahogany, walnut.

CONSTRUCTION

Standard methods employed. Work-bags seldom original, often missing altogether.

DECORATION

Fine stringing and inlay before 1800; then ebony or (after 1810) brass inlay of classical design. Many Victorian pieces with burr veneers; sometimes inlay or marquetry of floral or Renaissance-inspired design.

Handles: Generally brass or wood knobs.

FINISH

Varnish or stain followed by wax polish. French polish after 1820.

RELATIVE VALUES

Price related to complexity of design, presence of decoration, and original interior fittings. The best definitely in four figures, but many still in three. Most border the line between the two. Regency lyre-end supports by far the most desirable.

TEA-POYS

Very similar in appearance, but with a lockable lidded wooden box above the pedestal base, are tea-poys (about 1800-1860), large tea caddies, usually containing two small caddies and two glass bowls, one for sugar and one for mixing the leaves. Not common objects and expensive considering their lack of usefulness.

TABLES: SOFA

About

1790-1840

Sotheby's

Regency rosewood brass inlaid sofa table, about 1815.

A rather smart table for use while sitting on a sofa. The drawer may be fitted with compartments for gaming counters or cards. Less elegant variations were made throughout the Victorian period. Widely reproduced during the past 40 years.

STYLE AND APPEARANCE

On all types, a rectangular top with hinged, D-shaped flaps. A pair of full-depth drawers backed by dummy drawer fronts; usually one opening on either side, sometimes both on same side. Thick sides of underframe (see **CONSTRUCTION**, below) usually had a decorative motif.

The base was one of two types:

Trestle type, with standard end; about 1790 onwards: Standards with flat or turned uprights, usually with splayed or scrolled legs ending in castors. Early examples may have high, arched stretcher – or no stretcher at all – enabling table to be pulled right over end of sofa or day-bed. Some (and later) pieces with straight, turned stretcher. Lyre ends – sometimes with brass strings – fashionable from about 1815. (Beware post-war reproductions of these – check construction carefully.)

Plinth type: About 1810 onwards. One, two or four pillar supports on flat plinth with four splayed (sometimes kneed, later scrolled) legs, ending in castors (often cast paw). Alternatively semi-circular band support.

Sotheby's

Regency lyre-end sofa table, about 1815.

MATERIALS

Satinwood, rosewood, mahogany; occasionally walnut. Sometimes exotic woods such as amboyna, zebrawood. Birch as a cheap substitute for satinwood in late Victorian times. Pine or cheap Honduras mahogany for carcases; oak or mahogany for drawer linings.

CONSTRUCTION

Standard methods employed. Mortise-and-tenon joints to underframe; sides of frame thicker than average (to take weight of flaps). Top screwed from underneath. Flaps supported on fly brackets. Undersides veneered. Hinged with rule joints (to allow moulding to continue all around top. Grain of top *always* across width, never along length.

DECORATION

Mostly figuring of veneers; wide cross-banding on edges, continuing around flaps. Some inlay, mostly stringing lines, on drawers, occasionally on top too. Some restrained ebony or brass inlay during Regency period.

Handles: Brass or finely turned wood knobs; occasionally lion's mask or other ring handles.

FINISH

Varnish or stain followed by wax polish. French polish from about 1820.

RELATIVE VALUES

Despite being fairly numerous, always in demand; the best quality, early Regency pieces, with fine, preferably exotic, veneers, can fetch enormous sums, well into five figures. Even the simplest mahogany (the least desirable) are in four.

TABLES: SUTHERLAND

About

1850-1900

Christie's

Victorian walnut Sutherland table, about 1865.

A small, narrow occasional version of the gate-leg dining-table (see p. 163). Despite being very practical, never popular. Reputedly named after Queen Victoria's Mistress of the Robes, the Duchess of Sutherland.

STYLE AND APPEARANCE

Cheval base with one or two turned uprights to the side joined by turned stretcher. Splayed, often scrolled, feet, always on castors. Sometimes pendant finial under ends. A narrow top (maximum width 9 inches/22.5 cm) with deep hinged flaps, forming circular or oval (only occasionally rectangular) top when open. Flaps supported on two single legs, also turned but usually different and thinner than side supports. Cheap examples may have plain, square-sectioned legs and stretchers. Country versions barley-twist columns (like a 17thC gate-leg dining-table).

Christie's

Simple square-flap mahogany version, about 1880.

MATERIALS

Mahogany, walnut, oak, yew, elm, fruitwoods, either alone, or in combinations, for country versions. Generally solid timbers; occasionally maple veneered on pine for cheap, late pieces.

CONSTRUCTION

Gate-legs swing on wooden hinges and generally slot into a groove in the underframe when closed. Flaps were usually supported on more than two hinges (to support weight), with rule joints to allow moulding to continue all round top.

MARRIAGES

Sutherland tables are occasionally found made up from an adapted towel horse or from staircase balusters, with a new top and underframe. Look underneath for new timber and/or screws, and for plugged holes on inner sides of supports. The under-side of an old top will show uneven natural dirt stains caused by frequent handling around the edges; a faked one may show liquid stain.

DECORATION

Some inlay, usually around borders, occasionally in centre too. Fine stringing lines, formalised neo-classical patterns or foliage.

FINISH

French polish; sometimes stain – in natural colours (to simulate hardwoods) or black (i.e. ebonised).

RELATIVE VALUES

Cheap as tables go because generally unpopular. Prices for most in the lower part of the three-figure range. An early date and finely figured timber are an advantage.

WARDROBES AND CLOTHES (OR LINEN) PRESSES

About

1750-1940

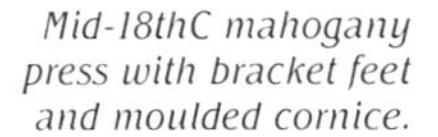

Mid-18thC mahogany press with bracket feet and moulded cornice.

A cabinet-made cupboard – uasually with drawers below – designed for the storage of the clothes. The wardrobe, which included a space for hanging items vertically, began to replace the press, with its horizontal sliding trays, in about 1850. Although Sheraton had designed a cupboard with a rail and 'arms to hang clothes on' in the 1790s, rails and coat-hangers – or shoulders as they were first called – did not appear until about 1870, and were not used universally until after 1900.

STYLE AND APPEARANCE

Presses: About 1750-1850. Tall, upper cupboard section with shelves on sliding trays (with rounded tops to front) enclosed by two panelled doors. Moulded cornice above, occasionally pedimented; sometimes a decorative frieze. Narrow moulding on right-hand door to conceal join.

The top sits within waist moulding on a chest of two or three layers of drawers, the top layer having one long or two short drawers; occasionally a secretaire drawer. Usually straight, sometimes serpentine-fronted.

Bracket feet (often ogee) to about 1780, then fashionably swept feet or a plinth base. Top and/or bottom may have canted corners.

From about 1790, presses were sometimes made with flanking wings, generally set back to form a breakfront. One of these usually contains further drawers, and the other a cupboard.

Presses were still made after 1850, but in dwindling numbers. Sometimes the upper interior was divided into two; shelves on one side, hanging space on the other.

Wardrobes: About 1850-1915. Generally made as one piece with one long drawer or a pair of deep drawers below, and a two- or three-door cupboard above. Sometimes there is a central door only, flanked by fixed panels (usually of equal size) fronting a large interior hanging space. From about 1870, the central door was fashionably fitted with a full-length mirror. The cupboard was fitted inside with wooden knobs, metal hooks and/or (after 1870) a brass rail. Fitted shoe and tie racks were introduced around 1900.

Late-18thC wardrobe with wings.

Christie's

***Above**, design for 18thC open wardrobe showing sliding trays.*

Elaborately inlaid late 19thC wardrobe.

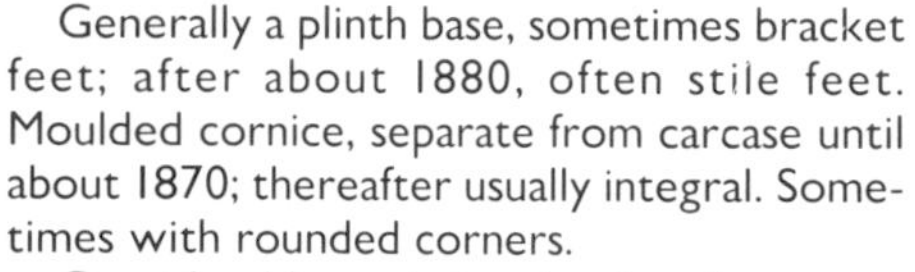

Generally a plinth base, sometimes bracket feet; after about 1880, often stile feet. Moulded cornice, separate from carcase until about 1870; thereafter usually integral. Sometimes with rounded corners.

Considerable variation in size, but many very large. Those forming part of suites (particularly cheap models) can be small.

Many pieces plain; some followed prevailing historic revivals and other styles.

MATERIALS

Principally mahogany, sometimes walnut, occasionally cedar. Birch or satin walnut in late-19thC: pine stained to simulate mahogany on cheap pieces. Pine or beech when japanned (though rare); pine or Honduras mahogany for carcases; oak or mahogany or cedar for drawer linings and interior shelves or trays.

CONSTRUCTION

Standard methods employed for carcases and drawers (see CHESTS OF DRAWERS, p. 93. and BOOKCASES, p. 37).

Sliding trays move on runners fitted to carcase. These slot into grooves cut in tray sides. Trays sometimes removed to make a more useful hanging wardrobe, but runners still in place.

Presses, particularly those with a secretaire drawer, were often converted to a more valuable bookcase. Large breakfronts sometimes reduced to single size by removal of wings: look for new timber, joints and staining on sides and back.

DECORATION

Presses generally plain with limited decorative effects achieved by figuring of veneers.

Some restrained carving or inlay on Victorian wardrobes denoting individual style; for example, crenellated cornice on Victorian Gothic, inlaid urns and swags on neo-classical. Pine and extensive marquetry of stylized foliage on art nouveau pieces around 1900.

Handles: Standard for their day, but generally the simplest form. Wooden knobs from about 1820. Right-hand surface cupboard opened with keys; skeleton escutcheon to about 1870, then surface-mounted metal. Left-hand side secured with sliding bolts. Small metal drop handles common from 1880.

FINISH

Stain or varnish followed by wax polish. Very occasionally, japanning (but only if part of a suite). French polish from about 1820. Cheap Victorian pine stained to simulate mahogany; sometimes paint (white or green) from about 1890.

RELATIVE VALUES

Value of presses is low when compared with other contemporary furniture of similar standard, mostly because their sliding trays are largely obsolete. Those with cupboards rather than drawers in the base are the least desirable. Prices for good quality versions in four figures, but lesser quality, and Victorian wardrobes, usually in three; art nouveau marquetry is the only common exception to the rule.

WHAT-NOTS OR ETAGERES

About

1790-1900

Bonhams

George III mahogany what-not, about 1800.

An arrangement of open shelves, usually, though not invariably, on castors. Designed to display books and bric-à-brac. Often made in pairs, but seldom found so now. Not often reproduced.

STYLE AND APPEARANCE

Most have four, sometimes three, shelves. Generally rectangular, but can be square. Victorian corner versions (about 1855 onwards) with rounded or shaped outer edge.

Many what-nots have a single drawer, usually under the lowest shelf, but on three-shelf versions, in the centre.

Uprights are formed as turned columns, often vase-shaped but during Regency straight and collared. Some double-collared to simulate bamboo. Victorian versions generally heavier than Georgian with heavier and broader legs. Sometimes spiral-turned.

Regency examples occasionally have brass gallery around top; after 1840 fretwork or spindled galleries more common, with turned finials at corners.

Christie's

Mid-Victorian walnut corner what-not, about 1855.

MATERIALS

Mahogany, rosewood, walnut. After 1880 occasionally bamboo.

CONSTRUCTION

Uprights can be set individually between the shelves, dowelling into their top and undersides. Alternatively can be continuous with legs, the sides of the shelves rebated into the blocks between the turnings.

DECORATION

Principally turning of uprights. Fretwork on Victorian pieces; usually naturalistic. Applied as galleries, aprons, brackets.

Victorian walnut examples sometimes have burr veneered shelves. Bamboo pieces can have lacquer or grass matting surfaces.

Small, turned knob handles on drawers.

FINISH

Polish.

RELATIVE VALUES

One of the few pieces of good quality furniture which can still usually be found for a three-figure sum. Elegant Georgian examples obviously more valuable than fussier and heavier Victorian versions.

WINE COOLERS (OR CISTERNS) AND CELLARETS

About

1750-1830

Containers to hold wine bottles in the dining-room. The terms are inter-changeable today although coolers were specifically for cooling wine before consumption, while cellarets were for short-term storage. Both were lead-lined and many cellarets were used for cooling too. Only briefly fashionable, as by 1800 both facilities were contained in the newly developed and rapidly universal sideboard. Valuable items in relation to their cost of manufacture, and widely reproduced and faked.

STYLE AND APPEARANCE

Coolers (surviving examples from about 1750-1800). Open-topped; oval or circular. The most fashionable construction was as a barrel, i.e. staved and bound with broad, flat, brass bands, but with straight, tapering sides. Usually a simple moulded rim and brass carrying handles at ends; sometimes no rim and one stave on either side raised above the others and pierced with a handle. Mounted on a stand with straight, slightly splayed legs. Sometimes a drainage tap fitted at base.

Cellarets (about 1760-1800): Lidded boxes with lock and key. Oval, circular, square, octagonal or hexagonal. Generally fixed tapering legs fitted with castors to enable easy movement from under the side-table or 'board' where they were kept. Plainly veneered but sometimes still brass-bound (for decorative effect only). Brass carrying handles on most.

Sarcophagus cellarets (about 1790-1830): Literally of sarcophagus form, a popular Regency Grecian shape for caddies, boxes. Some with raised lids, occasionally with chamfered sides. Short splayed legs or carved lion's-paw feet; occasionally bracket. Paw feet often heavier during late Regency period (post-1830). Usually designed to stand underneath a pedestal sideboard, and therefore of complementary appearance. Suites seldom found still together today.

MATERIALS

Mahogany; occasional satinwood, rosewood.

CONSTRUCTION

Staved pieces literally formed of solid mahogany staves. Later versions sometimes strengthened with inner bands of steel.

Quality of brass varied; latten (hammered brass) until about 1770; thereafter thinner and smoother rolled brass increasingly common; universal after about 1790.

DECORATION

Decorative veneers, some with restrained inlay (often stringing lines) or cross-banding. Carrying handles on all types popularly of lion's mask form.

Just a few with low-relief neo-classical carving such as paterae, swags, ribbons.

FINISH

Polish.

RELATIVE VALUES

Prices for those raised on legs generally around the middle of the four-figure range; sarcophagus types usually about half the price, even when of equal quality.

Sotheby's

__Above__, an open-topped oval cellaret, about 1780; __right__, hexagonal brass-bound cooler, about 1790.

Bonhams

Christie's

__Above__, Regency cooler of classical sarcohpagus form.

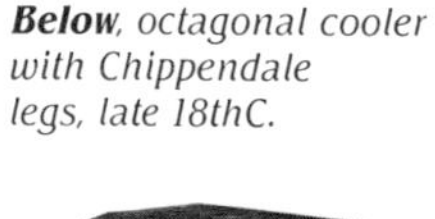

__Below__, octagonal cooler with Chippendale legs, late 18thC.

Sotheby's

EUROPEAN

GUIDE TO PERIODS AND STYLES: EUROPEAN

The major European furniture styles have all been related to other arts, fine and applied, and especially to architecture. Most were international, but subject to national and regional variations. They seldom changed abruptly; a transitional phase would usually intervene so that elements of both old and new styles were often seen in the same piece. Provincial and country work reflected these changes, but only after a delay – sometimes a lengthy one – while perpetuating both local traditions and styles that had, years before, been fashionable in the cities; and even there, revivals of earlier styles were promoted from time to time.

These factors, not to mention the modern reproductions and downright fakes that abound, make it unsafe to assume that any given piece is necessarily of the period its style implies. Familiarity with styles, important though it is, should ideally go hand in hand with a knowledge of the materials and methods in use at different times and in different places.

ANCIENT AND CLASSICAL

The private collector is unlikely to acquire an authentic piece of furniture from the ancient civilizations, but can hardly escape becoming the owner of something that derives from them; so it is helpful to have an understanding of the sources.

The Egyptians were making sophisticated furniture in about 3,000 BC and, by 1,500 BC, were employing mortise-and-tenon, dovetail and mitred joints to produce beds, tables, stools (including an X-shaped folding type), chairs and chests – many decorated with carving, veneering, inlay and painting. These methods were taken over and developed by the Greeks, Etruscans and Romans. Turning on the lathe, and casting in bronze and silver were added to the techniques of furniture-making.

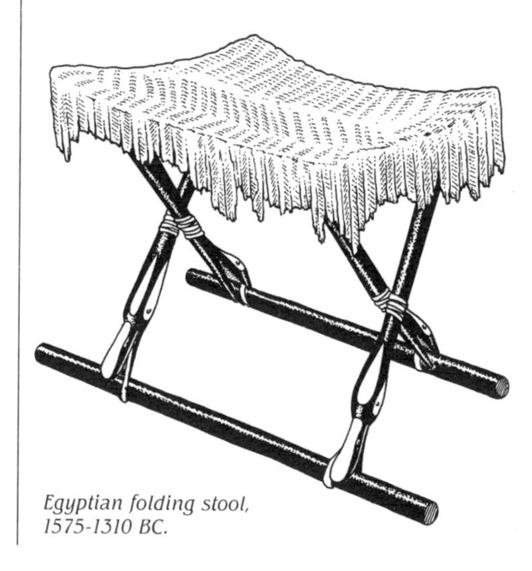

Egyptian folding stool, 1575-1310 BC.

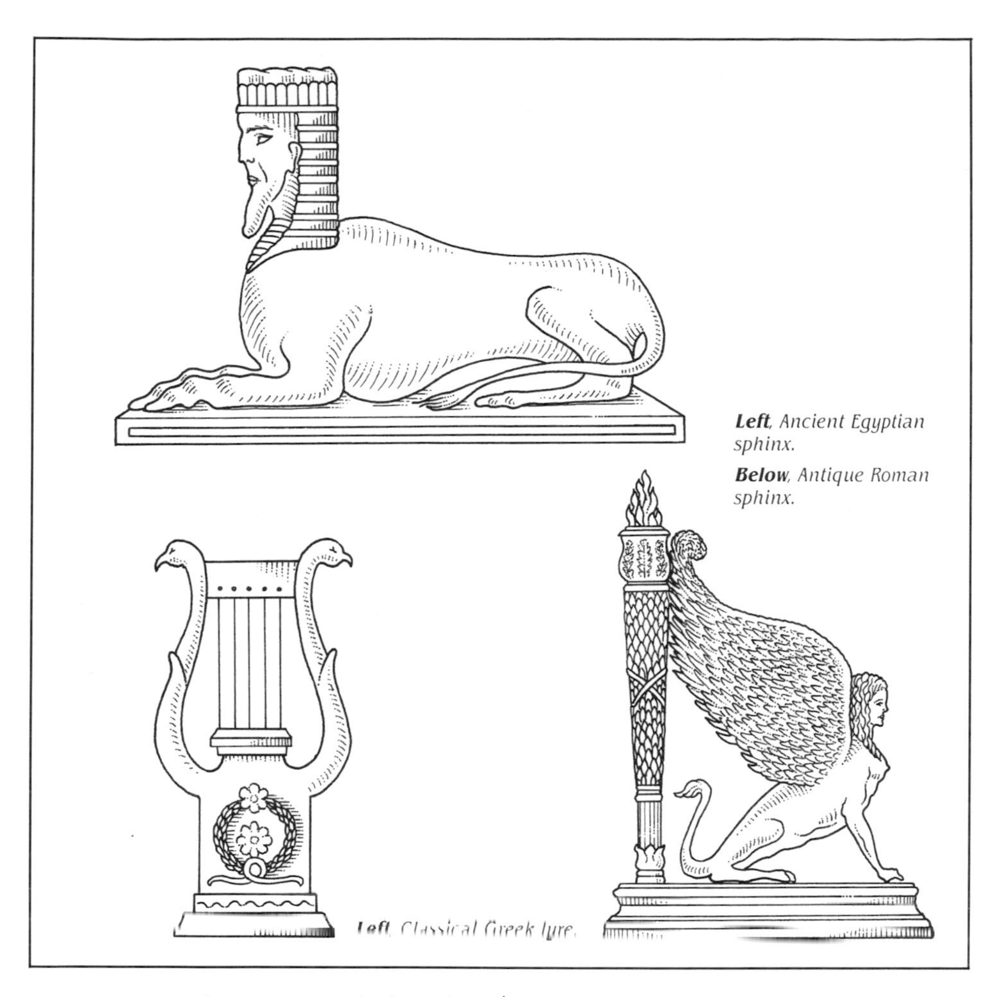

***Left**, Ancient Egyptian sphinx.*

***Below**, Antique Roman sphinx.*

***Left**, Classical Greek lyre.*

A repertoire of ornament was built up that included animal forms for legs and feet (lion paws, hooves); sphinxes and other mythological beasts; human and semi-human figures such as caryatids, used as decorative supports; leafy scrolls, wreaths and floral motifs including anthemion (honeysuckle) and acanthus; columns and pediments based on classical architecture.

Although the fall of the Roman Empire in the west in the 5thC AD resulted in the decay of furniture-making skills, not all were lost, and from the Renaissance onwards, their rediscovery led to a whole series of classical revivals, from the 16th to the 19thC.

BYZANTINE

Many of the old skills were retained in Constantinople, capital of the Eastern Empire, built in the 4thC AD near the Hellenic city of

***Below**, Byzantine carved ivory throne, 6thC.*

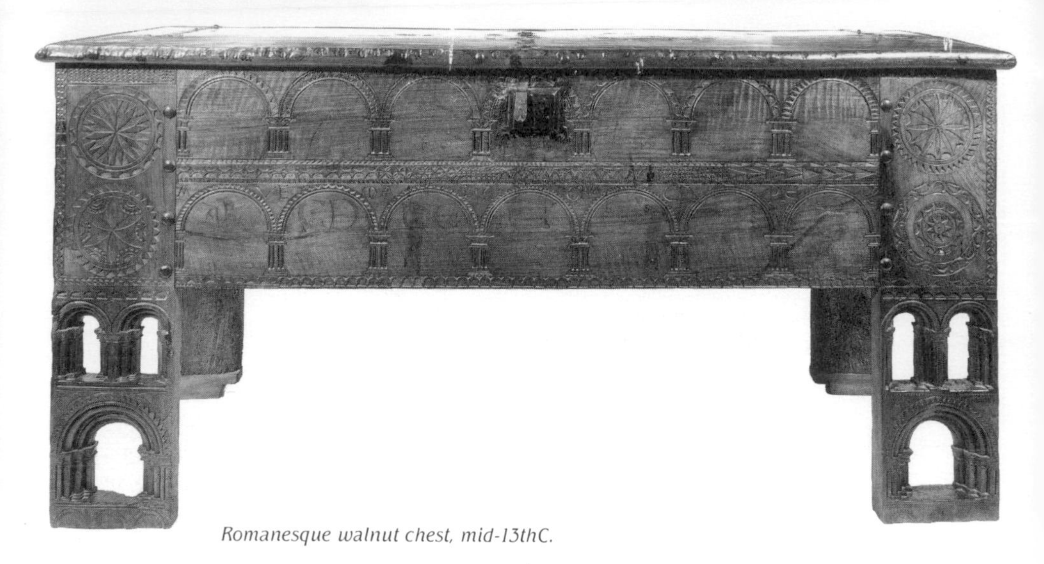

Romanesque walnut chest, mid-13thC.

Byzantium. To them were added those of Middle Eastern craftsmen who were adept at the intricate carving of religious figures, plants and animals, on ivory panels set in a frame, for chests and box-seated chairs. Similar subjects were painted on large wooden cupboards.

ROMANESQUE

Painted cupboards were among the furniture made in Italy in the early Middle Ages, probably by itinerant Byzantine craftsmen. The northern invaders also grafted their own ideas of decoration on to residual Roman types, and a composite style emerged which, by the 11thC, had slowly spread to France, the Netherlands and Scandinavia. The furniture, whether meant for churches or castles, was mainly ecclesiastic in flavour; box-seated chairs, functional stools on turned legs, carved ones that served as thrones and status symbols, massive chests carved with rounded arches supported by squat classical columns – a form of decoration that continued until after 1600.

GOTHIC

This style owed nothing to the Goths, who had been defeated 400 years before the first 'Gothic' church was begun in France in 1140. Another 400 years later, the term was used by an enthusiast for a new style (**Renaissance**), to decry medieval architecture. By the 15thC, the Gothic style had spread throughout most of Europe, surviving in some areas until the 16thC. Main features: pointed arches, tracery, carving of animals and foliage, panels carved to represent the folds of parchment or linen ('linenfold'), wrought-iron scrolls on chests, coats-of-arms. Much was painted in bright, heraldic colours. Main types: trestle tables, lidded chests, slab-ended stools, box-seated and X-framed chairs, posted beds.

V&A

RENAISSANCE

A revival of interest in ancient culture began in Italy in the 14thC, grew over the next hundred years into the Renaissance in Florence and spread widely. Little was known of Greek or Roman furniture, but decorative features from classical architecture were grafted on to existing forms, and new ones created. Carved, painted and gilded decoration on 15thC *cassoni* (lidded chests) bore coats-of-arms and depicted Olympian gods and goddesses as well as Christian saints; 16thC examples were shaped to resemble the Roman sarcophagus.

Columns and pilasters were applied to the credenza (low cupboard). Tables, copied from fragments of Roman originals in marble, were carved with animal subjects. Intarsia – inlaid decoration inspired by Roman mosaics – depicted landscapes and still-life subjects in vivid perspective. Carved strapwork – a flat, continuous geometric pattern – was popular in northern Europe.

Carved walnut meuble-à-deux-corps, 16thC.

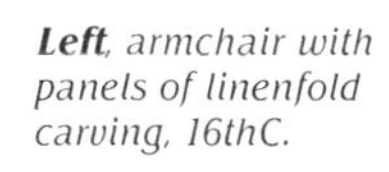

***Left**, armchair with panels of linenfold carving, 16thC.*

***Right**, 16thC carved caryatid with grotesque mask.*

The Mannerist movement in art led to the carving of the nude or semi-nude human figure with elongated, distorted limbs; an extreme version of this style, known as Auricular, involved demonic caryatids on bed-heads, and grotesque masks with huge ears as chair-backs.

Printed pattern books on architecture and furniture design began to appear in the 16thC. Works by Serlio, Vredeman de Vries, Flötner, Sambin, Du Cerceau and the German master known only as 'H.S.' were widely circulated and used by craftsmen internationally.

Some countries, however, developed very individual versions of the Renaissance style. Spain, at the height of its power and wealth in the 16thC, embellished furniture with silver from the New World, and abstract decoration derived from the Islamic culture of the resident Moors. Doors and drawer-fronts were

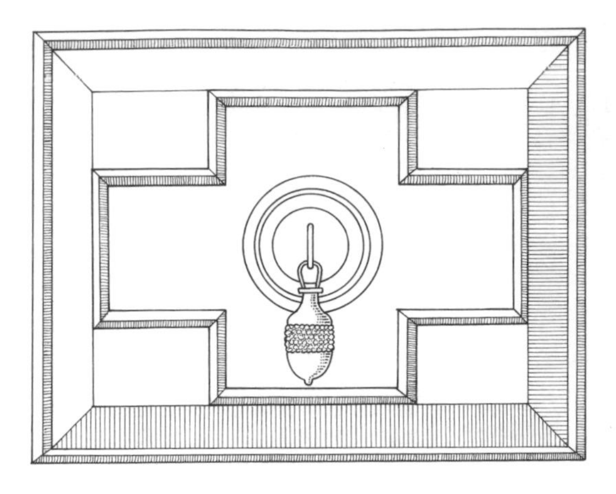

Drawer front with geometrical mouldings, fashionable throughout the 17thC.

decorated with mouldings arranged in geometric patterns – a fashion that spread to the Spanish Netherlands and thence to much of Europe in the 17thC, becoming a feature of many pieces regarded now as baroque.

BAROQUE

The word baroque means 'irregular pearl', and many pieces in the style are partly asymmetrical, being the work of sculptors such as Brustolon who carved life-size human figures in the round as supports for console tables and candle-stands. Most other pieces, however, were symmetrical, formal and heavy-looking.

The style first developed in Italy early in the 17thC, using classical architecture as a basis but adding bold, restless curves and rich decoration – gilding, painting in imitation of oriental lacquer, veneering and marquetry (inlaying into veneers) in exotic woods, *pietre dure* (hardstones) and metal.

In France, during the reign of Louis XIV (effectively 1600-1715), the royal cabinet-maker A.C. Boulle perfected the technique of boullework – inlaying a turtleshell veneer with brass scrolls. He also created new shapes, e.g. the commode (chest) with curved outline.

Christie's

Louis XIV boulle bureau Mazarin, about 1690.

Christie's

Flemish walnut upholstered armchair, late-17thC.

Chairs and settees were richly upholstered. Large mirrors, previously a Venetian monopoly, were produced in France for the Palace of Versailles which was imitated by the rich all over Europe. Those with less money to spend adopted a diluted version of the baroque style – one that involved (in Portugal especially) much bold turning on the lathe to produce baluster, bulbous and spiral profiles.

Right, *Louis XV marquetry bureau de dame, about 1750.*

ROCOCO

Known in France, where it originated, as rocaille, the rococo ('rock and shell') style was a reaction to the pompous, macho, Louis XIV version of baroque. Soon after the king's death in 1715, rococo was created by Meissonier and Pineau, and developed during the Rgence when Louis XV was still a child. The cabinet-maker Cressent perfected the bombé ('blown up') commode (see **CHESTS OF DRAWERS *p. 234-246***). The cabriole leg, with the delicate curve of an elongated 'S', replaced the turned or scrolled legs of the baroque. Surfaces were decorated with floral marquetry or lacquer. Carving and ormolu (gilded bronze) mounts were often asymmetrical, especially in some areas (Spain, Scandinavia) where the style was adopted almost too eagerly; but at its best, it was charming.

The Paris guild of cabinet-makers and joiners enforced quality control on its members who, from 1743 until the Revolution in 1789, had to stamp their products with their names. Foreign craftsmen and makers to the Crown were excused, so – contrary to popular belief – not all fine French furniture is signed.

Christie's

NEO-CLASSICAL

The rococo style was replaced in France several years before the death of Louis XV in 1774 by what is now known as the Louis XVI style. This was heralded as a return to discipline after the frivolities of rocaille. Shapes changed from sinuous curves to rectilinear, circular or oval outlines. Cabriole legs gradually gave way to straight ones, and bombé carcases were soon outmoded in Paris, though remaining popular in Holland and Sweden.

Once again, designers returned to the ancient civilizations for their inspiration. In the late 1750s, a cosmopolitan group mingled in Rome, Pompeii and Herculaneum, where recent excavations aroused fresh enthusiasm for classical ideas, although little more was known about ancient furniture itself than had been familiar to the men of the Renaissance. In the first phase of neo-classicism, it was only the ornament on neo-classical furniture – urns, rams' heads, masks and so forth – that owed much to antiquity.

Marquetry was as popular as ever, and although mythological figures were favourite subjects for it in Northern Italy, the French still liked their flowers, and many pieces were inset with Svres porcelain plaques painted with floral subjects. Some of the finest craftsmen in Paris were German, and one of the greatest – David Roentgen – supplied the Crown with furniture made in his Neuwied workshops. Famous for his marquetry, he was among the first to abandon it when fashion dictated a plainer style.

Louis XVI gilded fauteuil, about 1770-1780.

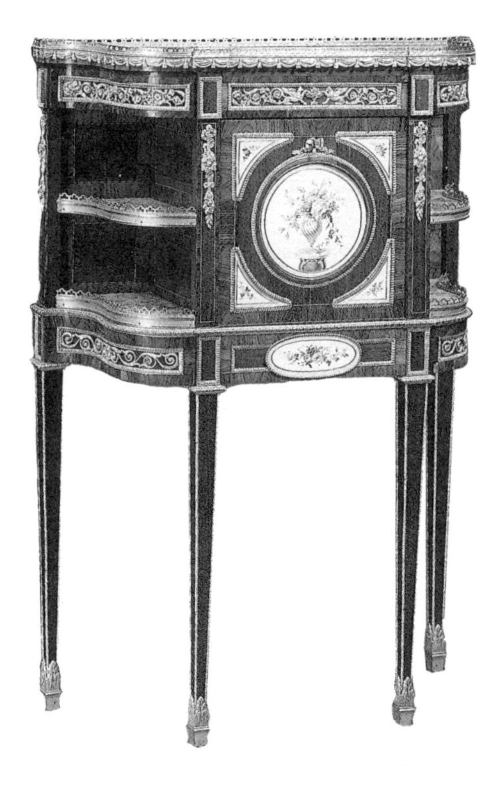

***Left**, kingwood secretaire incorporating Sèvres porcelain plaques, about 1780.*

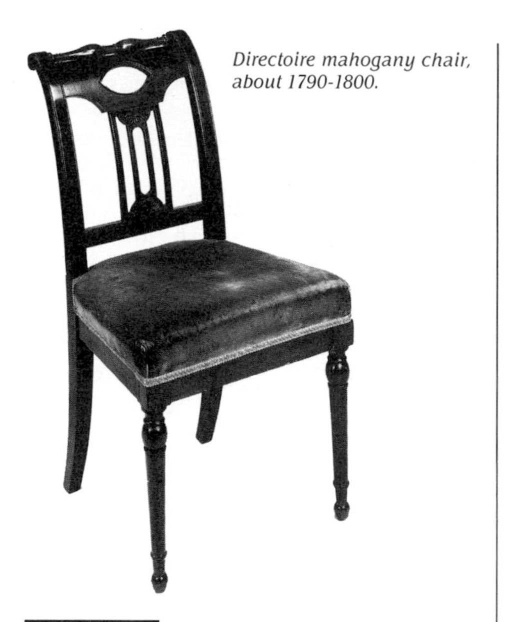

Directoire mahogany chair, about 1790-1800.

DIRECTOIRE

The first to attempt furniture based on ancient prototypes was the artist David, who copied couches and chairs from paintings on Greek vases and had them made for him, in about 1787, by the royal chairmaker, Jacob, an admirer of English furniture and the first major French craftsman to use solid mahogany – a wood that had been fashionable in England for 50 years. The severe, no-nonsense style continued after the Revolution in 1789, under the short-lived Directoire.

EMPIRE

A partial return to grandeur accompanied a new phase of neo-classicism in the early years of the 19thC, when Percier and Fontaine dressed it up with eagles, laurel wreaths and other imperial symbols to echo the glory of the Emperor Napoleon, and added sphinxes to mark his Egyptian campaign. These motifs were cast in bronze and applied to pieces of austere shape, some based on Roman or Greek prototypes. Great play was made with black and gold paint, and fabrics striped like the tents of the armies. The style was imitated across Europe, even in countries at war with France, so that terms such as 'Russian Empire' are sometimes used misleadingly to describe the French Empire style as it was interpreted elsewhere. In Paris, 10,000 hands were employed in the furniture trade, the Jacob family being the leading manufacturers.

Empire X-frame stool, about 1810.

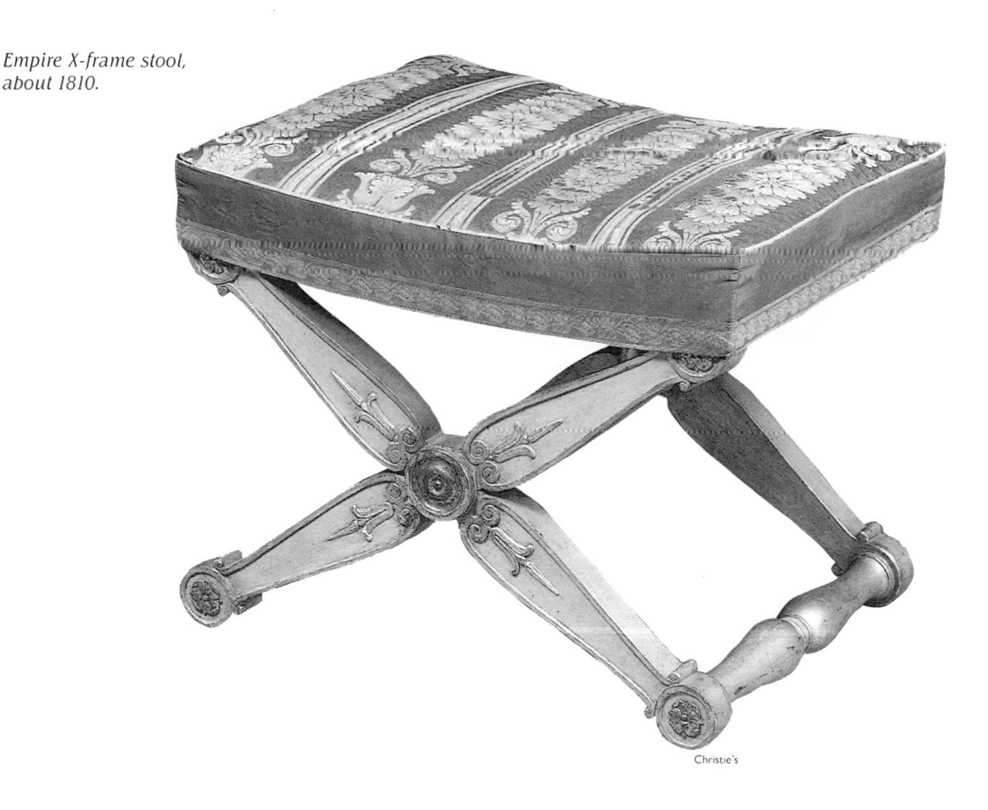

Christie's

BIEDERMEIER

This term should be confined to Austrian, German and Scandinavian furniture of 1815-50, but many pieces – Russian (Alexander I), Polish (the 'Simmler' style) and French (Charles X) – strongly resemble early Biedermeier, which followed the neo-classical principles of the Empire, but expressed them more soberly.

Light-coloured woods were favoured. Comfortable sofas with swan-neck arms, hefty fall-front secretaires, lyre-backed chairs and circular dining tables on central supports, were typical items designed mainly for the middle-class which the name originally satirised, though the most notable designer was the Berlin court architect Schinkel. The biggest manufacturers in Vienna were Danhauser from 1804 to 1838, and Thonet, who set up a factory in 1842 for making bentwood furniture.

'Late Biedermeier' and 'Second Empire' are terms used to describe the European bourgeois home in the later 19thC: over-stuffed seating and over-decorated woodwork in a medley of styles based on romantic revivals. In France, good copies of 18thC pieces were made, while a few designers – notably Viollet-le-Duc – attempted scholarly re-creations of medieval types. In Italy, magnificent pastiches in the Renaissance and baroque styles were produced.

ART NOUVEAU

This style takes its name from Bing's shop in Paris which, in the 1890s, sold both oriental imports and new, revolutionary furniture.

Plant-form inspired the 'whiplash line' and asymmetrical shapes reminiscent of the rococo. Marquetry decoration was used by Majorelle and Gallé of Nancy. Other leading designers were Endell of Germany and the Belgian, van de Velde. 'Viking' furniture was dreamed up in Scandinavia, while Munthe's off-beat chairs in black and white, based on peasant patterns, anticipated Art Deco.

French art nouveau cabinet, with marquetry decoration, about 1900.

Charles X dressing-table, about 1830.

Biedermeier birchwood sofa, about 1820.

Gerrit Rietveld Red and Blue chair, 1918.

MODERNIST

A reaction against art nouveau began in Vienna soon after 1900 and continued in Berlin with the setting up of workshops for producing good inexpensive furniture, using hand skills in association with machinery. During the 1914-18 war Rietveld worked in neutral Holland on angular chairs, put together without recourse to normal joinery, and painted in red, blue and yellow.

In the 1920s, the Bauhaus was set up in Germany, under the direction of Gropius, to create furniture suited to modern needs, to which Le Corbusier's concept of the home as a factory for living was first cousin.

ART DECO

Many people, however, still yearned for luxury. At an exhibition of decorative arts in Paris in 1925, Le Corbusier's display was in stark contrast to the lavish flavour of Ruhlmann's exhibits, which gave a new and very expensive twist to adaptations of 18thC design, using costly materials for items purporting to be functional.

Art Deco wrought-iron console table, 1920s.

Debased versions of jazzy Art Deco were soon being mass-produced, but there was much good, medium-range furniture made between the two world wars, especially that produced under Scandinavian influence. Plain and simple, modern but not ultra-modern, it owed – at least in spirit – as much to the Biedermeier tradition as to the Bauhaus and art nouveau.

Palisander wood card table and chairs, by Maurice Dufrene, 1930s.

BEDS

Before
1500

In the early Middle Ages, the bed was often no more than a shallow chest with curtains hung around it for privacy, in a room that served as living quarters. In colder areas, shutters took the place of drapes: 'shut beds' survived in peasant communities until the 19thC.

15thC bed with tester suspended from the ceiling.

STYLE AND APPEARANCE

Gothic (see **p. 190**): A French miniature of about 1400 shows a bedstead with a headboard of linenfold panelling; a tester (overhead canopy) has curtains hanging from it. Beside the bed is a baby's cradle on rockers with head and foot composed of turned spindles. In **Italy**, where the Gothic style was not so popular and the climate was warmer, the claustrophobic tester and curtains were used less often.

MATERIALS

Few early examples have survived, but local woods would have been used, typically oak in **France**, walnut or pine in **Italy**. The materials used for drapes varied, but were regarded as the most valuable part of the bed. The tester was panelled in wood or covered with cloth over a wooden framework, and suspended by cords from roof timbers.

DECORATION

In **France**, panels of headboard carved with linenfold or a heraldic device, and often painted. In **Italy**, less carving, more painting.

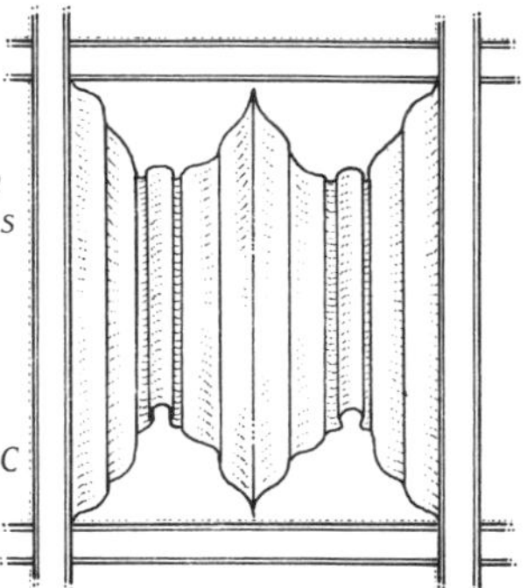

Panel carved in relief with 'linenfold' or 'parchment' pattern, of which endless variations occur. Used vertically on headboards and footboards of beds, northern Europe, late-15thC and 16thC, revived in 19thC.

FINISH

When not painted, wood was varnished or waxed.

CONSTRUCTION

Crude bed-frame jointed with mortise-and-tenon, strung with strips of leather for resilience. Panelled head and footboards.

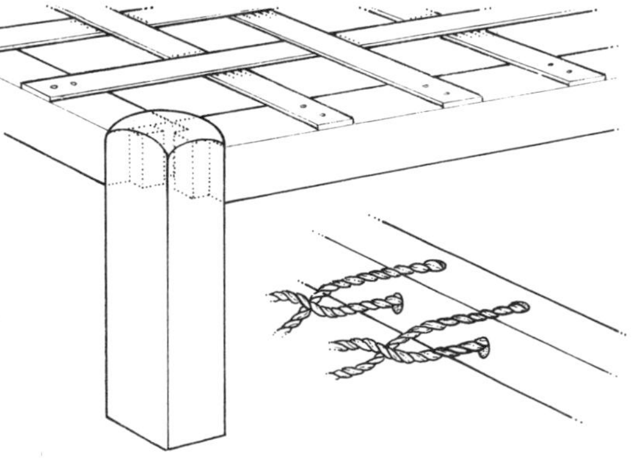

***Above right**, corner of a bedframe. Dotted lines indicate mortise-and-tenon joints; springing for mattress provided by strips of leather, interwoven and nailed to rails. **Right**, using similar construction, but alternative method of springing by threading cords through holes drilled at an angle in rails, and interweaving them. Both methods continued in use, in country areas especially, until the 19thC.*

BEDS

About

1500-1630

Engraved designs for bed by J.A. Du Cerceau, about 1560.

STYLE AND APPEARANCE

Renaissance (see **p. 191**): The four-poster bed is known from paintings to have existed in Venice 1490-1500. From then on, the influence of classical architecture is often evident in the capitals of the bedposts. Low beds, with headboards and footboards, were made with or without testers in some areas, **Italy** especially.

MATERIALS

Local timbers: Oak in **France**, **Germany**, **Netherlands**; walnut in **Italy**, **Spain**. The mattress, in **Scandinavia** and **Germany** especially, was often filled with feathers or down (eiderdown).

CONSTRUCTION

Early 'four-posters' – unlike later types so called – had four posts on pedestal bases, holding up a tester joined to them with tenons and secured by pegs, but easily dismantled. The bed itself was separate and similar to the Gothic type (**p. 190**). In the **Netherlands**, beds were sometimes built into the corner of a room, with a single post at the exposed angle and a headboard integral with the panelling of the walls.

DECORATION

Mythological figures in carved and painted decoration, carved strapwork in the Renaissance style (**p. 191**) lingering on in the **Netherlands** and **Germany** until well into the seventeen hundreds.

FINISH

Unpainted wood was oiled and waxed or varnished.

RELATIVE VALUES

Completely authentic examples of this period are very rare and expensive, and anything that appears to be going at bargain price is automatically suspect. Most of those that appear on the market are either downright reproductions made at any time from the early-19th century onwards, or are made up, using fragments taken from furniture (not necessarily beds) or interior woodwork.

Engraved design for bed by Vredeman de Vries, about 1580.

BEDS

About

1620-1730

Generally lavish and ornate, in keeping with a room where the aristocratic owner, while still in bed, received callers.

Italian carved and giltwood cradle, early-18thC.

STYLE AND APPEARANCE

Baroque: (see **p. 192**).

France: Little woodwork visible under hangings on posted beds. Another type, set sideways in an alcove, had head and foot of equal length.

Netherlands: Scrolled headboards on posted beds, drapes more elaborate after 1685 when the designer Daniel Marot (1663-1752), a Huguenot, fled France to serve under William of Orange.

Danish bed, about 1625-1650, with panelled headboard.

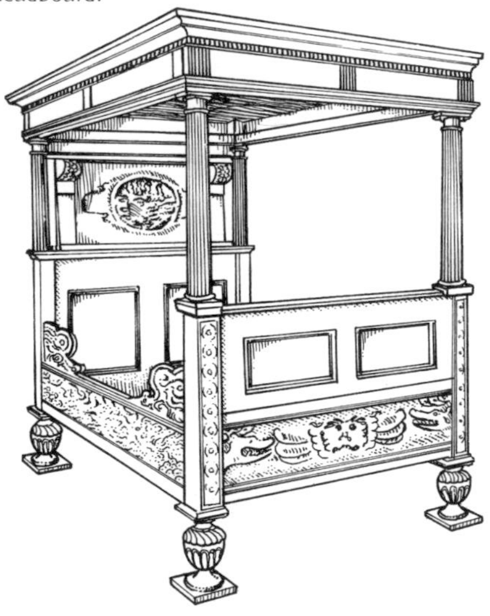

Germany: After 1650, magnificently upholstered beds in princely palaces; simpler, posted types for merchant classes.

Denmark: A popular type had four short posts rising from a box-like base.

Austria: State beds were kept in monasteries, ready for royal visits, for example one at St-Florian, carved with figures of captured Turks.

Italy: Except in Sicily, the posted bed was less popular than a tester canopy suspended from the ceiling.

Spain: Carved or turned posts, drapes not so heavy – some headboards of Portuguese type, composed of rows of arches.

Portugal: A posted bed (*cama de bilros*) consisted almost entirely of turned members, often spiral.

MATERIALS

Local timbers in country districts. Indigenous woods for frames hidden by drapes. For sophisticated work meant to be exposed, exotic hardwoods; for example, ebony from East Indies and jacaranda from New World. In **Sicily**, iron. **Italy** exported Genoa velvets and Lucca silks for use as drapes to most of Europe.

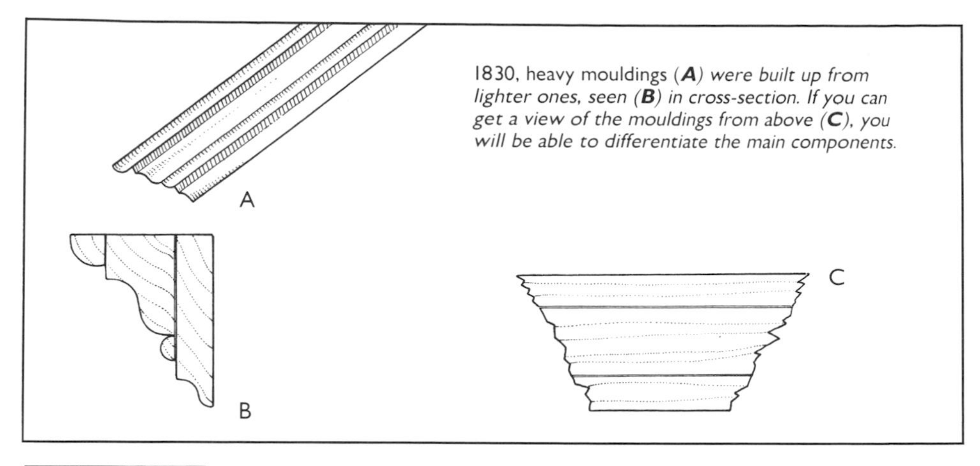

1830, heavy mouldings (***A***) *were built up from lighter ones, seen* (***B***) *in cross-section. If you can get a view of the mouldings from above* (***C***), *you will be able to differentiate the main components.*

CONSTRUCTION

The headboard of the four-poster became substantial enough, with a pair of posts at the foot, to support the tester. The bed itself was no longer a unit separate from the posts; these were jointed to the footboard, and side-rails were bolted to them. As often in the past, many beds were easily dismantled for removal.

Below, *Daniel Marot design for an 'Angel Bed', about 1690.*

DECORATION

Carving in the baroque style (**p. 192**), with *amorini* (cherubs) supporting a cartouche as a popular motif for headboards; painting and gilding in the same manner; embroidery and appliqué work on valances.

FINISH

Turned and carved hardwoods oiled and waxed or varnished. Softwoods, if exposed, were usually painted.

RELATIVE VALUES

Carved examples sell for the largest sums.

MARRIAGES

Few beds, especially four-posters, earlier than, say, 1700 are entirely original and allowances must be made. Many that now command six figure prices are made up from the residue of incomplete survivals, sections of panelling, odd lengths of moulding and fragments of carving. Expert advice is often needed, but in the first instance, check that carving is consistent in style and quality throughout, that the mitres at the angles of the tester do not look too fresh, and that surfaces not ordinarily visible at ground level have not been stained down to appear deceptively old; they should be free of stain and polish, and have a dry look.

BEDS

About

1730-1770

Elegant design dominated by the fashions in France under Louis XV.

Christie's

Bed of lit à la polonaise *type, popular in France and Germany in the mid-18thC. The bed has head and foot of equal height with curving frame and is upholstered in a way that relates closely to seat furniture of the rococo period.*

STYLE AND APPEARANCE

Rococo (see **p. 193**):

France: Beds in great variety – fewer posted types, more low examples with ornate, curving frames. Oriential themes – *à la chinoise* and *à la turque*.

Germany, Austria: Vast beds used only for state occasions, otherwise replaced by the French type called *à la polonaise* with low head and foot, set sideways against the wall with drapes suspended overhead; in peasant communities, pine bedsteads brightly painted with flowers.

Russia: Bedsteads of solid wood with no posts, but with shaped headboard, on scrolled legs.

Spain: No tester, the headboard painted in pastel colours.

Portugal: No posts, tester or visible footboard – headboard formed as a carved frame around a damask panel, the foot a board concealed by the bedclothes, joined to cabriole legs with reverse cabrioles forming upward projections.

MATERIALS

Walnut, oak and beech widely used for both unpainted and decorated frames. Lighter fabrics for drapes, matching other upholstery, and walls.

CONSTRUCTION

Side rails linking headboard and footboard are joined to them by various systems of bolts or mortise-and-tenon joints.

DECORATION

Carving is a more delicate, feminine style than that of the baroque, with great emphasis on shells, flowers and opposed C-scrolls.

FINISH

Painting in schemes usually contrasting two colours – for example blue and white, pink and green, yellow and silver. Gilding, both matt and burnished. Some carved frames left in natural colour and waxed. For regional variations, see **STYLE AND APPEARANCE** above.

RELATIVE VALUES

Good examples of this period are now scarce, and therefore expensive. Many posted beds were dismantled and cannibalized in the late-19th and early-20th centuries; posts were converted into torchères and standard lamps. Conversions of that kind which have survived in pairs are now being reinstated as posts for made-up beds; the price is usually still high, but not so astronomic as for an original. Peasant types are especially hard to find.

SIZES

Dimensions of 18thC beds are usually different from those of modern ones, and mattresses usually have to be made to special order.

BEDS

About

1770 to 1800

Discipline returns to design in the Louis XVI and Directoire periods, with most of Europe following French fashion, but taking note of English pattern books.

Louis XIV bed, which sits sideways in an alcove.

STYLE AND APPEARANCE

Neo-classical (see **p. 194**):

France: Alcove beds with rectangular headboards and footboards, turned and tapered feet.

Italy: Beds resembling enormous settees made in Siena.

Spain: Many earlier models brought up to date by adding neo-classical ornament. Portugal: Simple outlines, inlay on headboards with Louis XVI cresting; a folding bed-settee (*leito à Inglesa*), was based on an English mode.

Germany, Austria, Switzerland: Marriage beds painted and inscribed with names and dates.

Tyrolean painted bed, inscribed and dated 1778.

Scandinavia: Simple four-posters still made in country districts; English, German and Dutch influence strong in **Denmark**, French styles predominant in **Sweden**. **Norway** produced a provincial version of Danish types. Danish cradles often boat-shaped.

MATERIALS

As in the rococo period (see **p. 193**), but with the addition of bronze as a material for French beds in the 1790s.

CONSTRUCTION

Side rails jointed or bolted to cross rails on headboard and footboard. In some examples the side rails are meant to be concealed by bedclothes; in others, they are wide, shaped boards that provide a decorative feature in themselves.

DECORATION

Carving of neo-classical flowers, foliage, medallions and cartouches.

FINISH

Gilding and painting or oiling and waxing.

RELATIVE VALUES

Authenticity plus decorative effect will usually ensure a high price at auction for any bed of this period, whatever the type. Even a pair of posts, to which replacement rails and cornice can be added, will command a premium. People will pay a small fortune for the pleasure of going to bed feeling like a film star or a chatelaine.

BEDS

About

1800-1870

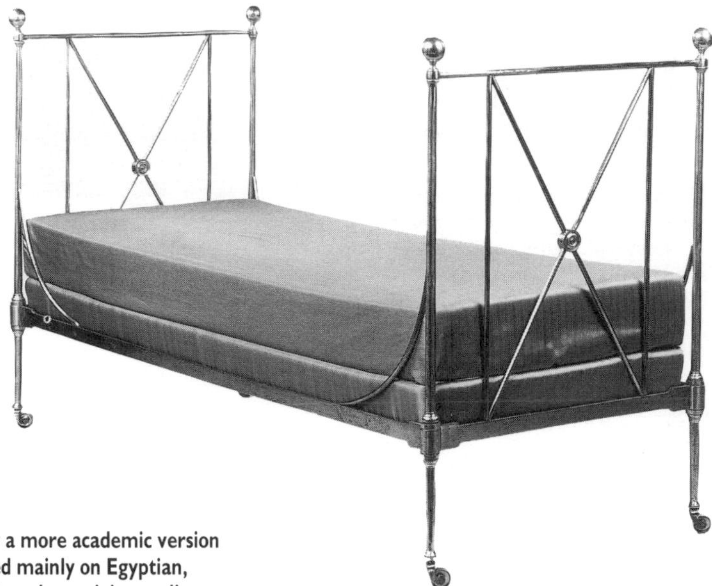

Directoire camp bed with castors.

Design is dominated by a more academic version of neo-classicism based mainly on Egyptian, Greek and Roman types, but also reviving earlier styles and adding oriental flourishes.

STYLE AND APPEARANCE

Empire, Biedermeier, Second Empire (see p. 196):

France: During Napoleon's Consulat (1799-1804) and Empire (1804-15), the main types, widely adopted throughout Europe, were the simple *lit droit* with triangular pedimented headboard, the classical *lit antique*, the *lit à la turque* with curved headboard and footboard of equal height, and the boatshaped *lit en bateau* which, mounted on a daïs, continued to be popular after the Restauration in 1815. Campaign beds, developed during the Napoleonic wars, were made for civilian travellers distrustful of accommodation at inns. During the Second Empire (1848-70), the main types altered little but hangings from testers and half-testers became generally heavier and richer.

Austria, Germany: From around 1815, the late, domesticated version of Empire known as Biedermeier produced beds in that style until around 1850, but in Vienna in the 1830s a long-lasting rococo revival began, with asymmetrical C-scrolls on headboards and cabriole legs on footboards.

Sweden: Adopted the French Empire style but also produced beds of some originality, looking like large settees with the 'arms' serving as headboard and footboard, the 'back' being placed against the wall.

Denmark, Norway: The 'Danish Empire' style used carved wood or moulded sawdust in place of bronze mounts, anticipating Biedermeier. Gothic and rococo revivals influenced Scandinavian beds from 1830.

Spain, Italy: Heavy versions of Empire beds, adorned with swans and other imperial symbols, prevailed long after the demise of Napoleon.

Holland: In 1808, Louis Napoleon converted Amsterdam town hall into a royal palace, with furniture supplied by Dutch craftsmen. The beds may have been produced by the upholsterer Joseph Cuel. Late Empire or Biedermeier beds continued to be popular until romantic revivals took over at mid-century.

Belgium: The Renaissance revival produced some remarkable beds. The Antwerp firm of Roulé showed an ebony bed carved with mannerist figures at the Great Exhibition in London in 1851.

MATERIALS

Mahogany fashionable during Empire period, but in short supply during wars, because of British blockade; so native woods such as oak, maple, beech, were exploited. Pale woods preferred during Biedermeier period.

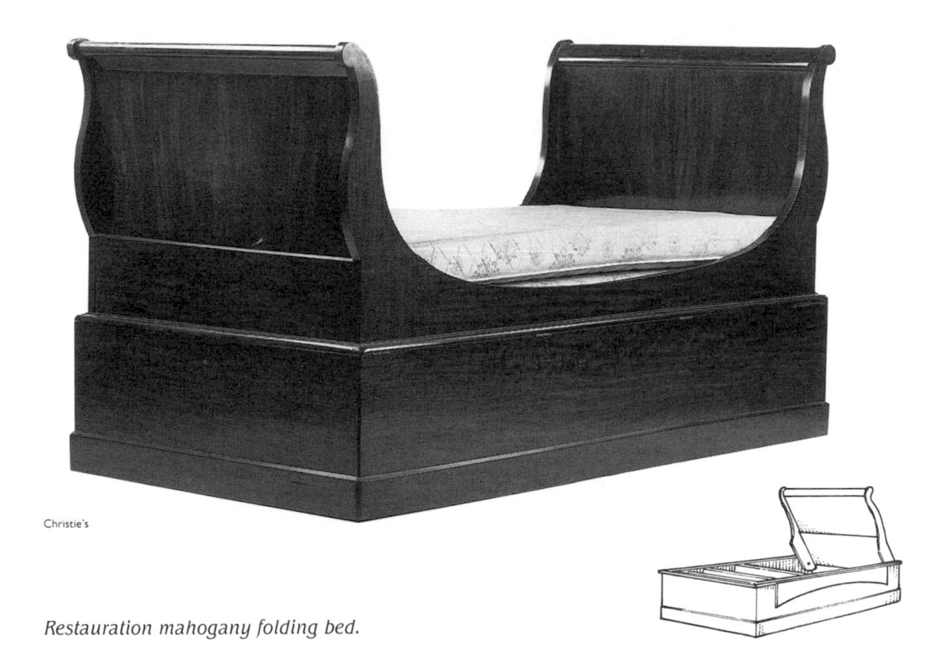

Christie's

Restauration mahogany folding bed.

CONSTRUCTION

Steam-driven woodworking machines reduced production costs, but led to gradual decline in quality. Coil springs, first invented by Georg Junigl, Vienna, 1822 (but patented by Pratt in Britain, 1828), used for box mattresses. Wire mattresses to support feather beds or flock mattresses made from 1850, when side irons began to replace wood.

DECORATION

Carving of classical motifs on Empire and romantic revival bedsteads. Gilded bronze mounts (imperial symbols) on Empire examples. Painted landscapes and flowers on Alpine peasant beds.

FINISH

From 1800, with increased use of mahogany, veneers used on bedsteads. High gloss achieved by French polishing.

RELATIVE VALUES

Attractively painted 'peasant' beds are now regarded as important examples of folk culture and can command higher prices than 'bourgeois' equivalents; but these, too, are becoming sought after by interior decorators, who tend to like ample turnery and heavy carving. Elaborate decoration does not always guarantee high quality. The growing interest in mid-19thC styles is pushing up prices of ornate beds with decoration that is often machine-carved.

Lit en bateau, in walnut and parcel gilt, possibly German.

Mallet at Bourdon House Ltd.

BEDS

About

1870-1940

Increased mechanization brings revolutionary changes in design, manufacture and distribution.

Late-19thC bed in Louis XV style. This type was much used in smart hotels.

STYLE AND APPEARANCE

Revivals, art nouveau, modernist, Art Deco (see p. 197):

France: Hotels built on the Riviera in the 1880-1900 era installed imposing beds, many in pastiches of 18thC styles now known collectively as 'Hotel Louis'.

As practised by Majorelle and other art nouveau designers, the asymmetrical curves and marquetry decoration on beds owed much to the rococo. Debased versions of art nouveau limped along until 1920.

By that time, industrial design as preached by Le Corbusier was eliminating decoration from modernist furniture, while Ruhlmann and other Art Deco designers produced beds veneered with exotic materials. In the 1930s, the low divan bed with headboard but no footboard became popular internationally.

Italy: Political unification in 1870 stimulated national awareness and a revival (Dantesque) that featured pseudo-Renaissance beds produced partly with machinery.

Wrought-iron bedsteads from Tuscany and Liguria have curving headboards and footboards inset with panels painted with landscapes. From 1900, beds in Carlo Bugatti's unique style were inspired by the Turkish divan. Beds in a cheaper version of the stile Liberty (art nouveau) continued into the 1920s.

Belgium: Scaled down, machine-made beds in baroque styles popular in the late-19thC. From 1890-1915 many show the influence of art nouveau designers, van de Velde and Horta, who used the whiplash line, and of Serrurier-Bovy who preferred the angular forms of the Arts and Crafts Movement (**p. 68**).

Austria: The Sezession, founded 1897, broke with prevailing historicism. Otto Wagner, Hoffmann, Moser and Olbrich anticipated and influenced both art nouveau and Bauhaus designs for beds. In Vienna and at their other factories the firm of Thonet manufactured bentwood bedsteads.

Germany: Heavily carved baroque-style bedsteads, 1880-1900. In Munich in the1880s, the Jugendstil (young style) movement led by Behrens favoured quiet curves. One of his students, Gropius, went on to direct the Bauhaus school of art and design at Weimar, where Breuer, inspired by the handlebars of his bicycle, designed furniture made of tubular steel that came to include simple bed frames.

Ethnic types: Peasant communities in many countries had, up to 1900, continued the tradition of the marriage bed, decorated with symbols of good fortune and fertility. Support came from folk culture enthusiasts in **Poland**, **Russia**, **Scandinavia** and **Hungary**.

Interior of box spring mattress; spiral springs are laced to webbings, covered with canvas supporting a layer of stuffing, which is in turn covered with ticking.

French art nouveau bed with inlaid decoration, abut 1900.

Christie's

MATERIALS

Native and imported timbers. Plywood developed in the late-19thC from the 18thC technique of lamination. Cast- and wrought-iron in the 19thC, tubular steel in the early 20th. Interior sprung mattresses on sprung bases from 1920s. Machine-cut veneers, thinner than earlier saw-cut kind.

Bedstead, about 1900, with wire mesh mattress, resting on cast-iron side-irons, and supporting an overlay that is stuffed with hair or wool.

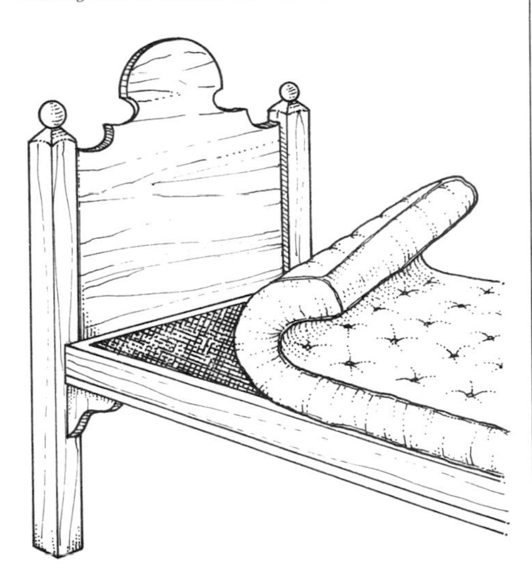

CONSTRUCTION

Machinery in use for cutting dovetail and other joints, but machine-made, tapered screws often used in place of joints.

DECORATION

Carving by machine, but fine handwork still practised.

FINISH

Many art nouveau beds painted white. Veneered surfaces French-polished. In the 1930s limed oak was fashionable: the lime was applied and left in the grain only.

RELATIVE VALUES

From about 1920 to 1970, ornate late-19th century bedsteads were regarded as monstrosities, but have now come into their own again and can often command high prices, as do luxurious Art Deco types. Simply designed 1930s beds can still be bought reasonably.

CUPBOARDS AND ARMOIRES

Before

1300

***Left**, painted sacristy cupboard.*

Vertical storage or display pieces with doors, as distinct from chests with lids, made from early Middle Ages onwards.

STYLE AND APPEARANCE

Byzantine, Romanesque, Gothic: Early surviving examples; armoire about 1176, arched doors and ends (Abbey Church of St Etienne, Obazine); sacristy cupboard, about 1200, massive plank construction, painted over coating of gesso with figures of saints (Cathedral Museum, Halberstadt); armoire, about 1240, since altered but originally composed of numerous small compartments, each with its own door (Bayeux Cathedral).

MATERIALS

Survivors mostly oak, but other local woods, including soft ones, probably used. Wrought-iron for hinges, scrollwork.

CONSTRUCTION

Mortise-and-tenon joints used but planks sometimes pegged to face of frame. Doors are planks joined edge to edge.

DECORATION

Painting over gesso ground. Wrought-iron scrolls nailed to doors on Gothic types.

RELATIVE VALUES

Survivors in churches and museums – not normally for sale.

CUPBOARDS AND ARMOIRES

About

1300-1630

The terms cupboard and cabinet are virtually interchangeable as applied to any pieces of this period with doors; armoire, dressoir and buffet are also freely substituted for each other and for their approximate English equivalents.

German marquetry cabinet, about 1610

STYLE AND APPEARANCE

Gothic and Renaissance: Design affected by Italian Renaissance in 14thC. Ideal described in 15thC as 'harmony and concord of all the parts', but Gothic persists in **northern Europe**. A **German** cupboard with doors above and below, carved with typical Gothic arches and tracery (National Museum, Munich) was made about same time (1470) as the study in the palace of Urbino, fitted with built-in cupboards matching walls decorated in

Renaissance style with intarsia (inlay). A later **German** cupboard (1541), made to a published design by Flötner, is similar in construction to the Munich example, but carved with Renaissance urns in place of Gothic arches. In 16thC **Spain**, Gothic merges with Renaissance and abstract Moorish patterns are carved on cupboard doors.

Shortly after 1500, Renaissance style promoted in **Burgundy**; mannerist elements in Sambin's designs are combined with architectural features in Du Cerceau's. French *armoire-à-deux-corps* is a two-door cupboard set on another, slightly larger. Some French types rest on stands with carved or turned supports. By mid-16thC **Italy** has developed a waist-high sideboard (credenza) with cupboards flanked by columns; heavier version in **Netherlands** about 1625, also a two-stage cupboard, upper stage smaller than the lower, often with carved figures supporting a canopy.

MATERIALS

Local timbers, e.g. oak, walnut in **France**, walnut and cypress in **Italy**, lime in southern **Germany**. Mixture of woods for cupboards meant to be painted. Doors are always wood, never glass (the term 'cabinet' might misleadingly suggest otherwise).

CONSTRUCTION

Panels of carcases and doors set in mortised-and-tenoned frames. When on stands, turned or carved supports end in squares with mortises into which rails are tenoned. No glue; joints secured with pegs.

Construction of stand for cabinet.

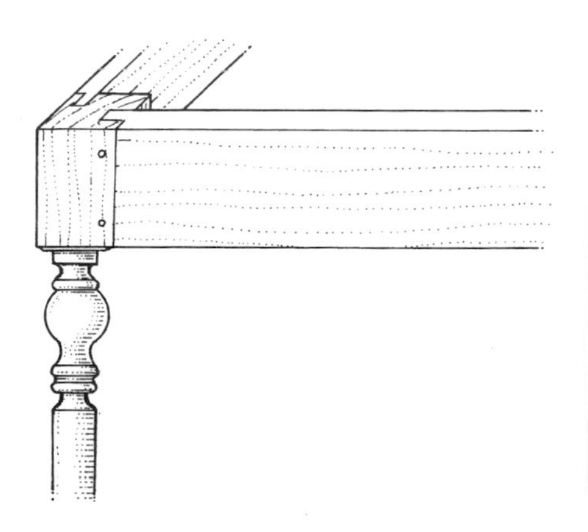

DECORATION

Gothic carving: Pointed arches, tracery, birds, animals, linenfold panels.

Renaissance carving: Classical urns with flowers, mannerist grotesques, nude or draped figures with elongated limbs, strapwork or scrolled borders.

***Above**, 16thC oak dwarf cabinet with carved panels.*

Renaissance: Intarsia; still-life and architectural subjects in wood mosaic, creating *trompe l'oeil* effects.

FINISH

Gothic: Many cupboards vividly painted; highly valued when new and probably kept in closed areas of churches.

Renaissance: Woods stained for intarsia work only. Otherwise oiled, varnished or left in natural state.

RELATIVE VALUES

Late Gothic cupboards appear on the market at prices within reach of anyone who can afford, as well as or instead of, a good car. Many late Renaissance cupboards sell for less than the price of a second-hand family saloon.

FRAGMENTS

In 1922, a collection of Italian Renaissance furniture, bought in Victorian times by a national institution, was found to have been largely made up from fragments. Sadly – because the fragments would be worth having – all were destroyed on the orders of an outraged Establishment; but many such pieces are still around.

CUPBOARDS AND ARMOIRES

About

1625-1725

French walnut armoire--deux-corps, early-17thC.

STYLE AND APPEARANCE

Mannerist, auricular and baroque:

Cupboards: In **Italy** slow development; baroque mouldings, spiral columns added to Renaissance types. In France, the *armoire-à-deux-corps* is substantially unaltered except for baroque carving covering entire front, not just panels; gives way slowly to armoire with full-length doors.

In the **Netherlands**, two-part cupboards still being made about 1650; type with full-length, arched doors a speciality of Zeeland; grotesque elements in mannerist style borrowed from silversmith Van Vianen – fleshy sea creatures, grinning masks and anatomical details, especially the human ear – thus *Knorpelwerk* or auricular style, taken up by Unteutsch, Frankfurt; seen in his designs for carving on cupboard doors.

The *Schrank* – **German** version of armoire with full-length doors – a status symbol, so heavily loaded with moulded cornices and arrangements of mouldings on doors that it is known as a *Barockschrank*. An asymmetrical Swiss buffet has an upper stage raised on turned supports, leaving a waist-high space with provision for basin and ewer at one end.

Cabinets: In this period, the term described pieces fitted with small drawers that may or may not be enclosed with doors, mounted on stands, often ornate. Nominally intended to hold collectors' items (coins, gems, geological specimens), but really prestige pieces valued as works of art in themselves. Regional differences mainly in decoration (see **DECORATION**).

MATERIALS

Local woods used in the solid for provincial cupboards and armoires. Exotic materials for veneering and marquetry, e.g. turtleshell, ebony, pewter, gilt bronze, hardstones, variegated marbles.

19thC copy of a late-17thC Portuguese cabinet on matching stand.

CONSTRUCTION

Large armoires: Massive but usually manageable: framework and panels assembled with loose-fitting tenons and pegs, easily knocked apart. Doors can be lifted off pin hinges.

Two-stage cupboards: Panelled. Usually two separate carcases, but some **Netherlands** types are, in spite of appearances to the contrary, made as one and not easy to move.

Cabinets: Early examples have panelled ends, later ones are flush. Tops flat, domed or, in rare, luxurious examples, surmounted by superstructures with clocks at their centres.

17thC Flemish table cabinet veneered with tortoiseshell and inlaid with bone.

Interiors fitted with small drawers set around miniature cupboard. Doors, if any, panelled or flush. Stands constructed either as cupboards or, more usually, as table-frames; but many cabinets exported from Florence, Antwerp and Augsburg without stands, which were made later at destination.

DECORATION

Cupboards: On early **Italian** types, carved motifs, e.g. lion masks, at centres of panels (often three to each door). The 17thC **German** *Schrank* relied mainly on arrangements of mouldings, sometimes with carved details or a central panel of marquetry. Finest late-17thC **French** armoires decorated with boulle marquetry – patterns cut out in veneer, or brass inlaid into turtleshell ground.

XIV French armoire with superb wood marquetry in the style of Boulle.

Cabinets: Florence specialized in *pietre-dure* – inlaying drawer-fronts with pictures of birds and flowers in hardstones – lapis, chalcedony, jasper, agate – and marbles, against an ebony-veneered carcase mounted with ormolu. Centre of activity was the Uffizi, under patronage of the Medicis.

At Eger in **Bohemia**, a highly complicated combination of intarsia and carving was used. Antwerp, Augsburg and Middelburg also decorated drawer-fronts and doors with intarsia, and veneered the sides and top with ebony. Macé, a skilled French craftsman, spent two years at Middelburg about 1620, learning the art of veneering in ebony and returned to Paris to work for the Crown. Louis XIV owned magnificent cabinets, both Italian and, later, French.

Amsterdam was noted for large cabinets decorated with floral marquetry. About 1690, Van Mekeren was the leading maker.

Stands were either turned or, for some of the finest cabinets, richly carved with scrolls, foliage, figures of cherubs, slaves, nymphs or tritons.

FINISH

East India trading companies brought in cabinets from Japan and China, decorated with figures in gilt on a ground built up with successive coats of lacquer made from sap of a tree (*Rhus vernicifera*); imitated in Europe by 'japanning' with a substitute (gum-lac, seed lac or shellac). Dutch examples considered best copies. Carved stands were silvered or gilded.

RELATIVE VALUES

Good examples of the German *Schrank* now sell at high prices, but bargains in big cupboards from other countries may be found. Highly decorated cabinets very expensive; a *pietre dure* example was sold in 1990 for £8,580,000 – a world record for any piece of furniture. Simpler types often reasonable in price. Early European copies of oriental lacquer cabinets can cost more than originals.

> **STANDS**
>
> Do not reject a good cabinet because the stand is not obviously 'original' – it may well be one of those originally made many hundreds of miles from the birthplace of the cabinet.

CUPBOARDS AND ARMOIRES

About

1725-1775

French provincial armoire made in restrained rococo style.

Bonhams

STYLE AND APPEARANCE

Cupboards: In **France**, heavy Louis XIV types gradually give way to lighter rococo style. Doors of armoires have shaped panels matching *boiserie* (wall panelling); some feature in *buffet-bas* (sideboard with cupboards and drawers), *buffet-vaisselier* or dressoir (buffet with rack of shelves above), and *buffet-à-deux-corps* (two-stage cupboard with doors above and below). Baroque armoire persists for many years in some regions (**Denmark**, parts of **Germany**); in other provincial centres (Liège, Aachen), rococo fully developed.

French provincial fruitwood buffet, mid-18thC.

Christie's

Cabinets: Baroque cabinet-on-stand goes out of fashion, new version in extreme rococo style developed in **Italy**, where architect Juvarra designs tall cabinets – lavish carving, gilding and inlay, mounted on cabriole-legged side tables – made by Piffetti of Turin. Rather similar cabinets made in **Germany** (see also Bureau-Cabinets, under **DESKS, p. 252**). French examples more restrained, much lower, e.g. the *encoignure*– waist-high corner cabinet with door(s) decorated in marquetry. Tall corner cabinets, some bow-fronted, made in Holland, where standard test-piece for cabinet-maker seeking entry into guild is a veneered cabinet mounted on bombé base. **Dutch** vitrines (display cabinets) have glazed doors and canted ends on cupboard or bombé bases (see **CHESTS OF DRAWERS, p. 241**).

MATERIALS

Provincial: Local timbers, e.g. oak, walnut and cherry main woods for **French** armoires and related types; walnut, fruitwood and chestnut in **Tuscany** and **Lombardy**; olive, poplar in **Sicily**.

Sophisticated: Exotic woods for veneering and marquetry, supplemented by mother-of-pearl, ivory, turtleshell. Ormolu handles and mounts.

Inlaid Italian corner cupboard, with bombé base, mid-18thC.

Phillips

CONSTRUCTION

Methods change little for solid cupboards (i.e. not veneered), except for panels of doors (see **FRENCH CANADIAN ARMOIRES, p. 285** for details). For doors and ends of sophisticated cabinets, veneers often matched or quartered (see diagram). The figure in all veneers cut from same piece of wood being virtually identical, if Sheet A is turned over and set edge to edge with Sheet B, a symmetrical, matched pattern is created. Taking the process a step further, if Sheets C and D are similarly treated but also turned upside down, and then set against bottom edges of A and B, a symmetrical, quartered pattern results.

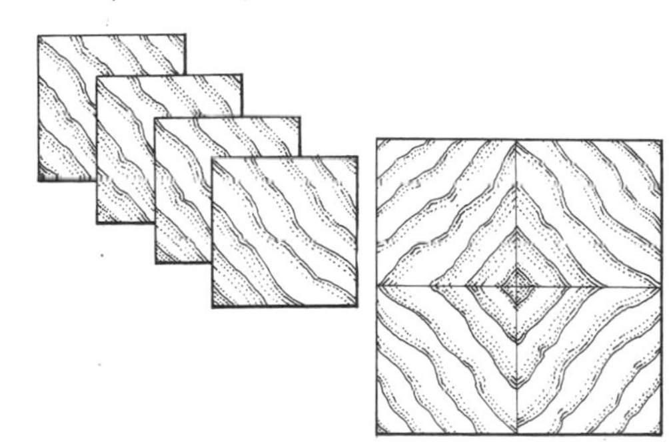
Matched and quartered veneers.

DECORATION

Carving of rococo motifs – C-scrolls, flowers, cherubs – reaches high standard on provincial and sophisticated pieces. On veneered cabinets – marquetry flowers, chinoiseries, landscapes – often partly obscured on drawers by ormolu handles placed with curious disregard for design.

FINISH

Alpine, **Dutch** and **Scandinavian** pine cupboards painted all over with ground colour, then in polychrome with flowers, figures, landscapes, within borders simulating exotic woods or marble. Many French cabinets decorated with chinoiseries or *fêtes galantes* scenes in the Watteau style with *vernis Martin* (generic term for translucent coloured varnish, originally invented early in the 18thC by four brothers after whom it is named).

Pine Alpine cupboard, painted, about 1775.

RELATIVE VALUES

In very wide field, good buys are simpler types of **French** Provincial armoire and **Danish** or **Alpine** cupboards in painted pine, both suitable – with shelves discreetly added to interior if necessary – for use in living-rooms as well as bedrooms.

19thC ARMOIRES

French Provincial armoires and buffets in Louis XV rococo style continued to be made well into the 19thC. Two-stage buffets with large glass panels in doors are usually found to be either 19thC entirely, or 18thC examples that have been modified.

CABINETS AND CUPBOARDS

About

1775-1800

***Right**, ormolu mount on neo-classical cabinet.*

STYLE AND APPEARANCE

Transition from rococo to neo-classicism (see **GUIDE TO PERIODS AND STYLES, p.194**) complete in Paris by accession of Louis XVI, 1774, and further encouraged by Marie Antoinette. Other royal families patronize Parisian cabinet-makers (many of them German) and style soon becomes international, with increasing use of straight legs, flat fronts and tops to cupboards, cabinets, glass-fronted vitrines for porcelain and free-standing bookcases (still mainly built-in fitments).

Louis XVI mahogany jewel cabinet.

Leading makers in **Paris** include Oeben, Riesener, Leleu, Weisweiler, Beneman, Stckel, Carlin. In **Turin**, Bonzanigo, sculptor and cabinet-maker, produces finely carved and painted cabinets, some mounted with busts of Bourbons. Haupt returns to **Stockholm** from Paris, 1769, versed in neo-classical trends. Copenhagen requires cabinet-makers to submit designs for test-pieces to the Academy, and in 1777 established Kongelige Meubel Maagazin as retail outlet for **Danish** cabinet-makers.

***Above**, Dutch marquetry corner cupboards, dating from about 1790.*

Louis XVI provincial armoire, about 1780.

Dutch mahogany buffet, about 1775.

MATERIALS

Cupboards: Local timbers, e.g. oak, pine, walnut, cherry.

Cabinets: Exotic veneers e.g. kingwood, tulipwood, satinwood, amboyna. Mahogany used in Paris after 1780. Porcelain, bronze, shell, used for plaques and inlay.

CONSTRUCTION

Flush surfaces simpler to construct by existing methods because fewer complex curves to contend with when bombé carcase and cabriole leg got out of fashion. Low, rectilinear *meuble d'appui* (pier cabinet placed against narrow wall between pair of windows)

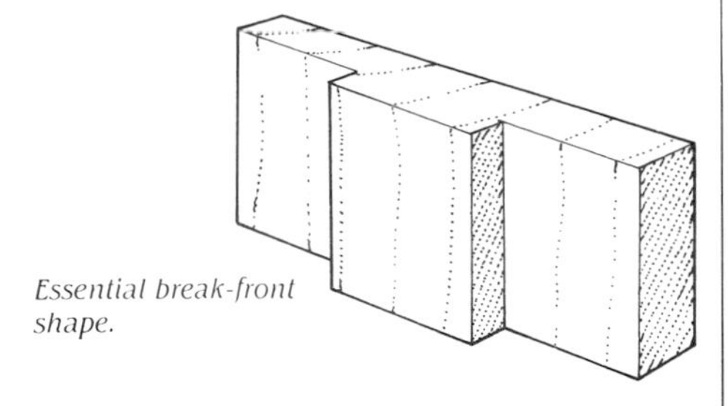
Essential break-front shape.

is outwardly similar to a type of commode with drawers enclosed by doors (see **CHESTS AND CHESTS OF DRAWERS, p. 241**); larger type has rounded ends or breakfront (middle section projects slightly). A Dutch type has a hinged, lift-up top and a sunken basin for washing drinking-glasses in living-room.

DECORATION

Cupboards: Carved rococo scrolls and flowers abandoned in favour of plainer style in some areas but retained in others (e.g. Normandy) regardless of city fashions.

Cabinets: Until 1780, extravagant use of marquetry, lacquer, boullework (revived by Leleu and others), caryatid figures in ormolu. Doors inset with plaques of Sèvres porcelain or bronze. Marie Antoinette fond of inlay in mother-of-pearl. After 1780, fashion for plain mahogany – supposedly prompted by need for economy but huge sums still spent on furniture. Marquetry on **Dutch** and **Spanish** examples usually fine.

FINISH

In **France**, more restrained use of *vernis Martin*. In **Italy**, painting of mythological figures, medallions, urns and wreaths.

RELATIVE VALUES

Decorated Louis XVI cabinets expensive, especially those with Sèvres plaques; plainer ones much less so. Severe Louis XVI provincial armoires cheaper than showier, florally carved Louis XV types.

DUTCH MARQUETRY

Dutch marquetry cabinets in neo-classical style seem to have been reproduced far less often than those with traditional floral marquetry; pale veneers used for ground make refreshing change.

CABINETS AND CUPBOARDS

About
1800-1850

Pier cabinet in post-Empire style, about 1830.

STYLE AND APPEARANCE

Cupboards: Architectural wardrobes and sideboards with cupboards in cities but in country districts, armoires, dressers continue 18thC traditions.

Cabinets: After French Revolution, the Directoire takes later, austere Louis XVI style a step further with functional cabinets and bookcases – doors with brass grilles or glass panes arranged with flat glazing bars in diamond patterns. From 1804, grand Empire ornament applied to simple, rectilinear shapes. Style adopted throughout Europe and continued after 1815, until 1850 but with ornament much reduced.

Biedermeier: In **Austria**, **Hungary**, **Germany**, **Scandinavia**, flat-fronted cases display bibelots. Bow-fronted corner cabinets with glass doors above, wood below, also popular. Similar style in Russian cabinets made by Gambs and Bobkov of St Petersburg.

Style Troubadour (Gothic Revival): Begins in **France** 1820, runs parallel with Biedermeier until 1850, reaching climax with vast bookcase designed by Cremer and Bernardis for **Austrian** stand at Great Exhibitions, London, 1851 – pointed arches, pinnacles, domes, cluster columns, tracery.

Louis-Philippe (Rococo revival): Serpentine-fronted vitrines with *vernis Martin* panels made from about 1830 when Louis-Philippe becomes King of France. Name applied recklessly to cabinets made long after his downfall in 1848.

MATERIALS

Directoire and Empire: Mahogany, cherry, maple, fruitwoods, walnut, oak, pine.

Biedermeier: As above but with preference for pale woods – birch, maple, poplar, cherry. In **Russia**, Karelian birch, poplar, Persian walnut, Brazilian amaranth.

Troubadour: Oak.

Louis-Philippe: Kingwood, ormolu often poorly finished.

Swiss cherry dresser with panelled doors.

CONSTRUCTION

Fashion for flush surfaces results in few panelled carcases in sophisticated furniture; most joints disguised. Ends joined to tops and bottoms with lapped dovetails, frames of doors tenoned and mortised, rebated to receive glass. Traditional methods increasingly assisted by steam-driven machines.

***Above**, Charles X bookcase, about 1825.*

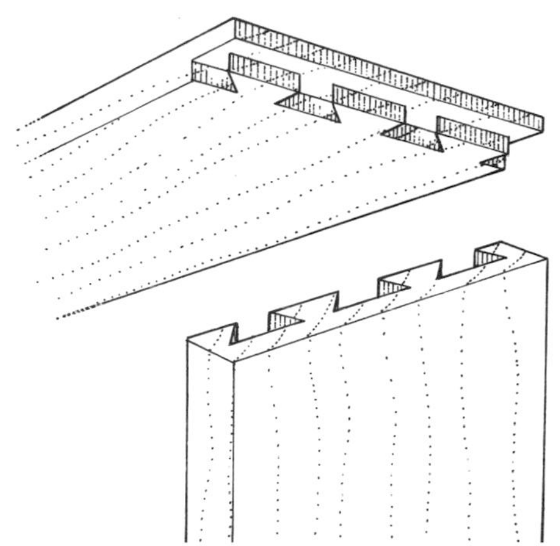

Lapped dovetails.

DECORATION

Empire: Turned columns or pilasters often surmounted by Egyptian heads, flanking doors. Ormolu or brass mounts on friezes.

Biedermeier: Ornament limited to sparse use of mounts, geometric marquetry, carved paw feet.

Troubadour: Carved and pierced details from Gothic architecture.

Louis-Philippe: Marquetry, ormolu mounts. *Vernis Martin* lacquer in Louis XV style.

FINISH

French polishing becomes general except for country pieces, still oiled and waxed, painted, varnished or left natural.

RELATIVE VALUES

Simple Empire and Biedermeier bookcases sometimes sell at reasonable prices but can take off alarmingly, especially if in pale woods liked by interior decorators. Louis-Philippe vitrines almost always sell at high prices, even though some arbiters of taste disapprove of them.

Louis Philippe vitrine, glazed door and Vernis Martin panels, about 1840.

SHELVES

Until about 1820, shelves in bookcases and cabinets were of wood, usually made adjustable by fitting freely in grooves cut in the ends. Shelves resting on cleats attached to ends, or on studs in holes, generally indicate a later date. Glass shelves in vitrines are usually modern, but may be replacements for wood ones in a period cabinet.

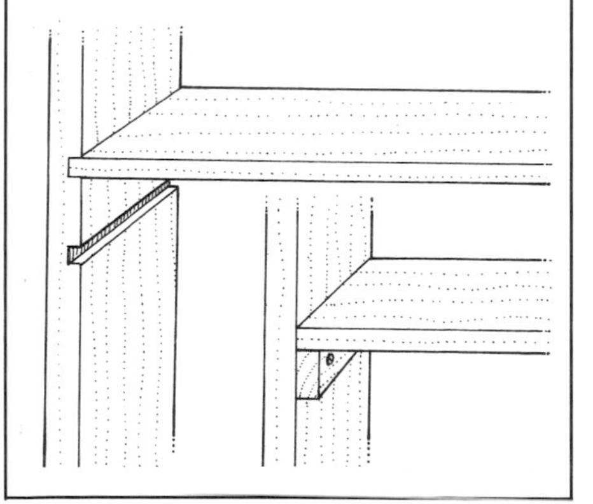

CABINETS AND CUPBOARDS

About
1850-1890

Sotheby's

Ornate cabinet inlaid with Renaissance ornament, about 1870.

STYLE AND APPEARANCE

Revivals of historic styles continue – Gothic, Renaissance, baroque, rococo – with a grand town-hall version of neo-classicism never wholly abandoned.

MATERIALS

Wide variety of veneers – some imported, many local, e.g. olive in **Italy** – laid on oak in **France**, pine in **Italy**, **Spain**, parts of **Germany**, **Scandinavia**.

CONSTRUCTION

Outwardly the same as in previous period, but growing use of dowels in place of mortise-and-tenon, machined dovetails in place of hand-cut ones.

DECORATION

Two-stage cabinets of 16thC Renaissance form, made in Germany about 1880 have fine Meissen (Dresden) porcelain plaques copies from 17thC paintings. Intricately carved Bavarian rococo cabinets have shelves and brackets unknown on 18thC types. In most countries, decorative features from different periods are applied to large cupboards and wardrobes. Leading makers: Pogliani, Milan, Fourdinois, Linke, Paris; Pssenbacher, Munich.

Austin Peare Studio

Late-19thC French vitrine in mid-18thC style, with ormolu mounts and panels of vernis Martin lacquer decoration.

FINISH

Copies and pastiches of French 18thC cabinets mounted in ormolu or imitations. True ormolu is cast, tooled bronze, gilded with amalgam of gold and mercury, fired to evaporate mercury and leave film of gold. Process repeated before final burnishing. Some areas

Ormolu-mounted maple bookcase, late-19thC.

may be left matt. Partly for economy, partly because mercury process highly poisonous, substitutes developed, e.g. bronze dipped in acid and lacquered; electrotypes (Galvano-plastics); and electroplated nickel.

Gothic revival cabinet, about 1870.

RELATIVE VALUES

Belgian reproductions of Renaissance and baroque cupboards, carved with genre subjects, lion masks, fairly reasonable; marquetry cabinets expensive.

JOINTS

Dowel joints in place of mortise-and-tenon (see **CONSTRUCTION**) can only be detected if join is slightly open due to shrinkage. Method used on Continent earlier than in Britain, but not before 19thC.

CABINETS AND CUPBOARDS

About

1890-1940

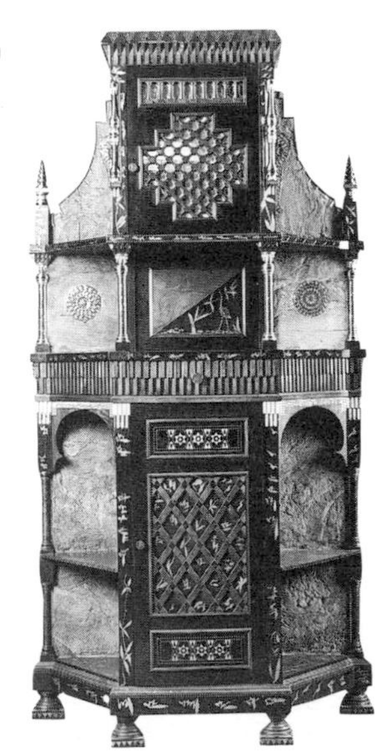

Inlaid cabinet by Bugatti, about 1900-1910.

Hotel de Ventes Horta

STYLE AND APPEARANCE

Walnut bookcases, asymmetrical and carved in the round with symbolist female nudes and plant forms are among only 20 pieces made in Paris by Carabin of Alsace that influence Messag's work in bronze for Linke, and anticipate art nouveau designers. These include Carabin's friend Gallé of Nancy, who utilizes plant forms, and Charpentier who uses nude figures and tree stems for his cabinets. Guimard,

Pair of two-part cabinets by van de Velde.

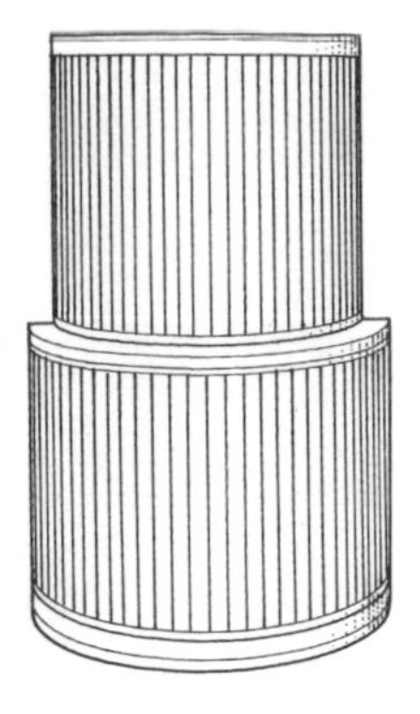

Christie's

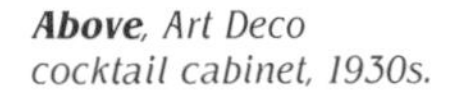

Above, *Art Deco cocktail cabinet, 1930s.*

Above right, pair of burr walnut bedside cupboards, 1930s.

Majorelle and van de Velde also design fine art nouveau case furniture for rich clients.

Bugatti of **Milan** displays cabinets of highly unusual designs, derived from Moorish and oriental sources, at Turin Exhibition, 1902, where art nouveau style peaks. After that, commercialized versions produced until about 1920 in most regions, but **Holland** rejects eccentricities in favour of sensible cupboards.

Meanwhile, in 1897, Viennese Sezessionist Movement is founded in reaction to prevailing academic approach. Two members – Hoffmann and Moser – start Wiener Werkstatte (Vienna Workshops) in 1903 to produce artistic furniture. Moser's cabinets very 20thC, their angularity anticipating Bauhaus and Le Corbusier functionalism, but relieving it with abstract decoration that paves the way for Art Deco.

Le Corbusier (C-E Jeanneret) works in partnership with Charlotte Perriand whose wall units are geometric assemblies of cubic compartments. Eileen Gray, an Irishwoman based in Paris, designs cabinets of adaptable form, richly lacquered. Art Deco wardrobes handsome and functional, sideboards with cupboards often lumpy blocks jutting aggressively into room.

MATERIALS

Mahogany less in favour except for reproductions, e.g. revival of Biedermeier, in **Germany**, early 20thC. Rosewood and walnut popular for art nouveau; oak, walnut, maple, for Art Deco.

CONSTRUCTION

Art nouveau: Good examples hand-made using traditional methods, cheaper ones factory-made with machined dovetails and so on. Many Bugatti pieces put together by his own idiosyncratic methods.

Modernist: Le Corbusier favoured machined work but many of his designs could only be carried out by hand.

Art Deco: Best cabinets hand-made, but popular, post-1930 versions mass-produced.

DECORATION

Art nouveau: Fine marquetry, good carving.

Modernist: Very little; Gropius (Bauhaus) inlaid mahogany wardrobes with brass lines.

Art Deco: Some marquetry and parquetry. Oxidized or chromium-plated handles.

FINISH

Art nouveau: Wax or French polishing.

Modernist: Painting,varnishing.

Art Deco: Varnishing, lacquering, French polishing.

RELATIVE VALUES

Important examples (all styles) expensive. Best buys: hand-made 1930s cupboards.

PLYWOOD

Plywood backs may indicate low standard throughout. Some makers used it to good effect, but if infected with woodworm, much more difficult to treat successfully than solid wood.

CHAIRS

Before

1630

Seat furniture ranging from simple stools to splendid thrones, some dating from about 1250 BC, have survived in Egyptian tombs. Greeks and Romans developed these types and added elegant couches. All these became prototypes for much later models, and will repay study, but the private collector is unlikely to acquire examples earlier than 16thC.

STYLE AND APPEARANCE

Gothic (12thC – mid-16thC), overlapped by Renaissance (15thC – early-17thC): Stools and benches main seating; gradually, backs added to form backstools, settles. Armchairs for use of master, mistress and honoured guests only.

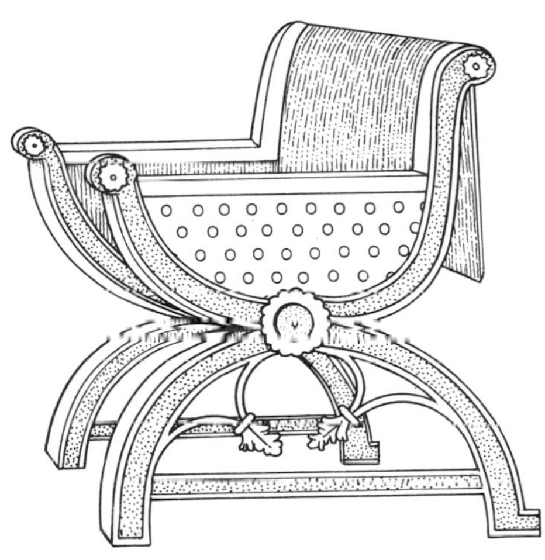

Norman throne stool of William the Conqueror, before 1100.

MATERIALS

Local timbers, especially oak, walnut, beech. Some German throne chairs in steel.

CONSTRUCTION

Stools, Gothic: Slab-ended, i.e. boards tenoned into seat at each end to form supports, with or without rails; usually with stretcher(s), the tenons projecting through ends, secured with key wedges.

Armchairs, Gothic: Mainly box-seated, panelled backs, enclosed arms.

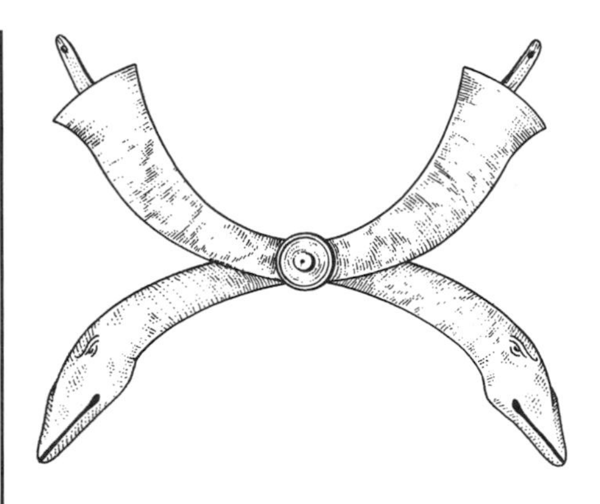

Roman bronze support for a stool.

Stools, Renaissance: Turned legs with rails and stretchers mortised, tenoned and secured with pegs.

Backstools, Renaissance: Italian *scabello* has slab supports back and front, and third slab, tenoned through the seat, forming the back.

Armchairs, Renaissance: 1 Turned legs and arm supports, panelled backs, open arms; **French** *caquetoire* (gossip chair) has wide seat to accommodate women's skirts. **2** X-shaped supports at back and front of Florentine ('Savonarola') type, and at each side of Venetian type; both types originally made to fold, but many rigid.

Settles, Renaissance: The *casapanca* is an **Italian** forerunner of the settee – a box-seated chest with back and arms added.

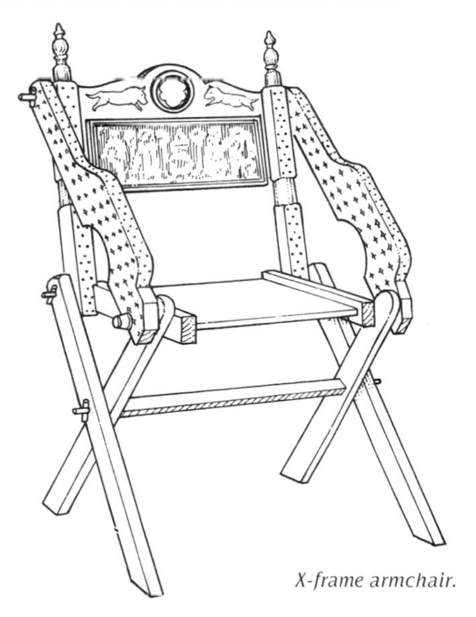

X-frame armchair.

Italian walnut casapanca, *about 1600.*

DECORATION

Gothic: Stools have buttress-shaped edges to slab ends, pierced rails. **Flemish** and **French** armchairs have linenfold panels to backs and box bases. **Portuguese** throne-chairs are delicately pierced and carved with pointed arches.

Renaissance: Legs turned, rails carved with lunettes, scrolls; back panels of some armchairs inlaid into the solid with floral subjects in contrasting woods. *Caquetoires* carved with 'Romayne' work (medallion portraits, often of owners grandly dressed up in Roman helmets).

FINISH

Armchairs often painted and gilded when new, but few retain original pigments. Most of these are now a mellow brown or silver-grey colour.

RELATIVE VALUES

Authentic Gothic examples rare, expensive. A Renaissance *scabello* or *caquetoire*, though not cheap, is a desirable and interesting object because it can make a powerful first impression in a well-lit and appropriately decorated entrance hall.

__Above__, Gothic bench, about 1500; __below__, 19thC bench reshaped to appear Gothic.

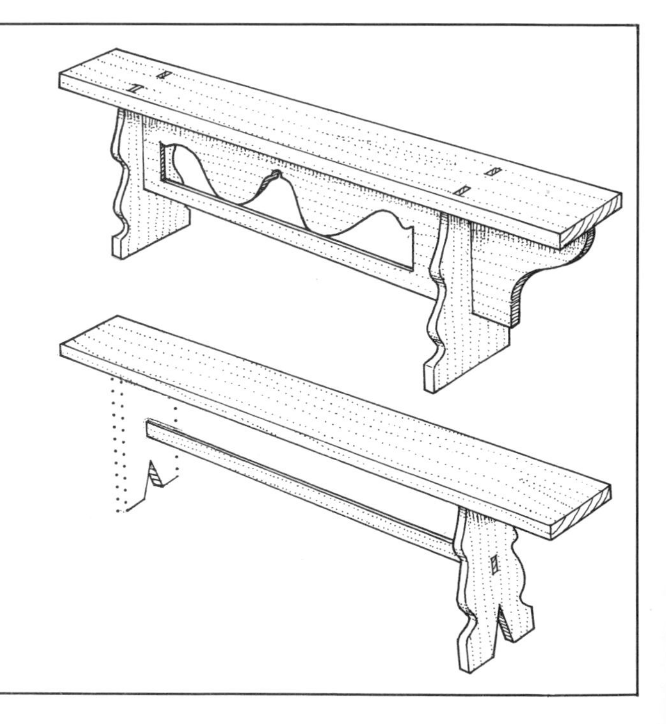

NATURAL WEAR

Early armchairs almost always show signs of natural wear – smooth and free of scratches – where countless hands have rested on the terminations of the arms. Sit in the chair, rub your own hands gently over them and ask yourself if they feel right.

CHAIRS

About
1630-1770

Mid-17thC Spanish walnut armchair with baluster turnings.

STYLE AND APPEARANCE

Baroque, 1630-1715 (Louis XIII/XIV): Until about 1650, chair legs are turned to baluster or trumpet shapes, then spirals, followed from about 1670-1700 by scrolled legs joined by matching front stretchers and accompanied by turned uprights to backs with high cresting rails.

Settees, either resembling three chairs joined together or fully upholstered, are popular from 1660, as are day-beds and sleeping chairs with adjustable headrests. Winged armchairs appear about 1670, when Louis XIV version of baroque developed by Le Brun for Versailles, begins to affect design throughout Europe. Stools with upholstered seats (*tabourets*) play role in court protocol – folding *pliants* on X-supports reserved for duchesses.

In 1685, religious discrimination in France drives out many craftsmen and designers, including Marot who settles in Holland and becomes noted especially for designs of grandiloquent seat furniture.

Rococo, 1715-70: Heavy, hook-like scrolled leg has gradually been smoothed into the elongated S-curve of the cabriole leg, which dominates the Régence and Louis XV periods. Cabriole leg terminates in various types of feet, e.g. scroll, hoof, in **France**, **Italy**; claw-and-ball in **Holland**, **Portugal**. Chair and settee backs lower. Notable chairmakers: Migeon and Cresson of Paris; Nogaret of Lyon.

Louis XIV carved and gilded tabouret.

Italian gilded rococo settee, about 1750.

Rococo style often exaggerated in **Italy**, **Spain** and **Scandinavia** by use of boldly curved cabriole legs and asymmetrical cresting rails; in **Russia**, by exuberant carving on seat furniture designed for royal palaces by the Italian, Count Rastrelli. **Portuguese** chairs about 1750 have fretted splats and claw-and-ball feet in English style.

MATERIALS

Mainly oak, walnut and beech for sophisticated *fauteuil* (chair with open arms), bergère (padded arms, cushioned seat), *canapé* (settee); *duchesse-brisée* (daybed in form of bergère

German walnut fauteuil, about 1750.

A Louis XV rococo canap, about 1750-1760.

with removable extension).

Frames usually exposed, seats and backs upholstered in velvet, tapestry, brocade, damask, needlework. Rattan, imported from the East, used from about 1660 for woven cane seats and back panels.

Ash, elm, pine, birch used for country chairs with wood or rush seats.

CONSTRUCTION

Baroque: Many high-backed, narrow-seated chairs have front legs socketed into flat seat frames; others mortised-and-tenoned.

Rococo: Most chairs totally devoid of straight lines; joining one curved section of frame to another entails masterly use of mortised joints.

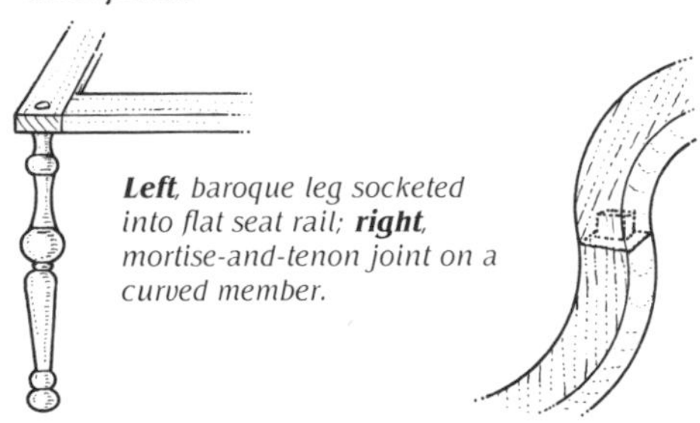

***Left**, baroque leg socketed into flat seat rail; **right**, mortise-and-tenon joint on a curved member.*

DECORATION

Baroque: Bold turning, bobbin and baluster shapes. Spirals ('twists') carved by hand until turners devise jigs for turning on lathe. Scroll legs shaped and decorated by carver. Cresting rails carved with cherubs' heads, vine leaves.

Rococo: Cabriole legs and curving frames shaped and decorated by carver, exploiting opposed C-scrolls, shells, flowers, moulded edges of frames.

FINISH

Baroque: Silvered, gilded or left natural. Water gilding more usual becuase it can be burnished or left matt; more expensive than oil gilding which cannot be burnished. Ground prepared with several coats of gesso (plaster mixed with size), coated with coloured mordant (blue, red or yellow) and, in case of water gilding, wetted before application of gold leaf over very small areas at a time. Cheap substitute for gilding is 'Dutch gold', using copper in place of gold leaf. Silvering uses same process as gilding, with silver leaf instead of gold.

French provincial child's chair.

Rococo: Left natural, gilded all over or painted, often with details in gold. Venetian seats brightly painted with flowers.

RELATIVE VALUES

Louis XV seat furniture, especially if upholstered in original tapestry, much more expensive than 17thC baroque.

FRAMES

Frames of Louis XV seat furniture, as distinct from other types, e.g. tables, were very rarely veneered or mounted in ormolu, whereas 19thC pastiches sometimes were.

CHAIRS

About

1770-1815

Christie's

Louis XV fauteuil by Georges Jacob, about 1770.

STYLE AND APPEARANCE

Designers converging on Rome in 1750s absorb ideas of classical Roman decoration and begin to apply them in 1760s to seat furniture with square, rectangular or oval backs; straight legs in place of cabriole. Neo-classical style international by 1770. Identified with reigns of Louis XVI in France, Friedrich Wilhelm II in Prussia, Joseph II in Austria, Catherine II in Russia, Maria I in Portugal, Charles IV in Spain and George III in Britain. In spite of Italian source, English and French interpretations most influential.

In 1780s, the painter David commissions chair-maker Jacob to produce chairs with sabre legs and wide top rails, and couches with scroll ends on turned feet derived from paintings of Greek originals – basis of Directoire style (1790-1800), Empire (1800-15). Notable makers: Sen and the Jacob family of Paris.

Russian steel chair showing Sheraton influence.

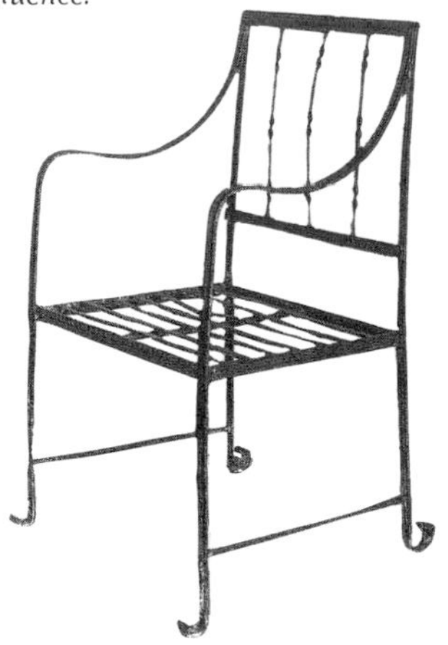

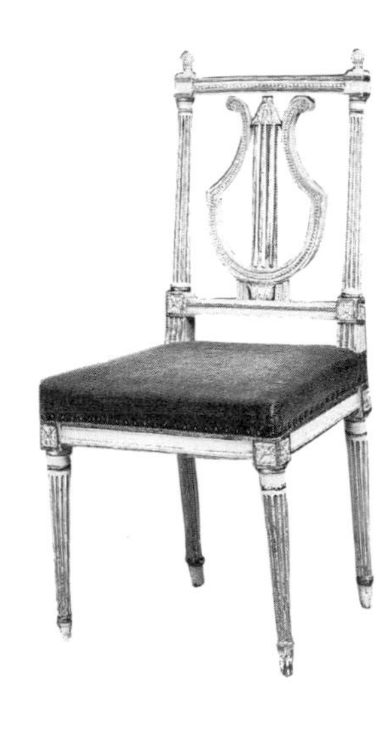

Christie's

Directoire chair with lyre back, in the manner of Jacob and Sen, about 1800.

MATERIALS

Mainly as in rococo period until 1780s, but timber used more economically – one reason advanced for abandoning cabriole leg being waste of wood in shaping. In 1780s, mahogany introduced by Jacob and 'Etruscan' (Greek) style which becomes international Empire style, identified with Napoleon I.

CONSTRUCTION

Return to discipline, after excesses of baroque and rococo, makes for sounder construction, especially in chairs with angular backs; but oval backs, composed of four segments joined by mortise-and-tenon, still difficult to make.

Etruscan style introduces innovations – wide top rail to chairs sometimes set against, rather than between, uprights. Stools have

Directoire chair with broad top rail, sabre legs and Greek key decoration, based on a klismos chair.

Early-19thC X-frame stool based on ancient Roman model, probably Austrian.

curved X-supports. Guilds disbanded following French Revolution, but standards remain high in cities. In country districts, unaffected by guilds, traditional methods followed. Many provincial chairs have 'ladded' ('slat') backs, with shaped rungs or rails tenoned into rounded uprights, legs socketed into seat frames (see also **NEW WORLD, SLAT-BACK CHAIRS, p. 293**).

DECORATION

Neo-classical, first phase (Louis XVI): Legs square-tapered or turned and tapered, often fluted. Delicate, restrained carving of beads, acanthus, on frames; backs sometimes surmounted by a trophy of arms or musical instruments within a wreath.

Neo-classical, second phase (Etruscan): Fretted, lyre-shaped splats from 1780s. Egyptian sphinxes, carved or cast in metal, on Empire armchairs, some of which have rounded backs and arms carved as crouching lions.

***Above**, Russian mahogany bergre with ormolu mounts, about 1810.*

FINISH

Louis XVI: Woodwork left natural, painted or gilded. Seats caned, or webbed and padded before being upholstered, but not sprung.

Etruscan/Empire: Mahogany polished, beech stained black and parcel-gilt.

RELATIVE VALUES

Louis XVI and Empire chairs and settees survive in sufficiently large quantities for them to be bought at sensible prices, unless in the category described as 'important'.

JACOB

Georges Jacob and his sons, leading chairmakers of the Louis XVI, Directoire and Empire periods, very often carved a pair of marguerites on the frieze of a chair, above the front legs.

CHAIRS

About

1815-1860

French Charles X mahogany armchair, about 1825.

STYLE AND APPEARANCE

Biedermeier (post-Empire) style in **Austria**, **Germany**, **Scandinavia**, 1815-35. Chairs – mostly without arms – have square-section legs, straight or slightly splayed, and low backs with top rails projecting at sides beyond uprights, enclosing lyre, vase, dolphin or triple reed motifs, or simple horizontal rails. Balloon-back chairs, 1835-50. Armchairs

Russian Karelian birch chair in Biedermeier style, about 1820.

***Above**, an Austrian Biedermeier sofa, about 1820.*

ousted by settees, mainly Empire in style with sabre or cornucopia-shaped feet; turned feet after 1830. One type has compartments in arms for magazines. Highly original designs with serpentine supports by Danhauser of Vienna.

In 1830, Thonet of Boppard, **Prussia**, begins experiments that lead to factory in Vienna producing bentwood chairs, rocking-chairs, stools, settees, at first Biedermeier in style but developing unique curvilinear character by 1850 – still in production. In Poland,

***Above**, French Louis Philippe rosewood sofa with neo-classical marquetry decoration.*

'Simmler' style (named after Warsaw family firm founded in 18thC) influenced by Biedermeier, French and English styles). In Russia, upholstery embroidered with flowers.

France retains many Empire elements following restoration of monarchy in 1815 (Restauration) e.g. *la méridienne* – couch with scrolled ends, one lower than the other; *fauteuil à gondole* – armchair with rounded prow-like back. Gothic revival about 1840 adopts chair-backs with pointed arches, cluster columns in *troubadour* style, otherwise known as *cathédrale* when applied to *prie dieux* with low sloping seat. Rococo chairs and settees in Louis XV style reproduced.

A Napoleon III mahogany side-chair in Gothic style.

Christie's

Italy continues Empire style, toys with Gothic revival; burgeoning nationalism favours Dantesque chairs and stools on X-supports, echoing Italian Renaissance.

Spain follows semi-classical 'Fernandino' phase at mid-century with full-blooded revival of baroque ('Isabellino' style).

MATERIALS

Pale woods (*bois clairs*) – cherry, bird's eye maple – fashionable until return about 1840 to mahogany, ebony, oak, walnut. Wide range of upholstery fabrics.

19thC Alpine walnut chair, the back in the form of a grotesque mask.

Christie's

CONSTRUCTION

Steam-driven machinery makes for cheaper production, but mainly confined to sawing boards and veneers. Most joints still cut by hand, except in large factories. Thonet's patented method of steaming birch rods into curved shapes makes mortise-and-tenon joints obsolete for his chairs; e.g. No. 14 in his range is composed of six sections screwed together; components exported for assembly at destination.

DECORATION

Biedermeier: Carving of swans, dolphins. Ebonised classical columns applied to fronts of settees.

Restauration: Marquetry in dark woods on light grounds. Fewer ormolu mounts.

Troubadour *(Cathédrale)*: Carving and piercing of Gothic motifs.

Dantesque: Carving in Renaissance style.

Rococo revival: Carving in Louis XV style.

FINISH

Biedermeier: Polished, never stained.

Restauration: French polishing. Some legs of seat furniture veneered.

Troubadour: Oak left natural or waxed.

Dantesque: Walnut sometimes 'antiqued' with black stain.

Rococo revival: Painted and/or gilded.

RELATIVE VALUES

Sets of Biedermeier chairs expensive but odd ones often very reasonably priced. Anything in *bois clairs* is now appreciably dearer than the mahogany equivalent.

SEAT CONSTRUCTION

Chair-seats may be either 'stuffed over', the upholstery being fixed to the frame of the chair with small tacks, or 'drop-in', the seat fitting within, but not fixed to, the frame. If, as often happens, a drop-in seat is re-upholstered without removing the existing cover, the fit is usually too tight; this may result in loosening of mortise-and-tenon joints, leading to splits.

CHAIRS

About

1850-1890

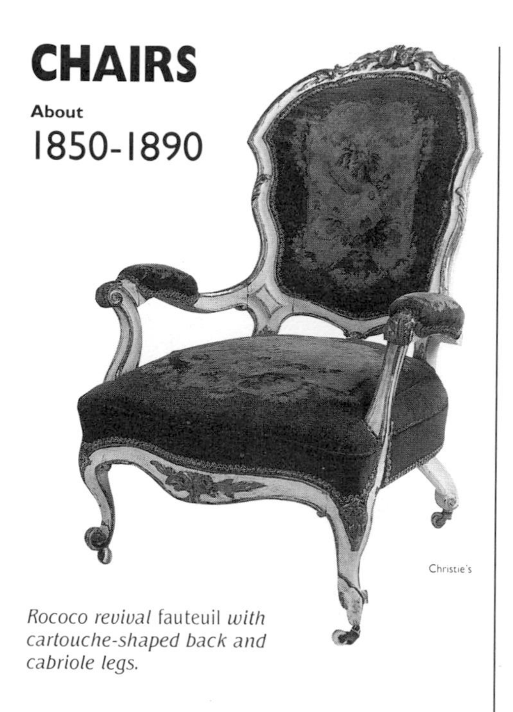

Rococo revival fauteuil *with cartouche-shaped back and cabriole legs.*

Revivals of historic styles abounded, but were often interpreted in new ways, so despite all the slavish copying that went on, most seat furniture of this period can hardly be mistaken for any other.

STYLE AND APPEARANCE

Rococo revival chairs combine cabriole legs with baroque twists, while *chaises longues* and sofas have backs with curves bolder than anything known in 18thC.

***Below**, rococo revival sofa with elaborate carving, about 1860.*

From 1850s, Napoleon III (Second Empire) side chairs have tapered legs derived from Louis XVI types, but turnings are more pronounced and ringed with gilt metal beadings. A suite comprises sofa, two armchairs, four or six side-chairs with exposed frames, often ebonised, the legs with gilt flutes. Balloon backs, familiar since 1830s, remain popular.

Napoleon III chair with turned, tapered and fluted legs.

New types include *le confident* (S-shaped sofa – occupants whisper to each other while facing in opposite directions); *le canapé capitonné* (prototype of modern settee, with sausage-shaped arms); *le pouf* (circular stool); *la chauffeuse capitonné à roulettes* (low, armless chair on wheels for drawing up to fire); *'le*

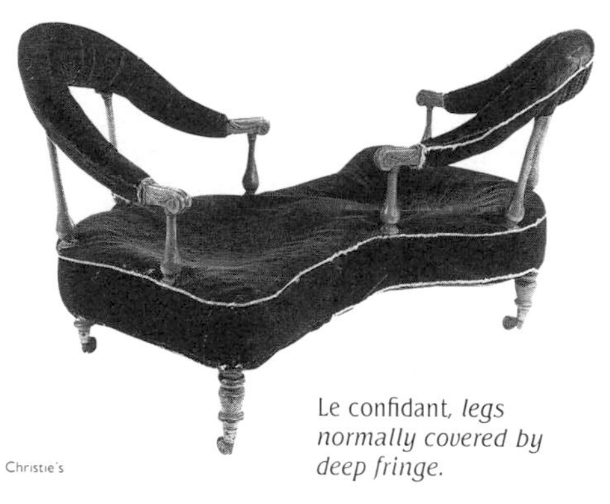

Le confidant, *legs normally covered by deep fringe.*

crapaud' (vernacular name for fully-upholstered armchair). All heavily stuffed, deep-buttoned and with long fringes hiding their turned feet.

'Sociable' used at centre of salon, about 1860.

Christie's

MATERIALS

Mahogany, walnut, beech for side chairs and armchairs with exposed woodwork, beech for frames of fully upholstered types. Horsehair and flock for stuffing. Steel for spiral springs. Bamboo for chairs in oriental styles. Rich upholstery fabrics, especially plush (wool velvet as distinct from silk).

CONSTRUCTION

Apart from mass-produced, screwed-together Thonet products (see CHAIRS about 1815 to 1860, **p. 227**), traditional methods assisted by machinery are employed for seats with exposed woodwork. For frames of fully upholstered types, dowels increasingly used in place of mortise-and-tenon joints, and towards end of century for chairs with show-wood (exposed) frames. Most important development is spiral springing, first invented in Germany, patented in Britain in 1828 but not in general use until about 1850.

DECORATION

Revivals: Carving, sometimes rather coarse, of motifs more or less appropriate to the style imitated.

Contemporary: Turning, carving, fluting of legs, marquetry on top rails. Main decorative feature is rich upholstery and fancy trimmings, especially fringes.

FINISH

Much exposed woodwork ebonised, otherwise French polished.

RELATIVE VALUES

Taste swings periodically for and against ebonised furniture. If Napoleon III types are bought in a bear market, complete or part salon suites in need of re-upholstery can be picked up at bargain prices.

EBONISED SEATS

The fashion for ebonised seats spread to Britain in the 1860s and it is often difficult to be sure about the country of origin. A useful but not infallible guide is that most Continental (especially **French** and **Italian**) examples have small leather-covered wheels; **English** have brown or white porcelain castors. English castors, however, were imported in bulk by furniture manufacturers in Germany. It is fairly safe to conclude that chairs of this period with porcelain castors are not French, and that ones with leather wheels are not English – unless, of course, they have been replaced.

CHAIRS

About

1890-1920

Walnut chair by van de Velde, 1895.

Christie's

'Sitzmachine', 1914; bentwood.

Christie's

Declining quality of commercial products blamed – often unfairly – on machine work. Reformist movement partly inspired by folk culture, but culminates in 1890s with international style taking its name from main outlet, la Maison de l'Art Nouveau in Paris.

STYLE AND APPEARANCE

Art nouveau: Paris designers; de Feure, noted for rich upholstery on neo-Louis XVI style frames; Gaillard, whose functional chairs covered in leather have legs and stretchers that resemble trees; Guimard, who also uses leather for asymmetrical banquettes.

At **Nancy** in 1901, Gallé founds school of design inspired by Symbolist movement and drawing heavily on natural forms. Now best known for engraved glass; chairs derived partly from Louis XV types, partly from organic forms. Influences Majorelle, maker of reproduction furniture, who adopts new style; his chairs are elegant, finely made (but utilizing machines), ormolu-mounted.

In **Brussels**, van de Velde of Antwerp is associated with La Libre Esthétique and practises principles of organic unity in design, before moving to Germany in 1898. Some of his chairs have rush seats, some batik upholstery (see MATERIALS). Horta, Brussels architect famous for whiplash line, designs seat furniture upholstered in velvet. Serrurier-Bovy, Liège cabinet-maker, uses both continental art nouveau curves and more austere forms inspired by British Arts and Crafts; cane-seated settles in ash show influence of Mackintosh.

In **Vienna**, same principles followed when Wiener Werkstätte is set up in 1903 by Hoffman and Moser, members of Sezessionist movement. The *'Sitzmachine'* – bentwood

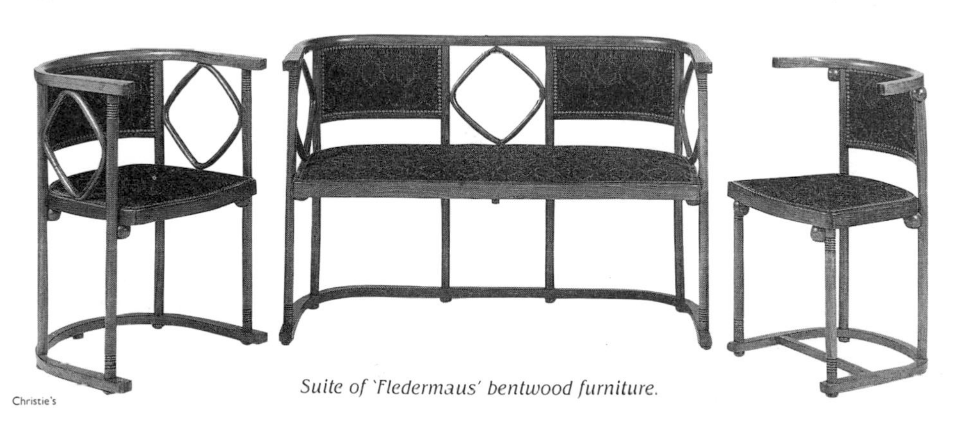

Christie's

Suite of 'Fledermaus' bentwood furniture.

armchair – designed by Hoffmann and made by Kohn, owes much to Thonet. Moser's chairs – angular, with flat, solid backs decorated in marquetry in maple and mother-of-pearl – anticipate Art Deco.

Ebonised side chair; vellum, copper and pewter inlay by Bugatti.

Christie's

In **Milan**, Bugatti's workshops produce fantastic seat furniture: a bench seat, Moorish in flavour, comprises a pair of low armchairs on X-supports linked by a high-backed centre section; frame inlaid with metal, seats and backs covered in vellum and hung with tasselled fringes.

Austrian Secessionist armchair (with table).

Christie's

In **Barcelona**, Gaudi designs equally strange chairs that appear to be made of human bones or tentacles of sea creatures, but are, disappointingly, only wood.

MATERIALS

Oak, ash, rosewood, beech, palisander, walnut, ebony. Bugatti uses vellum, leather, copper. Van de Velde uses batik fabrics – technique, derived from Java, for negative dyeing, using wax to resist dyes and leave pattern in original colour of cloth.

CONSTRUCTION

Best examples hand-crafted by established methods, but some makers, e.g. Majorelle, use machines to good effect for producing component parts; others, e.g. Hoffmann, adapt Thonet's system of assembling steam-bent section with screws. Commercial, 1920s chairs and settees in art nouveau style mainly machine-cut and assembled by hand. Cheapest type, intended for bedrooms, has turned legs socketed into seat-frame.

DECORATION

Frames carved as stems and branches; flowers in marquetry, especially by Gallé. Floral subjects in ormolu by Majorelle. Islamic-style inlay by Bugatti. Silvered metal inlay by Moser. Later commercial products in mahogany inlaid with lilies in contrasting woods, mother-of-pearl.

FINISH

French polishing, waxing.

RELATIVE VALUES

As with other periods, important art nouveau items expensive, but quantities of late, commercially produced seats – tall-backed, leggy – available at modest prices.

INFERIOR QUALITY

Lower quality chairs and settees, mostly forming drawing-room suites originally, continued to be made (in **Italy** especially) until about 1925. Though decorative, they are often flimsy in construction and unsuitable for heavy use.

CHAIRS

About

1920-1940

Painted chair designed by Rietveld for a military club in 1932.

Christie's

STYLE AND APPEARANCE

Modernist and Art Deco: About 1917, **Dutch** architect Rietveld, trained by father as a joiner, designs his first chair under influence of Lloyd Wright, dispensing with traditional joints – type that becomes known as 'Red and Blue' (see CONSTRUCTION.) With other members of group associated with *de Stijl* magazine, believes 'the machine contributes to the spiritualization of life'.

In 1919, Gropius established Bauhaus school of art and design at Weimar, moving to Dessau, 1925. Breuer designs steel-framed 'Wassily' chair, 1925; Stam makes tubular metal cantilevered chair, 1924-6, with versions by van der Rohe and Breuer also contending for first place. Van der Rohe designs Barcelona chair as exhibition piece, 1929 – still in production. Equally famous is Breuer's steel and wood *chaise longue*, 1932.

In **France**, Le Corbusier works along similar lines, but pushed to perimeter of 1925 Paris Exposition Internationale des Arts Décoratifs et Industriels Modernes – more decorative than modern industrial – devoted mainly to what is now known as Art Deco: Ruhlmann's elegant armchairs and sofas with inlaid frames, Defréne's three-piece suites upholstered in tapestry, the frames carved and gilt. Le Corbusier and Perriand design *grand confort* easy chair (1926) with tubular steel frame, leather upholstery, consistent with 'beautiful equipment' concept.

Art Deco chair, influenced by primitive African furniture, 1920s.

Christie's

Oak lath and leather chair by Breuer, 1924.

Christie's

Late 1920s and 1930s seat furniture combines best and worst of functional modernist and extravagant Art Deco styles, best elegantly streamlined, worst flashy and vulgar. Most distinguished work from **Scandinavia**, where trim chairs with seat and back forming continuous curves are designed about 1925 by Asplund, followed by Klint's hand-made look, and Aalto's use of steamed and bent plywood for cantilevered frames.

MATERIALS

Modernist: Oak, ash, beech, walnut; birch plywood; tubular steel, leather, woven textiles.

Rosewood stool by Eileen Gray, 1920s

Art Deco: Mahogany, walnut, rosewood, steel, fine leathers, suede, tapestry, printed textiles, wool moquette, uncut moquette.

CONSTRUCTION

Modernists reject traditional methods. Rietveld – a competent joiner – abandons mortise-and-tenon joints, making 'Red and Blue' armchair by screwing together, face to face, six uprights, four stretchers, two seat rails, a back rail, two narrow boards as arms and two wide ones as seat and back. Breuer, Stam, van der Rohe, Le Corbusier devise continuous shapes in tubular steel, thus obviating joinery. In 1930s, Breuer uses aluminium strips.

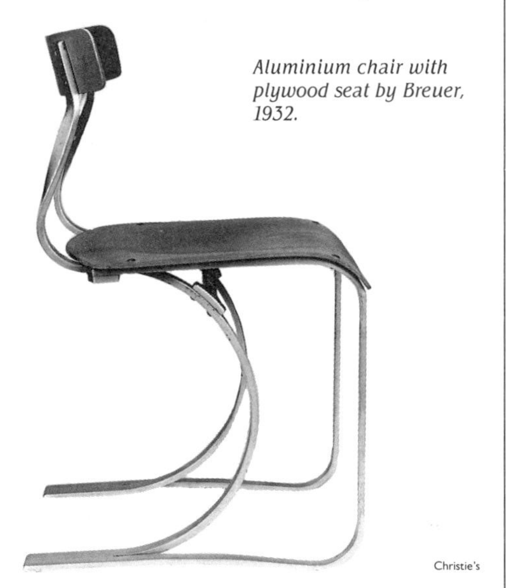

Aluminium chair with plywood seat by Breuer, 1932.

Art Deco essentially traditional, however novel in appearance; frames joined with mortise-and-tenon or dowel joints.

DECORATION

Modernists reject extraneous decoration, but are not brutalists as has been said; they see chairs, settees, *chaises longues* as forms of abstract sculpture, beautiful in themselves. Some designers, e.g. Rietveld, make use of contrasting colours; others, e.g. Klint, rely on the natural grain of the wood and on undyed leather.

Art Deco, while not neglecting line and form, puts great emphasis on decoration – marquetry in exotic woods, metal inlay, carving, lacquering. When cheap furniture trade attempts to reproduce effect of faintly decadent glamour, the result has all the charm of smeared lipstick.

FINISH

Modernist: Natural woods, waxed or French polished and rubbed down to semi-matt. Early tubular steel nickel-plated, later types chromium-plated. Upholstery often made as separate units – squab cushions, pads.

Art Deco: Woods either natural colours or stained. Cheaper versions highly polished or cellulose sprayed. Better types very skilfully upholstered, cheaper ones badly finished. More traditional types, neither distinctly modern' nor 'Art Deco', often supplied with loose covers (for further details, see the **BOX** at the foot of this page).

RELATIVE VALUES

Being the 'antiques' period nearest to the present, and the one in which mass-production came into its own, the 1920-40 period might be expected to offer a wide and inexpensive choice. In practice, the best modernist and Art Deco seat furniture is at least as expensive as that of other periods, and second-best that is worth having is hard to find; but auction sales in houses furnished in 1930s can provide excellent opportunities.

LOOSE COVERS

The practice of fitting loose covers dates back to 18thC, when – especially in France – sets were changed with the seasons. Nothing that early now likely to be concealed, but interesting chairs and settees dating from 19thC onwards can be found with original upholstery hidden and protected by tatty chintz covers.

CHESTS

Before about

1450

The lidded, box-like chest was one of the earliest articles of furniture, made over a very long period and in many parts of the world.

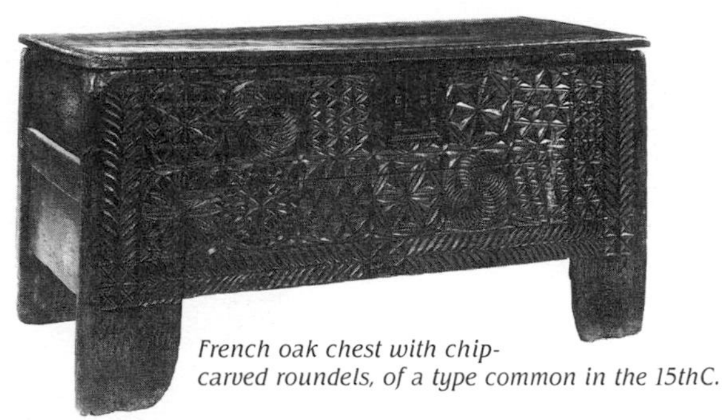

French oak chest with chip-carved roundels, of a type common in the 15thC.

STYLE AND APPEARANCE

The first chests were hollowed out logs, but more advanced types survive from the 13thC, when the Romanesque style was being overtaken by the Gothic in Northern Europe, while Italy was more influenced by Byzantine styles of the Eatsern Roman Empire (see **GUIDE TO PERIODS AND STYLES p. 189**).

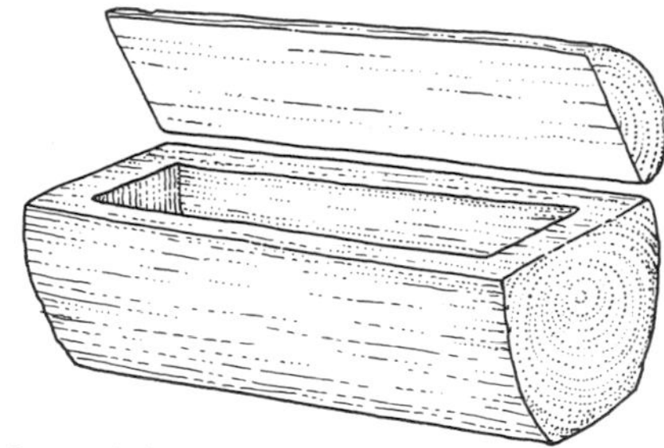

Dug-out chest.

MATERIALS

Local timbers, e.g. walnut in **Italy**, **Spain**, southern **Germany**; oak in **France** and the **Netherlands**. Iron hinges, straps, scrolls.

CONSTRUCTION

Dug-out: Log hollowed out with adze (axe with horizontal cutting edge). The lid was formed from a slice of tree-trunk (thus 'travelling trunk').

Boarded (or 'plank'): Five boards – front, back, two ends bottom – nailed together, with sixth as lid.

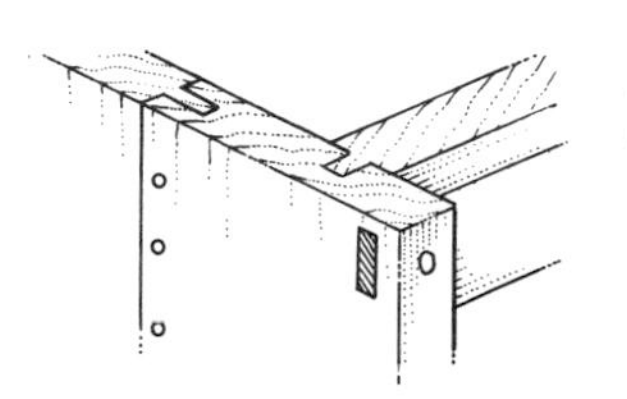

Housed construction for chest.

Housed (or clamped): Front, back and ends tenoned into mortises cut in uprights; ends sometimes strengthened with framing. Lid often pivoted with wooden pins in sockets without recourse to metal hinges.

DECORATION

Romanesque: Rounded arches on stumpy columns carved in rows across front, and pierced through feet.

Early Gothic: Chip-carved roundels on fronts, the placing of the roundels symmetrical but the patterns within them varying in random fashion. In France, birthplace of the style, carved figures of saints, knights in armour, pointed arches, or elaborately scrolled ironwork used both to strengthen and decorate.

FINISH

Often painted in vivid colours originally but little trace of them remains. Present colour and appearance depend on environment and treatment over last 500 years, and may be dark, light or something in between.

RELATIVE VALUES

Most chests earlier than 1450 are now in churches or museums, and when decorated examples in reasonable condition appear on the open market, they are expensive.

Roundels

Plain boarded chests were made well into the 17thC, and some have been chip-carved in recent times in the Gothic style. In genuine examples, the roundels were marked out with a compass, and faint traces of the incised circles can often be discerned. These are not usually apparent in chests carved later.

CHESTS

About

1450 to 1600

V&A

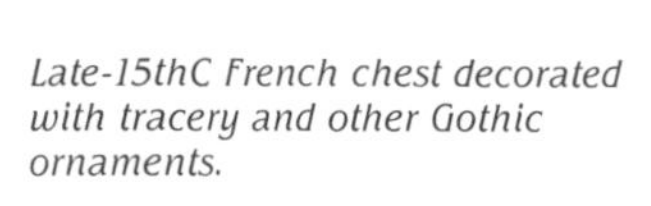

Late-15thC French chest decorated with tracery and other Gothic ornaments.

STYLE AND APPEARANCE

Late Gothic persists in Northern Europe, but is gradually influenced by the Renaissance in Italy where, from the late 15thC, classical Roman shapes and decorative features are reintroduced.

MATERIALS

Oak in **France**, northern **Germany**, the **Netherlands**; pine and fir in **Scandinavia**; walnut, cypress in **Italy**; walnut, oak, chestnut in **Spain**; various fruitwoods where grown. Gesso (plaster hardened with size). Iron hinges, carrying handles, locks and keys.

CONSTRUCTION

Panelled: Framework mortised and tenoned, secured with pegs, rebated to receive panels bevelled at edges and fitted to allow play for unequal expansion and contraction, thus minimizing warping and splitting. Lids either panelled or flush planks nailed to cross-members.

Housed: Lighter versions of this method (see **CHESTS, p. 235**) continued to be used in many areas.

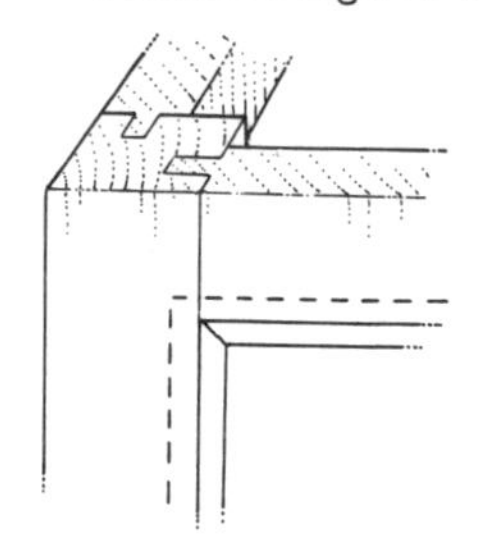

Panel rebated into mortised and tenoned frame.

Curvilinear: From late 15thC, some Italian *cassoni* (chests), imitating Roman sarcophagi, were built up sectionally and shaped to curved outline, leaving joins to be covered with gesso.

DECORATION

Late Gothic, Northern Europe: Panels carved with pointed arches, tracery, animals, foliage, linenfold (see **BEDS, p. 198**).

Renaissance: In Italy, some carving, more painting in tempera and gilding on gesso ground of biblical subjects and scenes from classical mythology. Gifted artists employed on decoration of marriage chests, often made in pairs from about 1470, when intarsia – inlay depicting architecture and still life groups – was also used. In the 16thC, intarsia was practised in the **Netherlands** (Antwerp) and **Germany** (Augsburg and Nuremberg). In **Spain** and **Portugal** – both immensely rich in the 16thC – chests were lavishly decorated with carving and inlaid abstract patterns derived from Moorish sources. **France** and **Burgundy** adopted an Italianate style in the early 16thC (François I). Mannerist (late Renaissance) elements, grotesque masks, elongated figures and 'Romayne work' – heads of men and women in carved medallions – were popular.

FINISH

Painting on gesso and directly on to wood. Oiling, waxing, varnishing; much woodwork in Northern Europe left in natural state.

RELATIVE VALUES

Many 16thC chests still survive and can be bought at prices that are modest in comparison with those of later pieces. Beware of 19thC fakes of painted Italian *cassoni*.

CHESTS AND CHESTS OF DRAWERS

About
1600-1675

Christie's

Italian Renaissance cassone.

STYLE AND APPEARANCE

Lidded chests continued to be the main storage pieces until about 1650. From then on, they were largely replaced with armoires (see **CUPBOARDS, p. 210**) and chests of drawers, but in many rural areas the lidded chest survived as a traditional type. By about 1620, baroque (see **GUIDE TO PERIODS AND STYLES, p. 192**) had begun to replace Renaissance in Italy as the dominating style for much furniture, and soon travelled north. Many Italian *cassoni* are of the sarcophagus type (see **CHESTS** 1450-1600, **opposite**) with curved carcases that suited the baroque style of decoration, but 17thC chests of drawers were angular.

Christie's

17thC carved Italian cassone.

MATERIALS

Usually, a timber near to hand (see **CHESTS** before 1450, **opposite**) as the principal wood and sometimes throughout (e.g. oak in the **Netherlands**), sometimes with a secondary one (e.g. chestnut in **France**) for drawer-linings (sides, back and bottom). Iron.

CONSTRUCTION

Chests (wood): Framed, housed or built up. Germany made an iron type now popularly known as 'armada', with a large escutcheon around a false keyhole, the true one being concealed at the centre of the lid, under which a steel mechanism operates as many as 12 spring-loaded bolts.

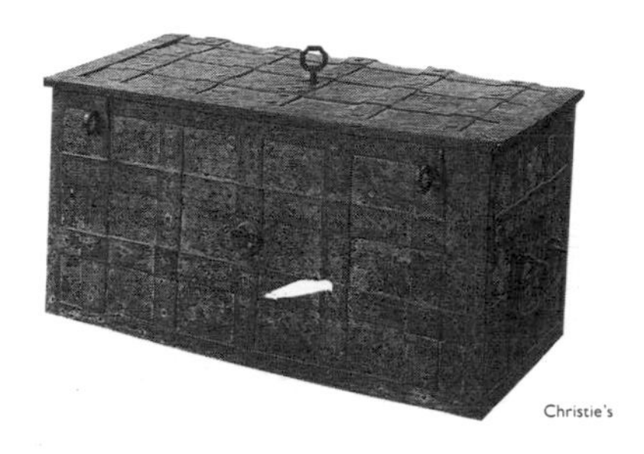
Christie's

***Above**, early-17thC German steel 'Armada' chest, locking at 14 points.*

Chests of drawers: Panelled ends joined by mortise-and-tenon joints to horizontal rails between the drawers at the front, panelled or boarded back. Drawers usually full width, but often moulded to appear narrower. In the **Netherlands**, lower ones often enclosed by doors. Drawers made with lap joints or, at best, two or three coarse dovetails. Drawer-sides grooved to slide on side runners fitted inside ends. Feet are either continuations of stiles (corner posts) or separately turned on the lathe to ball or bun shapes, and dowelled into the base.

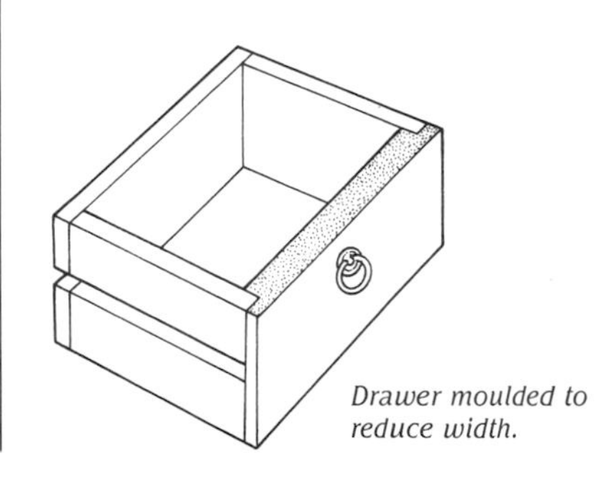

Drawer moulded to reduce width.

DECORATION

Chests: Early-17thC Italian *cassoni* often have one large front panel with figures, scrolls or coats-of-arms carved in bold relief. In **Denmark**, chests of boarded construction were carved with love tokens (e.g. twin hearts) or with repeat patterns simulating the strapping on German iron chests (see the information on CONSTRUCTION above).

Chests of drawers: In Italy, drawer-fronts were sometimes decorated with *certosina* – inlay into the solid with small pieces of bone to form geometric patterns. In the **Netherlands**, floral patterns were inlaid with bone, ivory, mother-of-pearl. In most regions, mouldings were applied to drawer-fronts in geometric patterns – an Islamic style that spread from Moorish Spain. Patterns may be different on each drawer-front. Some mouldings and small areas veneered in ebony, imported from the East Indies; thus, the ability to veneer led to the French calling cabinetmakers *ébénistes*, to distinguish them from the *menuisiers* (joiners) who worked with solid wood.

Handles: Turned wood, iron rings or brass drops. Italian wood knobs sometimes carved with heads of humans or animals.

Handles: ***below right****, wooden knob, turned and hatched;* ***below left****, iron ring.*

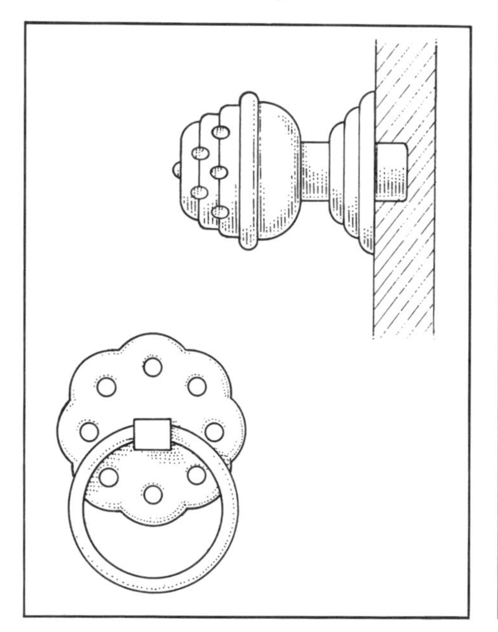

FINISH

If grain was meant to be seen, varnish made of resin dissolved in linseed or poppy oil was used until about 1660, when lac in spirits of wine became popular. Country-made pieces oiled and polished with beeswax dissolved in turpentine. In **Spain**, **Italy**, the **Alpine countries** and **Scandinavia**, pine was painted in colours, with scrolls, foliage, flowers or figures, or left in natural state and scrubbed.

RELATIVE VALUES

Best buy for those with space to fill: large Dutch chests of drawers, partly enclosed by doors; high quality, oak throughout. There are 19thC copies around, but the quality is often even better than the 17thC originals.

A.T. Sylvester & Sons

Dutch chest of drawers, mid-17thC.

WHAT TO AVOID

Small Italian and Spanish chests of drawers in painted pine are often crudely constructed and later in date than they appear – sometimes so much later that they are best avoided unless backed by a worthwhile guarantee.

CHESTS AND CHESTS OF DRAWERS

About

1675-1760

Polychrome boulle commode, about 1700.

STYLE AND APPEARANCE

Lidded chests continue to be made, but mainly in rural areas; regional variations become firmly established.

Chests of drawers in mid-17thC styles also made in provinces until well after 1700, but in major centres, panelled ends give way to flush surfaces, applied mouldings disappear from drawer-fronts, veneering, parquetry and marquetry are widely practised. Chests on stands with turned legs in the **Netherlands**. Rectilinear carcases until after 1700.

France is leader of fashion under Louis XIV, for whom a pair of curved chests of drawers – *commodes en tombeau*– were made by Boulle in 1708-9, derived from Roman sarcophagus shape already re-created for Italian Renaissance *cassoni*. During the transitional baroque/rococo period (Régence, 1715-30, covering childhood of Louis XV), serpentine-fronted and bombé (blown up) three-drawer commodes are made, until the Louis XV rococo form, with only two drawers, raised on cabriole legs, is created by Cressent. In the 1730s the full bombé shape, with gently undulating curves from top to bottom and side to side, has become popular throughout most of Europe, but provincial types often have curve on one plane only. In some centres, curves are exaggerated, e.g. 'high-bosomed' in **Venice**, 'low-bellied' in **Holland**.

MATERIALS

Local timbers for country types, exotic woods for veneers, e.g. varieties of *Dalbergia* – rosewood, kingwood ('prince wood'), palisander (purpleheart). Pine or oak as foundation for veneering and with chestnut and poplar, as drawer-linings. Marble in various colours was used for tops of commodes, ormolu for handles and mounts.

CONSTRUCTION

1675-1720: Flush ends made with rub joints (glueing boards edge to edge, rubbing them together until surplus glue is expunged, clamping until set). Rails between drawers tenoned into ends. Drawers dovetailed, not always very finely; fronts extended to overlap rails; side-runners abandoned in favour of runners on bottoms of drawers.

Cross-section of drawer-fronts of bombé commode, extended to conceal rail.

1720-1760: Serpentine and bombé shapes built up (see NEW WORLD, TABLES 1790-1840, **p. 323**). By about 1750, drawer-fronts in fine examples overlap rails sufficiently to conceal them and present a virtually uninterrupted surface for decoration.

DECORATION

Marquetry: Inlaying veneered surface with a figurative design composed of other veneers. The usual material was wood, sometimes tinted with coloured stains; but other materials were used, e.g. ivory, while Boulle per-

Boulle marquetry: ***left*** *motif cut from sheet of brass;* ***right*** *motif in tortoiseshell.*

fected the technique of inlaying arabesques of engraved metal (brass, pewter) into a turtleshell veneer backed with coloured mica.

Christie's

Top of Louis XIV boulle commode.

The pieces of shell were fitted into the spaces left after cutting out the brass, and vice versa, to produce pairs of commodes with the decoration of one the reverse of that of the other. The Spindler family and Müller of Bayreuth were among the many German craftsmen who made bombé commodes with fine marquetry.

Parquetry: Small diamond-shaped pieces of contrasting veneer laid in juxtaposition to create intriguing illusions of three-dimensional perspectives.

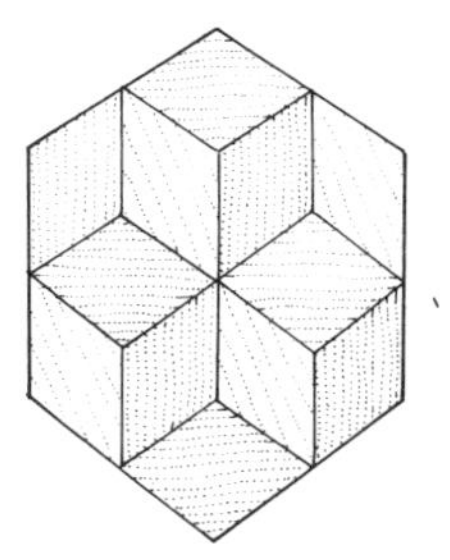

Parquetry.

Ormolu: Cast bronze, chiselled, gilded and burnished, used for handles and mounts. Commodes made by the Spindlers for Frederick the Great were loaded with ormolu mounts made by the Swiss-born Kambli.

Carving: In some areas, e.g. **Scandinavia**, carved and gilt mounts substituted for ormolu. Carved scrolls, flowers, foliage decorate fine French provincial commodes.

FINISH

Marquetry was brought to a brilliant colourful finish by sanding down and coating with varnish before waxing. Coloured varnishes patented by the brothers Martin (*vernis Martin*) were used for special effects on fronts and ends of commodes, e.g. imitating oriental lacquer (see also **EUROPEAN CUPBOARDS AND CABINETS, p. 213**). Venetians used their own varnish – *lacca*– to paint vivid flowers on coloured grounds. A cheaper version, *lacca povera*, was executed by glueing prints to surfaces before colouring and varnishing. The interiors of Venetian commodes – even the best – are often very poorly finished.

Christie's

Marquetry decoration.

RELATIVE VALUES

A first-class signed French commode is a millionaire's status symbol, but many lesser items made in the provinces or in other parts of Europe sell at much more modest prices and can be every bit as agreeable.

MAKERS' STAMPS

From 1743 every piece made in Paris was supposed to be stamped with the maker's name and, after vetting by a member of the guild's jury, with their stamp – 'J.M.E.' (Jure des Menuisiers et Ebnistes). If the marble top is lifted off, these marks are frequently found stamped in the woodwork of a commode made between 1743 and 1791, but their absence is not necessarily damning (see **GUIDE TO PERIODS AND STYLES, ROCOCO, p. 193**).

CHESTS AND CHESTS OF DRAWERS

About

1760-1800

Transitional French commode with neo-classical mounts and marquetry decoration, about 1770.

STYLE AND APPEARANCE

First stage of neo-classicism brings discipline to design of sophisticated commodes. Bombé shape unfashionable in Paris during reign of Louis XVI but survives in **Germany** and **Holland**, often in modified form (with curve from top to bottom only) into 1770s. Full bombé shape is continued in **Sweden** with gilt channels in rails between drawers.

Many country-made lidded chests and provincial chests of drawers – especially in **Denmark** – interpret new style in naïve ways, sometimes showing English influence in crisp, economical shapes.

MATERIALS

Mainly as in previous period; mahogany added to French repertoire in 1780s.

CONSTRUCTION

Full bombé shape (curved on two planes) difficult for all but best craftsmen to manage – only a few made drawer-sides with curves following line of ends – so its abandonment in favour of rectilinear shapes, or of bowed or serpentine fronts (curved on one plane only, from side to side) results in more attention to sound construction. Even basic features, e.g. dovetailed joint, show improvement. The cabriole leg is retained during the transitional Louis XV/XVI period but is eventually discarded and a variety of straight, tapered legs, square or turned, is adopted. Some commodes more like cabinets, with doors concealing drawers.

Bombé shape.

Serpentine lines.

Bowed shape.

DECORATION

Marquetry: From about 1760 to 1780, still lavish but with growing tendency to restriction within defined areas, e.g. an oval or octagon at centre of commode front by Maggiolini of Milan inlaid with figures from classical myth-

Sotheby's

North Italian marquetry commode, 1790-1800.

ology. David Roentgen of Neuwied, supplier to French and Russian royal families and supreme practitioner of marquetry, is quick to jettison it when plain mahogany becomes fashionable in 1780s, shortly before French Revolution.

Carving: Delicately carved commodes on slim legs produced in **Rhineland**, richly carved flowers on angles of serpentine-fronted commodes in **Portugal**.

Ormolu: Handles and mounts first features to exchange asymmetrical rococo squirls for neatly balanced, neo-classical masks, acanthus leaves and wreaths, but high quality maintained.

Bronze workers had own guilds guarding demarcation lines until disbandment of all guilds in 1791.

***Below**, porcelain plaques and neo-classical mounts on Louis XVI commode.*

Christie's

FINISH

Painting: Delicate trellis patterns painted with coloured varnishes in **France**, panels painted with Pompeiian figures in **Spain**.

Pietre dure: Florentine mosaic panels in coloured hardstones – often cannibalized from earlier cabinets – used to decorate Louis XVI commodes (see **CUPBOARDS AND CABINETS, p. 211**).

Folk art: Country-made chests of drawers in many areas (e.g. **Switzerland**, the **Tyrol**, **Denmark**) painted in bright colours with flowers, landscapes, formally arranged, in keeping with the neo-classical style.

RELATIVE VALUES

Highly-decorated Louis XVI commodes almost as expensive as Louis XV types; plainer ones much less so and easier to live with, whether French or of another nationality in the French-dominated style.

Christie's

***Above**, a plain mahogany commode with ormolu mounts and secretaire drawer, about 1790-1800.*

FRENCH COMMODES

In French commodes of the Louis XV/XVI periods, it is usual, though not essential, for the top edges of drawer-sides to be slightly rounded. This is not a guarantee of authenticity, nor is it conclusive evidence of French nationality (the same feature is found on many of the best 18thC English chests of drawers), but it is a favourable sign when present in French commodes, as it is not usually evident on 19thC copies.

CHESTS AND CHESTS OF DRAWERS

About
1800-1850

German commode in French Empire style, about 1810.

STYLE AND APPEARANCE

The lidded chest continues to be made as a purely utilitarian article – e.g. blanket chest, tool chest; and as a decorative one also in some areas – **Scandinavia**, **Russia**, **Poland** and the **Baltic countries**. Chests made by peasant communities in **Catalonia** in the mid-19thC can easily be mistaken for 17thC examples.

French mahogany commode, the drawers flanked by monopodia, about 1820.

The grand, commode-type chest of drawers survives as a salon piece in French Empire style, current throughout most of Europe, 1800-15; but from then until about 1850 (excepting revivals of Louis XV) is made in plainer, more functional fashion and banished to the bourgeois bedroom, where it is seen at its best in the Biedermeier style, originating in **Austria** about 1815, spreading to **Germany**, **Scandinavia** and **Russia**, so carrying on a sober version of Empire neo-classicism until about 1830, after which historic revivals (Gothic, rococo, Renaissance, baroque) begin to intrude.

MATERIALS

Mahogany popular at first but British blockade of Napoleonic Europe creates scarcity, thus stimulating use of native timbers – cherry, birch, pine, walnut, fruitwoods, poplar, ash (but not oak) – with growing preference for pale woods.

CONSTRUCTION

Empire-Biedermeier: Usually rectilinear, but semi-bombé shape used by Danhauser, Vienna, about 1815. In popular type, top drawer projects as if resting on a pair of cylindrical columns. A tall, slim type (called *semainier* in France) has seven drawers – one for each day of the week. Although guilds had been disbanded in France, Germany and Aus-

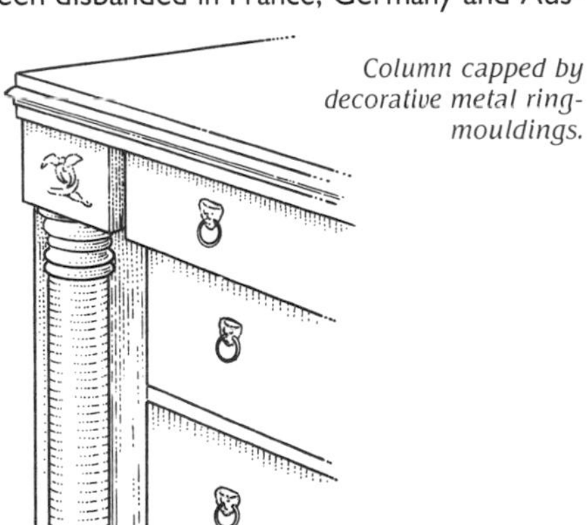

Column capped by decorative metal ring-mouldings.

tria, the strict training of apprentices continued as before, resulting in a high degree of craftsmanship, aided from the 1820s by English inventions, e.g. glass paper, improved saws and planes. New machines for planing, drilling, cutting mortises and producing veneers in large sheets were introduced during the Biedermeier period, and large factories set up (notably Danhauser's, Vienna); but methods of assembly with traditional mortise-and-tenon and dovetail joints remained much the same as before. They are always concealed, the Biedermeier ideal being a flush surface, sometimes broken by a recessed arch set at the centre of the drawers, the rails also sometimes hidden by overlapping drawer-fronts.

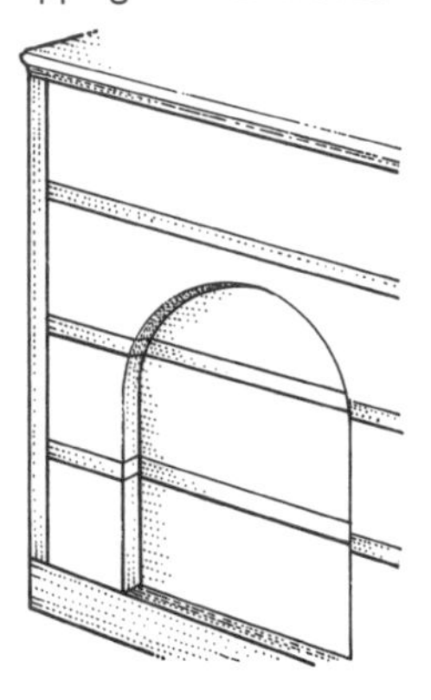

Recessed arch, sometimes found on Biedermeier furniture.

DECORATION

Empire: Imperial symbols as gilt bronze mounts, imitated in brass for cheaper products. Marquetry in dark woods on light ground revived after restoration of French monarchy in 1815.

Biedermier chest of drawers, about 1825.

Sotheby's

Biedermeier: Marquetry and mounts similar to Empire; ivory or bone escutcheon plates around keyhole – perhaps as an aid to finding key; it is often the only thing to grip, handles being sacrificed to Biedermeier passion for flatness.

FINISH

French polishing introduced in **France** during Empire period. **Austria** and **Germany** used stains for first time during Biedermeier period, especially to simulate ebony (for bandings) and mahogany. Even then, walnut never stained. Grain of veneer on drawer-fronts runs vertically. Top edges of drawers masked with thick veneer except in **Sweden**, where pine foundation is usually visible; this also applies to many 18thC Swedish bureaux.

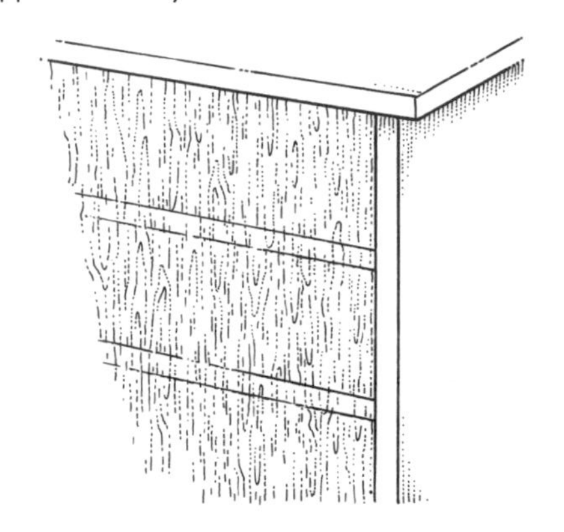

Continous vertical grain of veneer.

RELATIVE VALUES

Chests of drawers of this period in pale woods not very fashionable but still not over-expensive. Darker woods, especially mahogany (the most expensive when new), now wanted rather less – excellent value.

MOCK-BIEDERMEIER

Much pretentious, poorly made, post-1850 Germanic furniture is now sold under the fashionable Biedermeier label. The best was made before 1830, is of high quality and severe-looking. Anything made after the 1840 revolution is unlikely to be true to the Biedermeier ideal of beauty – best expressed, someone once said, in the music of Schubert.

CHESTS AND CHESTS OF DRAWERS

About

1850-1890

Christie's

19thC Swiss traditional dough trough.

STYLE AND APPEARANCE

Contemporary **chests of drawers** commodious but not very elegant. **Commodes** in 18thC rococo style, but with original touches, produced by Leistler of **Vienna**, Linke and Zwiener of **Paris**, followed by revival of Louis XVI style. Copies of originals by Carlin (18thC *ébéniste*) incorporating oriental lacquer panels, made by H. Dasson but signed with own name. In **Holland**, bombé commodes reproduced and marquetry flowers and birds added to plain old ones.

Lidded chests: French Provincial or **Swiss** dough trough (*maie* or *pétrin*) – a tapered chest resting on a stand, with Louis XIII-type turned legs and, very often, with Louis XV-type cabriole feet.

Christie's

Swiss mahogany chest of drawers, about 1865.

MATERIALS

Contemporary type: Mahogany, oak, walnut veneer.

Reproductions: Wide variety of exotic woods.

Rural types: Local timbers.

CONSTRUCTION

Traditional methods employed with great attention to detail on fine quality reproductions. Some contemporary types hand-made, many machine-assisted.

DECORATION

Veneered types: Marquetry, ormolu mounts (often poor).

Rural types (solid): Carving.

FINISH

Veneered types: French polished.

Rural types: oiled and waxed or left in natural state. Painting of figures and flowers in **Scandinavia** and **Eastern Europe**.

RELATIVE VALUES

Good quality 19thC copies of Louis XV and Louis XVI commodes now sell at fairly high prices, especially if signed by well-known maker, e.g. Linke or Dasson. Bulky, contemporary types often well-made, inexpensive but not easy to re-sell when they have outlived their usefulness.

19thC COPIES

The interiors of 19thC copies are generally better finished than those of the originals. Signatures, when present, are more conspicuous, and some (Linke's especially) have been forged in recent years.

CHESTS AND CHESTS OF DRAWERS

About

1890 to 1940

Macassar ebony chest of drawers, 1930s.

STYLE AND APPEARANCE

1890-1920: Sinuous **art nouveau** line lends itself to leggy items – tables, chairs – more readily than to carcase pieces. Leading practitioners (Majorelle, Gallé) adapt bow-fronted types by framing within stem-like mouldings, placing them on swept plinths and decorating with stylized plant forms, carved or inlaid – reminders that original chests were hollowed-out trees.

1910-40, Industrial Design: Theories of Le Corbusier and the Bauhaus, combined with practicalities of mechanized production, reduce chest to angular carcase.

1920-40, Art Deco: In reaction against industrial design, commode is treated by designers (Ruhlmann, Dunand, Follot) as item fit for drawing-room of a princess rather than cubicle of an institution. About 1930, price of one by Ruhlmann, Paris, higher than an important 18thC example – often source of inspiration exploited in novel ways. Style soon becomes debased, with flashy ornament added to angular or boldly curved shapes; but between extremes of machined austerity and Art Deco kitsch, are many hand-made, simply designed and discreetly decorated chests of drawers.

MATERIALS

Except for birch plywood and Scandinavian pine used as secondary woods, most of the main timber for furniture of all types is imported into Europe from the tropics. Art Deco designers also use ivory, semi-precious stones and silver for inlay.

CONSTRUCTION

Although much woodworking machinery now in use, old techniques survive, hand-skills being essential for fine Art Deco commodes; but by 1930s, most dovetail joints and mortises cut by machines.

Rear view of hand-made drawer with lipped front.

DECORATION

Art nouveau and Art Deco: Marquetry, carving.

Industrial design: Almost none.

FINISH

Mainly French polishing. Some Art Deco commodes lacquered. Industrial design favoured natural finish paint, cellulose.

RELATIVE VALUES

Art nouveau and Art Deco commodes, expensive when new, now command very high prices. Best buy: medium range 1930s chests of drawers in natural wood, hand-dovetailed.

VENEERS

Before paying a high price for an Art Deco commode, check that any veneers are in reasonably good condition. They were usually knife-cut very thin and prone to cracking and peeling.

DESKS

Before about

1630

South German walnut writing-box inlaid with bone, about 1600.

Pieces of furniture designed specifically for writing have taken many different forms, the work-surface sometimes being the most important feature, sometimes little more than a hidden accessory in a prestige piece designed to proclaim the owner's power and cultural pretensions.

STYLE AND APPEARANCE

Byzantine: Desks combining flat surfaces with sloped lecterns fairly commonplace.

Romanesque: The few literate people (mainly monks) used a writing-slope – often a portable box with hinged, slanted lid, but sometimes on a fixed base. A desk dating from about 1200 at Valstena Church, Gotland, **Sweden**, has a simple sloping lid on a chest-like carcase and with turned corner-posts forming the legs.

Gothic: Writing-slopes sometimes supported on panelled stands with some carved decoration.

Renaissance: In **Italy**, scholars' studies were fitted with desks, sometimes flat-topped and free standing but more often fixtures with sloped tops. A painting in Venice by Carpaccio, about 1502-08, shows St Augustine seated at a table with one end attached to wall, the other on a turned support.

Desk and chair of Romanesque form, probably Swedish, from about 1200.

Craftsmen in Augsburg, southern **Germany** produce elaborate writing cabinets, e.g. one made for Charles V in 1554 by Strohmeier, with numerous drawers, carved with figures symbolic of literature and history. A less grandiose German type is a free-standing table with a compartment placed below the top. Many tables used as desks in **Germany**, **Low Countries**, **Scandinavia** are based on designs by Vredeman de Vries published about 1588. In that year, **Spanish** power suffers setback, but rich decoration continues to be lavished on the *vargueño* (writing cabinet) with vertical fall- front serving as a work surface, the interior fitted with many small drawers grouped around a central cupboard. Related type (*papeleira*) has drawers for papers but no writing-leaf. Both types have Portuguese equivalents.

Spanish iron-bound walnut vargueño.

Spanish bone-inlaid papeleira.

MATERIALS

Mainly local woods for construction. Augsburg craftsmen use great variety for intarsia work. After 1500, **Spain** and **Portugal** import ebony, rosewood, mahogany, jacaranda, silver from New World.

CONSTRUCTION

Writing-slopes simply constructed, using nails or coarse dovetail joints. Augsburg **writing-cabinets** finely constructed with mortise-and-tenon, dovetail joints. Spanish ***vargueño*** assembled with flush boards forming tops, bottoms and ends, coarsely dovetailed together; drawers crudely made; early stands on turned legs or shaped supports with wrought-iron stretchers.

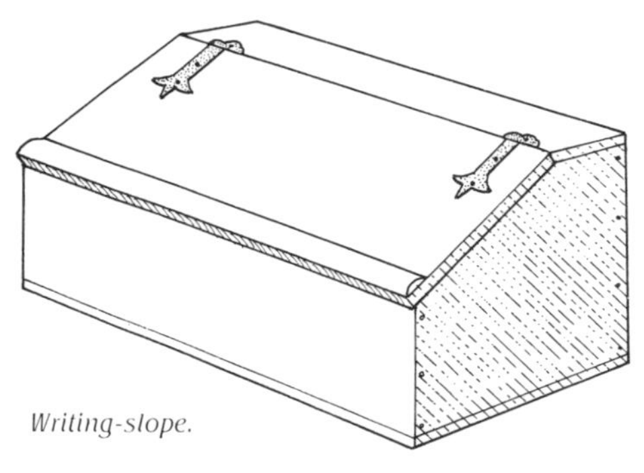

Writing-slope.

DECORATION

Renaissance **writing-slopes** often carved with strapwork; interior surface of slope in Italian examples sometimes painted naïvely with religious subjects. Augsburg **writing cabinets** inlaid with architectural fantasies.

Panel of marquetry.

Drawer-fronts of Spanish ***vargueños*** faced with carved 'Romayne' heads in boxwood or ivory, overlaid with fretted silver, inlaid with abstract patterns with strong *Mudjar* (Moorish) influence.

FINISH

Simpler types oiled, waxed or varnished. Carvings on luxurious types often gilded. Exteriors of *vargueños* sometimes covered with velvet and mounted with wrought-iron.

RELATIVE VALUES

Very few authentic examples earlier than 16thC appear on open market. Attractive writing-slopes often sell at modest prices. **German** writing cabinets expensive. **Spanish** *vargueños* not really dear considering the wealth of decoration and indeed their decorative value.

VARGUEÑOS

The *vargueño* continued to be made in Renaissance style until 19thC. Later examples should be regarded not so much as fakes or reproductions – more as traditional status symbols.

DESKS

About

1630-1715

Louis XIV boulle bureau Mazarin.

Christie's

STYLE AND APPEARANCE

Table types: Still in late-Renaissance, mannerist style of Vredeman de Vries, brought up to date with richer carved decoration by son's designs – *Versheyden Schrynwerk* – published 1630, widely used in northern Europe throughout 17thC. By about 1650, legs developed heavier, baroque turnings, very busy-looking in **Portugal**. In **Holland**, from about 1660, writing-tables on spiral legs fitted with one drawer in frieze.

From about 1680, the flat-topped *bureau Mazarin* – prototype pedestal desk with knee-hole – appears in **France**, well after death in 1661 of Cardinal Mazarin. Made also in **Italy**, especially Piedmont.

Cabinet types: In **Holland** from about 1675, medieval form of desk is adapted by moving hinges of slope from top edge to bottom so that it opens out as flat writing-surface supported by lopers (sliding bearers) or, a method soon abandoned, with gates forming part of separate stand with turned legs. About 1700, stand may still be table type (cabriole legs from about 1710), or chest of drawers type, often with cabinet above. In early 18thC bureau-cabinet develops complex features: concave drawer-fronts in **Germany**; double-dome tops in **Holland**.

Dutch slope-front bureau.

Christie's

Northern Italian bureau cabinet, about 1715.

Bonhams

Fall-front secretaire has a flat top above vertical fall, with drawers filling space below. Spanish version – *vargueño*– continues as obligatory status symbol, but is often mounted on chest of drawers type base which, in many examples now on market, is old but not original.

MATERIALS

Favourite wood internationally is walnut, used in solid and veneer forms, with ebony and wide variety of woods for marquetry and banding. Veneers laid on foundation of oak or pine which, together with walnut, chestnut, elm and poplar, according to regional availability, are used for drawer linings. Some **Dutch** bureau-cabinets have mirror glass doors, similar to English. Ivory and bone for inlay; brass, pewter and turtleshell for boullework. Brass handles, lockplates; locks fitted with brass screws (see below).

CONSTRUCTION

Bureau-Mazarin: Eight scrolled or square, tapered legs, arranged in sets of four, each set joined by X-shaped stretchers, support carcase fitted with three drawers (fronts often slightly bowed) each side, one at centre, and a recessed cupboard in kneehole. In northern **Italy**, the number of legs is sometimes reduced from eight to six.

Bureau-cabinet: Originally constructed in three separate sections – chest of drawers base supporting sloped desk with two-door cabinet above; about 1700, base and desk are integrated; cabinet always separate.

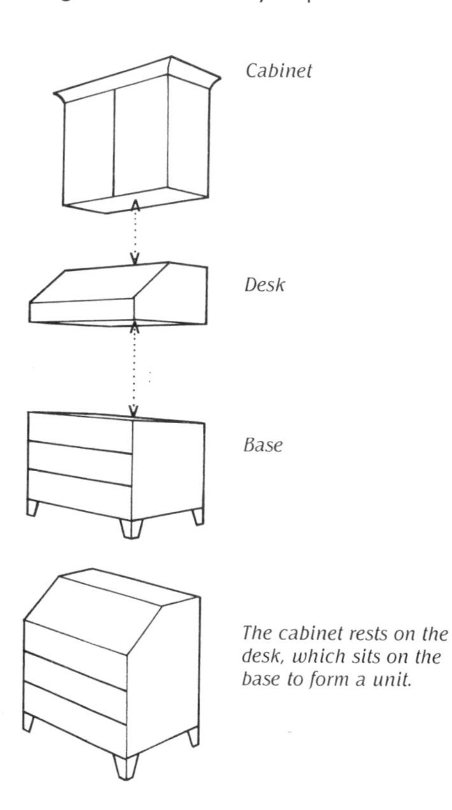

The cabinet rests on the desk, which sits on the base to form a unit.

Fall-front secretaire: Carcase in one piece, lower part fitted with drawers; large writing-leaf, in vertical position when closed, supported on iron stays when open. Shallow 'map drawer' in frieze, disguised as moulding.

Secret drawers, when found behind overt ones in interiors, often appear new and unused since the day they were made.

DECORATION

Bureaux-Mazarins: Boullework or floral marquetry in **France**; inlaid figures in bone or ivory in northern **Italy** (Turin especially).

Bureaux, bureau-cabinets, secretaires: Some provincial types in solid wood have carved decoration in baroque style, but most are veneered in walnut inlaid with geometric bandings; floral or 'seaweed' marquetry in **Holland**, banded in boxwood ornamented with penwork in black ink. Heavy moulding, especially in **Germany**.

FINISH

Solid types oiled, varnished or left natural. Veneered types varnished, waxed.

RELATIVE VALUES

Really fine *bureaux-Mazarins* and bureaux-cabinets for the seriously rich. Bureaux can be bought at sensible prices. Fall-front secretaires often reasonable because large writing-leaf creates problems in small rooms.

SCREWS

From late-17thC onwards, screws used for fixing locks, hinges. Early screws usually brass, only slightly tapered, with irregular threads filed by hand. Lathe-turned screws with regular thread from about 1750, but still without much taper, and slot across head to receive screwdriver is rarely centred precisely. Sharply tapered, machine-made steel screws with slot usually dead centre not in general use until about 1850.

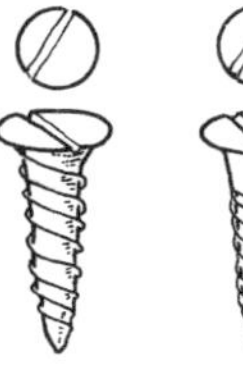
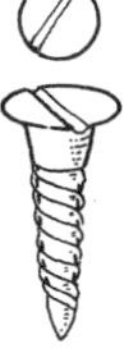
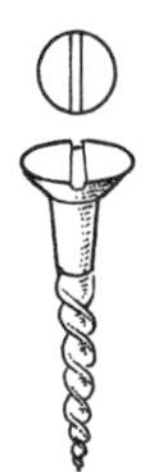

***Left**, before 1750; centre, 1750-1850; **right**, after 1850.*

DESKS

About
1715-1770

Louis XV kingwood bureau plat with serpentine top.

Christie's

STYLE AND APPEARANCE

In **France**, about 1715, the *bureau-Mazarin* with eight legs and banks of drawers is replaced, probably by Boulle, with the *bureau plat* (flat-topped writing-table) on four cabriole legs with only three drawers set in line in the frieze, the centre one slightly recessed. Veneers are protected, especially on outside angles of legs, with ormolu mounts. By 1750, *bureau plat* in fully developed Louis XV style is an assembly of flowing curves, sometimes without drawers in frieze to detract from its elegance, sometimes with cartonnier (separate, matching rack of shelves for documents) placed at end next to wall. Flowing lines followed in solid French provincial and Swiss versions.

About 1760, the *secrétaire-à-capucin* (or *à-la-Bourgogne*) is made by Vandercruse and others; a small table on cabriole legs when closed, but when folding top is extended, a mechanism releases a bank of drawers. The *bonheur-du-jour* is also a lady's desk, but with bank of drawers and/or pigeonholes permanently in position. The *bureau-de-dame* is on cabriole legs and in its early form has a sloped fall, modified by Oeben who replaces it with a tambour composed of slats glued to fabric and running in curved grooves. He invents cylinder-top desk for Louis XV – solid, curved lid moving in grooves – unfinished on Oeben's death in 1763 and completed by Riesener, 1769; considered finest piece of French 18thC furniture extant.

The *secretaire-à-abattant* is a revival of late-17thC secretaire with vertical fall, but carcase often has bombé curves. Rococo curves become less marked during transitional period In 1760s, when royal mistresses, de Pompadour and (later) du Barry help steer court taste in direction of neo-classicism.

Louis XV kingwood and parquetry bureau de dame.

Bonhams

German birch bureau-cabinet, mid-18thC.

Christie's

Finnish oak bureau-cabinet, mid-18thC.

Christie's

In **Germany**, the bureau-cabinet remains favourite form of desk. Rococo decoration is applied to heavy, shaped carcases. In some, cabinet section has cabriole feet resting on top of bureau. Makers include Schnell in Dresden and Hermann of Bamberg, who also produces writing-table in French style about 1765 with tambour top. Lighter types of bureau without cabinet produced by Roentgen family at Neuwied. **Danish** and **Finnish** examples mostly follow German. In **Holland**, bureau-cabinet retains heavy baroque flavour with rococo touches; base has boldly canted corners, top of cabinet is often stepped to hold oriental vases. In **Italy** bureau-cabinet reaches dizzy heights of rococo extravagance, notably at hands of Piffeti, Turin. Simpler bureaux were made in Tuscany.

Northern Italian walnut bombé bureau, mid-18thC.

Christie's

MATERIALS

Sophisticated types: Exotic veneers, e.g. kingwood, tulipwood, citrus.

Provincial types: Solid cherry, walnut.

CONSTRUCTION

Bureau, bureau-cabinet: Basically as for previous period, but elaborate shaping of carcase in **German** examples achieved by 'brick' system – building up with small sections.

Bureau plat: Rails tenoned into tops of cabriole legs; top of sophisticated type framed up and fixed to rails with pegs and glue-blocks. Top of **French** provincial type made up with solid boards, tongued and grooved.

DECORATION

French: Delicate marquetry on fall of *bureau-de-dame* and *secrétaire-à-abattant*; *bureau plat* more reliant on fine veneers and elaborate ormolu mounts; e.g. Cressent, cabinet-maker to Regent during minority of Louis XV, sets fashion for *espagnolettes*– mounts cast as busts of nymphs and fauns.

German and **Italian:** Elaborate carving and marquetry for bureau-cabinets; cresting on cabinet can be wildly asymmetrical. Best Dresden work has very fine ormolu mounts.

FINISH

Veneers varnished, sanded down and waxed. **German** carving parcel-gilt – i.e. details gilded in contrast to woodwork. In Italy, painting with *lacca*; Venice specializes in *lacca povera* (*lacca contrafatta*) – prints by Bassano del Grappa of Remondini, glued to coloured ground and varnished.

RELATIVE VALUES

Ostentatious pieces bring very high prices and demand handsome settings. Best buy is probably French provincial *bureau plat* in cherry or walnut.

ORTMANN PIECES

Principal maker of bureau-cabinets in mid-18thC Copenhagen was Ortmann, who numbered all his products and pasted a trade label inside. Some were disposed of as prizes in lotteries, and could turn up anywhere.

DESKS

About

1770-1800

Louis XVI secretaire-à-abattant in satinwood with marquetry decoration.

Christie's

STYLE AND APPEARANCE

Neo-classical, first phase: 'Louis XVI' style already established in France by 1771, four years before death of Louis XV. Sinuous shapes replaced by rectilinear carcase for secretaire, straight tapered legs (square or round section) on *bureau plat* and cylinder-topped desk. Many pieces still highly decorative but trend towards plainer style was marked in the 1780s.

Dubois makes arguably the first *bureau plat* on tapered legs about 1768; Riesener noted for type of small writing-table with projecting central panel of frieze, also for a lady's work-table with writing-slide on end supports. Many *ébénistes* work to instructions from a *marchand mercier* (intermediary between maker and customer). After 1789 Revolution, an austere version of the style continues under the Directoire.

Germany adopts rectilinear carcase for bureau-cabinet on turned and tapered legs, but rococo shaping retained in pediment, e.g. one made in Berlin, 1775, by Fiedler for Frederick the Great. Cylinder-top bureau popular 1780-1820 in Mainz.

Vienna produces elegant version of *bonheur-du-jour*, showing French and English influences; these also evident in **Italy** where decorative elements of style are emphasized in tall bureau-cabinets, and **Spain** where neat knee-hole writing-tables have richly ornamented drawer-fronts.

Louis XVI mahogany table à transformations, ***left**, in closed and **right**, in open positions.*

Christie's

In 1771, **Holland** prohibits imports of furniture to protect Dutch craftsmen who produce fine fall-front secretaires and writing-tables in neo-classical style. In **Sweden**, Haupt makes magnificent examples of *bureaux plat*; in Denmark, bureaux and bureau-cabinets with slope fronts are simple in outline but colourfully painted.

Catherine the Great imports numerous desks into **Russia**, some by Roentgen, which serve as models for simplified versions by craftsmen in St Petersburg and on country estates. In Poland, chunky slope-front bureaux with very wide crossbandings produced in Kolbuszowa (Little Poland).

MATERIALS

Mainly as in the previous period but with the important addition of mahogany to the French repertoire.

CONSTRUCTION

Mainly as in previous period but with revived use of stretchers to strengthen slim-legged stands for heavy carcases, e.g. in Paris, Weisweiler makes secretaires raised on legs joined by interlaced stretchers.

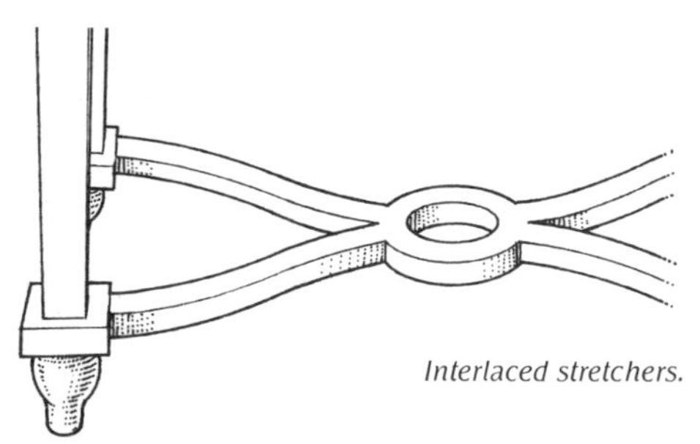

Interlaced stretchers.

DECORATION

Marquetry still highly popular (until fashion for plain mahogany desks takes off), but subjects are neo-classical – e.g. in **Milan**, Maggiolini uses marquetry panels depicting Greek gods and goddesses.

Parquetry – geometric arrangements of small pieces of contrasting veneer – also used in many countries, e.g. for falls of cylinder bureaux by Tenuta, Lisbon, one of few **Portuguese** cabinetmakers to sign work; signature found in secret drawers, embossed on leather panels.

Neo-classical motifs also used for carved decoration, e.g. urns, swags, Roman busts surmounting secretaires by Bonzanigo, **Turin**; also for ormolu mounts of very high quality in **France** and **Germany**.

Louis XVI bonheur du jour.

King & Chasemore

Handles and mounts are first feature to be adapted to the change from rococo to neo-classical.

FINISH

Many small French writing-tables painted with flowered trellis patterns using coloured varnishes (*vernis Martin*). **Danish** bureaux painted with formal patterns in bright colours on cool ground. Marquetry brought to very high finish by varnishing, sanding down and waxing; colours of various woods, now mellow, vivid when new and some made more so with stains. What English collectors now prize as 'patina' is result of fading, waxing and dirt; less appreciated on Continent where many pieces are re-finished to restore former glory.

RELATIVE VALUES

Grand pieces understandably expensive but many lesser bureaux and writing-tables of this period can be bought reasonably, e.g. cylinder-top bureaux in plain mahogany of late-Louis XVI or Directoire vintage, or Dutch secretaires decorated with marquetry or lacquer panels.

ORMOLU

Although the word 'ormolu' derives from French meaning "ground gold", in France the mounts are described as *les bronzes dors* or simply *les bronzes*.

DESKS

About

1800-1850

Dutch mahogany secretaire-à-abattant made in Empire style.

STYLE AND APPEARANCE

Consulat and Empire: The brief period (1799-1804) known by Napoleon's title of Consul, marks transition between slightly anæmic, late-Louis XVI/ Directoire style and full-blooded grandeur of Empire (1804-15), created for Napoleon by Percier and Fontaine and simplified for bourgeoisie by Mésangère's designs, serialized from 1802 to 1835 in a women's magazine.

Writing-tables with curved X-supports, based on Graeco-Roman type, produced by Jacob-Desmalter and others, but favourite form of desk is *secrétaire-à-abattant*, severely architectural but enriched with mounts. Style persists into Louis Philippe period; heavy desks with columnar supports and sphinx mounts still being produced in 1840, by which time *bonheur du jour* type with superstructure of drawers, on end supports with cabriole feet, has become fashionable.

Flat-topped desks in Empire style made throughout Europe: French craftsmen brought to **Italy**, where Socchi of Florence makes ingenious writing-table with concealed chair that moves into position when mechanism is operated. In **Spain**, flat-topped desks made with carved swan supports in Fernandino style (version of Directoire/Empire). In **Sweden**, secretaires by Berg of Stockholm have Egyptian caryatids flanking writing-section. In **Denmark**, the bureau-cabinet (*chatol*) is principal living-room piece, accompanied by a sofa table – originally a writing-table with drop leaves at ends but also used with sofa for meals. This grouping common in **Scandinavia**, **Germany**, **Austria**, **Russia** in Biedermeier period.

Russian walnut Empire pedestal desk with ormolu mounts.

Christie's

Scandinavian mahogany sofa table.

Biedermeier, about 1815-50: In its way, often eccentric, the fall-front secretaire is most interesting contribution of Biedermeier style to history of furniture design. Conservative examples are rectilinear, with recessed, arched panels to exterior of fall and cupboard or drawers below; stepped superstructure above. Adventurous types about 1820-30, e.g. by Brandt and Beissner of Thuringia, are like nothing seen before or since: outline of whole structure inspired by lyre form – U-shape with rounded base resting on platform, and overhanging scrolled pediment. Sofa tables much nearer to English Regency type.

MATERIALS

Much mahogany, but growing preference for pale woods – maple, birch, poplar – used in solid form for supports and as veneers on flush surfaces. Beech used for carved supports (e.g. swans) meant for gilding.

Bronze and brass for mounts, leather for insets of writing-surfaces.

CONSTRUCTION

Usually very strong and sound, using traditional joints (mortise-and-tenon, dovetail), in spite of disbandment of guilds in Paris, where work force in furniture trade numbers about 10,000. Factories in **Paris**, **Vienna**, **Berlin** use machines to assist hand work. Secretaires either single carcase or desk section resting on stand with pillar supports; backs of carcases panelled. Biedermeier sofa tables were mounted on centre columns with platform bases, or on end supports.

DECORATION

Empire: Little marquetry, some carving but heavy reliance on gilt mounts (bronze or brass) using typical Empire motifs – anthemion, sphinx, caryatid, bee, imperial eagle, swan, trophy of arms, lyre. In some areas, carved and gilt wood was substituted for cast metal.

Christie's

Biedermeier satin birch secretaire.

Biedermeier: Some Empire motifs, e.g. swan, sphinx, lyre, persist to mid-century. Architectural emphasis on columns and pilasters. Marquetry used discreetly in neatly confined patterns. Country-made versions of secretaire, especially in Alpine regions, have rural scenes on exterior of fall, inlaid into solid wood (as distinct from marquetry inlaying into veneer).

FINISH

Veneers used extensively throughout period in cities, very seldom in country districts.

Empire: French polishing.

Biedermeier: Varnishing, waxing.

RELATIVE VALUES

Simpler Empire or Biedermeier secretaires good value for money. Sofa tables on end supports usually command higher prices than centre column types.

INFERIOR REPRODUCTIONS

Many secretaires made in late-19thC revival of Empire style; quality often poor – very thin veneers, poorly constructed drawers, tinny mounts, backs made of matchboard (tongue-and-grooved) instead of being panelled as in Napoleon I period.

DESKS

About

1850-1890

King & Chasemore

Mahogany secretaire-à-abattant, about 1860.

Bureau de dame in Louis XV style, about 1870.

STYLE AND APPEARANCE

Chiefly remarkable for revivals, pastiches and direct copies, especially of Louis XIV *bureau Mazarin*, Louis XV/XVI *bureau plat*. English pedestal desk widely adopted as model for study and grand office; modest businessman more likely to have imported American roll-top (see **NEW WORLD, p.317**). For bourgeois homes, many variations of sloped bureau and bureau-cabinet.

MATERIALS

Preponderance of mahogany, but walnut also popular, both used in solid form and as veneer. More prosaic types in oak.

CONSTRUCTION

Ever increasing use of machinery, but decline in quality, where it occurs, due more to price-cuttiing. Many desks still well-made with hand-cut dovetails for drawers. Copies of *bureau plat*, though stylistically lifeless, can be technically superior to 18thC originals.

DECORATION

Too much in many cases, e.g. boullework *bureau plat* with poor quality gilt metal mounts; 'late Biedermeier' bureau-cabinet with fretted pediment; machine-carved linenfold panels for 'Gothic' partners' desks.

FINISH

Passion for high gloss finish, achieved by French polishing, reaches fever pitch.

RELATIVE VALUES

Good copies of 18thC types expensive. Many opportunities in better quality, less ornate bureaux and bureau-cabinets.

VICTORIAN COPIES

Some 19thC copies of Louis XV *bureau plat* so good that expert advice is necessary. In general, quality high but decoration, especially marquetry, too fussy and lacking verve. Difference only becomes evident when eye has been trained by looking closely at numerous examples of both originals and copies.

DESKS

About
1890-1940

Belgian art nouveau desk by Gustave Serrurier-Bovy, about 1910.

Hotel de Ventes Horta

STYLE AND APPEARANCE

Art nouveau, 1890-1920: About 1898 van de Velde designs desk with kidney-shaped top mounted on pedestals with drawers and bookshelf extensions. Majorelle's 1905 writing-tables with dished tops on heavy, semi-cabriole legs reinterpret rococo. Many commercially manufactured bureau-cabinets are asymmetrical, with shelving on one side of fall.

Modernist, 1920-40: Functional flat-top desks for home and office, including some asymmetrical types – pedestal of drawers on one side only – prototype for typist's desk. Built-in fitments often combine writing-surfaces with bookshelves.

Art Deco, 1920-40: Running concurrently with modernist functionalism, Art Deco designers frequently borrow from it – e.g. asymmetrical arrangements of drawers, but for dramatic effect rather than practical convenience. Rich materials lavished on domestic writing-tables and vast office desks for tycoons. Period also offers many unspectacular but satisfying desks of all types, simply designed and well-made.

MATERIALS

Art nouveau: Main preferences walnut and mahogany; variety of woods for marquetry.

Modernist: Oak, ash, elm. Glass or leather for tops, tubular steel frames for desks in Le Corbusier's style.

Art Deco: Mahogany, walnut, figured ebony, fine skins and leathers for tops. Plywood for drawer-bottoms and backs of cheaper products.

CONSTRUCTION

Art nouveau: Best examples almost entirely hand-made, though Majorelle uses machinery for shaping complex curves.

Modernist: Ideologically non-traditional, many makers use screws or bolts in place of mortise-and-tenon joints. Attempts at producing inexpensive furniture often fail because capable machines not yet developed.

Art Deco: Best work, e.g. desks by Ruhlmann of Paris, hand-crafted; flashy types mass-produced by using machines for planing, dovetailing, cutting mortises, but hand-assembled.

DECORATION

Almost by definition, modernism avoids decoration. Good art nouveau and Art Deco use carving, marquetry, inlay in silver and semi-precious stones, ormolu mounts (Majorelle's speciality). Cheaper art nouveau bureau-cabinets have leaded light glass doors, large bronzed metal hinges.

FINISH

Art nouveau: Better examples waxed, secondary ones French polished.

Modernist: Often brightly painted.

Art Deco: Better pieces hand-finished, using thin skins (skivers) for writing surfaces. Cheap products sprayed with cellulose; writing-surfaces inset with imitation leather.

RELATIVE VALUES

Top quality desks, if suitable for executive suites, are disproportionately expensive because they are being paid for out of company funds rather than private money. Best private buys are probably simply designed 1930s desks and bureaux using mostly solid hardwoods.

LEATHER TOPS

Never reject a basically good flat-topped desk because the leather top is shabby. Re-leathering is not unduly expensive, and transforms the appearance.

TABLES AND STANDS

Before about

1500

Refectory table, late-15thC.

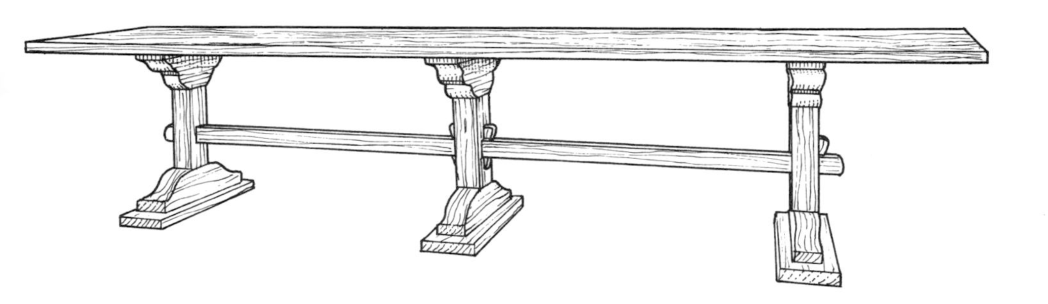

STYLE AND APPEARANCE

Ancient civilizations provide prototypes for later models, e.g. **Egyptian** gaming tables have tops inlaid with squares for a game like chess, on bull or lion legs. Ancient **Greeks** have small, round table on three legs with hoof feet; **Romans** have large marble serving-tables on end supports carved as winged lions.

Romanesque: In hall of medieval castle, dining-tables with loose tops on trestle supports, dismantled after meal. Also in 9th-10thC, semi-circular dining-tables with curtains hung from rails.

Gothic: Tables on trestles of various types (see CONSTRUCTION), also type with central support on platform base, late 15thC – early examples no longer extant, but type re-emerges early 19thC.

MATERIALS

Ancient world: By 1500 BC, **Egypt** is using native and imported timbers, ivory, bone, faience and semi-precious stones for inlay. **Greeks** and **Romans** use wood, marble, bronze.

Medieval (Romanesque-Gothic): Cypress **south of Alps**; walnut in **Italy**, **Spain**, **France**, **Germany**; oak in **Low Countries**, **France**, **Germany**. Local stone, iron.

CONSTRUCTION

Mortise-and-tenon, dovetail, mitre joints mastered by **Egyptians**. **Greeks** add lathe and plane to range of tools. Bronze casting perfected by **Etruscans**. Medieval side-table (*table dormante*) has vertical legs tied by stretchers. Dining-tables have removable tops on trestles, some A-shaped, mortised or nailed together; some X-shaped using halving joint; some columnar with cruciform bases, also using halving joint.

DECORATION

Ancient world uses carving, inlay, veneering, painting, decorative features cast in silver, bronze. Many skills lost in West after fall of Rome, some preserved in Byzantine Empire.

Medieval: Mainly carving, painting.

FINISH

Painting.

RELATIVE VALUES

Ancient tables for museums only. Late Gothic examples, especially Germanic, appear on market but bring high prices.

FRAGMENTS

Fragments, e.g. carved ivory legs of Egyptian tables, sometimes appear at auction – interesting collectors' pieces.

TABLES AND STANDS

About

1500-1630

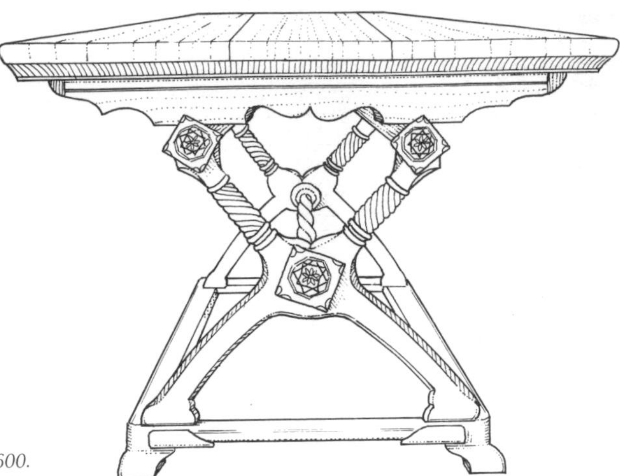

German table on X-supports, before 1600.

STYLE AND APPEARANCE

Renaissance: After about 1530, mannerist influence in some examples. No dining-rooms as such in 16thC **Italy** – meals served wherever convenient, so many tables were still on trestles and easily dismantled; tops spread with damask cloths, oriental rugs, or covered with velvet, nailed on or draped. In some, new interest in classical architecture reflected in columnar legs or end supports based on Roman marble types.

Both features seen in **French** Renaissance designs by Du Cerceau (about 1550 – shaped ends, decorated with mannerist monsters, and connected by row of turned columns.

In **Netherlands**, dining-tables on bulbous legs joined by stretchers, some with extending leaves sliding under main part of top when not in use, decorated with carved brackets derived from engravings by Vredeman de Vries, published 1580 (updated by son, 1630), circulating in **Sweden** and **Germany**.

Before 1600, trestles of **Spanish** tables made with turned members, attached to top with curved, wrought-iron stretchers. Peasant type with plain legs, crudely-made drawer under top – still being made in 19thC.

MATERIALS

Walnut in **Italy**, **France**, **Spain**. Oak in **France**, **Netherlands**, **Germany**. Chestnut in **Spain**. Pine in **Alpine countries** and **Scandinavia**. Lime in **Germany**. Ebony and other exotic woods for inlay, especially in **Netherlands**, **Germany**. Wrought-iron for stretchers in **Spain**.

CONSTRUCTION

Mortise-and-tenon joints secured by pegs for fixed frames and most trestles; X-shaped trestles made with halving joint. Tops, if not one board, made by joining planks with tongue-and-groove or rub joints, sometimes with butterfly ties. For construction of draw-leaf tables see **NEW WORLD TABLES, p. 328**.

DECORATION

Tops of most tables plain, but some rare examples with intarsia – inlay using very small pieces of wood – practised in **Florence**, **Augsburg**, **Nuremberg**, **Würzburg**, **Antwerp**. Simple stands plain or turned, grander ones carved. In **Netherlands**, stretchers inlaid with ebony stringing.

FINISH

Mainly oiled and waxed, or varnished.

RELATIVE VALUES

Simpler types not outrageously expensive. Elaborate Italianate types with shaped end supports in Roman style highly priced.

REPLACEMENT TOPS

Because so many tops were made to be lifted off, it is often difficult to be sure whether they are originals. Look for marks left by previous stands that do not tally with existing frame.

TABLES AND STANDS

About

1630-1730

Portuguese side table, panels from 16thC Spanish cabinet forming the top.

Christie's

STYLE AND APPEARANCE

Until about 1640, Louis XIII style still late-Renaissance with elaborately turned legs – a feature surviving until end of century in provincial **France** and other regions, e.g. **Portugal**. Simultaneously, dramatic **Italian** baroque spreads through Europe, expressed in sculptural supports for tables and stands for cabinets.

After about 1660, equally grand but more classically disciplined version created in **France** for Louis XIV – fewer scrolls, more vertical legs. Low stands (*guéridons*) and taller ones (*torchères*) for candelabra carved to represent blackamoors or Nubian slaves – finest by Brustolon in Venice, 1685-96. Engravings of palace interiors published in Augsburg and Nuremberg show side-tables surmounted by mirrors, and grand centre tables in entrance halls.

French walnut torchère on spiral stem.

Christie's

Christie's

Pair of Venetian Blackamoor torchères, 17thC style, actually mid-19thC.

MATERIALS

Turned leg types: Hardwoods, native (e.g. oak) or imported (e.g. ebony, jacaranda).

Carved types: Softwoods, e.g. pine, lime. Exotic woods for veneered and marquetry tops, hardstones for *pietre dure* (see **DECORATION**), marble for tops of side-tables.

CONSTRUCTION

Turned legs joined by mortise-and-tenon to frieze, which may have drawers made with coarse dovetails.

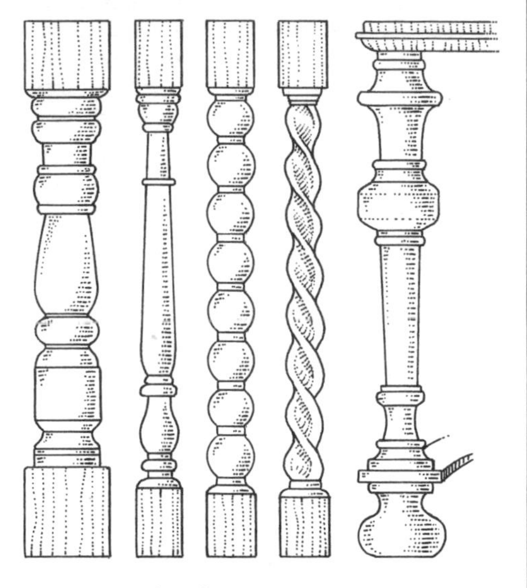

Common designs for turned legs and supports.

Carved types: necessarily unorthodox variations of traditional methods for joining sculpted figures of humans or animals to frame supporting marble top. Console table is fixed to wall and has leg(s) at front only. Small Venetian tables supported on upturned feet of blackamoor pageboys doing handstands.

Various designs for carved and scrolled feet.

DECORATION

Turning: Baluster, bobbin, twist patterns.

Carving: Often in the round for caryatid supports resembling mermaids with scroll tails; water nymphs holding giant shells; chained slaves pretending to hold up top; gods, goddesses, and cherubs frisking in foliage.

Marquetry: Arabesques, chinoiseries and (especially in **Holland**) floral subjects in exotic woods, ivory, mother-of-pearl.

Boullework: Brass arabesques inlaid into turtleshell.

***Pietre dure*:** Florentine mosaic (see under CUPBOARDS AND CABINETS).

Flemish draw-leaf table, early-17thC.

FINISH

Hardwoods oiled and waxed or varnished.

Softwoods painted, gilded. Italian *lacca*(coloured varnishes) for *torchères* carved as nubile Nubians wearing turbans, harem trousers, not much else.

RELATIVE VALUES

Turned-leg side-tables, e.g. **Portuguese** type with fat turnings, often sell at prices comparable with good modern or reproduction furniture. Fine sculptural pieces usually expensive but not easy to place, so surprising things can happen at auction.

BLACKAMOORS

17thC blackamoor or Nubian figures usually have thin lips, later ones thick lips – but fakers know this, so pay high prices only if guarantee forthcoming. Convincing copies made in Venice in 1970s from redundant French telegraph poles.

TABLES AND STANDS

About

1730-1770

***Above**, a Portuguese side-table, made in the English style, about 1750.*

STYLE AND APPEARANCE

Rococo: After French and Dutch success at end of 17thC in correcting baroque excesses by the use of straight, slightly tapered legs terminating in bun feet, the elongated S-shaped cabriole leg becomes, by 1730, universally adopted for most tables and stands.

***Below**, a French rococo gilded console table, about 1750.*

Wide variety includes gaming-tables with fold-over tops, writing-tables (see **DESKS, p. 253**), *guéridons, étagères* (stands with two or three tiers), *tables ambulantes* (small, oval or round), tea and toilet tables. Notable Paris *ébénistes*: Dubois, van Risen Burgh, Criaerd, Roussel. Dining-tables, however, even in châteaux, still plain and square-legged in farmhouse manner, were covered at mealtimes with fine napery.

Carved and gilt side-tables, especially by Corradini, **Venice**, retain opulence of baroque, but render it with lighter touch; supports are ornate versions of cabriole leg with sculptural details, e.g. console table in Royal Palace, **Stockholm**, designed by French-trained architect Harleman about 1750, and one for the Residenz, Munich, designed by Civillis, made locally by Pichler, 1761.

Dressing-table of the King of Poland, 1769.

In **Holland**, tripod tables have three cabriole-curved feet splaying from central stem; drawers in side-tables have bombé shaped drawer-fronts.

MATERIALS

Veneered types: Exotic woods, e.g. kingwood, rosewood, usually laid on oak foundation. Wide variety of woods for marquetry.

Carved types: Oak or walnut for console tables left in natural state, pine for gilding or painting. Specimen marbles for tops prized by connoisseurs in 18thC.

Dutch tripod table, mid-18thC, with painted top.

CONSTRUCTION

Widely adopted Louis XV type of cabriole leg is joined by mortise-and-tenon to frame with smooth, concave curve on under edge; in **Holland**, parts of **Germany** and **Scandinavia** (as in England), more often a convex bulge, or wing, made from separate piece of timber.

In **Denmark**, one type of gateleg table has main section on shaped end supports, and flat, profiled uprights of gates; another type has turned legs split down centre, separating when table is opened up.

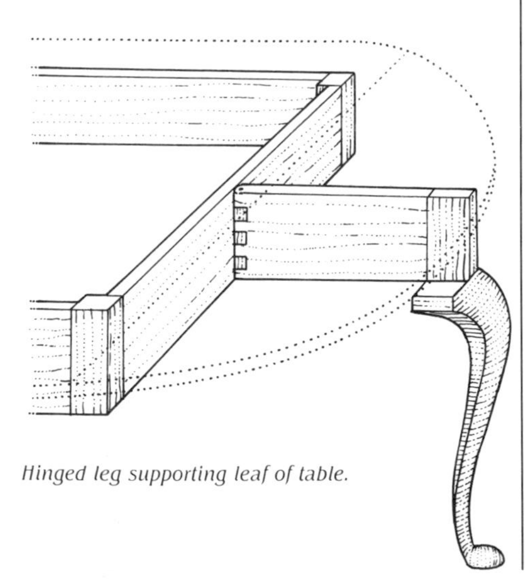

Hinged leg supporting leaf of table.

DECORATION

Veneered types: Marquetry flowers, trellis patterns, landscapes. Veneer on legs arranged with grain forming chevron pattern.

Carved types: Cabriole leg itself produced by carver, edged with C-scrolls continued along 'apron' (front rail forming decorative frieze); legs joined by curving stretchers with carved *putto* (cherub) at centre.

Right, a painted and silvered Venetian pedestal, mid-18thC.

Christie's

FINISH

Veneered types: Varnished, sanded down, polished with wax to bring figured grain and especially marquetry to brilliant finish. Ormolu mounts.

Carved types: Oak or walnut left natural. Pine painted and/or gilded.

Lacquered types: Painted with coloured varnished (e.g. Italian *lacca* or French *vernis Martin*) in formal patterns or chinoiseries imitating oriental lacquer.

RELATIVE VALUES

Highly sophisticated examples, especially if with marquetry, expensive. Provincial types in solid wood rather less so, but vogue for country style has pushed up prices.

19th CENTURY COPIES

Skilful 19thC copies of Louis XV tables often veneered on softwood and relatively light in weight. Authentic examples, even of nominally portable *table ambulante*, usually veneered on oak and surprisingly heavy to lift.

TABLES AND STANDS

About

1770-1790

Christie's

Louis XVI ormolu and Sèvres-mounted gueridon.

STYLE AND APPEARANCE

Neo-classical, first phase (Louis XVI): Most obvious development is abandonment of cabriole leg in favour of straight, tapered types, either square-section or turned, but process is gradual. *Le goût grec* – taste for classical decoration – fashionable in **Paris** from late 1760s, but some makers (e.g. Topino, Lacroix) retain cabriole leg with modified curves for *tables ambulantes* until about 1775.

In **Italy**, sculptural tradition persists. In 1769 Piranese published engravings of side-tables as he correctly imagines Roman ones to have been, featuring sphinx and monopodia supports (*monopodium*: single animal leg surmounted by head of lion or griffin). Centre table made for Villa Borghese about 1780 has marble supports carved as winged lions; another, designed by Baladier in 1789, is supported by eight bronze figures of Hercules modelled by Pacetti (Vatican library). Provincial side-tables have heavy, tapered legs.

Christie's

Detail of carved satyr mask on leg of Italian side-table.

Louis XV tricoteuse (knitting table) on end supports.

Christie's

In **Germany**, Roentgen's workshops devise tables with mechanical devices operating concealed compartments that intrigue Louis XVI. Roentgen also supplies Catherine the Great with tables copied by serf craftsmen on Russian estates. Arms factory at Tula produces occasional tables in cut steel with fretted decoration.

Christie's

Italian scagliola panel, late-18thC.

Christie's

Russian games table, about 1770.

In **Austria**, Viennese guild enforces high standards; members produce side-tables on rather high legs, giving stilted look.

In **Sweden**, narrow console tables appear even narrower than they are, because mirrors over them are often very high; Haupt's small tables on slim turned legs reflect experience in Holland, Germany, France and England. Strong English influence on work of Iwersson and Masreliez brothers; English-type tea-tables very popular in **Stockholm**, also in **Copenhagen**. In **Norway**, heavier versions of Danish types.

In rural regions everywhere, functional tables of traditional type made with few acknowledgments of new style, cabriole legs continuing to be popular after 1800.

MATERIALS

As in previous period, but with increased use of bronze and marble. *Scagliola*, made by mixing marble chippings with plaster and size, substitutes for *pietre dure*; *stucco lustro* – painted plaster – simulates marble (see below).

CONSTRUCTION

Simplified by abandonment of cabriole leg; less shaping by carver, more by turner. Otherwise, business as usual.

DECORATION

Carving and marquetry – acanthus, wreaths, swags, pendant husks, oval and round shields. Same motifs cast in ormolu.

FINISH

Many side-tables painted, gilded. Carved oak or walnut left natural.

RELATIVE VALUES

Scandinavian console tables usually less expensive than **French** or **Italian**, and of a size suitable for small entrance halls.

SCAGLIOLA AND STUCCO LUSTRO

See MATERIALS, above. These were brought to level of fine art in 18thC, can easily deceive the eye but are warmer to the touch than real thing.

TABLES AND STANDS

About

1790-1850

Christie's

Russian table, early-19thC.

STYLE AND APPEARANCE

Neo-classical, second phase: In late 1780s a more severe neo-classical ('Etruscan') style emerges in France, continues after Revolution as Directoire, later becoming basis of Empire (1804-15) and Biedermeier (1815-48). Leading designers: Percier, Fontaine, Mésangère in Paris, Schinkel in Berlin. Leading makers: Jacob-Desmalter in Paris, Danhauser in Vienna.

Christie's

Empire guéridon.

New types include: small circular tables (*guéridons*) with marble tops, standing on cylindrical columns or monopodia supports; *l'athénienne*, based on tripod excavated at Pompeii, bowl serving as either jardinière or wash-stand, side-tables on columns or monopodia; dressing-tables on curved X-supports, with attached mirrors (usually circular).

Most important development, originating in late 1780s but coming into general use until after 1800, is large circular table on centre pedestal with platform base, used both as centre-piece and for meals, essential feature of Biedermeier living-room in **Germany**, **Austria**, **Russia**, **Scandinavia**.

MATERIALS

Mahogany, either in sold form or veneer, fashionable in France in 1780s; becomes scarce during Empire, often replaced in Napoleonic Europe with native oak, walnut, birch. Oak hardly ever used for Biedermeier.

CONSTRUCTION

Although steam-driven machines gradually introduced in early 19thC, especially for sawing veneers, construction still traditional – heavy reliance on mortise-and-tenon joints, largely concealed in Biedermeier period by veneering entire surface. Large circular tables usually made with top pivoted to base, so that it can be tipped on vertical position.

DECORATION

Carving of monopodia supports – lions, griffins, sphinxes. Ormolu and cast brass mounts – Roman, Greek, Egyptian motifs.

FINISH

French polishing after 1800. Monopodia stained black and part-gilt to create effect of antique bronze. Biedermeier tables wax polished, walnut examples never stained.

RELATIVE VALUES

Circular tables on centre pedestals – type known in English-speaking countries as 'loo', from card game, 'lanterloo' – made over very long period (about 1785- 1885) and in most countries. Prices depend on quality and size rather than age; much higher prices if capable of seating more than four in comfort.

FRAME TOP

Until about 1810, top of large circular tables does not have frame around circumference; after 1810, screwed to a frame about 3-4 inches/8-10 cms deep.

TABLES AND STANDS

About

1815 to 1890

(overlapping previous period)

French kingwood and marquetry centre table, 19thC, in Louis XVI style.

STYLE AND APPEARANCE

Restoration of monarchy in France in 1815 provides excuse for reviving Louis XVI neo-classicism; fashions follow for neo-everything else, often mixed together in eclectic frenzy – octagonal tables with boullework tops, Gothic stands; *guéridons* on baroque spiral columns with rococo enamel tops. Napoleon III style (Second Empire) distinctive with tapered, fluted legs, black and gilt – but even these are derived from Louis XIV, XVI types. Each country resurrects features from its past. International exhibitions stimulate makers to vie with each other, no expense spared, but pieces imitated for middle market with as much expense spared as possible.

Leading craftsmen and/or designers:

France: Viollet-le-Duc (medievalist); Biardot (manufacturer of Renaissance, oriental).

Italy: Barbetti, Baccetti (carvers of Renaissance types).

Spain: Maeso (designer of Neo-Gothic, painted white and parcel gilt)

MATERIALS

Great variety of woods, with preference for strongly marked grains, e.g. burr walnut, figured ebony (Coromandel wood), amboyna, kingwood, mahogany. Walnut in Scandinavia. Bar tables with marble tops on cast-iron, cabriole-legged stands.

CONSTRUCTION

Industrialization gradually undermines craftsmanship. Dowels and glue, screws and bolts often substitute for mortise-and-tenon joints. In country districts, traditional types, e.g. farmhouse dining-tables, were still produced by hand.

DECORATION

Lavish carving, marquetry, gilt metal mounts, porcelain and enamel plaques.

Table with porcelain top, legs inlaid with ivory, 1887.

Christie's

FINISH

Painting, japanning, French polishing.

RELATIVE VALUES

Decorative pieces of exhibition quality now much sought after and very expensive. Simple, country-made tables – **French**, **Austrian**, **Swiss**, **Scandinavian** – not cheap but easier to live with.

MAKER'S STAMPS

The mere presence of a maker's name stamped on a table in Louis XV/XVI style does not always indicate 18thC work. Although 19thC French makers were no longer required by law to stamp their products, some – e.g. Dasson – chose to do so, and their signed pieces are well worth having.

TABLES AND STANDS

About

1890-1920

Christie's

Walnut and marquetry table by Gallé.

STYLE AND APPEARANCE

Art nouveau: Centres in Paris, Vienna, Nancy, Munich, Brussels, St Petersburg, Milan, produce tables original in design but not entirely divorced from past or devoid of exotic influences. A *guéridon* by Gallé, though impossible to confuse with anything earlier, has three legs like neo-classical monopodia, with dragonflies in place of lions or griffins; tables by Majorelle have cabriole legs mounted with orchids in ormolu, owing much to early rococo, while Bugatti's coffee-tables are unashamedly Moorish/Turkish in flavour.

Many art nouveau table legs are carved to represent stylized stems of plants, the tops decorated with flowers in marquetry; others, purely abstract, have asymmetrical, curvilinear supports. A much more austere style, showing British Arts and Crafts influence, was adopted by Dijsselhof, one of whose dining-tables at Gemeente Museum, The Hague, has pierced end supports.

In 1903, Hoffmann and Moser, members of anti-academic **Viennese** Sezession, founded Wiener Werkstätte to produce popular furniture. Hoffmann favoured angular tables inlaid with black and white squares in ebony and mother-of-pearl. Another black-and-white enthusiast, Munthe of **Norway**, designs triangular, three-legged tables with sun-ray brackets that, as early as 1895, anticipate Art Deco.

Sotheby's

Nest of tables by Gallé, about 1900.

MATERIALS

Wide range of fine timbers, indigenous and imported, used in solid and as veneers by **French** art nouveau makers. **Austrians** and **Germans** tend more to use of native timbers for solid construction, with exotic materials (e.g. ebony) for inlay.

CONSTRUCTION

Luxurious **French** work largely hand-made, with adjustment to traditional joints, e.g. mitres, for more eccentric shapes. Wiener Werksttte uses some machinery.

DECORATION

Carving, marquetry, inlay in solid wood. Ormolu and bronze mounts.

FINISH

Mainly wax polishing. Cheaper grade of late art nouveau types French polished.

RELATIVE VALUES

Top quality art nouveau and secessionist pieces now very expensive. Commercial products in medium price range.

FAKE MAJORELLE

Small tables with marquetry tops bearing Majorelle's signature have been faked in recent years. Marquetry lacks quality, timber often inferior (Majorelle usually worked in fine mahogany).

TABLES AND STANDS

About

1920-1940

Art Deco walnut dining-table.

Christie's

STYLE AND APPEARANCE

Modernist, Art Deco: Foundations of modernism already exist in geometrically designed Wiener Werkstätte tables; those of Art Deco in more decorative art nouveau examples. Some art nouveau designers, e.g. Majorelle, continue working into 1930s.

Purely functional tables produced in post-Revolutionary **Russia**; main impetus for industrialized types comes from **Bauhaus** design school after Gropius moves it from Weimar to Dessau in 1925, and in France from **Le Corbusier**, who rationalizes furniture into three categories – storage units, chairs and tables – meant to be mass-produced and appear untouched by hand.

Factory-for-living concept lacks appeal for public, who are catered for by Art Deco designers, e.g. Ruhlmann of Paris. Dressing-tables often asymetrical, dining-tables slab-ended; domestic card tables suggest well-heeled decadence of casino.

Flemish birch table, 1930s.

Christie's

MATERIALS

Many modernist tables are glass-topped, on tubular steel frames. In 1930, **Danish** school uses steamed and bent plywood in place of steel to achieve similar jointless appearance. Art Deco designers use expensive timbers, silver, ormolu, for tables combining traditional feeling of luxury with modern approach. Plywood and Bakelite now used for the tops of cheap products.

CONSTRUCTION

Modernists use traditional joints when necessary, but often substitute screws and bolts to strengthen shouldered joints attaching legs to friezes. Nuts and bolts used for assembly of tubular steel tables.

DECORATION

Modernist: Philosophical attitude summed up in aphorism of the time – 'decoration is a crime'. Nevertheless, many tables of the period add Art Deco details to severe modernist shapes – restrained marquetry or a fanciful handle on a drawer.

Art Deco: No inhibitions – indeed, some pieces with painted or inlaid decoration, depicting nude figures in mildly erotic poses, were for long considered immoral and hidden away; now displayed in museums.

FINISH

Modernist: Tubular metal frames nickel or chromium plated.

Art Deco: Best work wax polished. Cheaper tables – the vast preponderance – sprayed with cellulose or French polished.

RELATIVE VALUES

Good modernist tables on tubular metal stands buyable at reasonable prices. Top quality Art Deco expensive, kitsch comparatively dear for what it is.

COMBINATIONS

Although originally diametrically opposed to each other, modernist and Art Deco pieces can blend together very well in a room devoted to them, especially in association with modern hi-tech equipment.

NEW WORLD

GUIDE TO PERIODS AND STYLES: NEW WORLD

As furniture in the conventional sense hardly figured in the cultures of the Indians, any review of American work must begin with what was made for, and mainly by, the early colonists and immigrants who followed them – Spanish, Portuguese, British, French, Italian, Dutch, German and Scandinavian – bringing traditions and skills, but little furniture. Craftsmen had largely to rely on memory.

Differences from remembered models developed in various regions, partly because materials were available that, in Europe, had been unfamiliar (for example,red oak and hickory in North America), or too expensive (for example, Peruvian silver). Mexican Indian woodcarving added a strange, often grotesque element to pieces of basically Spanish design.

French Provincial types of furniture persisted in Canada long after the British had achieved supremacy. In Pennsylvania, German immigrants created a style often wrongly called Pennsylvania Dutch – a corruption of *Deutsch*; but a type of Dutch *kas* (cupboard) remained popular in New York from the early-18thC until the mid-19thC. In the Shenandoah Valley, Italian settlers re-created a mid-18thC Piedmontese dresser with plate-rack. Scandinavians in Minnesota and Wisconsin kept up a tradition of carved and brightly painted decoration.

Some religious sects maintained close-knit communities and made their own distinctive furniture – notably the Shakers (United Society of Believers in Christ's Second Appearing), whose work was severely plain. The German Zoarites did not allow strict religious beliefs to prohibit the making of vividly painted pieces and, later, decorated versions of English designs, mainly Hepplewhite and Sheraton. In this respect they were close to the mainstream of American furniture which, despite the mix of nationalities, was predominantly English in flavour, at least until around 1800, and is classified accordingly; but some of the dates (for example 'Queen Anne') do not always coincide with their English counterparts.

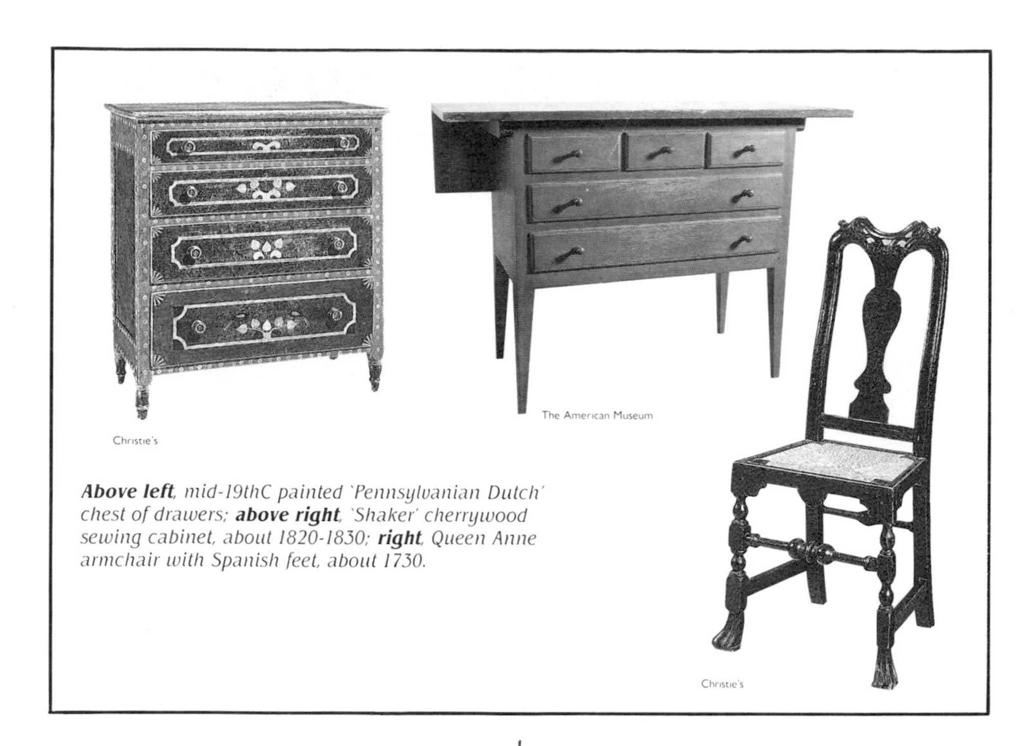

Christie's

The American Museum

***Above left**, mid-19thC painted 'Pennsylvanian Dutch' chest of drawers; **above right**, 'Shaker' cherrywood sewing cabinet, about 1820-1830; **right**, Queen Anne armchair with Spanish feet, about 1730.*

Christie's

PILGRIM 1620-90

Although a permanent colony was established at Jamestown, Virginia, in 1607, little furniture was made in the south in the 17thC, the rich planters preferring to import it. The Pilgrim Fathers landed at Plymouth, Massachusetts, in 1620 with little furniture other than chests used as packing crates. They had no seasoned timber suitable for joinery, but there was green wood in plenty, used by the turners for pieces in provincial versions of the English baroque style. By 1640 houses were, according to one contemporary source, 'well-furnished', but construction was fairly crude.

***Left**, 17thC mulberry wood chair with bobbin and sausage turnings.*

The American Museum

WILLIAM AND MARY 1690-1725

(England 1689-1702, see **p. 19**)

Construction and decoration became more sophisticated with the use of dovetail joints, veneering in walnut and burr maple, and japanning in imitation of oriental lacquer. Boston became a recognized centre supplying other areas. Typical pieces: the highboy (chest of drawers raised on a stand with turned legs); the fall-front desk.

William & Mary burr-veneered highboy, about 1720-30.

Christie's

QUEEN ANNE 1725-60

(England 1702-14, see **p. 20**)

The curvaceous lines of the rococo were adopted as individual centres of production grew up in Newport, Rhode Island, New York and Philadelphia, all developing distinctive styles. Typical pieces: cabinets with 'bonnet tops', chairs with cabriole legs and vase-shaped splats.

Above, Queen Anne maple highboy, about 1770-1800.

CHIPPENDALE 1760-90

(England 1755-75, see **p. 56**)

Mahogany from Honduras permitted crisply carved rococo pieces in the style of Chippendale's *Director*, made by Affleck and Randolph in Philadelphia. From the 1740s, the Townsend and Goddard families of Newport, Rhode Island, developed 'block and shell' fronts on chests of drawers and related pieces. 'Kettle' shapes (bombé' – 'blown up'), popular in Boston until 1780, derived from European rather than English sources.

Chippendale-style walnut highboy, about 1779.

FEDERAL 1785-1810

After the War of Independence, styles remained mainly English, with reliance on the designs of Adam, Hepplewhite and Sheraton, blended by Seymour of Boston to produce a personal manner. As sideboards grew in popularity, mahogany became more generally used; but away from the big towns, native woods – maple, walnut, cherry, birch – continued to be used.

Federal mahogany lolling chair, about 1795-1810.

CLASSICAL 1800-40

The 'Grecian' style, as practised by Phyfe of New York, owed something to English Regency but more to French Empire. Immigrant French cabinet-makers settled in Boston, New Orleans, Philadelphia, Charleston and New York, where Lannuier used Louis XVI designs until 1810.

Sotheby's

Laminated rosewood Belter settee, about 1870.

REVIVAL & INNOVATIONS 1840-1890

Revivals of old styles – Gothic, rococo, Renaissance, baroque and neo-classical – in that non-historic order – ran parallel to the many mid-19thC innovations. Belter of New York combined rococo extravagance with new techniques in his laminated, steam-bent, carved and pierced confections, while Pabst specialized in carved pieces in the Gothic style.

During the Civil War, deep-buttoned, heavily-fringed upholstery in the French Second Empire manner was fashionable. Cast-iron furniture was made by Barnum of Michigan. (Grand Rapids, Michigan, had now become the centre of the furniture manufacturing industry.) 'Patent' pieces included the Wootton desk and improved types of rocking chair. In the West, chairs and hallstands were made of antlers and buffalo horns, or carved in mahogany to simulate them. Even the Shakers commercialized their output.

1840-1890

This period is the most likely to provide the modest collector with opportunities for buying affordable, authentically American antiques. Examples from the earlier periods are rare and usually expensive. Pieces of British origin, genuine in themselves, are often described as 'Early American', but unless there is a sound provenance, anything not peculiar to America in design, material or construction should be regarded as a doubtful candidate for American citizenship.

Late-19thC Wootton desk.

Phillips

MACHINEWORK & ART MODERNE 1890-1940

In the 1890s, Lloyd Wright, trained in Chicago, reacted against the weird confusion of historic revivals and began to design furniture that owed much to the British Arts and Crafts Movement, yet succeeds as an original statement. The principle was to design good, clean pieces that could be made by machine.

'Mission' furniture, inspired by chairs in a Spanish mission house in California, was first produced in the 1890s by McHugh and shortly after by the Roycroft Community, Stickley's Craftsmen Workshops and others, remaining popular until the outbreak of World War I.

In the 1920s, the Art Moderne style (Art Deco) inspired designers such as Deskey, who made imaginative use of Bakelite and aluminium. In the 1930s vast quantities of kitsch were produced, and good, simple pieces are quite rare.

Craftsman oak desk with open-end shelves, about 1900.

Christie's

BEDS AND CRADLES

About

1660-1760

New England maple cradle, swinging on upright ends.

Examples survive from the late 17thC. Some of the earliest types continued to be made with little change until well into the 19thC, making it difficult to date them with certainty. Many space-saving constructions, some dual-purpose.

STYLE AND APPEARANCE

Low posted bed: Turned posts, headboard, New England, late-17thC. Similar types made about 1840 by Shakers at Lebanon, New York, and by slaves in Louisiana.

Trundle (truckle) bed: Bed-frame on feet, pushed under posted bed when not in use.

Settle bed (French Canadian *banc-lit*): Box-seated settle by day; seat tips forward to disclose bed – the prototype bed-settee. Made in country districts throughout 18thC.

Press bed: Hinged to tip up against wall in daytime, and enclosed by doors or drapes. Persisted, with some improvements, from early 18thC down to modern times.

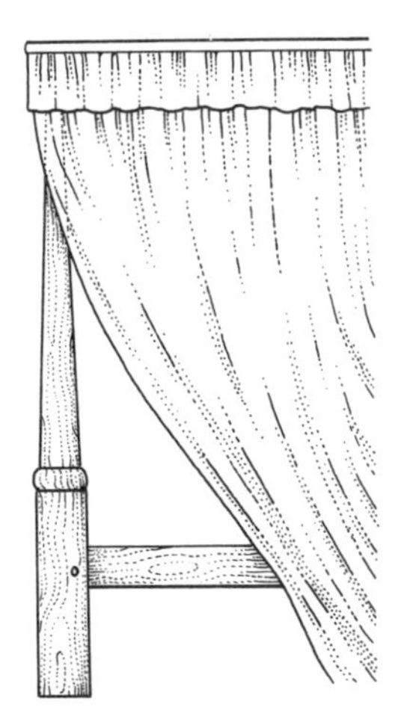

Early-18thC tester bed with post square to floor from bed-rail.

Tester bed: The English type of four-poster bed with carved decoration does not seem to have been produced in 17thC New England, but many 18thC American tester beds have survived. Early examples have simple posts that were hidden by hangings, providing privacy and protection from the night air, believed to be poisonous. Posts came square to the floor until the claw-and-ball foot was introduced about 1760.

Slaap banck: A bed built into a curtained alcove, with panelled sides and ends; some were imported from the Netherlands by Dutch colonists, others made to order, mainly in New York area.

Cradles: Late-17th and early-18thC types made like lidless, panelled chests mounted on rockers, with turnings at the foot to provide the mother with a hand grip for rocking. Many have a complete hood or a three-sided screen at the head – again for protection against poisonous night air – but some (Pennsylvania German especially) are open. A New England type was suspended from uprights at the ends, so that it could swing instead of rock.

MATERIALS

Pine panels, birch posts, not much oak. Walnut in Pennsylvania. Fabrics for drapes.

CONSTRUCTION

Low posted bed: Solid headboard with two tenons at each side let into mortises cut in posts. Rails attached to posts at head and foot, also with mortise-and-tenon joints. Rope interlaced through rails to form a resilient platform for mattress.

Tester bed: Basically similar to above, but tenons of rails secured with bolts through posts for ease in dismantling.

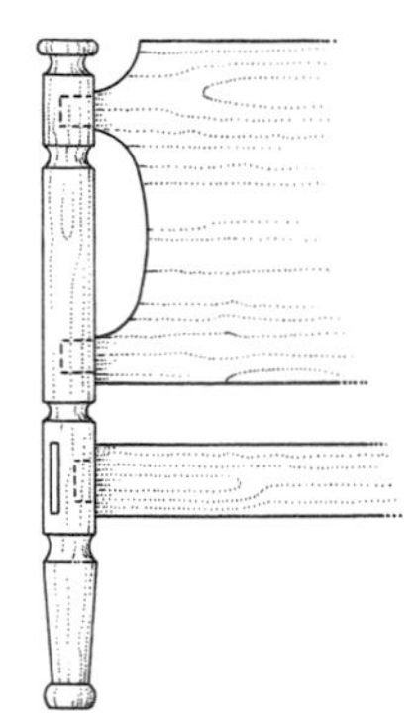

Left, construction of bedstead, 1650-1850.

Right, detail of a crewelwork bed hanging, late-17thC.

V&A

Bed settle, press bed: Action usually based on dowels moving in sockets.

Cradle: Boarded or panelled.

Pencil bed frame.

DECORATION

Simple turning of posts, some headboards with cyma scrolls on top edge. Tester beds before mid-18thC relied for decoration on crewelwork drapes – floral patterns, some with sampler-like texts or verses, embroidered in long-stitch by the women of the house, using the long, blunt crewel needle to produce what was called, in the 19thC, 'painting with the needle' – raised to a fine art in Colonial America.

Cradles: Some Rhode Island examples have rows of turned spindles. Pennsylvania German types without hoods have a heart motif cut through headboard, and are brightly painted with stylized patterns.

Headboard of Pennsylvania German open cradle, pierced with heart motif

FINISH

Woodwork painted, varnished, waxed or left raw.

RELATIVE VALUES

Even the simplest beds can bring high prices if an early American origin can be substantiated; if it cannot, the bed should be assessed on its merits, bearing in mind the problems of dating (see above). Cradles are fashionable furnishing pieces for putting plants in, or logs if there is an open fire. Not much used for babies.

Surprisingly, people do pay fancy prices for beds in which some celebrity is supposed to have slept. Association value can be a valid factor, but it needs more than a one night stand to establish it.

BEDS AND CRADLES

About

1760-1790

Chippendale carved mahogany four-post bedstead, Massachusetts 1760-1780.

Christie's

STYLE AND APPEARANCE

With the introduction of the **Chippendale** style, more trouble was taken with the posts of the full tester, as they were exposed to view, at least during the day, the drapes being drawn back to hang at the head. Headboards more shapely with top edge scrolled in the rococo style. Tester sometimes exposed, sometimes hidden by valance. Low beds and cradles much as before.

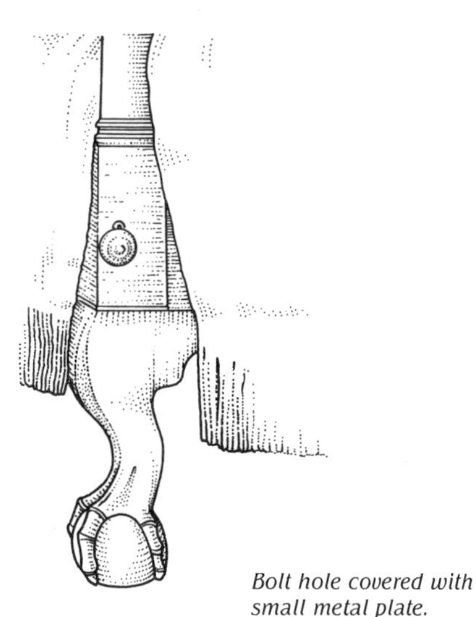

Bolt hole covered with small metal plate.

MATERIALS

As before, except for the use of mahogany for the best quality tester beds.

CONSTRUCTION

Little change.

DECORATION

Posts – especially those at the foot – no longer treated as merely functional supports but as objects for decoration – turning, fluting, carving – terminating in turned feet or, exceptionally, cabriole legs with claw-and-ball feet. Headboards shaped, sometimes upholstered.

FINISH

Exposed woodwork wax polished. Because posts were exposed, bolt holes were covered with small metal plates.

RELATIVE VALUES

Good tester beds of this period, with decorated posts, tend to be more expensive than earlier, plainer examples.

Check that the decorated parts – posts, headboard, tester (if exposed) – are all of the same period and really belong to each other. Replaced rails are much less important.

BEDS AND CRADLES

About

1790-1820

Christie's

Federal cherrywood tent bed, American eagle carved on headboard.

STYLE AND APPEARANCE

First phase of neo-classicism: Hepplewhite and Sheraton styles – restrained elegance. Tent beds and Windsor cradles popular – see **CONSTRUCTION**. Some half-testers with posts at head only.

The American Museum *Early-19thC mahogany tent bed.*

MATERIALS

Tent beds: Mahogany, birch, pine. Fine fabrics for drapes on grander beds, cotton gingham, striped or checked, for more modest types.

Windsor cradles: Birch, beech, ash, pine.

CONSTRUCTION

Tent beds: Four posts supporting frame of canopy, curved at head and foot, sometimes at sides, using thin, bent laths with fabric draped over.

Half-tester beds: Canopy cantilevered.

Windsor cradles: Lightly built, made like Windsor chairs, using turned spindles socketed into holes in frame of bent ash.

DECORATION

If meant to stand against wall, the posts at the head were sometimes turned but not fluted and/or carved, being partly hidden by drapes; but when the ceiling sloped too steeply for that, the bed had to be free-standing at, or near, centre of room; all four posts were exposed to view and were decorated to match each other. Do not, therefore, reject a four-poster too readily as a made-up piece because the posts at the foot are decorated and those at the head are not.

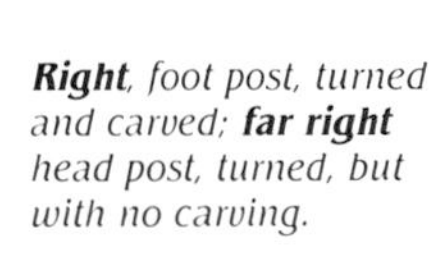

Right, *foot post, turned and carved;* ***far right*** *head post, turned, but with no carving.*

FINISH

Many beds of this period were painted in pale colours, otherwise wax polished.

RELATIVE VALUES

Tent beds with well-turned, fluted posts are expensive but so agreeable that they are unlikely ever to become unfashionable and may be seen as sound investments.

BEDS

About

1820-1890

Sotheby's

Late-19thC Empire-style gilt and bronze-mounted bed.

STYLE AND APPEARANCE

The **Empire** style (second neo-classical phase) lasted from 1820 to 1840 but by about 1825 was already being elbowed out by Gothic and rococo revivals, soon followed by Elizabethan (Renaissance/ baroque). Tent beds continued to be made but with heavier posts. New types included:

Sleigh beds: A type modelled on Franch *lit-en-bateau* (see **EUROPEAN BEDS, p. 204**) with scrolled head and foot, sometimes with suspended, draped canopy.

***Below**, Renaissance-style mahogany bed, about 1870.*

The American Museum in Britain

Gothic: Massive posts formed as cluster columns set on square pedestal bases. (One example is reputed to have been made about 1825 for the visit of Lafayette.)

Rococo: No posts, ornate head and foot-board, reaching apogee about 1850 with J. H. Belter's creations in carved and pierced types made from laminated boards. Baudouine and Meeks worked in a similar style. Brass bedsteads were equally ornate using brass (or brassed) tubes combined with rosettes in gilt metal and mother-of-pearl. Iron bedsteads were much simpler.

Meanwhile, more austere beds, little different in appearance from 18thC types, were made by country craftsmen and by Shaker communities. The latter included trundle, folding and easily dismantled models in their range.

***Below**, painted poplar bedstead, New York 1830.*

Sotheby's

Christie's

Aesthetic movement ebonised bed, New York, about 1880.

MATERIALS

Variety of timbers. Brass, iron. Belter's patented laminated timber (from three to 16 laminae) was surfaced with rosewood, steamed and pressed into moulds to shape it into curves. Shakers used cherry, pine and maple. Less emphasis on drapes, but much loving care devoted to quilts, especially patchwork.

CONSTRUCTION

Whether machined or hand-cut, the mortise-and-tenon joint remained mainstay of most makers of beds. Shakers made ingenious use of lapped joint secured with key wedges for a type that could be easily taken apart, the legs mounted on castors.

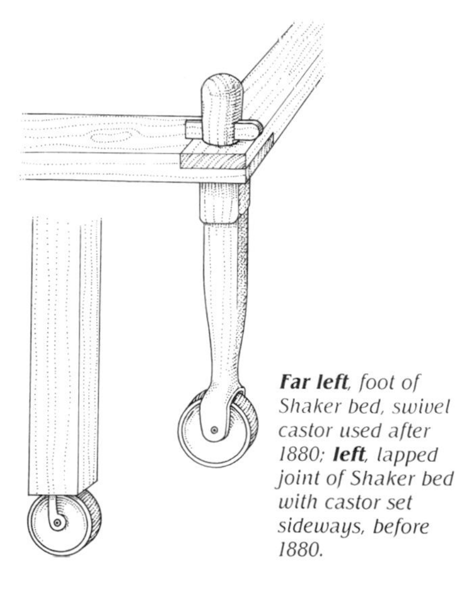

***Far left**, foot of Shaker bed, swivel castor used after 1880; **left**, lapped joint of Shaker bed with castor set sideways, before 1880.*

Shaker beds can be difficult to date, but one clue is to be found in the castors or roller wheels. Before about 1880, they were set sideways so that bed could not run away from wall: after 1880, they swivel.

Late in the century, wire mesh mattresses were introduced as supports for overlays in sophisticated circles, but rural and western types either continued to use the cross-rope system or replaced it with lath supports slotted into mortises in frame.

DECORATION

Empire style: Turned bar, resembling a rolling pin, set above panel of headboard. Sleigh beds were carved with swans.

Gothic: Carved tracery in pointed arches on headboards, cluster-column posts.

Rococo: Lavish carving (and sometimes piercing) of C-scrolls, flowers and foliage on headboards.

Elizabethan: Headboards set between spirally turned uprights.

FINISH

Sophisticated beds French polished. Country and Shaker types left neutral, painted or stained.

***Below**, craft style bed-head, with through tenons, about 1910.*

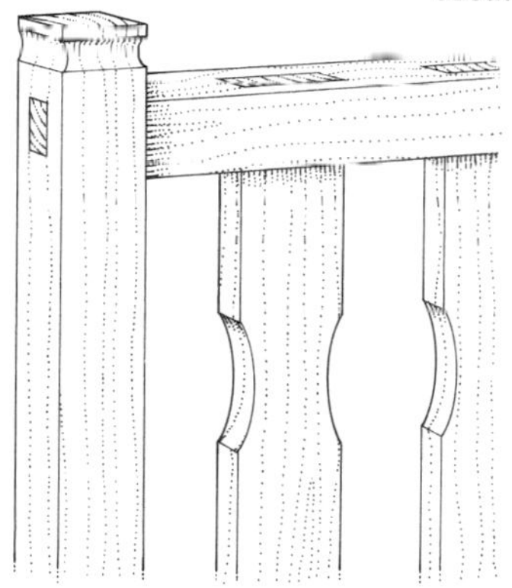

RELATIVE VALUES

Belter's lavish beds highly collectable, but many attributed to him were probably made by Meeks or Baudouine, both of whom imitated his style and came close to infringing his patents. Money better spent on simpler, solid types, e.g. Shaker.

BEDS

About
1890-1940

Gradual move towards greater simplicity, with emphasis on comfort and practicality rather than appearance.

Headboard of Sheraton revival bedstead.

STYLE AND APPEARANCE

Craft movement favoured bedsteads with head and foot composed of vertical bars set into horizontal rails between low, square-section posts.

Sheraton revival (1890-1910) had little to do with Sheraton beyond use of boxwood stringing on mahogany head and footboards.

Jacobean revival followed, using caned panels, often oval, set between turned uprights. Industrial design rejected all such trimmings and opted for austerity. Art Moderne went in opposite direction, applying luxurious and sometimes garish headboards to low divan beds.

***Below**, carved headboard of Jacobean revival bedstead.*

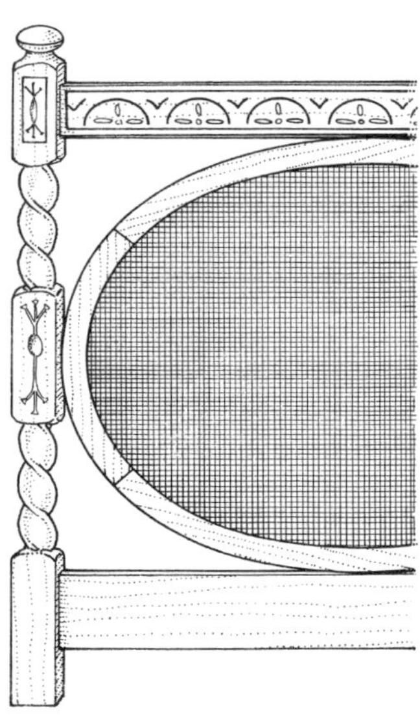

MATERIALS

Oak, ash, for **Craft** and **Jacobean** types, mahogany for **Sheraton** revival. Industrial designers liked hygienic, painted surface on headboards, or chromium-plated steel tubes. **Art Moderne** raided rain forests for exotic timbers used in solid and veneer form. Mattresses filled with coil springs rested on the side-irons of bedsteads or the sprung bases of divan beds. Headboards often upholstered.

CONSTRUCTION

Traditional types made by traditional methods. **Industrial** and **Art Moderne** used new techniques, machine processes, to achieve flush surfaces, bold shapes.

DECORATION

Sheraton: Inlaid stringing, crossbanding.

Jacobean: Turning, simplistic carving.

Art Moderne: Marquetry, quartered veneers (SEE EUROPEAN CABINETS, p. 213).

FINISH

French polish, cellulose, paint, lacquer.

RELATIVE VALUES

Best buys: **Craft** bedsteads, **Art Moderne** divan beds.

PRESS AND COURT CUPBOARDS

About

1670-1700

Oak court cupboard, 1670-1680.

Originally, a cupboard was literally a Cup Board – an open, three-tiered side table for displaying silver cups. The earliest American examples date from after 1670 and are partly enclosed with panels and doors – cupboards in the modern sense – but clearly meant as status symbols. Known variously as 'press' or 'court' cupboards

STYLE AND APPEARANCE

Late Renaissance style. Heavy turnings support tiers. Arrangement of doors and drawers between tiers varies. In some examples, the whole of the lower stage is enclosed and closely resembles the front of a chest (see CHESTS, 1620-1740 **p. 305**).

MATERIALS

Oak, pine, curly maple.

CONSTRUCTION

Panelled, mortise-and-tenon joints. Drawers, if any, crudely dovetailed. Built in two stages, upper and lower. Each support, however bulky, turned from one piece of wood – not built up – with a dowel at each end for socketing into hole in cornice above and ledge below.

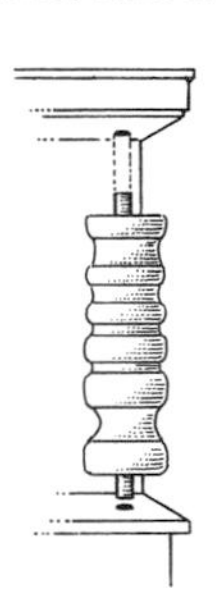

Turned and dowelled support for cornice.

DECORATION

Carving: Strapwork in the manner of T. Dennis, Ipswich, Massachusetts; tulips, sunflowers.

Applied: Geometric mouldings, split banister turnings.

Handles: Wooden knobs, round or turtle-back (see CHESTS **p. 306**).

FINISH

Oiled and waxed. Applied decoration often stained black.

RELATIVE VALUES

Prices very high for authentic American examples. English and Welsh types offer a cheaper alternative if patriotism permits.

FAKES

Fakers of American types have been known to re-carve the four legs of a Victorian dining-table and set them around cupboards made up of old panelling decorated with split banister turnings, new but camouflaged with black stain.

CUPBOARDS: DUTCH *KAS*

About
1770-1850

The *kas*, a Dutch-American version of the Netherlands *kast*: Full-length cupboard made in New York and New Jersey for more than 100 years.

Painted pine schrank, about 1780.

Sotheby's

STYLE AND APPEARANCE
Baroque, with heavily moulded cornice and turned ball feet.

Door of kas, *arched and fielded panels.*

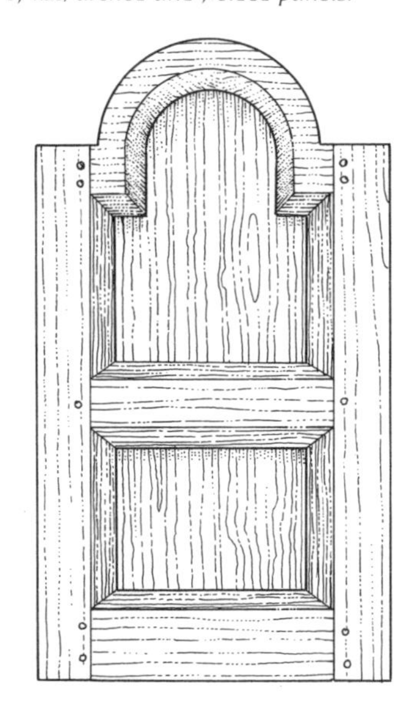

MATERIALS
Fruitwood, gumwood, walnut, pine.

CONSTRUCTION
Panelled, the panels often arched and fielded. Usually two or three drawers in base.

DECORATION
Mouldings around panels.

FINISH
Many painted with still life subjects of fruit and flowers *en grisaille* (tones of grey), within *trompe l'oeil* panels.

RELATIVE VALUES
Examples with good, original grisaille decoration expensive. Plain, late-18th or early-19thC examples are buyable. Old but plain pine cupboards, often imported from Europe, are given the grisaille treatment by skilled decorators who tend to copy the fruit painted on the doors of a well-known museum example. If no guarantee is promised, the advice of an expert should be sought.

CUPBOARDS: FRENCH ARMOIRE

About

1680-1800

Mainly French Canadian, but influence felt along Mississippi to New Orleans.

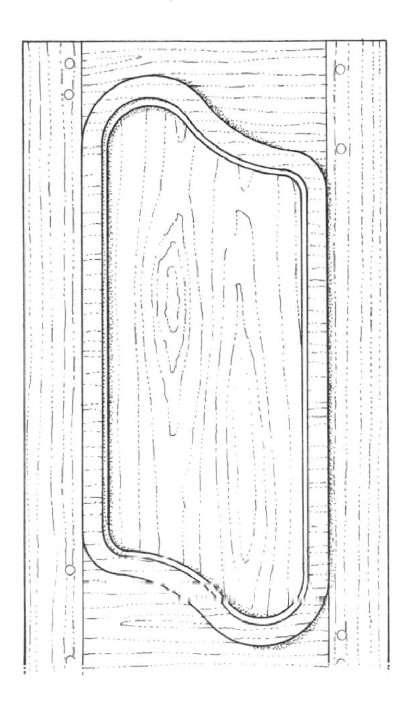

Above, *carved panel, typical of mid-18thC French rococo armoires and boiseries.*

STYLE AND APPEARANCE

Louis XIII-XV. **See p. 210**.

MATERIALS

Canadian examples usually pine.

CONSTRUCTION, DECORATION AND FINISH

As in France. See **p. 210**.

RELATIVE VALUES

Plainer types with shaped panels but no carving can be very good value.

CUPBOARDS: CORNER CUPBOARDS AND CABINETS

About

1720-1850

The American Museum

Above, *painted and grained Federal corner cupboard, Pennsylvania, about 1810.*

Unglazed types known as cupboards, glazed ones as cabinets, but the terms tend to be interchangeable.

STYLE AND APPEARANCE

Rural versions made with little change over long period. Sophisticated types adapted slowly to changing fashions.

MATERIALS

Oak, pine, walnut, maple, mahogany.

CONSTRUCTION

Some single door width, some double. Both types include the following variations:

1 Full-length, standing: Wooden door(s) above and below. Doors panelled.

2 Full-length, standing: Glazed door(s) above, wood door(s) below. Wood doors panelled, glazed doors before 1800 always composed of separate panes puttied into a framework of glazing bars (astragals).

3 Full-length, standing: Wood or glazed doors above, or open shelves often framed with cyma scrolls; wood doors below. Arched, architectural types built in.

4 Half-length, hanging: Wood doors.

5 Half-length, hanging: Glazed door(s), glazing bars as in 2 above.

6 Half-length, hanging: Open shelves, often cyma-scrolled as in 3 above.

7 Half-length, hanging: Bow-fronted wood doors.

Full-length types sometimes made in two stages, sometimes in one piece. Backs; boards (tongued-and-grooved from early 19thC), nailed on.

A 'blind' door is often converted to a glazed one by replacing it with glass – a time-consuming process if done correctly with small panes. A short cut is taken by glueing strips of moulding to a single sheet of glass – easy to see if a careful examination is made. Large sheets of glass were not used for cases until about 1800, and only complex, curved astragals were glued on.

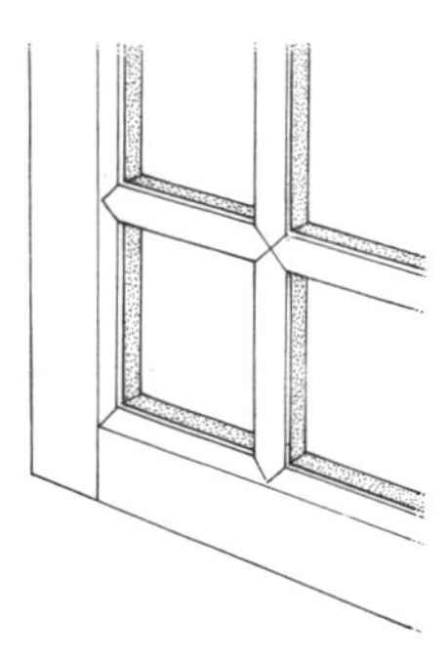

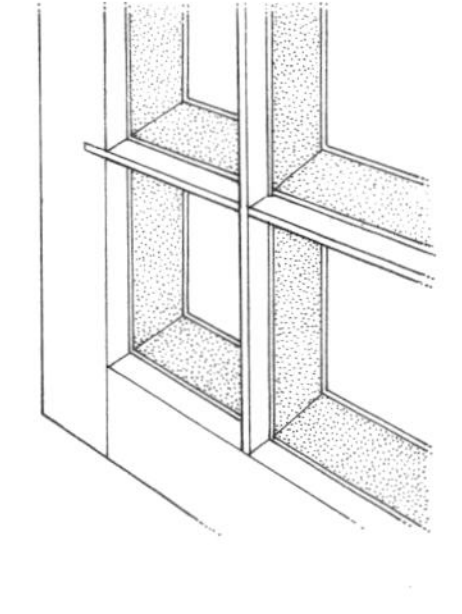

***Above**, front view of glazed door, glazing bars mitred into frame. **Right**, rear view of glazed door, bars tenoned into frame and separate panes fitted into bars.*

Painted and grained corner cabinet, about 1810.

American museum

DECORATION

Geometric mouldings on doors of early oak cupboards. Later rural types usually plain. Architectural, arched type usually has a rounded back and 'umbrella' top that is either ribbed or, in exceptionally fine examples, carved with a large shell; this type is flanked by a pair of fluted pilasters crowned with classical capitals. Some mahogany **Chippendale** types carved with rococo scrolls. In **Federal** period, more often decorated with neo-classical motifs in marquetry.

FINISH

Architectural types in pine often painted to match woodwork of room. Pennsylvania, 1820-50, grained effects and swirling patterns in sponged and spattered paint.

RELATIVE VALUES

It has been said that, if you furnish the corners of a room, the centre will look after itself. It is worth paying a fairly high price for a good cupboard that will bring an awkward corner to life.

MARRIAGES

A full-length corner cupboard in two parts may be a marriage of two hanging ones – a glass-fronted one above and a wood ('blind') door below. Check that the grain of the wood follows through, i.e. that there is consistency in the materials top and bottom.

CUPBOARDS: DISH DRESSERS

***Right**, simple painted dresser, Pennsylvania, early-19thC.*

STYLE AND APPEARANCE

Country sideboards: Regional variations of a cupboard base with a rack of open shelves above.

MATERIALS

Oak, pine, any suitable local wood.

CONSTRUCTION

Oak: Usually panelled.
Pine: Carcase often boarded (planks nailed to frame).

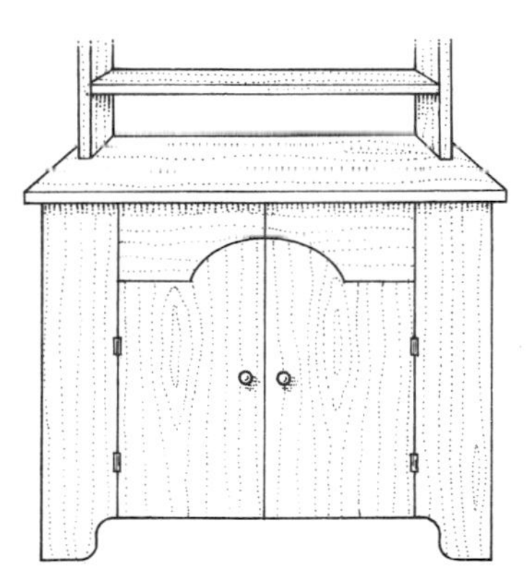

Base of dresser, boarded construction.

DECORATION

Shaping of rack-ends and sometimes of frieze below cornice.

FINISH

Painted, waxed or left raw.

RELATIVE VALUES

Surprisingly expensive when compared with average quality of the sophisticated equivalent, e.g. a good but not important mahogany sideboard of the late Empire period.

REPLACEMENT RACKS

The rack of a dresser may not belong originally to the base. If it does not, it will probably have been reduced in width to achieve a good fit. Examine the shelves where they join the ends for signs of recent cutting – slightly open joints with raw edges that may be camouflaged with vacuum cleaner dust mixed with glue, forming a kind of cement. Even the oldest encrusted dust is not as hard as that.

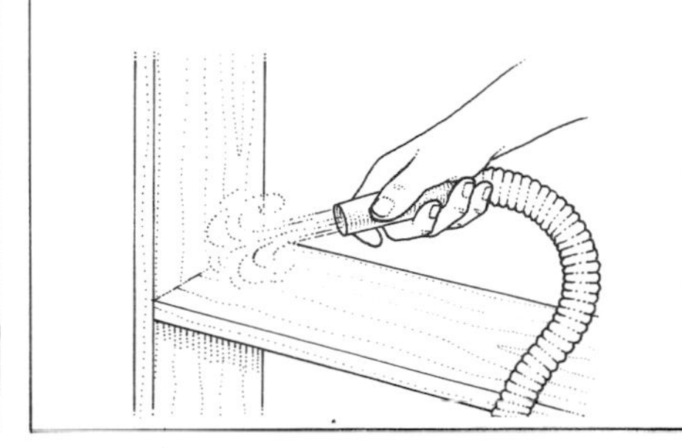

BOOKCASES AND CABINETS

About

1760-1840

Federal mahogany bookcase with butler's fall-front desk drawer, about 1790-1810.

Christie's

A desk in the base would suggest the case was intended for books, but in its absence it is difficult and a little pointless to distinguish arbitrarily between display cabinets and bookcases of the Chippendale, Federal and Empire periods. **See also CORNER CUPBOARDS AND CABINETS, p. 285 and secretary desks under DESKS, p. 313**

STYLE AND APPEARANCE

Dignified, often massive; the rococo element played down in the **Chippendale** period, the neo-classical style asserting itself in the **Federal** and **Empire** periods.

MATERIALS

Mahogany for sophisticated pieces; pine, poplar, for country pieces.

CONSTRUCTION

Chippendale breakfront: Centre section deeper back to front than wings; upper stage glazed, shallower back to front than lower, usually with cupboards and/or drawers, but sometimes on a stand e.g. the cabinet on Marlboro' legs made in 1771 by J. Folwell, Philadelphia, to house an orrery.

Federal breakfront: As above, but lower stage sometimes serpentine-fronted.

Empire: Sophisticated bookcases often in one piece with doors glazed with single sheets of glass, flanked by classical columns or pilasters.

Country: Pennsylvania produced two-stage types, glazed doors above divided into square panes; many made 1830-1840 appear earlier, stylistically.

DECORATION

Chippendale: Carving mainly confined to blind fret on friezes and, if on stands, the legs. Fine fretting within scrolls of pediments.

Federal: Marquetry in the Sheraton style.

Pennsylvania German: Carved demi-lunes arranged in series around door panels.

Painted bookcase, early-19thC.

The American Museum

FINISH

Mahogany types waxed or, later, French polished. Country types often painted and grained or painted in contrasting colours, with the occasional motif – e.g. an eagle – in gilt.

RELATIVE VALUES

Good examples much in demand both for books (especially in lawyers' offices) and for collections of ceramics, so prices are high, even for cases too large for normal domestic requirements.

BOOKCASES, CABINETS AND WARDROBES

About

1840-1890

The battles of the styles is followed by an attempt to discipline design and introduce new ideas.

STYLE AND APPEARANCE

Many pieces were nondescript – no style at all; but the more fashionable cupboards and cabinets in the mid-19thC were influenced by the passion for reviving, and often debasing, historic styles. Serpentine-fronted 'Louis' display cabinets had large glass doors and *vernis Martin* panels (see **EUROPEAN, p. 213**). Massive wardrobes and bookcases were built to look like Renaissance palaces or medieval fortresses. The Eastlake style of the 1870s purported to follow the structural honesty of the Gothic period, and was seen at its best in pieces, including bookcases, designed and made by the artist-craftsman L. E. Scott, but at its worst led to such travesties that in 1878, Eastlake disowned them.

The House Beautiful (1878) by C. Cook praised furniture of the Colonial period, provoking an antique-collecting craze and some copying of Early American cupboards. The book included furniture in Japanese style designed by A. Sandier and made by Herter Brothers of New York. It has some affinities with European art nouveau, as have cabinets produced in the 1880s by L. C. Tiffany.

Below, ash side-cabinet, with wooden inlay and brass mounts, mid-19thC.

Sotheby's

V&A

Ebonised cherrywood cabinet, about 1876.

Left, ebonised side-cabinet, about 1865.

Sotheby's

MATERIALS

Nondescript: Mahogany.
Louis: Kingwood.
Renaissance: Walnut.
Gothic: Oak.
Colonial: Oak, walnut, mahogany.
Japanese: Cherry, various woods for marquetry.

CONSTRUCTION

Fine craftsmanship using orthodox joinery for best items in Gothic style, some with exposed joints, e.g. through tenons. Increasing use of machined dovetails for commercial products.

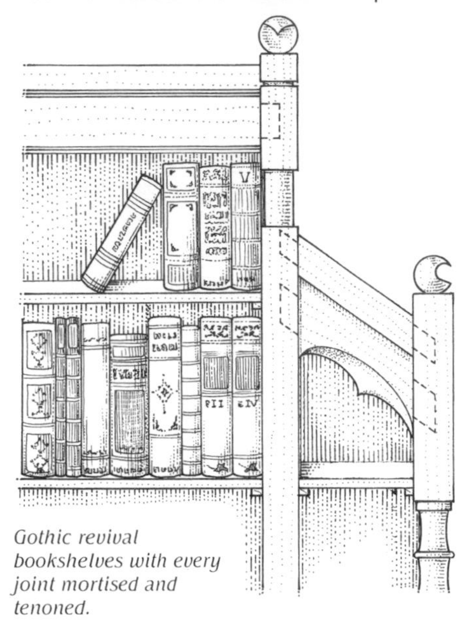

Gothic revival bookshelves with every joint mortised and tenoned.

19thC copies of Federal bookcases can be very deceptive. The give-away in some examples is the use of mahogany instead of oak for the sides of large drawers.

DECORATION

Nondescript: Fretted shelves, carved brackets, turned spindles.

Renaissance: Broken arches, split banister turnings (machined).

Gothic: Carved and pierced tracery, inlay of stylized flowers, birds and animals.

Colonial: Often inaccurate renderings of Early American decoration.

Japanese: Flowers in marquetry.

FINISH

Heavy-handed varnishing and French polishing. Herter's Japanese-style cherrywood pieces ebonised. Ormolu mounts on Louis cabinets.

RELATIVE VALUES

Louis cabinets sought after and expensive. Large cases of this period, out of fashion until 1980, now wanted.

CABINETS AND WARDROBES

About

1890-1920

Christie's

Oak corner display cabinet, Stickley, c.1910.

The end of the 19th and the beginning of the 20thC see traditional craftsmanship gradually giving way to the new age of industrial design and mass production.

STYLE AND APPEARANCE

By 1887, the Phoenix Furniture Company of Grand Rapids, Michigan, was said to have the most advanced machinery in the country, devoted to turning out a huge range that included cupboards, wardrobes and cabinets in all the popular period styles, as well as simple types that anticipated the work of the craft communities in the Mission style. From 1907, the Greene brothers designed furniture made by the Peter Hall company, Pasadena, combining Eastlake's principles with those of G. Stickley's Craftsman Workshops, and including glass-fronted cabinets built into panelled rooms.

MATERIALS

Craft communities: Mainly oak, some ash.
Manufacturers: Mainly mahogany; ebony.

CONSTRUCTION

Craft communities: Traditional methods, leaving tenons, dovetails and butterfly joints exposed.

Manufacturers: Machine-cut dovetails, increased use of dowels in place of tenons; doors glazed with single sheets of glass.

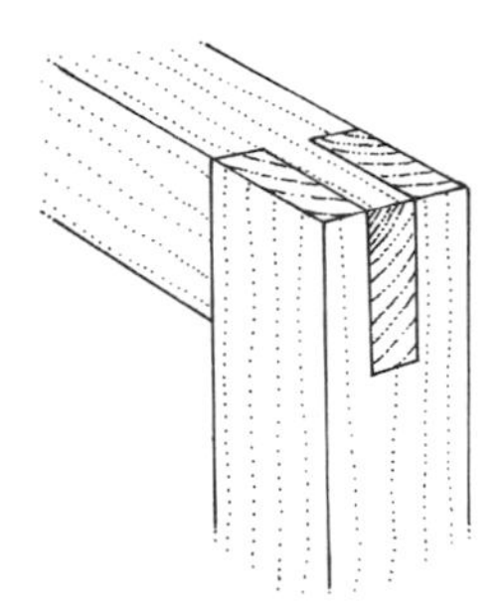

Exposed tenon.

DECORATION

Craft communities: Carving used sparingly.

Manufacturers: Carving and marquetry, some of it machine-work. Greene brothers used inlay in ebony, silver and semi-precious stones.

FINISH

Roycroft Comunity, East Aurora, used a finish that was kept secret, and hung the doors of cupboards with exposed copper hinges. Other craft centres used stains, some of them coloured. Traditional pieces French-polished.

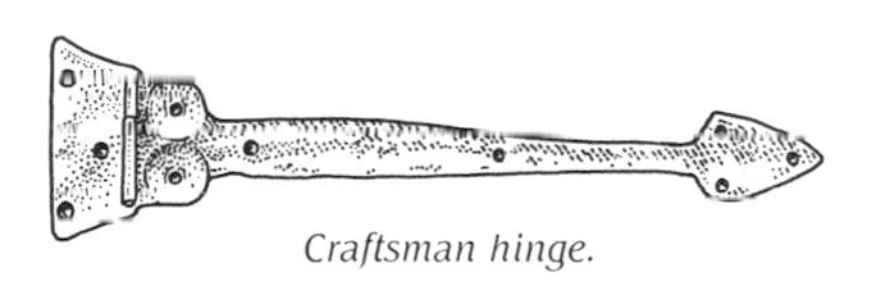

Craftsman hinge.

RELATIVE VALUES

Some of the best designer bookcases, cabinets and wardrobes of this period were built-in and difficult to remove, but many free-standing items appear on the market and if awkwardly proportioned, may sell reasonably. Stickley pieces still under-priced.

If cabinets in the neo-classical style are more to your taste than craft furniture, but authentic Federal items are beyond your budget, give serious thought to the reproductions made 1890-1920. The earlier ones are now over 100 years old and qualify as antiques in their own right.

CABINETS AND WARDROBES

About

1920-1940

Sotheby's

Painted cabinet, about 1929.

Industrial design rationalizes cabinets and wardrobes to the point where they would all be as featureless as the broom cupboard, were it not for the sometimes garish but humanizing influence of Art Moderne.

STYLE AND APPEARANCE

Wardrobes have flush surfaces and tend increasingly to be built-in units. The functional style is best expressed in display cabinets and bookcases with sliding, plate-glass, frameless doors. The Art Moderne style is typified by a 20thC invention that may be seen as a symbol of the jazz age – the cocktail cabinet.

MATERIALS

Plywood, veneered in pale woods – maple, satinwood, birch – used extensively for flush surfaces, especially for curved ends of cocktail cabinets. Fine timber used in the solid almost exclusively for architect-designed, custom-built pieces. Plate glass widely used for shelves, mirror glass for lining backs of display and cocktail cabinets, both types very often electrically illuminated.

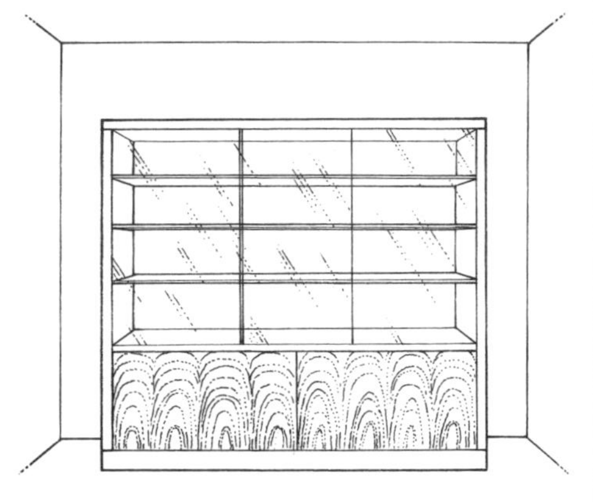

***Above**, built-in display cabinet with sliding doors, 1930s.*

CONSTRUCTION

Plywood used for backs and drawer-bottoms and in three different ways for exposed surfaces: **1** pinned to front of solid frame; **2** as panel set in rebated frame; **3** pinned to back of frame to give false impression of panelled construction.

***Below**, 1930s wardrobe.*

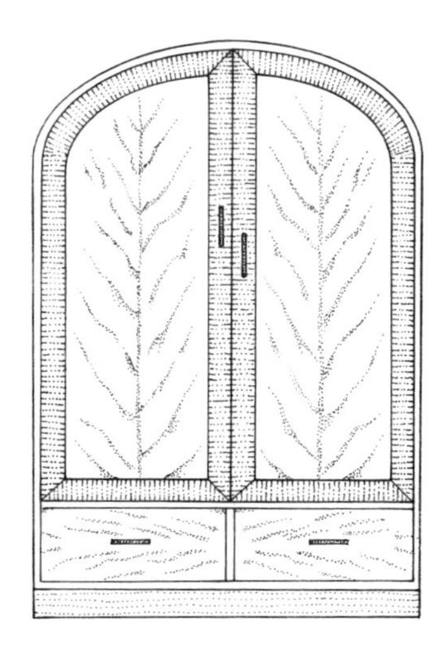

DECORATION

The functional school rejected decoration on principle; Art Moderne used marquetry in exotic materials, occasional carving of futuristic motifs.

FINISH

Clear cellulose spray. Bold use of paint or lacquer in contrasting colours. Chromium plated handles and fittings.

RELATIVE VALUES

Better pieces made between the wars are no longer mere 'second-hand' and should be assessed according to their merits like those of any other period. No serious collector – not even a total abstainer – should be without a '30s cocktail cabinet.

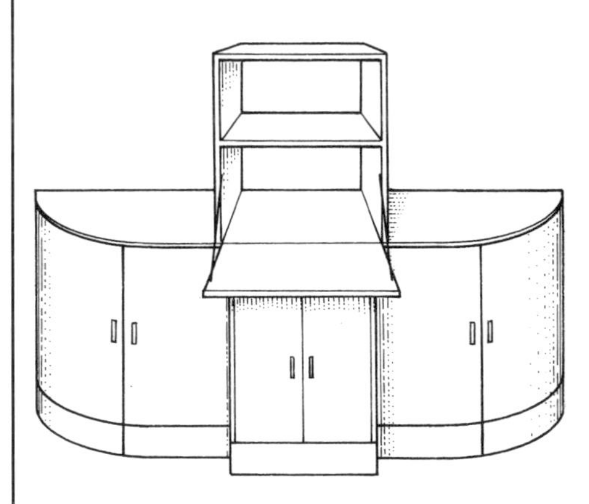

***Above**, 1930s cocktail cabinet.*

MODERN FAKES

Anything that is fashionable is liable to be faked. This is now beginning to apply to Art Moderne, but most of the copies are of kitsch. The good pieces were of high quality and expensive when new, so are less easy to reproduce cheaply, but do not assume that, because a thing belongs to a time within living memory, it must necessarily be genuine.

CHAIRS

About

1620-1690

An oak 'Carver' chair, about 1650.

The American Museum

Most of the seat furniture surviving from this period dates from after 1650 and chiefly comprises stools, chairs and armchairs.

STYLE AND APPEARANCE

Stools: **1** Fairly crude variations of the milking stool or 'peg-leg' type. **2** 'Joyned' or joint-stools, also called coffin stools because a pair was often pressed into service to form a bier.

Chairs: **1** Rare, early 'wainscot' types with panelled backs and seats have turned legs, but were made by joiners. **2** 'Stick' chairs made entirely by turners. The Brewster armchair has spindles under seat, the Carver does not. **3** 'Slat-backs', also stick type, have shaped slats set between the uprights of the backs, and turned legs.

BENCHES

Long benches of this type were much less common in America than in England and Holland, and should be accepted as of American origin only if the evidence is very strong indeed.

MATERIALS

Stools: Maple, oak, pine.

Wainscot chairs: Oak frames, pine panels in backs and seats.

Stick chairs: Maple, ash, oak frames; rush seats.

CONSTRUCTION

Peg-leg: Legs are turned or, more often, roughly rounded with a draw-knife, and driven through holes bored in the seat, so that their upper ends project very slightly above the surface; the fixing is tightened by driving a small wedge from above into the end grain of the leg.

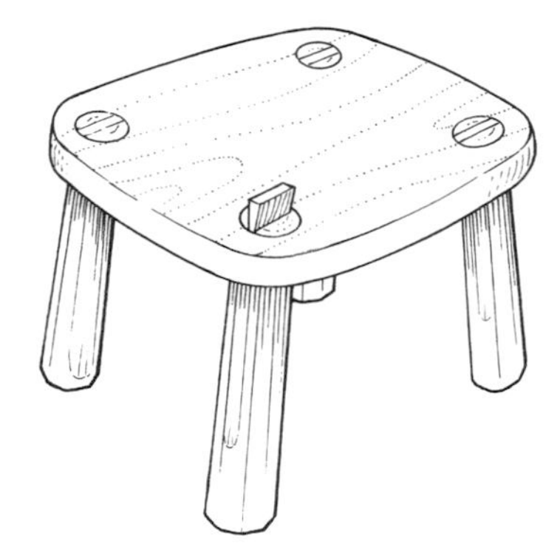

Peg-leg stool with wedge.

Joined stools and chairs: Seat rails and stretchers have tenons cut at their ends which slot into mortises in the square sections, top and bottom, of the turned legs; the joint is secured with pegs driven through holes to penetrate the tenons (not to be confused with peg-leg construction, see above). The seat is similarly pegged to the seat rail.

Turned leg, mortised to receive tenons.

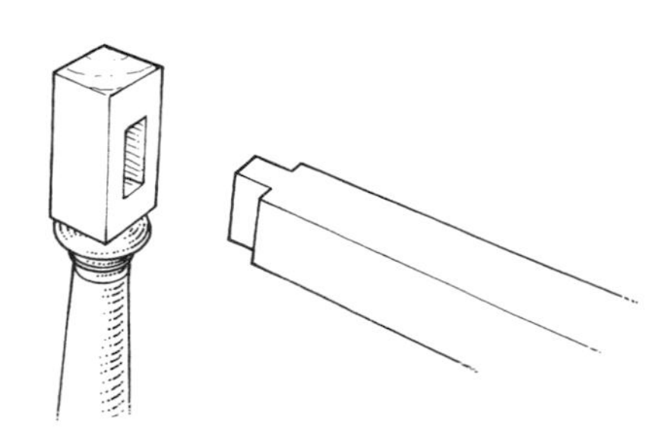

Stick: Stretchers, turned or rounded by hand, are driven into holes bored in the legs. Shaped slats, thin enough to be bent to curve outwards, are set in mortises cut in uprights of the back. In early armchairs, the arms are turned bars that slot into holes in the uprights and the arm supports. No pegging needed.

Replacement stool seats

Many experts (though not all) reject stools where the seat is secured by pegs driven in at the corners so that they penetrate the end grain of the legs, threatening to split them; such positioning, it is argued, occurs only when the original seat has been replaced clumsily.

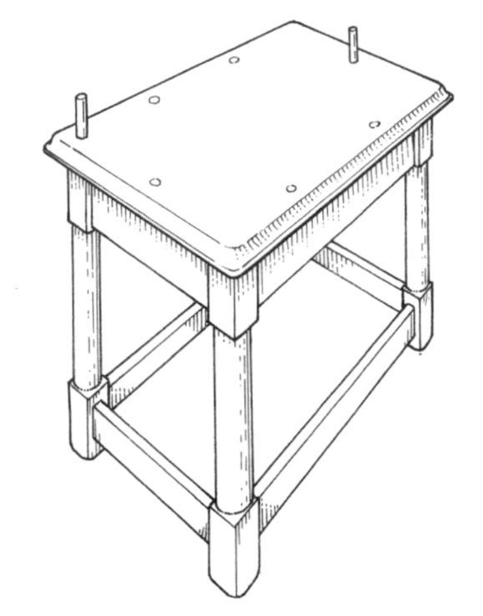

Pegs on joint stool. The peg on the right is correctly placed.

DECORATION

Wainscot chairs: Carved top rails occur only rarely, e.g. one at the Winterthur.

Stick chairs: Varied turnings include 'mushroom' finials to arm supports. Slats shaped to several different patterns.

FINISH

Oiled and waxed, varnished or painted.

RELATIVE VALUES

Joined stools and wainscot chairs now too expensive to sit on. Peg-leg stools difficult to date, but good for a gamble. Stick and slat-back chairs can still turn up unexpectedly at bargain prices.

CHAIRS

About

1690-1725

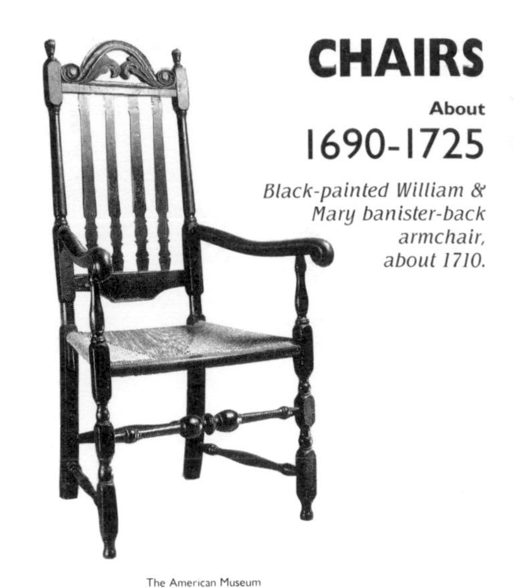

Black-painted William & Mary banister-back armchair, about 1710.

The American Museum

American interpretations of the European and English (Charles II and William and Mary) baroque style are expressed in several new types of seating.

STYLE AND APPEARANCE

Slat-back chairs (see **p. 293**) continued to be made in great variety. New types included: square-backed **Cromwell chairs** with turned front legs, the seats and back upholstered, before 1700; a small number of **high-backed** chairs in the Charles II (Anglo-Flemish) style, with caned backs and seats, turned or scrolled legs, the armchairs with 'ram's horn' arms, before 1700. **Corner chairs** with turned members and bowed backs, also in small quantities, from 1700. **Banister-back** chairs, from 1700 (see DECORATION). The **day-bed** – a couch for lounging on – before 1700 (see CONSTRUCTION). The New York **waggon seat** from 1720 (also made in other regions, such as Connecticut, Massachusetts); a crude prototype of the chair-back settee that served as seating in the house and, when lashed to a wagon, converted it into a makeshift carriage.

WAGGON SEATS

The waggon seat continued to be made well into the 19thC. Many offered for sale, though not fakes, are not as old as they are sometimes claimed to be. The hard use to which they were put means that early examples are seldom in pristine condition.

William & Mary maple day-bed, about 1725.

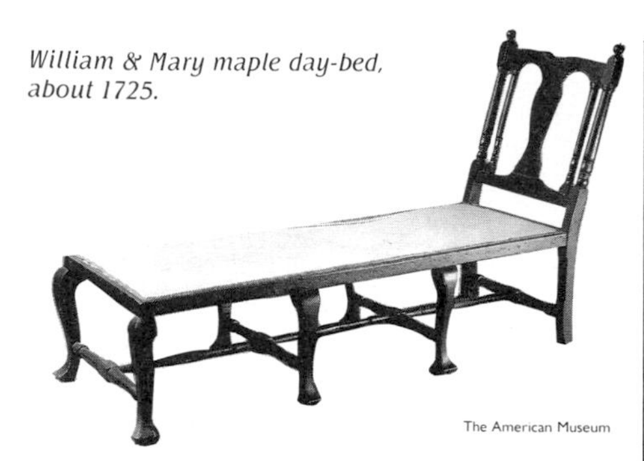

The American Museum

MATERIALS

Frames: Oak, walnut, beech, ash, maple.

Slats: Hickory or ash (easily bent to shape when still green).

Turned spindles: Juniper.

Upholstery (for Cromwell' chairs): Leather or 'Turkey work' – a hand-knotted imitation of Turkish carpets.

Caning (for baroque chairs and day-beds): Split and woven rattan cane.

HISTORICAL EVIDENCE

A large Turkey work Carpet for the table and *two doz. arm'd Cain Chairs* are mentioned in the Journals of the Burgesses of Virginia, 1702-12, in reference to the furnishing of the Council Chamber of the Capitol (first building) at Williamsburg.

CONSTRUCTION

High-backed baroque chairs: Front legs, whether turned or scrolled, often socketed into a flat seat-frame, instead of being jointed with mortise-and-tenon; likewise, the cresting rail of the back may be set *on to* uprights, instead of between them.

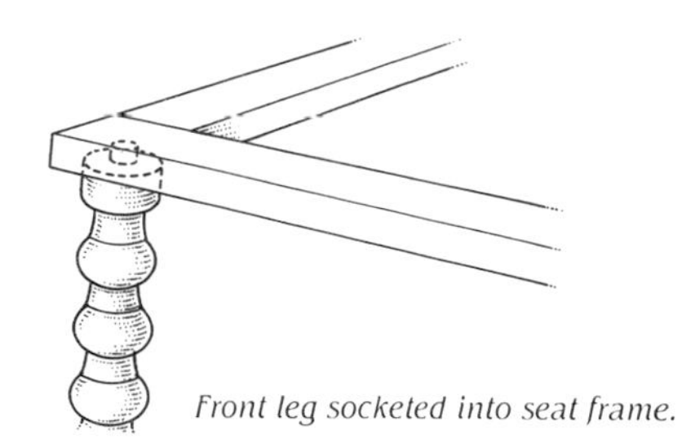

Front leg socketed into seat frame.

The day-bed: Essentially a chair with elongated seat and additional legs; the back, or bed-head, often hinged and fitted with a ratchet for adjustment.

DECORATION

Baroque chairs: Members turned, cresting rails arched and carved, 'Spanish' (also known as 'Braganza') feet shaped and carved.

Cromwell chairs: Varied turnings; 'barley twists' (spirals) were known as Crosswicks after the district near Philadelphia where this speciality was practised.

Spiral twist leg.

Banister chairs: The back composed of split banisters (also known as balusters), produced by sawing the wood in half, lengthwise, lightly glueing the two halves together, turning on the lathe to the desired shape, then splitting them apart again. They are then set into the upper and lower rails of the chair-back with their flat sides facing inwards, so that no protuberances make for discomfort.

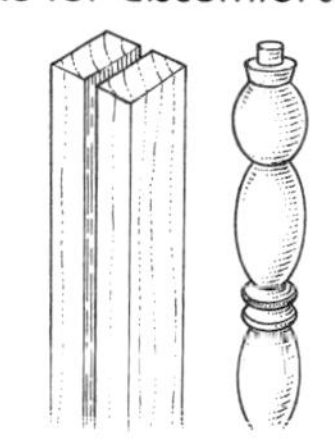

*Split banisters: **right**, length of timber sawn in half; **far right**, halves reassembled for turning on lathe.*

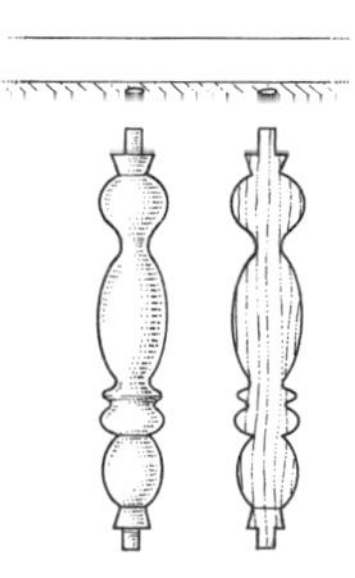

***Right**, rounded face; **far right**, flat face.*

FINISH

Baroque types often stained black and varnished, or japanned in imitation of oriental lacquer. Rural types oiled and waxed or painted.

RELATIVE VALUES

Cromwell, **high-backed** and **corner chairs**, also **day-beds**, rare and highly priced. Best buy: individual **slat-backs**.

CHAIRS

About

1725-1790

Christie's

Left, Queen Anne walnut side-chair, New York, about 1760.

Growing wealth created a demand for comfort, even luxury. Between 1725 and 1760, Boston alone gave employment to 38 chair-makers and 23 upholsterers. Regional differences became more marked in the work of Boston, Philadelphia, New York and Newport – the chief centres; for instance, New England side-chairs were taller and thinner than those of New York.

> **ATTRIBUTIONS**
>
> Attributions in this period are made by comparing examples with makers' labels, for example William Savery of Philadelphia; but names are sometimes bandied about for no better reason than to boost the price.

STYLE AND APPEARANCE

The **Queen Anne** style – merging, from 1760 into **Chippendale** – emphasised the S-shaped curve of the cabriole leg, a rounded seat and a swan-neck back with shaped centre splat ('fiddle back') – a feature seen in many country-made chairs still retaining turned legs. In more sophisticated examples, the splats are ergonomically designed to suit the human spine. In the Chippendale period, the splat was fretted and pierced, and the cabriole leg slowly gave way to the **Marlboro'** – straight, square in section but chamfered on the inside angle. Easy chairs have draught-excluding wings; a child's version in solid timber has a hole in the seat to hold a pot.

Christie's

Right, Chippendale mahogany side-chair, Philadelphia, about 1765-1770.

Christie's

Queen Anne walnut easy chair, Rhode Island, about 1735-1760.

In the 1780s, Daniel Trotter of Philadelphia was probably the maker of **ladder-back** chairs – sophisticated versions in mahogany of the country slat-back, with shaped and pierced slats and Marlboro' legs. Country chairs of **Windsor** type, made with spindles of green timber socketed into bent frames, succeeded earlier **stick** types. Windsor **settees** were an alternative to the settle, high or low in the back, boarded or panelled.

Sotheby's

Windsor settee, about 1775.

Sophisticated **settees**; two main types:

1 Fully-upholstered, with only the feet ex-

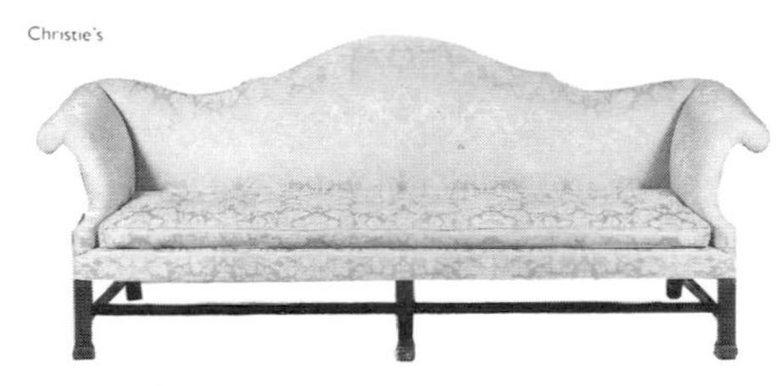

***Above**, Chippendale sofa, Philadelphia, about 1775.*

posed (and sometimes the rail). **2** The 'chair-back' or 'frame', conceived as two or three chair-backs conjoined.

Day-beds continued to be popular in the Queen Anne period, with fashionable splat-backs and cabriole legs.

MATERIALS

Native maple and cherrywood substituted for walnut, the most fashionable wood 1725-50, and for mahogany, 1750-90. Upholstery materials ranged from leather and local worsted cloth to imported damasks, velvets and brocades. Stools, promoted to the parlour, had seats that, whether stuffed-over or drop-in, were often covered in needlework made by the lady of the house.

***Above**, Queen Anne maple stool, about 1750-1760.*

***Left**, mahogany side-chair, Philadelphia about 1765-1785.*

CONSTRUCTION

Craftsmen did not at first trust the strength of cabriole legs with no underframing, and until 1740, many – in New England especially – continued to be united with turned stretchers.

As a means of joining the cabriole leg to the front of a curved seat, the mortise-and-tenon joint could be made to work only at the risk of weakening it, as too much of it had to be cut away to achieve the shape. Some makers compensated for this weakness by fitting a block inside. Others used a halving joint (a half-thickness of the side rail overlapping and glued to a half-thickness of the front rail). A cavity was then cut in the joint to receive the square at the top of the leg, shaped to a dovetail or tenon.

After 1760, the balloon shape of the seat was discarded in favour of an angular one, and in mahogany chairs of the Chippendale period, a conventional mortise-and-tenon joint is usual.

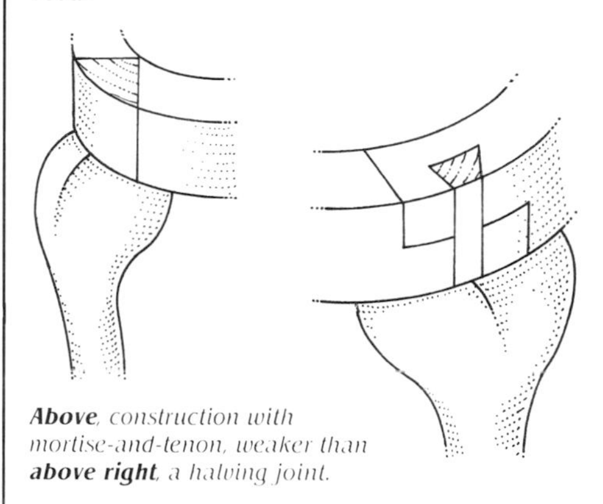

***Above**, construction with mortise-and-tenon, weaker than **above right**, a halving joint.*

MADE IN PHILADELPHIA

In Philadelphia in the mid-18thC, the regular method of joining the side-rails to the rear uprights was by means of a through-tenon, secured with pegs driven through holes in the side-rail. If the ends of the pegs and the through-tenon are visible, this is a sign of Philadelphian origin.

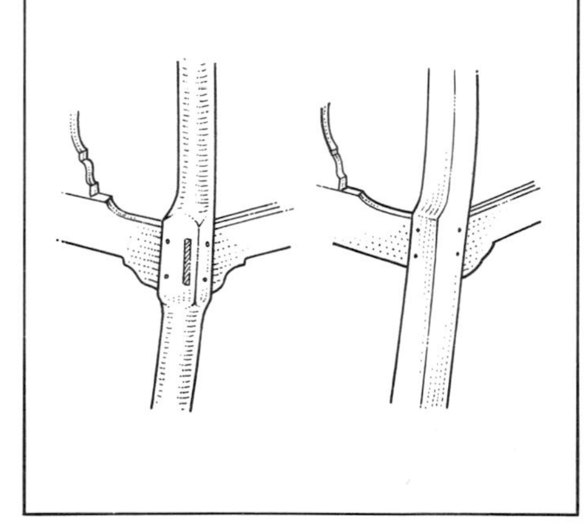

DECORATION

Queen Anne: Shells carved on knees of cabriole legs and often at the centre of the cresting rail which, in many New York examples, is pierced with two spaces flanking the shell. Feet were plain pads, carved lion paws or claw-and-ball. The Queen Anne style survived in Newport to the end of the Colonial period.

Chippendale: Splats fretted and pierced. Marlboro' legs headed by Chinese fretted brackets, but cabriole legs with claw-and-ball feet persisted; in New York, they were carved with foliage down to the feet.

CORRECT CLAWS

In a well-carved claw-and-ball foot, the claw should appear to be grasping the ball with the strength of an eagle clutching its prey – a feature naturalistically rendered in Philadelphia, where the ball is flatter than in the rather square New York version. Newport claws have been unflatteringly described as limp. The differences are sufficiently marked to be acceptable criteria when making attributions.

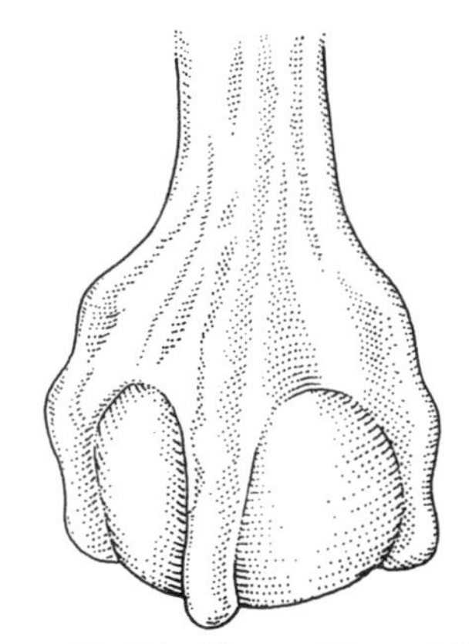

Claw and ball foot from a Chippendale side-chair, about 1765-70.

FINISH

Queen Anne: Walnut veneers often used in splats and seat rails. Others with japanned decoration, usually in gold on a black ground.

Chippendale: Mahogany seldom used in veneer form on chairs. Walnut and mahogany surfaces rubbed down with sand or brick-dust, varnished, rubbed down again and wax-polished.

CABRIOLE LEGS

Wing chairs with cabriole legs tend to command higher prices than ones with straight legs. Many of the latter type (**A**) have been glamorized by sawing off the legs and replacing them with cabriole legs (**B**), using dowels and/or hefty screws. The head of a screw may be visible but is more likely to have been countersunk and camouflaged with stopping wax. Dowels are out of sight, but if a flap of the upholstery is carefully lifted (**C**), it is possible to prove whether the cabriole leg and the square above it are of one continuous piece of wood, as they should be. If they are not, a human hair, pulled from your head and held taut, will penetrate the join (marked with arrows) that should not be there.

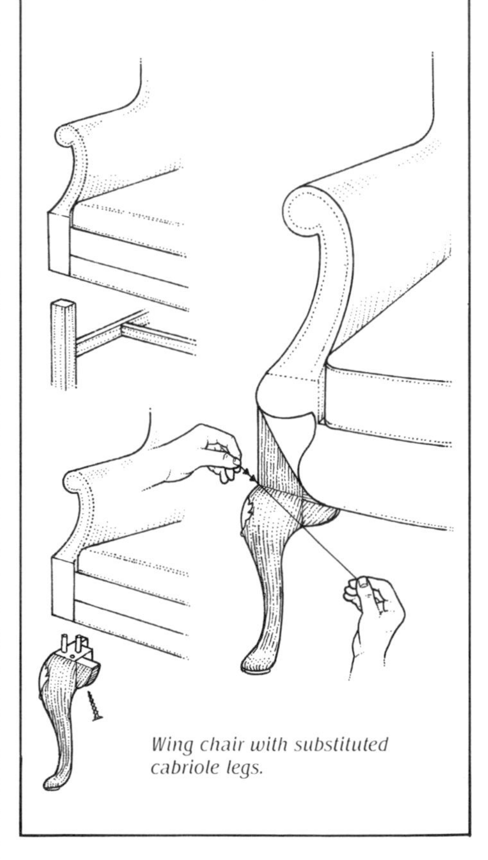

Wing chair with substituted cabriole legs.

RELATIVE VALUES

Cabriole-legged types tend to fetch more money than Marlboro', but much depends on detail. Windsor chairs made in great quantity and variety, but not cheap.

CHAIRS

About

1790-1810

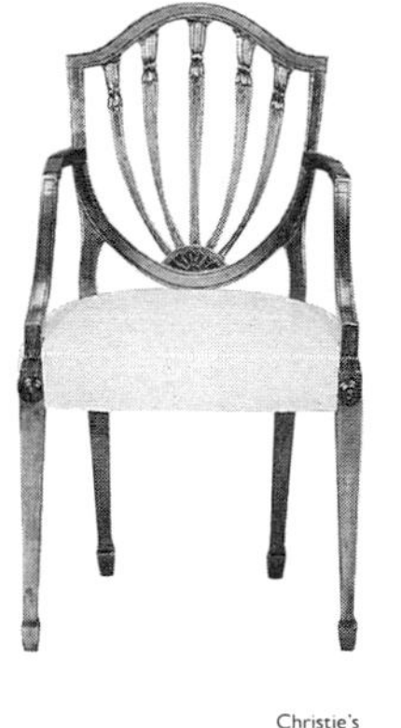

Mahogany armchairs in Hepplewhite style, Massachusetts, about 1790-1810.

Christie's

The publication of Robert Adam's neo-classical designs was delayed by the War of Independence, but by 1790, those of Hepplewhite and Sheraton were available and being interpreted by chair makers, notably John Aitken of Philadelphia (where the *Journeyman Cabinet and Chairmakers' Book of Prices* appeared in 1794-5); John Seymour of Boston; Samuel McIntire of Salem; Duncan Phyfe of New York (though the latter was more subject to French Directoire influence – see p. 195). From 1795, Baltimore became a centre for furniture that included 'fancy' (painted) chairs.

STYLE AND APPEARANCE

The Federal style is identified with the first phase of neo-classicism.

Side-chairs: 1 Rectangular, oval or shield-shaped backs, the splats pierced and carved; legs straight and tapered, often terminating in 'spade' feet. **2** Square-framed backs with a series of vertical bars replacing the splat; straight, tapered legs. **3** After 1805, square-framed backs enclosing straight or X-shaped bars. Phyfe also used X-shaped supports in place of conventional legs for chairs and settees.

'Fancy' chairs: Legs socketed into the seat frame, painted panels in the backs.

Easy chairs: stuffed backs and seats, tapered legs; **Martha Washington** chair with high back, low seat and open arms a speciality of New Hampshire.

Frame settees: Chair-back types with oval or shield shapes conjoined, on tapered legs, open arms.

Fully upholstered settees (sofas): 'Camel' backs rising to a hump, scrolled arms.

Country chairs and settees: Windsor types in greater variety and more elegant than English. Some turnings simulate bamboo.

Slat-backs include the early rocker, said to have been invented by Benjamin Franklin around 1770, but becoming general during Federal period and developing into a national institution. The Shaker communities produced two main types – the light-weight 'Sister's' rocker, and the heavier 'Brother's' version with mushroom tops to the arm-supports.

MATERIALS

West Indian mahogany the principal wood, but a wide mixture of native timbers used for seat furniture meant to be painted, for instance a set of 24 oval-backed maple chairs made in Philadelphia 1796 for Elias Derby of Salem.

CONSTRUCTION

Chairmakers had to perfect existing methods to meet the exacting demands of the neo-classical style with its emphasis on slim proportions and purity of line. Mortise-and-tenon joints had to be cut skilfully to create the fragile oval, heart and shield shapes of the backs.

FAKE MARRIAGES

The fragility of Federal chairs has necessitated legitimate repairs to many, but this has often led to abuse. An incomplete set is knocked apart and reassembled with a number of new parts copied from the originals. Thus, three chairs magically become six – each of them 50 per cent genuine; the new parts, if detected, are explained away as replacements. Look for differences in colour, texture, craftsmanship and finish.

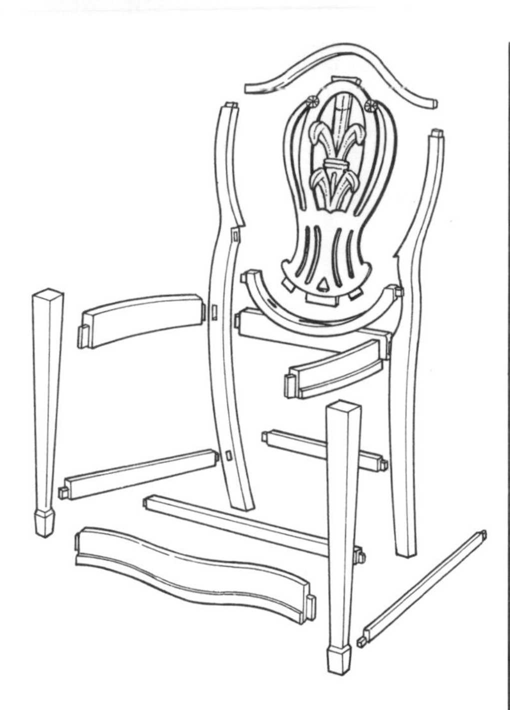

Shield-back chair, taken apart for repair or cannibalization.

DECORATION

Delicate carving of neo-classical motifs: urns, swags, paterae, formally arranged flowers. Some craftsmen practised what amount to signatures; for example, Samuel McIntire of Salem carved a trailing vine down legs of shield-back chairs. Sparing use of satinwood inlay.

FINISH

Mahogany was varnished to fill the grain, sanded and waxed until the early 1800s, when French polishing was introduced. **'Fancy' chairs** were painted in polychrome, either with conventional neo-classical motifs or, in the case of the panel-back types produced in Baltimore and New York, with romantic landscapes. **Windsor** chairs were often painted black or green.

RELATIVE VALUES

Heavy demand for sets of dining-chairs keeps prices high; collect odd ones of similar design to make a harlequin set – more fun and much cheaper.

CHAIRS

About

1810-1840

The American Museum

Federal mahogany dining chair, about 1815.

Following the War of 1812, American furniture was more influenced by the French Empire style than by English Regency.

STYLE AND APPEARANCE

The American Empire style (see ***p. 275***) introduced the second phase of neo-classicism – an academic approach to Ancient Greek and Roman shapes as well as ornament.

Side-chairs: Greek ***klismos*** type with sabre legs, favoured in Philadelphia; less so in New York, with the exception of a few makers, in particular the highly successful Duncan Phyfe (who had changed his name from the more prosaic Fife).

'Roman' versions with turned front legs, more popular in New York. James Madison, President at the time of the War of 1812, ordered a set designed by the architect Benjamin Latrobe for the White House.

Left, *painted 'fancy' chair, Connecticut, about 1820-1830.* ***Right,*** *early-19thC rocking chair.*

The American Museum

Hitchcock chairs: Vernacular versions of late Sheraton on turned, slightly splayed front legs with wide seats, caned or rushed – factory-produced from 1820 by Lambert Hitchcock at Barkhamsted (now Rivington), Con.

Boston rockers from 1835: Purpose-built with rolled seats and arms to correspond with the action, as distinct from slat-backs mounted on rockers.

Couches (*chaises longues*), 'lounges': Updated versions of the day-bed, based on the Greek couch, with scrolled head, asymmetrical back and either sabre or turned feet; more popular around 1820 than the settee or sofa.

The American Museum

Carved mahogany settle, New York, about 1800-1810.

Upholstered settees (sofas): Similar in line to the couch but with symmetrical back and scrolled arms.

Window seats: Stools with arms but no back, on high legs or scrolled 'dolphin' supports, fashionable from 1825.

MATERIALS

Mahogany, maple and exotic woods for visible parts of sophisticated seat furniture; beech for upholstered seat frames; ash, beech, birch, oak, hickory, juniper, pine, elm for Windsor and other 'country' types. A developing textile industry made home-produced, luxurious upholstery fabrics more widely available.

SEAT COVERINGS

During the Colonial period, apart from some not very successful attempts at silk production, mainly in Georgia, the weaving of expensive fabrics had not been encouraged, the colonies being regarded by Britain as a profitable market for manufactured goods. Few antique chairs, couches and sofas retain their original coverings anyway, but at the time, duty-free fabrics put good upholstery within the reach of a large public, and the quantity of seat furniture now surviving is that much greater.

CONSTRUCTION

Sound, traditional craftsmanship until 1830, growing reliance on machinery thereafter, leading to decline in craftsmanship. Backs of side-chairs were constructed in three different ways:

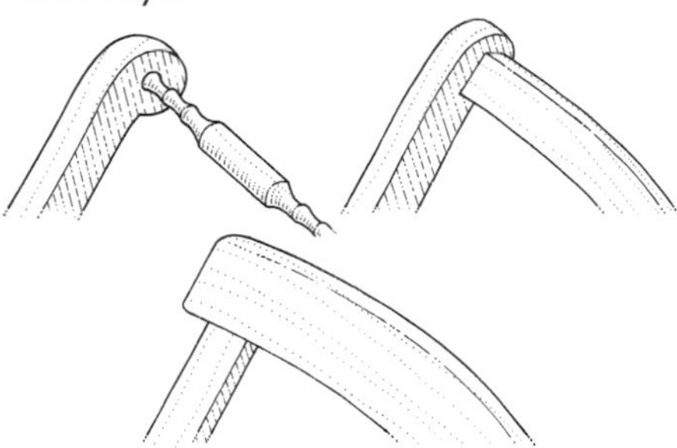

*Top rails: **top left**, turned bar between uprights; **top right**, flat rail tenoned between uprights; **above**, flat top rail (tablet) set against uprights and dowelled.*

1 Turned or hand-carved rounded bar as top rail, set *between* uprights, and socketed into them. **2** A flat top rail, plain carved or inlaid, set *between* uprights and tenoned into them. **3** Flat top rail ('tablet') set *against* the uprights and dowelled into them. Although nearest to Greek original type, this is the most prone to damage.

DECORATION

Chairs: Pierced and fretted lyre backs; brass inlay. Mainly stringing (thin strips to accentuate the line), but also complex patterns in top rails.

Sofas: Carving of cornucopiae as faces to arms, bold scrolls as supports.

FINISH

Increased use of veneers on seat rails of chairs. Hardwoods French-polished (see **p. 16**). Carved details picked out in gilt. Painted decoration of neo-classical motifs, flowers, fruit and landscapes on chairs of Hitchcock type.

RELATIVE VALUES

Sabre-legs usually dearer than turned. Armchairs good as desk chairs and as extra seating – elegant but comfortable. Never buy a chair (as many do) without sitting in it and checking for comfort, unless your interest in it is only as an object to look at.

CHAIRS

About

1840-1890

Settee from a suite of Renaissance revival furniture, about 1870.

With the development of railways, the established centres of production in the East lost ground to Grand Rapids, Michigan and Cincinatti, Ohio. From 1840, trade catalogues began to appear. A.J. Downing's *The Architecture of Country Houses* (1st. ed. 1850) and Charles Eastlake's *Hints on Household Taste* (originally English but published in Boston, 1872) were also influential.

STYLE AND APPEARANCE

Not one style but many, seemingly in conflict yet melding to produce an American flavour from ingredients similar to quasi-historic revivals current in Europe: **Classical** ('pillar and scroll'); **'Modern French'**) (rococo curves, followed by Second Empire opulence); **baroque** (called 'Elizabethan' but heavily reliant on twist legs); **Renaissance** (prominent at Philadelphia Centenniel Exposition, 1876, with emphasis on machine-worked, trumpet-shaped turnings); **Gothic** (pointed arches in chair backs, cluster column legs) vied with a **Japanese** craze in 1870 (bamboo, real or simulated, asymmetrical frets). From this medley, it was the 'Modern French' styles that most affected seat furniture.

MATERIALS

Exotic hardwoods such as rosewood, imported in growing quantities. Steam-bent, moulded **laminates** patented by J.H.Belter, active in New York from 1844. Cast iron used for garden and office chairs, from 1850. Moulded **papier mâché** chairs and settees produced at Litchfield, Connecticut from 1850. Printed **chintzes** and **cretonnes** fashionable for deep-buttoned upholstery. Natural **branches** and **roots** utilized for rustic seats. Grotesque chairs assembled from **buffalo horns** and **stag antlers**.

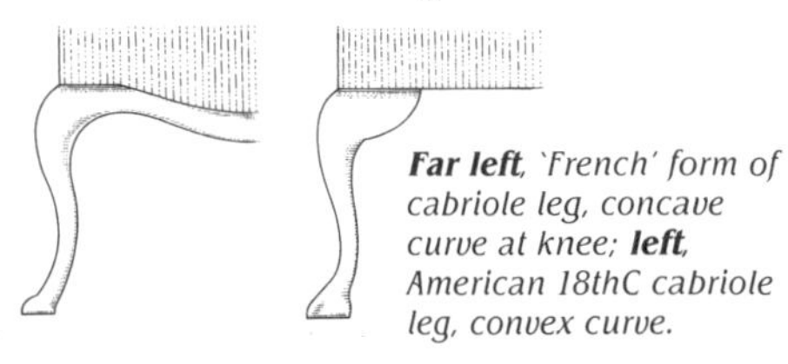

***Far left**, 'French' form of cabriole leg, concave curve at knee; **left**, American 18thC cabriole leg, convex curve.*

CONSTRUCTION

Side-chairs: 1 Rococo; balloon backs, open or padded. French form of cabriole legs, i.e. the under-side of leg joins seat frame with concave curve, as opposed to convex curve of 18thC English and American type. **2** 'Louis XVI' – in reality Napoleon III; oval back, open or padded; turned, tapered legs.

Sofa: *chaise longue;* love seat (sofa for two); **tête-à-tête** (two seats facing in opposite directions); **sociable** (three or four seats facing in varied directions); all heavily upholstered, usually deep-buttoned to hold padding in place over spiral springs laced to webbed platform. Many with show-wood (exposed) frames; cabriole or turned legs on castors.

Rococo rosewood settee, New York, about 1855.

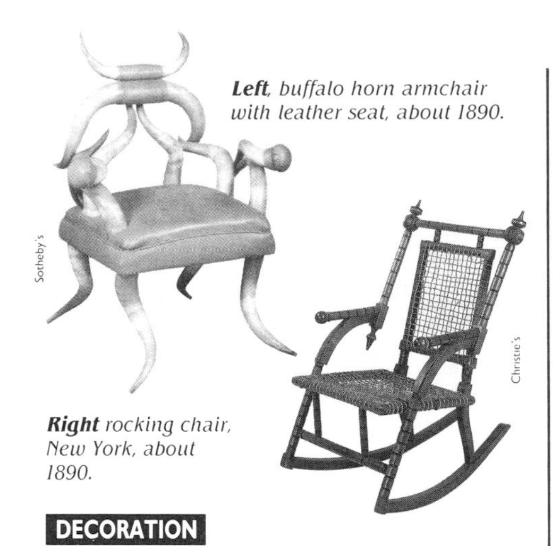

***Left**, buffalo horn armchair with leather seat, about 1890.*

***Right** rocking chair, New York, about 1890.*

Sotheby's

Christie's

DECORATION

Carved scrolls and flowers in exaggerated version of Louis XV style. Belter's moulded, laminated wood frames elaborately pierced and hand-carved, with high crests to chairs and sofas – a style imitated in cast iron. The lavish American version of plush Second Empire (Napoleon III) style out-frenchified the French, the turned and fluted legs hidden behind a curtain of fringe.

FINISH

Woodwork varnished, French polished or ebonised with details in gilt. Travesties of Eastlake's simple designs, purporting to be Gothic, incised with geometric patterns and ebonised. Black japanned papier mch painted with flowers and scenes in brilliant colours.

RELATIVE VALUES

Modern French style decorative, decadent, and, some think, delightful; can be bought cheaply in tatty condition. Cast-iron garden seats worth investigating.

FAKE 'EARLY AMERICAN'

The cult of collecting 'Early American' furniture was already established by around 1880, but the supply, even then, was inadequate. In 1884, the *Journal of Cabinet Making and Upholstery* reported that *the making of antiques has become a modern industry.* These copies have now had over 100 years to mellow. The quality of many is high but the proportions, when compared with authenticated specimens, are often wrong and the decoration is overdone.

CHAIRS

About

1890-1940

Oak reclining chair, designed by Frank Lloyd Wright, about 1902.

Christie's

Grand Rapids, Michigan, became the centre of the furniture industry, with Chicago as a breeding ground of reformist designers including Frank Lloyd Wright who stressed the need for good furniture that could be mass-produced with machinery and sold at reasonable prices.

STYLE AND APPEARANCE

In the 1890s there was a reaction against the historicism of the past half-century. American designers absorbed the principles of the Arts and Crafts Movement (see **p. 68**) and added touches from art nouveau (see **p. 196**), to which style **C. Rohlf's** elaborately carved chairs, around 1898, were, perhaps, nearest.

In 1894, **D.W. Kendall** designed for the Phoenix Furniture Co. an oak armchair with cane seat and flat arms that proved popular well into the 1920s. Simply-made chairs, sold off from a Spanish mission in California, inspired **J.P. McHugh**, who worked in oak and ash; **E. Hubbard** at the Ryecroft Community, East Aurora; **Gustav Stickley** at his Craftsman Workshops, Eastwood. Comfort was catered for with club easy chairs and deeply sprung 'Davenport' sofas.

Following World War I, industrial design created the cantilevered, tubular steel chair, but a public preference for something glamorous was catered for with **Art Moderne** (see **p. 275**) which, at its best, combined traditional craftsmanship with modern streamlining. The low sofa and easy chair with deeply sprung seats and backs, padded arms and minimal feet, took the term 'fully upholstered' to the point where woodwork was seldom visible. A sofa designed by the Spanish surrealist Dali, inspired by the lips of the American sex symbol, Mae West, is a classic example of the high Art Moderne style.

MATERIALS

Crafts Movement: Native hardwoods such as oak, ash. Cane, rush for seating. Folk weaves for upholstery.

Industrial Design: Tubular metal, mainly steel. Serviceable upholstery fabrics.

Art Moderne: Exotic woods and expensive textiles.

CONSTRUCTION

Crafts Movement: Construction frankly exposed to view. Some makers, influenced by Wright, abandoned conventional joints in favour of screwing sections together.

Industrial Design: When steel tubes took the place of timber, traditional methods were supplanted by metalwork techniques such as welding, bending.

Art Moderne: Traditional joints – mortise-and-tenon, dovetail – though often cut by machine.

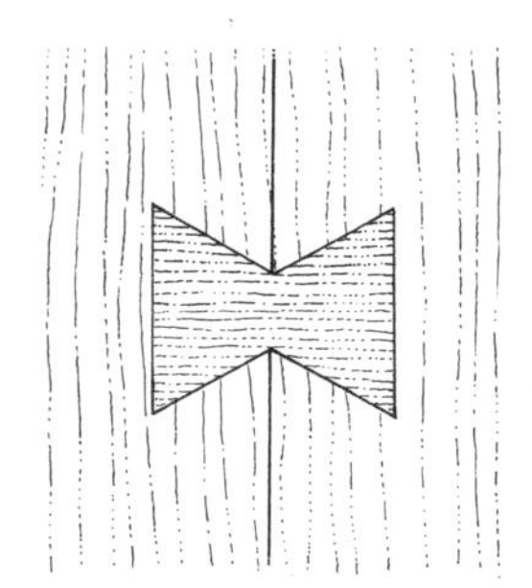

Butterfly joint exposed.

DECORATION

Crafts Movement: Exposed construction sometimes exploited as decoration, for instance butterfly joints and dowel ends stained by Rohlfs in contrasting colours. Carving was used by some craftsmen, but rejected by the puritanical.

Industrial Design: Puritanism of a slightly different kind saw decoration as superfluous, but often achieved – almost by accident – a decorative effect from elegant lines and fine proportions.

Art Moderne: Essentially a decorative style, exploiting every available means to achieve its ends – disastrously so at the lower end of the market.

FINISH

Crafts Movement: Veneers little used. Coloured stains, green expecially, as well as the usual browns. Varnish on cheaper lines, wax on up-market products.

Industrial Design: Chromium plating on tubular steel. Cellulose sprays on 1930s woodwork.

Art Moderne: Veneered panels often used to face the fronts of arms on sofas and easy chairs upholstered in futuristic patterns popular in the jazz age.

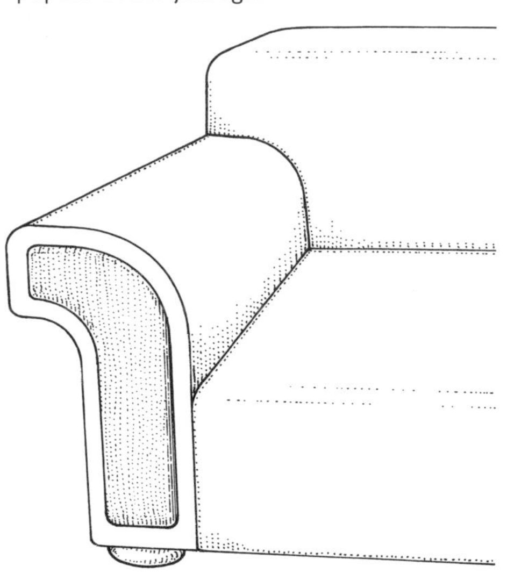

Veneered panel on front of arm.

RELATIVE VALUES

Best buys: Mission chairs, especially Roycroft, Stickley – but go for good craftsmanship rather than labels. Many opportunities in Art Moderne seating that needs re-upholstery.

CRAFT MOVEMENT

Craft Movement chairs are often difficult to date because some designs, such as Kendall's, remained in production for 30 years. Chairs by Stickley are often labelled and can still be bought at reasonable prices.

CHESTS AND CHESTS OF DRAWERS

About

1620-1740

Christie's

A painted and carved oak 'Hadley' chest, Connecticut, 1710-1715.

The box-like chest, serving as a crate or travelling trunk, is one of the few pieces of furniture brought with them by the Pilgrim Fathers. By 1660, panelled chests were being made with drawers below the box; their number increased until they occupied the whole space, and the top was no longer hinged. The chest became the chest of drawers.

Chests and chests of drawers of 17thC type continued to be made in country districts well into the 18thC as indicated by the overlapping dates of this section and the next.

***Below**, an oak and pine painted and ebonised chest, Connecticut, about 1675-1710.*

The American Museum

STYLE AND APPEARANCE

Before 1675, angular forms decorated in Anglo-Dutch Renaissance and baroque styles. New England types with regional differences then appear (see DECORATION below). Known makers include: W. Searle and T. Dennis of Ipswich, J. Allis and S. Belding of Hadley and Hatfield, Massachusetts; P. Blin of Wethersfield, Connecticut.

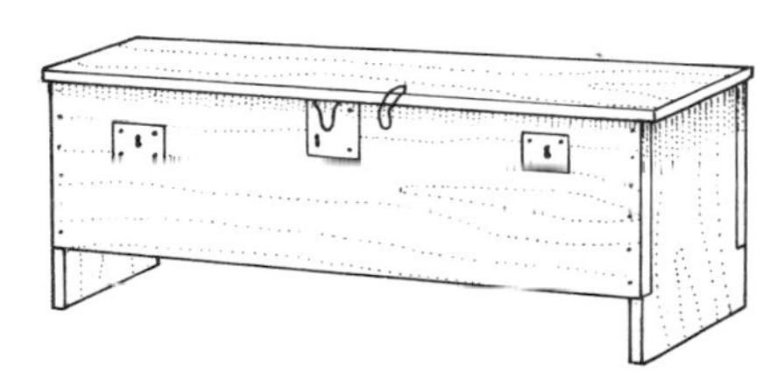

***Above**, simple boarded chest.*

MATERIALS

Oak, tulipwood; wide pine boards for lids of chests, linings of chests of drawers.

CONSTRUCTION

Boarded (or plank) chest: Simple type, the boards nailed to edges of ends.

Panelled chest: Panels bevelled at edges and inserted into rebates (rabbets, rabbits) in frame joined by mortise-and-tenon joints

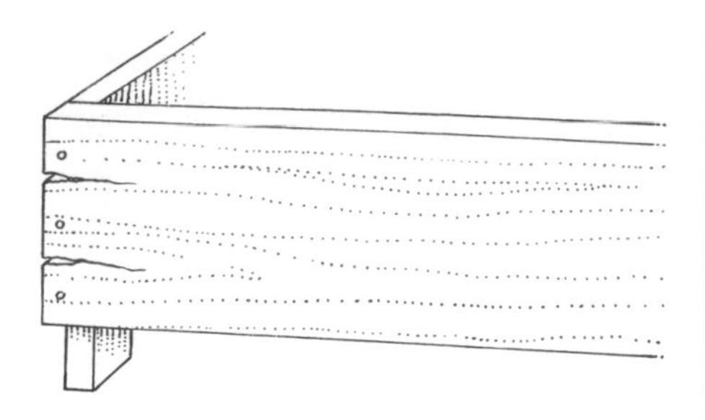

Above, boarded construction, splits in wood.

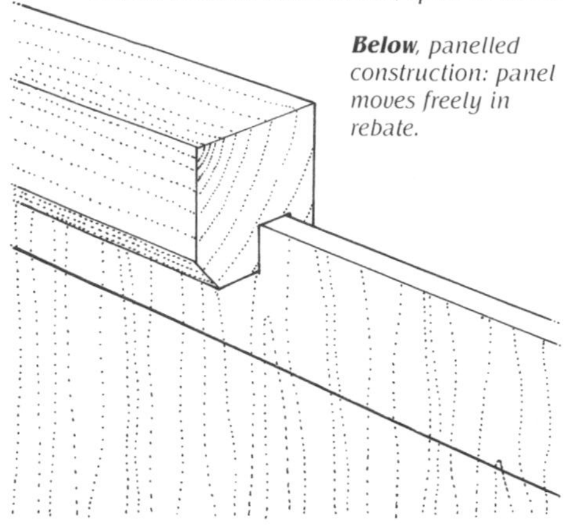

Below, panelled construction: panel moves freely in rebate.

secured with pegs. Lid not panelled – solid board(s) moulded on edge.

Panelled chest of drawers: Ends as for chests, above. Top fixed with nails, pegs or blocks glued inside. Back boarded or panelled.

Drawers assembled with nails and/or crude dovetails, grooves cut in sides to run on runners nailed to frame.

Drawer with grooves for side runners.

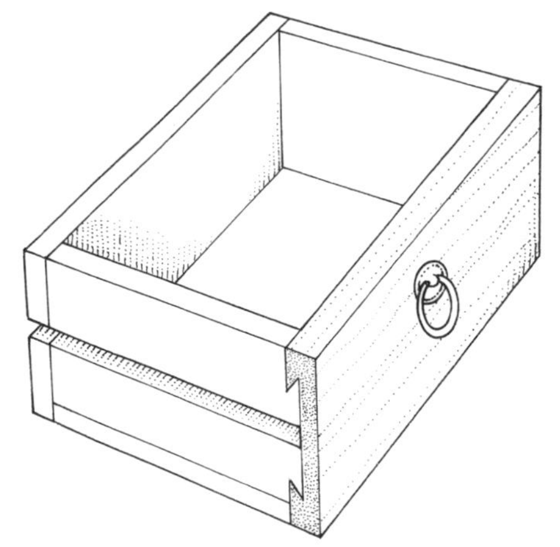

DECORATION

Chests, before 1675: Flat carving of foliage. Regional differences then develop.

After 1675, Hadley, Massachusetts: Flat carving of tulips, palm leaves, covering whole of front – frame as well as panels.

Hartford County, Connecticut: Carved sunflowers and applied split turnings.

Chests of drawers, from 1675: Essex County, Massachusetts: Drawer-fronts moulded on edges and divided into small areas by split turnings, also applied to stiles (see SEATS 1690 to 1725, p. 294).

The American Museum

A painted and ebonised oak and pine chest, about 1675-1710.

FINISH

Handles: Iron, or wood painted black. Wood handles turned or shaped to an oval and set at an angle ('turtle-back').

Painting and staining in black, red and blue with local or imported pigments used at first mainly to decorate carving but, in some districts, replacing it by 1700. Split turnings painted black to imitate ebony.

RELATIVE VALUES

American chests and chests of drawers pre-1740 are rare and expensive, but some have made a trip to the UK and got lost. A 17thC English oak chest was seldom carved all over its front like the Hadley type; neither did it have a pine top. Such features might be treated by English buyers as evidence of later carving and a replaced top. They might be right, but you could get lucky.

HIGHBOYS AND LOWBOYS

About
1700-1790

A Queen Anne walnut lowboy, about 1750-1760.

Christie's

As the 18thC begins, the joiner's lidded chest and the panelled chest of drawers continue to be made, but mainly in country districts; in the larger towns their place is taken by cabinet-makers' pieces with flush surfaces.

STYLE AND APPEARANCE

William and Mary, 1690-1725: Chests of drawers on turned feet, lowboys with cyma scrolled kneeholes and turned legs, highboys that are essentially chests of drawers on stands resembling lowboys. Half round mouldings on edges of frames.

Queen Anne, 1725-60: Similar to William and Mary but with bracket feet on chests, cabriole legs on lowboys and highboys. The finest highboys have bonnet tops. No half-round mouldings on frames.

Mahogany block-front chest of drawers, Boston, 1760-1770.

Christie's

Chippendale, 1760-90: Despite the name attached to this period, neither the block and shell fronts of the Newport, Rhode Island, chest of drawers, nor the curvaceous kettle base type in which Boston specialized, owes very much to Chippendale's designs. English highboys and lowboys were usually less elaborate and seldom – if ever – made to match, as they frequently were in America, where versions of the chest-on-chest (double chest of drawers) were also more complex than their English counterparts.

MATERIALS

William and Mary, Queen Anne: Walnut or curly maple veneers on foundation of pine; solid walnut cabriole legs; oak, pine, poplar and cedar used for drawer-linings.

Chippendale: Mahogany, maple used in the solid and in veneers, walnut and cherry in the solid. Secondary woods as above.

CONSTRUCTION

Ends of carcases not panelled but built up with boards glued edge to edge ('rub' joint), or made from a single wide board of solid mahogany or pine. Back panelled or boarded. Drawers with fine dovetail joints; no grooves at sides – they run on strips of wood glued to bottoms. Great variety in drawer arrangements of lowboys, the number varying from one to seven.

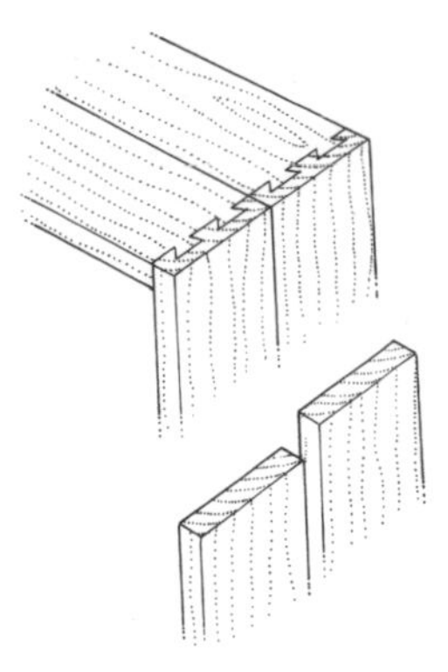

Construction of flush-ended chest end: boards glued together for width, then dovetailed.

DECORATION

William and Mary: Chests of drawers plain; legs of lowboys and highboys are turned to trumpet and cup shapes, and united by flat, curving stretchers.

Queen Anne: Chests of drawers plain; highboys and lowboys have cabriole legs carved with shells on knees, Dutch (pad) or Spanish (paintbrush) feet; highboys are surmounted by scrolled pediments (bonnet tops).

Christie's

A Chippendale-style mahogany dressing-table, Philadelphia. about 1779.

Chippendale: Rococo carving, especially in kneeholes of Philadelphia lowboys and highboys, influenced by Chippendale's *Gentleman and Cabinet-Makers' Director*, first published in 1754 in London, where cabriole legs and claw-and-ball feet were already out of fashion while continuing to be popular in America until about 1780.

FINISH

William and Mary, Queen Anne: Veneers of walnut, curly maple. Japanning in gilt on black ground in imitation of oriental lacquer.

Chippendale: Mahogany sometimes used as veneer especially on shaped drawer-fronts, e.g. kettle base chests of drawers. Brass handles and keyhole escutcheons.

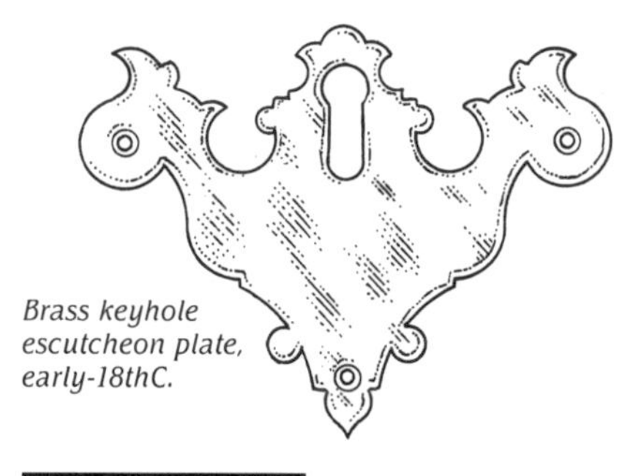

Brass keyhole escutcheon plate, early-18thC.

RELATIVE VALUES

Highboys command high prices, those with bonnet tops and carved detail highest of all. **Lowboys** vary according to quality and condition, but are usually expensive. Large, plain **chests of drawers** are much cheaper than small, decorative examples.

VENEER

Many plain, solid chests of drawers have been promoted to a higher price bracket by veneering them. The thickness of the veneer can be seen by examining the back edge of the top. In the 18thC veneers were saw-cut and much thicker than the modern knife-cut, paper-thin kind; but do not jump to conclusions either way. Even in the 18thC, the veneer was often not more than 1/16inches/1.5 mm thick before sanding down, and many pieces have been drastically cleaned off in the name of refurbishment, leaving them suspiciously thin. A thick veneer is not in itself a guarantee of authenticity. It may have been cannibalized – stripped from an old piece of little value – or it may be relatively new; saw-cut veneers are still available. Nevertheless, taken with other evidence, the relative thickness of veneers can be a useful guide.

This type of chest of drawers often veneered later in walnut or maple to increase the value.

CHESTS OF DRAWERS AND HIGHBOYS

About

1790-1890

Christie's

Right, *Federal mahogany and birch-veneered bow-front chest of drawers, about 1810-1820.*

Neo-classical principles dominate for 50 years, to be followed by eclecticism for the next 50; all the while, ethnic minorities preserve their heritage and religious communities reject worldly extravagance.

STYLE AND APPEARANCE

Federal, 1790-1810: Published designs of Hepplewhite and Sheraton favour chests of drawers with bow or serpentine fronts, commodes of half-round shape. Noted makers; McIntire, Seymour, both of Boston.

Above, *Federal inlaid maple bow-front chest of drawers, about 1790-1815.*

Empire, 1810-40: Flat fronts flanked by columns or pilasters. Top drawer often projects slightly. Many simplified country versions. Noted makers: Belter, Lannuier, both of New York.

Revivals, 1840-90: Louis XV/XVI commodes copies. Massive, mass-produced chests of drawers, commodious but inelegant. Noted makers: Meeks, New York.

Shaker, best period 1790-1840: Chests of drawers with flush fronts, flush or panelled ends, turned or slightly tapered feet, wooden knobs (brass handles rejected as vain and sinful); blanket chests, box type, sometimes with one or two drawers below, were commoner in northern than in western communities. Tall, slim, six-drawer chests made by Massachusetts communities.

The American Museum

Above, *Shaker cherrywood sewing chest, about 1820-1830.*

Gothic, 1790-1860: French Provincial commodes made in Quebec recall Louis XV styles but are in solid wood, as distinct from veneered New York reproductions. Califor-

***Above**, painted pine dower chest, Pennsylvania, 1794.*

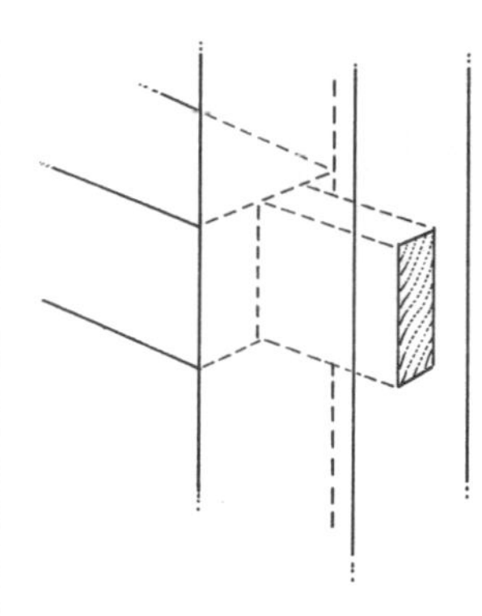

Through tenon construction with the end exposed.

nian chests of drawers show strong Spanish influence in use of through-tenons for joining rails to stiles. Pennsylvania German chests with painted decoration and inscriptions often bear late-18th and early-19thC dates.

MATERIALS

Sophisticated types: Mahogany, rosewood, maple, satinwood.
Country types: Oak, pine, poplar, walnut, butternut.

CONSTRUCTION

Sophisticated types: Very fine cabinetmaking in Federal and early Empire periods, giving way to machine work in mid-19thC. (For methods of shaping bow and serpentine drawer-fronts, see TABLES AND SIDEBOARDS, 1790-1840, **p. 323**).

Country types: Traditional joinery, varying from one area to another, e.g. through-tenons, California (see STYLE AND APPEARANCE above).

DECORATION

Sophisticated types: Carving confined to details, leaving main surfaces free for veneering, marquetry, painting.

Country types: Mostly plain but some ethnic communities painted flowers, birds, in bright colours.

FINISH

Sophisticated types: French polished.

Country types: Oiled and waxed, varnished or painted.

RELATIVE VALUES

Fine Federal highboys and chests of drawers so obviously valuable, they can hardly help commanding big prices. Simple late-Empire pieces much more reasonable. Good Shaker and country types very collectable; their unpretentiousness makes a boot sale bargain possible but improbable.

After 1840, Shaker design gradually succumbed to the hunger for excessive decoration, and by 1890 some pieces were sporting fretwork galleries and fussy turnings; a late piece could thus be rejected as too decorative to be genuine. Conversely, plain pieces have recently been reproduced, so beware the Shaker faker.

Late-19thC Shaker decoration above traditionally plain chest.

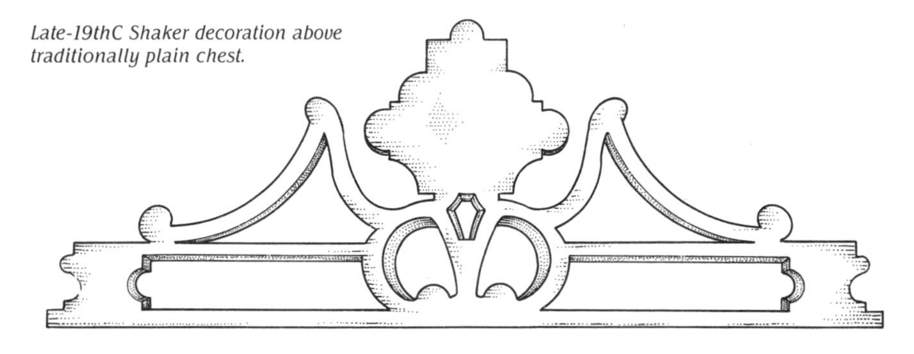

CHESTS OF DRAWERS (BUREAUX) AND DRESSING CHESTS (DRESSERS)

About

1890-1940

Nine-drawer oak chest designed by Frank Lloyd Wright, about 1902.

Christie's

In modern American usage, a bureau is a chest of drawers; in Britain it is a slope-front desk. In the USA, a dresser is a dressing-table or dressing-chest with a mirror; in the UK it is a kitchen cupboard or country-made sideboard, usually with shelves above.

From their positions of honour in the living-room, where they were repositories of heirlooms and dowries, epitomized by the 'bottom drawer' in which the bride-to-be tucked away her trousseau, chests of drawers were relegated to the bedroom, eventually to become 'storage units'.

Below, oak chest of drawers by Stickley, about 1901-1902.

Christie's

Right, oak dressing bureau by Stickley, 1910.

Sotheby's

STYLE AND APPEARANCE

1890-1910: The chest of drawers survived as an independent piece of furniture, often bow-fronted with pilasters and turned feet, but was also adapted to form part of a bedroom suite as a drawing-chest (dresser) with mirror attached.

1910-25: The need to economize on living space made the bulky chest of drawers a prime candidate for rationalization.

1925-40: The Art Moderne style did little in its defence beyond lavishing expensive veneers on it. Under reformist influence, it became at first purely functional but still autonomous, until absorbed into a storage system of shelving, hanging and drawer space composed of units, either built-in or flexible, often put together by early DIY enthusiasts.

For them, a New York cabinet-maker wrote a book called *How to Make Your Own Bedroom Furniture*. In the first six months, it sold 11 copies. The publishers changed the title to *How to Do It in the Bedroom*, and it be-

Below, dressing chest with asymmetrical mirror.

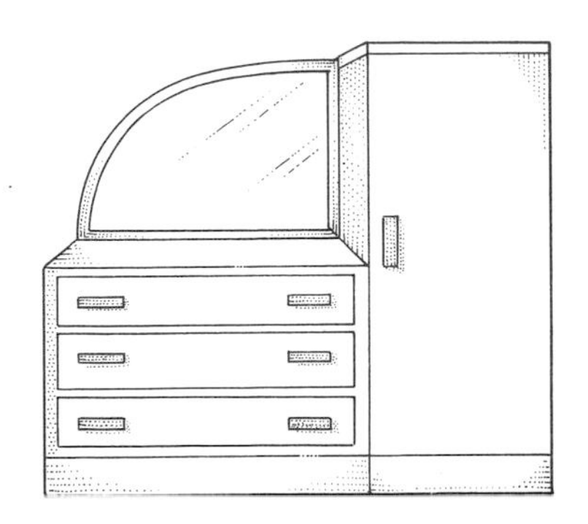

came a best-seller. DIY was not really a 20thC invention. From the days of the Pilgrim Fathers, much was made by unskilled home-makers, and in the late 19thC, amateur wood-work became a cult that accounts for many otherwise inexplicable departures from the norm.

MATERIALS

1890-1910: Mahogany, walnut, oak, used in the solid or as veneers on pine base. Drawers often lined with cedar.

1910-40: Oak, ash, walnut, mahogany, satin birch, Canary whitewood, used in the solid for drawer-fronts. Veneered plywood on soft-wood frames for carcases.

CONSTRUCTION

Custom-built pieces hand-made, mass-produced merchandise heavily reliant on machines. Some DIY artefacts remarkable for methods previously unknown and never repeated, e.g. a highboy converted from an upright piano, the drawers assembled with screwed-on angle irons.

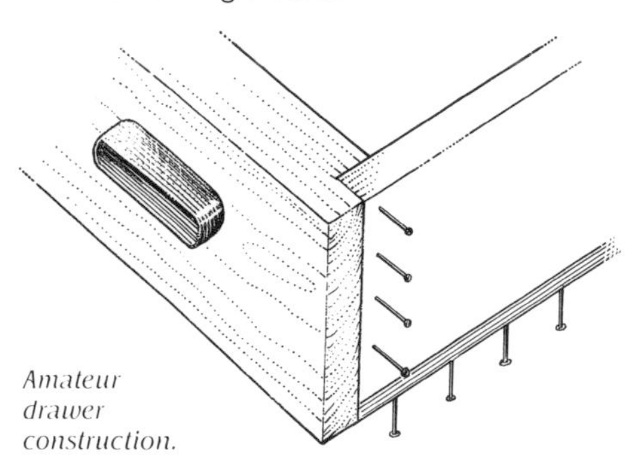

Amateur drawer construction.

DECORATION

1890-1925: Carving, by hand or machine; mass-produced marquetry motifs, many in pseudo-Federal style, available by the dozen for insertion at furniture factory.

Below, *18thC-style marquetry shell.*

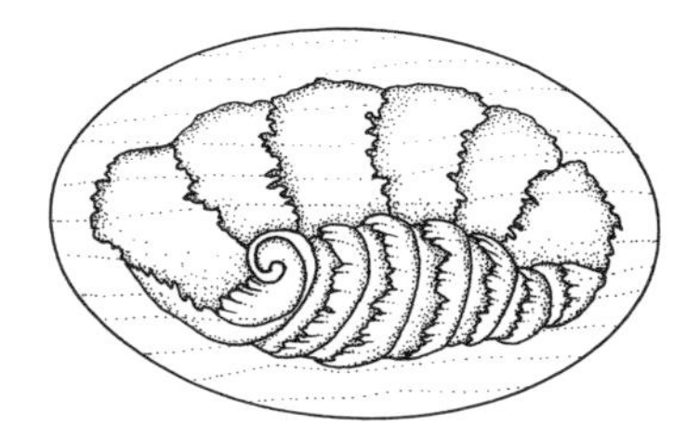

1925-40: Little decoration other than on reproductions and pastiches of 'Jacobean' (vaguely 17thC) chests of drawers with geometric mouldings and split banister turnings on drawer-fronts.

FINISH

Traditional types stained dark and French polished; dressing-chests fitted with mirrors in matching frames.

Handles: Turned wood, ornate metal simulating brass or bronze.

Art Moderne types veneered in exotic woods or, if solid, limed or painted and cleaned off, leaving pigment in grain. Dressing-chest fitted with frameless, bevelled mirrors, sometimes of eccentric shape.

Handles: Wooden bars, oxidized or chromium-plated metal grips.

RELATIVE VALUES

Late-19thC mahogany chests of drawers with cedar drawer-linings a good buy for those who like their rich, heavy look. Good examples of Art Moderne highly priced, poor ones not worth having.

FEDERAL FAKES

Many a late-19thC chest of drawers with bow front, heavy pilasters, turned feet and wooden knobs has been made into a Federal type by removing the pilasters, reducing the width, replacing the turned feet with brackets and the wooden knobs with reproduction brass handles.

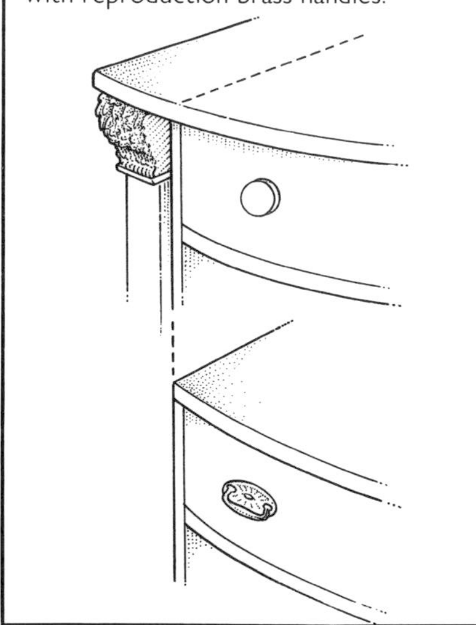

DESKS

About

1620-1680

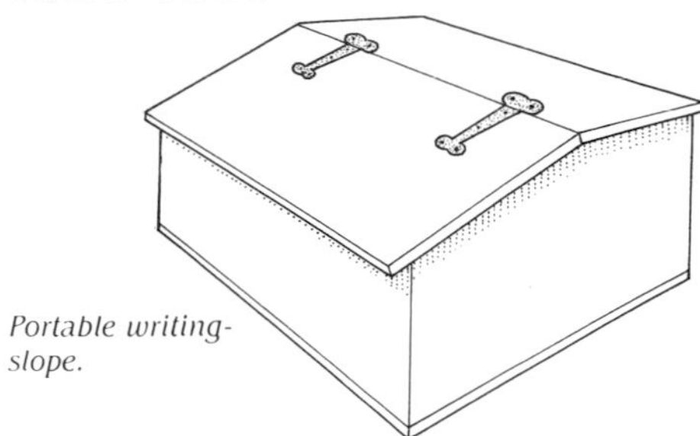

Portable writing-slope.

The Pilgrim period: Desks in the sense of specialized, substantial pieces of furniture are virtually unknown, but a portable writing-slope of the kind used since the Middle Ages is commonplace.

STYLE AND APPEARANCE

A shallow box about 24 inches wide, 20 inches deep and 12 inches high (60 cm by 51 cm by 30 cm), with sloping lid hinged at the top to a fixed ledge.

MATERIALS

Oak, pine, walnut or any other available timber, about ½ inch/1.75 cm thick.

CONSTRUCTION

Early examples nailed, later ones jointed with coarse dovetails at the corners. Lid attached by wrought-iron strap hinges.

DECORATION

Scroll, arcaded or floral patterns carved or incised. Painted flowers and figures.

FINISH

If not painted, oiled and waxed.

RELATIVE VALUES

It is often difficult to distinguish rare American examples from relatively plentiful British ones. Too high a price should not be paid for what is claimed as Americana, without convincing proof. Not outrageously expensive unless elaborately decorated and/or with sound provenance.

DESKS

About

1680-1760

Queen Anne walnut slant-front desk on stand, about 1760.

Sotheby's

As the American colonies become more prosperous, more people became literate and in need of better facilities for writing. Desks as pieces of standing furniture begin to appear in the late 17thC.

STYLE AND APPEARANCE

Simplified baroque giving way, after 1740, to restrained rococo. Types:

1 The desk on a stand with 'slant' (sloped) fall, hinged at its lower edge to provide a writing-surface on its interior surface, instead of the exterior as in the writing-slope. The stand was separate at first, attached from 1720, with turned legs 1680-1720, cabriole from 1720.

2 The fall-front secretary-desk (from 1700) with vertical fall and drawers below; an example made in 1707 by E. Evans is the earliest known signed piece of Philadelphia furniture.

3 The slant-front desk with drawer below that developed in the early 18thC.

4 The slant-front secretary-desk with bookcase above. Pennsylvania produced this type in William and Mary style, with double dome top, 1700-30.

> **GLASS**
>
> Before 1750, secretary-desks had wooden panels or mirror glass in the doors. Some have been modified by replacing these with clear glass, thus reducing the interest and commercial value.

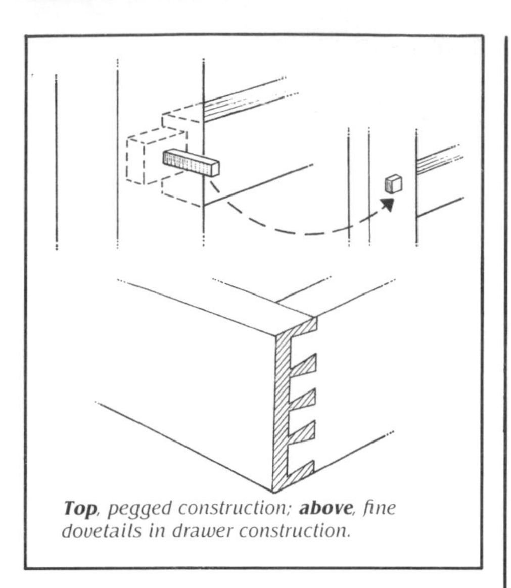

Top, *pegged construction;* ***above***, *fine dovetails in drawer construction.*

MATERIALS

Oak, maple, walnut, pine, cherry; after 1730, mahogany from San Domingo and Cuba; after 1750, from Honduras. Secondary woods used for drawer-linings and (after 1720) as foundation for veneers – pine for oak exteriors, oak for mahogany exteriors.

CONSTRUCTION

Mortise-and-tenon joints secured with hardwood pegs (see **p. 236**) on early work and on later country-made pieces. From the early 18thC, fine dovetails for drawers, most other joints (e.g. mortise-and-tenon) concealed in best quality work. Carcases on bracket feet or dwarf cabriole legs; after 1730, claw-and-ball.

DECORATION

Carving on mahogany items, for example, claw-and-ball feet, reached a high standard.

FINISH

Early-18thC: Burr walnut, maple veneer; japanning on Boston secretary-cabinets.

RELATIVE VALUES

Enormous range, and age not always the criterion. Starting relatively low for a plain pine slant-front, rising to dizzy heights for a fine mahogany secretary desk. A good 1750 example may be dearer than a poorly-proportioned one of 1720.

DESKS

About

1760-1785

Chippendale period: American makers achieve distinctive character and quality. Some work signed or labelled.

Right, *Chippendale-style mahogany desk and bookcase, about 1765-1780.*

Christie's

STYLE AND APPEARANCE

Many plain slant-front desks, but also block-front types with shell decoration, at their best in Newport, Rhode Island, where the interrelated Townsend and Goddard families dominated production. In Boston, Coggswell made secretary desks with bonnet tops and 'kettle' (bombé) bases.

MATERIALS

Mahogany, maple. Oak and other secondary woods as drawer-linings. Mahogany was used for lining very small drawers only, until late 19thC.

CONSTRUCTION

Drawer-fronts shaped to follow 'block' outline; ogee curve to bracket feet.

DECORATION

Concave shell motifs carved out of solid convex shells carved separately and applied to surfaces. Exaggerated shells on New Hampshire versions.

FINISH

Surfaces varnished, sanded and waxed.

RELATIVE VALUES

Block front types very expensive. Slant fronts, plain design, much cheaper.

DESKS

About
1785-1810

Federal period: Independence having been gained, the return to normal life fostered a desire for new furniture.

***Right**, secretary bookcase in mahogany, rosewood and maple, about 1810.*

STYLE AND APPEARANCE

In New England, regional types continued. In New York and Philadelphia, Hepplewhite, Shearer and Sheraton designs favoured straight lines, ovals, circles; splay feet and classical pediments.

MATERIALS

Mahogany from Honduras, pale yellow satinwood from West Indies.

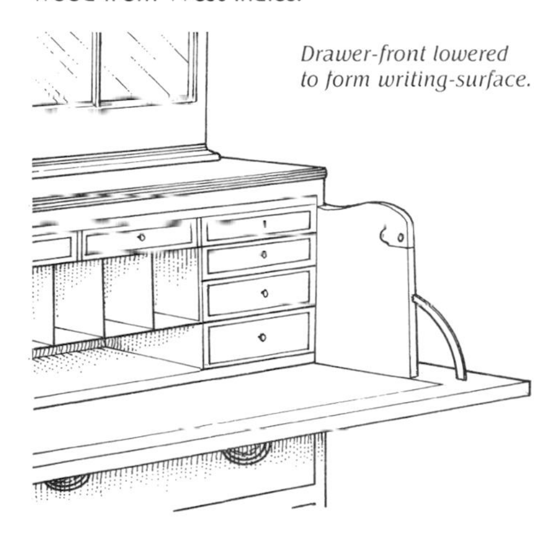

Drawer-front lowered to form writing-surface.

CONSTRUCTION

The Philadelphia secretary desk had a writing-section disguised as a drawer, with cupboards above and below. The 'Salem secretary' – a speciality of Nehemiah Adams – has a bookcase above with clear glass doors divided by curved astragals, resting on a base with a pair of cupboards flanking a secretaire drawer over a kneehole. Baltimore produced a *bonheur-du-jour* (lady's desk) on tapered legs, with flat writing surface and superstructure of small cupboards. Seymour of Boston made similar type with the superstructure enclosed by tambour front (flexible shutter constructed with narrow fillets of wood glued to a linen backing, running in grooves).

DECORATION

Husks, urns and swags in marquetry.

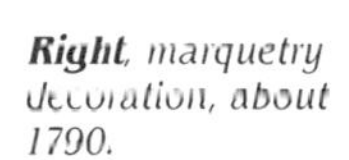

***Right**, marquetry decoration, about 1790.*

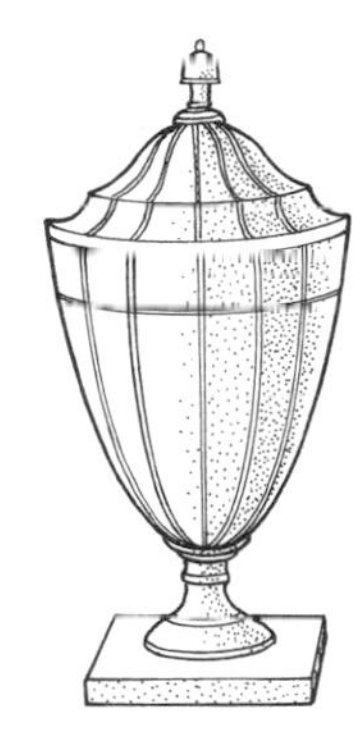

FINISH

Figured mahogany and satinwood veneers. Polishing with shellac dissolved in spirit (French polish) after 1800.

RELATIVE VALUES

Wide range and greater quantity offer better choice, but expect to pay for quality and elegance.

DESKS

About

1810-1840

Classical period (known at the time as 'Grecian'): Immigrant craftsmen – notably Lannuier in New York, Bouvier and Quervelle in Philadelphia – introduce French Empire style.

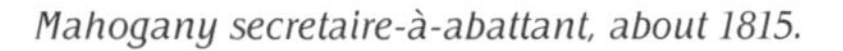

Mahogany secretaire-à-abattant, about 1815.

STYLE AND APPEARANCE

Desks embody features of the grand Napoleonic manner. Some are flat, leather-topped library tables, others are a new version of the secretary desk with a vertical fall. French influence felt after 1830 (see **p. 255**).

MATERIALS

Honduras mahogany, Brazilian rosewood, gilt bronze mounts.

CONSTRUCTION

Massive forms mounted on flat plinths or low feet of 'dolphin' or 'paw' type, in carved wood or case bronze.

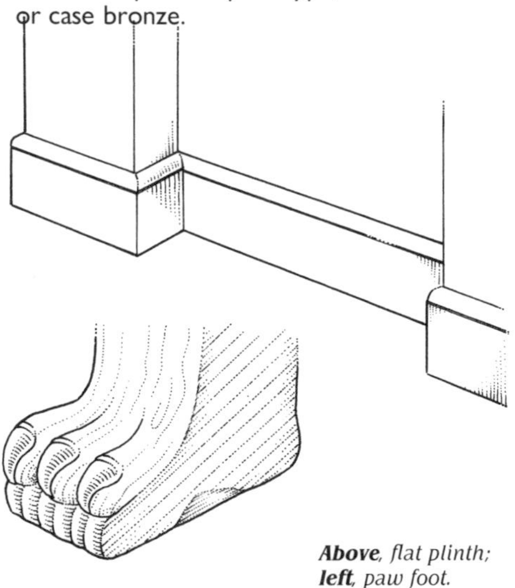

***Above**, flat plinth;*
***left**, paw foot.*

DECORATION

Columns or pilasters flanking fronts. Classical motifs – anthemion, lyre – figure in ormolu mounts.

***Above**, lyre ormolu mount;*
***right**, column mounted in gilt metal.*

FINISH

All top-quality work veneered in choice woods such as figured mahogany, rosewood, maple – and French polished.

RELATIVE VALUES

Chippendale, **Federal** and **Empire:** Top quality desks expensive, especially anything related stylistically to a name such as Townsend, Adams, Lannuier. Rich decoration attracts rich buyers. Fairly plain, wholly anonymous desks are much more affordable. Best buy is type with vertical fall-front.

DESKS

About

1840-1890

Right, *interior of late-19thC patent 'Wootton' desk.*

Phillips

Commerce creates an increasing demand for wide variety of office desks.

STYLE AND APPEARANCE

Office types included a writing-slope on tall legs; the American roll-top and the patent Wootton type; grand types in historic styles for successful businessmen. Hand-made, dual-purpose desks such as the sewing desk continued to be produced by Shakers for themselves and for sale.

MATERIALS

Pine for **clerks' desks**, oak for **roll-tops**, walnut or mahogany for **Wootton patents**; mahogany and rosewood for status symbols; walnut, cherry, maple, butternut, pumpkin pine for **Shaker pieces**.

CONSTRUCTION

Machine-cut dovetails, dowel joints often used in place of mortise-and-tenon. Plywood for drawer-bottoms, late 19thC.

DECORATION

Machine production camouflaged to look hand-made – Renaissance-style turning and carving favoured at mid-century (see **p. 191**).

FINISH

Rosewood and kingwood veneers on 'Louis' style *bureaux plats*. Leather or baize insets on writing-surfaces. Varnish, French polishing.

RELATIVE VALUES

Many good buys among plainer pieces. The more decorative they are, the higher the price. High prices paid for free-standing grand types – to impress the clients. Wootton and roll-top types increasing in value.

19th CENTURY REPRODUCTIONS

The Philadelphia Centennial Exposition (1876) sparked off a craze for reproductions of 18thC American furniture, slant-top and fall-front desks included, but most over-decorated and out of proportion.

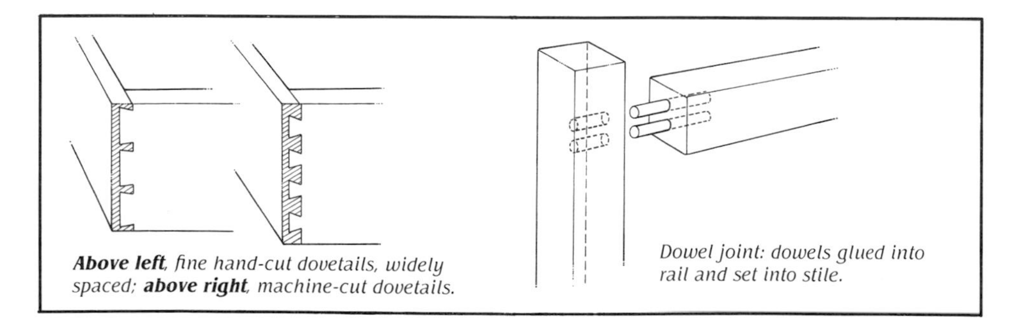

Above left, *fine hand-cut dovetails, widely spaced;* ***above right***, *machine-cut dovetails.*

Dowel joint: dowels glued into rail and set into stile.

DESKS

About
1890-1940

A striving after simpler, more functional styles, often bedevilled by a desire to impress the client, culminating in the vast executive-type desk with a battery of telephones. Smaller versions of this office type invaded the home.

__Above__, pedestal desk, about 1900.

STYLE AND APPEARANCE

1895-1901: Simple types, conforming to Arts and Crafts Movement principles, made by the Stickleys and others.

1900-40: Overtly simple, covertly sophisticated designs by followers of Lloyd Wright, for example the Pittsburgh office he designed for Kauffman, 1937. Art Moderne writing tables often asymmetrical – drawers on one side only.

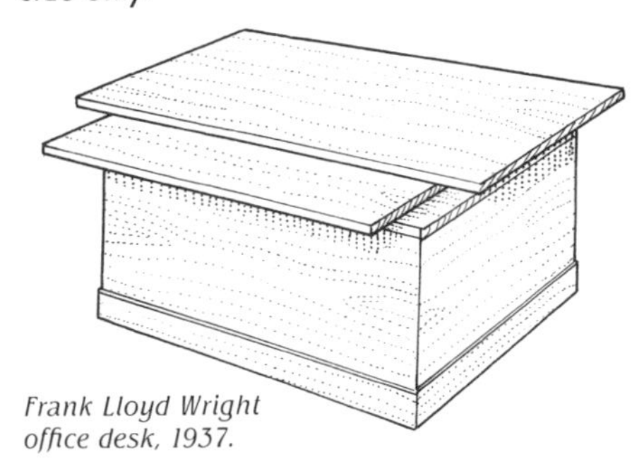

Frank Lloyd Wright office desk, 1937.

MATERIALS

Arts and Crafts types usually in oak. Art Moderne designers used great variety of woods, often veneered plywood for flush surfaces, also glass or Bakelite tops on tubular steel frames.

CONSTRUCTION

More machinework, less handwork after 1910. Panelled construction largely abandoned in favour of flush surfaces, most easily achieved by nailing or screwing sheets of plywood to solid frames.

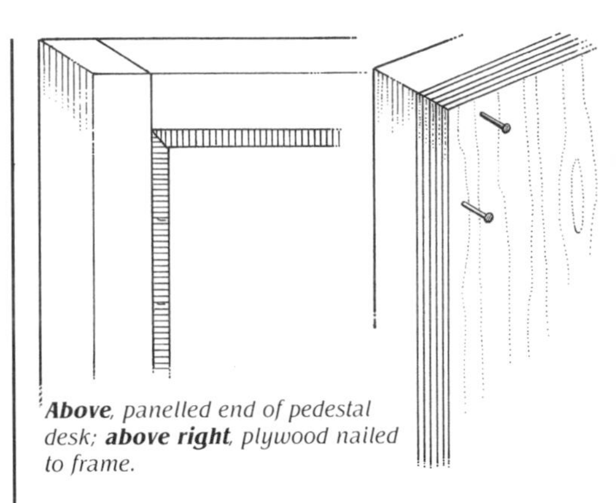

__Above__, panelled end of pedestal desk; __above right__, plywood nailed to frame.

DECORATION

Very little carving or applied decoration, but decorative effects achieved with veneers (see below), coloured leather tops, chromium or Bakelite handles.

FINISH

Veneers extensively used for flush surfaces, whether plywood or solid. Cellulose lacquer sprayed on. Chromium plating on tubular steel frames.

RELATIVE VALUES

Named pieces, such as by Lloyd Wright, for the rich only. Roll-tops and other mass produced types often reasonably priced. Good opportunities here for unlabelled Craft and Art Moderne types. Go for the article rather than the name.

TABLES

About

1620-1700

The American Museum

Late-17thC trestle table with pine top and oak trestles.

The settler's home in the 17thC often had only one large, multi-purpose table, supplemented, when circumstances allowed, by a few smaller ones.

STYLE AND APPEARANCE

Long tables (popularly but inaccurately called 'refectory'): Narrow tops, turned legs or trestle supports (T-shaped in New England, often X-shaped in Pennsylvania).

Gateleg tables: Varying sizes, some large enough for dining, with drop-leaves, on turned legs. Tops oval or rectangular.

Draw-leaf tables: Rigid frame, leaves slide out from under main part of top. Few Colonial examples now seen. Many 20thC versions (see **TABLES** 1890-1910, **p. 327**).

Butterfly tables: Recognized as an American type; mostly small, with bracket supports for drop-leaves.

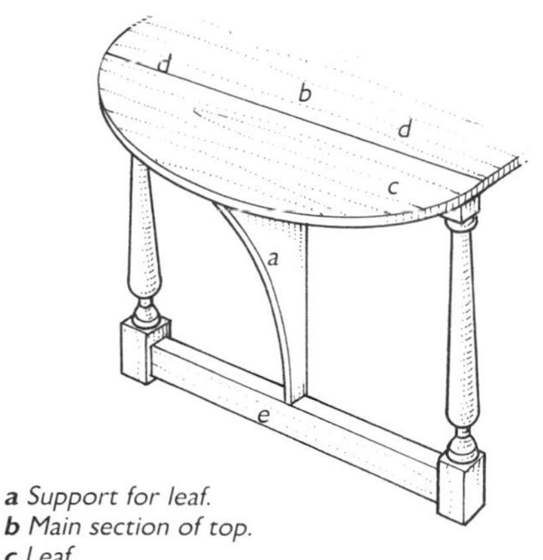

a *Support for leaf.*
b *Main section of top.*
c *Leaf.*
d *Iron hinges.*
e *Dowel cut in end of support, rotating in hole bored in stretcher.*

Tavern tables: Vague term used to cover all early tables small enough to be easily moved for individual use.

MATERIALS

New England: Pine tops on oak or maple frames.

Pennsylvania: Oak, walnut.

CONSTRUCTION

Long tables, New England, from mid-17thC: Plank top rests on frame, the legs united by rails above and stretchers below, with mortise-and-tenon joints.

Trestle tables, New England: Earliest known examples about 1650. Two or three T-shaped trestles, each comprising a post tenoned into a 'sledge' base and a bearer above. The trestles are united by a stretcher passing through them and secured with key wedges. The top – three boards tenoned into cleats at the ends – may rest loosely on the trestles or be fixed to them with oak pegs.

Trestle tables, Pennsylvania ('sawbuck' – term derived from the shape of saw bench): Made by German immigrants from end of 17thC through to 19thC. The X-shaped trestles are joined by a centre stretcher secured with key wedges.

TRESTLES

A New England trestle type with a row of turned spindles set above the stretcher is claimed as 17thC, but most examples of this type were made by the Shakers in the 19thC.

Gateleg tables made from mid-17thC to early 19thC. Main frame comprises four turned legs (vertical or splayed) united by rails above and stretchers below, with mortise-and-tenon joints secured with pegs. On each of the two long sides, a 'gate' made of two uprights and two cross-members is pivoted between the rail and the stretcher, to swing out and support the drop-leaf hinged to the centre section with iron hinges.

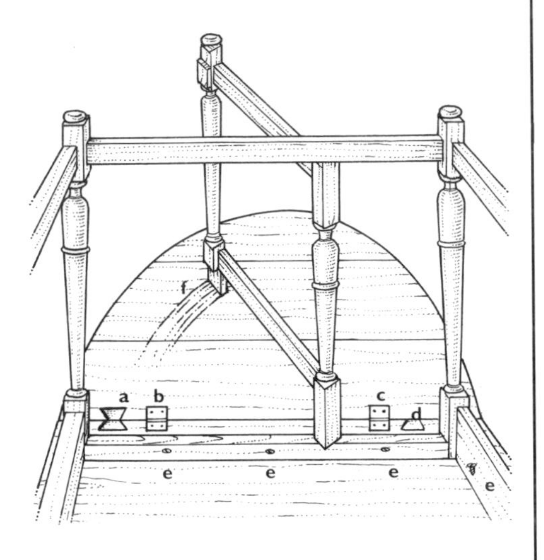

a Slots for previous hinges, matching on main section and leaf.
b/c Replacement hinges.
d Slot for previous hinge on main section, with no matching slot on leaf, indicating that leaf is not original.
e Screws driven up through frame into top – a method used in England from about 1700 but in America not until about 1780.
f Old scars consistent with action of gate, indicating that leaf is probably original.

GATELEGS

In early gatelegs, the top is always fixed with oak pegs driven through it into the frame. It was not until the late-18thC that tops were fixed by screwing up from below, through the frame. The leaves, or parts of them, have often been replaced. Check:

1 Are there marks of previous hinges on the under-side of the top?

2 Are there natural scars made by the top of the gate on the under-side of the leaf?

3 Do they coincide with its present action?

'Butterfly' tables, New England, from late-17thC through the 18thC. Several forms: all have a bracket swinging on iron hinges from rail of centre section and pivoting on a dowel sunk in the stretcher. Bracket either a solid, shaped board or a triangular construction of turned members. Centre section usually has four turned, splayed legs, but in some small examples only two, positioned vertically on a sledge base.

Tavern tables: 1 Frame comprising four turned legs vertical or slightly splayed, united by rails above and stretchers below. Top (circular, rectangular or square) is pegged on. Rectangular types often have a drawer, nailed together and/or crudely dovetailed.

2 Only two turned legs united by two stretchers, the upper plain, the lower turned; sledge feet, parallel bearers above, supporting top.

3 A small version of the sawbuck with X-shaped supports.

DECORATION

Lathe-turning in great variety, little carving other than on rails of rare side (possibly communion) tables on turned legs. The X-supports of some sawbucks have shaped outlines.

FINISH

Pine tops left in natural state and scrubbed. Walnut, oak and maple oiled and waxed, varnished or painted.

RELATIVE VALUES

Early trestle tables rare and expensive. Wide variety of tavern and gateleg types, some reasonably priced – but be on guard against replaced tops.

WEAR OF STRETCHERS

The stretchers of tables at which people sat were inevitably used as footrests and show wear towards the centre and mainly on the outer edges. Apparent wear too near the legs or on the inner edges is usually the work of the faker, using a spokeshave. Try sitting at the table and putting your feet on the stretchers to check whether the wear is natural or not.

TABLES

About

1700-1790

As early as 1685, William Penn had ordered 'two or three eating tables for 12, eight and five persons with falling leaves to them'. From 1700, William Penn's trend becomes a stampede. Long tables of various kinds (see TABLES, 1620-1700, p. 00) continue to be made in country districts but in more sophisticated homes are increasingly replaced by folding types.

Maple drop-leaf table, Connecticut, 1740-1750.

The American Museum

STYLE AND APPEARANCE

Drop-leaf tables: From 1700 to 1720 (William and Mary period), gateleg type, turned legs, larger ones with two gates to each leaf. Inconvenience caused to diners by undergrowth of stretchers, combined with arrival of S-shaped cabriole leg, led to adoption of Queen Anne (1720-60) and Chippendale (1760-90) drop-leaf tables.

Side tables (see also LOWBOYS, *p. 307*):

1 William and Mary, trumpet-shaped or twist legs.

2 Queen Anne and Early Chippendale: cabriole legs, pad ('Dutch') or claw-and-ball feet.

3 Later Chippendale (after 1770): square legs, chamfered on inside angle.

Card tables/tea-tables: Basically side-tables, as **2** and **3** above, but with fold-over tops opening to expose either a baized surface for playing cards or a polished one for serving tea. Often made in pairs, one of each kind.

Tripod tables, Chippendale: Top usually circular, occasionally square, on turned pillar terminating in three cabriole feet. Various diameters from candle-stand, about 10 inches, to tea-table, about 30 inches. Quality also very variable.

MATERIALS

1700-40: Oak, maple, walnut.

1740-90: Oak, maple for country pieces, mahogany for sophisticated items. Marble occasionally used for tops of side-tables.

CONSTRUCTION

Drop-leaf tables: Four or six cabriole legs, one or two on each side being hinged by a knuckle joint to the rail: leaves hinged to fixed centre section of top with iron hinges concealed by rule joint.

Side-tables: Cabriole or square legs mortised-and-tenoned to rail, joints strengthened with corner blocks glued or screwed across angle.

Card/tea-tables: Same leg action as with drop-leaf; fold-over top has specialized hinges set at the sides.

Tripod tables: Top fixed to round block fitting over head of pillar, or to two cleats pivoted on dowels to square block enabling top to tip from horizontal to vertical. Top secured when in horizontal position with a spring catch – thus the popular term 'snap table'. In superior models, a two-tiered,

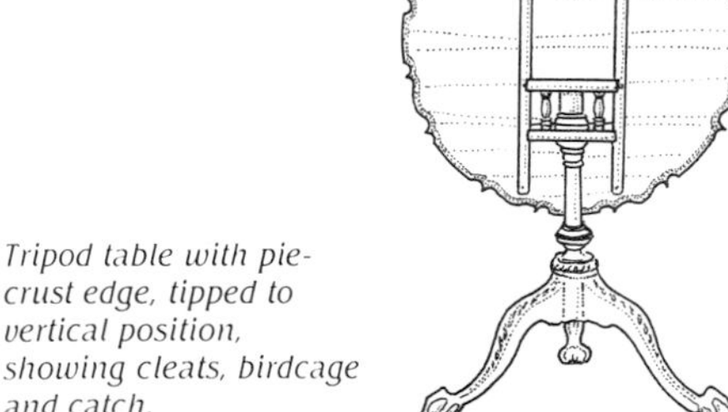

Tripod table with pie-crust edge, tipped to vertical position, showing cleats, birdcage and catch.

The American Museum

Mahogany tripod tea table with birdcage support, about 1760-1770.

square 'birdcage' about 5 inches high, with a small, turned column at each corner, takes the place of the block. Cleats under the table-top are pivoted on dowels to upper tier of the birdcage, which fits loosely round head of pillar, permitting top to rotate and become, when laden with food, a gourmet's carousel. A wedge inserted in a mortise in the pillar prevents accidents.

DECORATION

Cabriole-legged **drop-leaf tables:** Carving on legs (shells, foliage) and feet (claw-and-ball, paw).

Cabriole-legged **side-tables:** Skirt of frieze sometimes cyma-scrolled.

Square-legged **card/tea-tables, side-tables:** 'Blind fret' carving in 'Gothic' or 'Chinese Chippendale' styles on legs and friezes (see **p. 124-125**).

Tripod tables: 'Piecrust' tops shaped with moulded edge carved out of the solid – not applied to the surface.

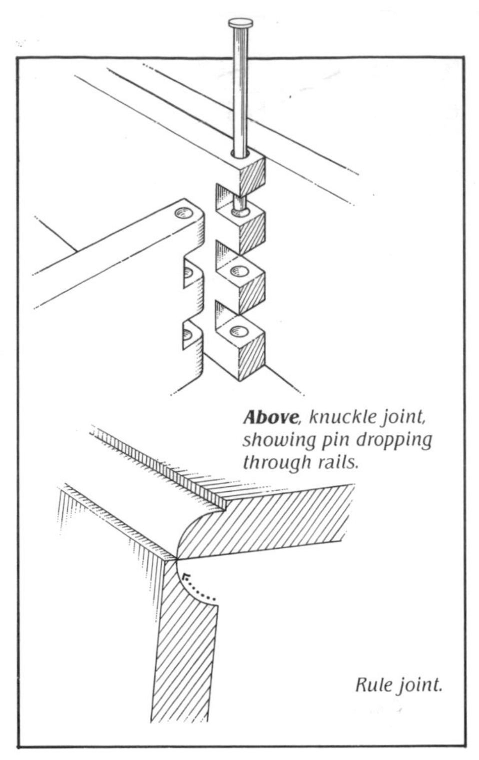

***Above**, knuckle joint, showing pin dropping through rails.*

Rule joint.

FINISH

William and Mary, Queen Anne: Walnut veneers used for tops and friezes of card/tea-tables.

Chippendale: Mahogany veneers often used on friezes, seldom on tops.

RELATIVE VALUES

Drop-leaf types of simpler kind are practical and worth substantial investment. Card tables more fragile and prone to warping if placed near central heating radiator without the precaution of a humidifier.

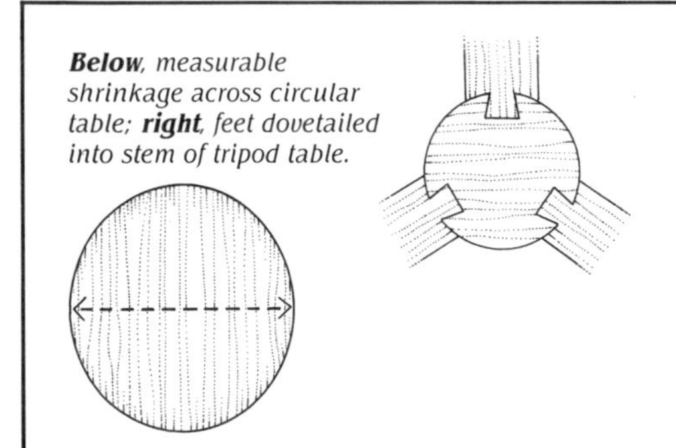

***Below**, measurable shrinkage across circular table; **right**, feet dovetailed into stem of tripod table.*

DETAILS

The feet of an 18thC tripod table are always dovetailed into the pillar, never dowelled; the lower ends of the dovetails can be seen if the table is turned upside-down – unless they are concealed by an iron strengthening piece which should show signs of age. A circular top should be cut from one piece of timber and, because of shrinkage, the diameter should be slightly narrower across the grain.

TABLES AND SIDEBOARDS

About

1790-1840

During the Federal period, dining-rooms became more formal, with elegant tables and matching sideboards in the Hepplewhite and Sheraton manners, followed after 1820 by the more bellicose Empire style. In rural areas and among poorer town-dwellers, it was the joiner rather than the cabinet-maker who supplied mainly traditional types, with few concessions to city fashions.

STYLE AND APPEARANCE

First and second phases of the neo-classical.

Dining-tables:

Federal: Typically, a drop-leaf centre section with rectangular leaves, capable of further extension by placing a half-round side-table at each end. Legs square-tapered, often terminating in spade feet, or turned, tapered.

Empire: Again sectional, but more often with pillar supports terminating in three or four cabriole or sabre feet. In some examples, the main section is on turned legs, while the extensions at the ends are on pillar supports.

Sideboards:

Federal: Square tapered or turned legs, the carcase bow- or serpentine-fronted, with a cupboard or deep cellaret drawer at each end, and a shallower drawer at the centre with a cupboard below it.

Empire: Heavy, architectural carcase, with drawers and cupboards almost to floor level,

The American Museum

Federal mahogany sideboard, Boston, about 1805.

on turned feet; applied classical pilasters and low backboard of Greek arch form.

Card/tea-tables: against wall when closed.

Federal: Rectangular, half-round, or serpentine fold-over tops on tapered legs.

Christie's

Federal inlaid mahogany dining-table, about 1790-1810.

Empire: Rectangular top, rounded corners, swivelling on centre support (no hinged legs) that rests on a platform with four sabre legs terminating in brass paw feet; many in 'pillar and scroll' style.

Mahogany card table, New York, about 1800.

The American Museum

Pembroke tables: Free-standing whether open or closed. A small drop-leaf on each long side, supported by hinged brackets.

Federal: Tapered legs, small drawer at one end only, 'dummy' drawer at the other.

Empire: Heavier turned legs or centre support similar to card/tea-tables.

Sofa tables: Free-standing.

Late Federal/Empire: On centre pillar or end supports; drop leaf on short sides.

Ladies' work ('bag') tables:

Federal: Rectangular, oval or octagonal tops, compartmented drawers for silks and a sliding bin or bag below for needlework.

Empire: Turnings heavier; some examples have pillar supports.

Shaker: Functional, on tripod bases.

Federal mahogany astragal work table, about 1800-1820.

Christie's

MATERIALS

Federal: Mahogany, satinwood, maple.
Empire: Mahogany, rosewood.

CONSTRUCTION

Legs supporting leaves of drop-leaf and fold-over tables hinged to frame with knuckle joints (see **TABLES**, 1720-90, **p. 321**).

The tops of serpentine and half-round tables were screwed from below, through the frame, and glue-blocked.

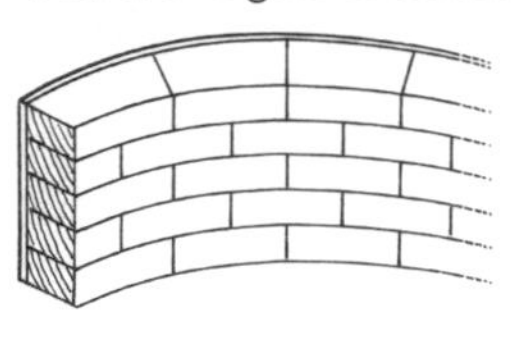

Left, rear view of curved drawer-front, front veneered; below, construction of curved door, using caul.

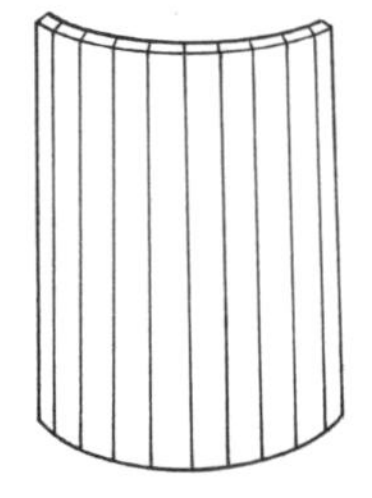

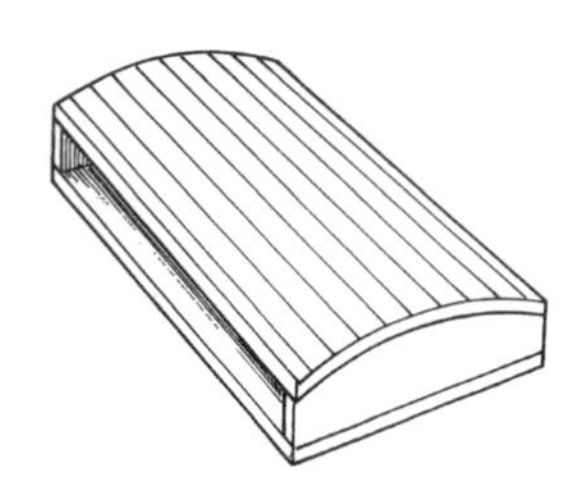

Boldly curved friezes and drawer-fronts had to be built up from small sections laid horizontally and glued together, rather like a brick wall, the outer surface of which was then veneered. Similarly, curved doors and panels had to be built up from vertical strips laid over a caul – a reverse mould carved out of the solid – before veneering.

Pillar supports were constructed in the same way as stands of tripod tables (**p. 175**).

DECORATION

Federal: Delicate carving and marquetry – husks, swags, urns. Some makers noted for distinctive decoration, for example, John Shaw of Annapolis, Maryland, used a moulded edge (as distinct from usual right-angle) for tops of sideboards, also exceptionally wide bands of satinwood cross-banding (see **FINISH**).

Left, conventional edge of sideboard top; below, moulded edge, typical of Baltimore.

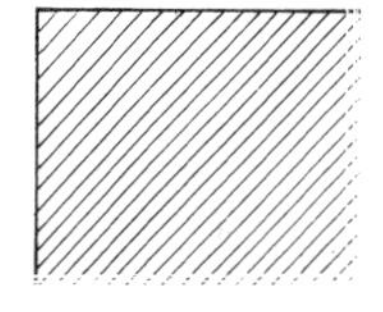

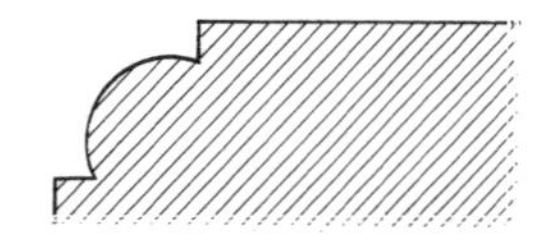

Glass panels painted on their reverse surfaces in black and gold were a highly original feature of Baltimore sideboards.

Empire: Less marquetry in wood but brass inlay used, for instance by C.H. Lannuier in New York, where card tables were favourite subjects for elaborate decoration. Carved eagle supports characterize those by Phyfe. Lannuier used caryatid and swan supports with massive lion paw feet.

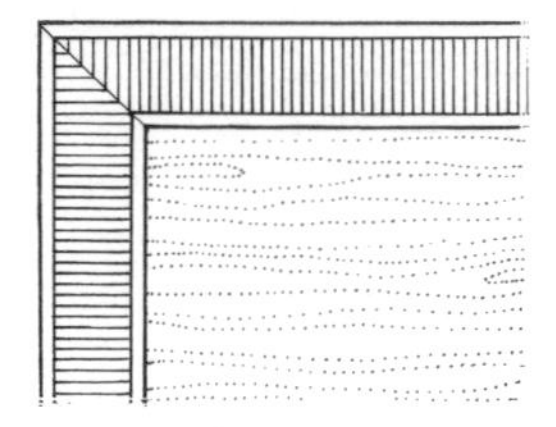

Cross-banding and stringing.

FINISH

Federal: Cross-banding on veneered table tops and drawer-fronts – short lengths of contrasting wood, for example satinwood, set with grain at right angles to that of principal timber (usually mahogany). Cross-bandings were often accompanied by stringing – narrow, contrasting lines. Drawers fitted with octagonal, oval or round brass handles with neo-classical motifs, such as a lion's head, in relief. Shaw of Annapolis used cut-glass handles.

Empire: Carving 'parcel' (part) gilt. Gilded bronze 'Grecian' mounts.

RELATIVE VALUES

Empire Pembroke tables on turned legs cheaper than tapered Federal types, and can be graceful. Empire sideboards much cheaper and more commodious than Federal, but much less elegant.

KNEEHOLES

The 'kneehole' feature seen in many English Hepplewhite/Sheraton sideboards is far less common in American examples. Whichever the nationality, however, the method of construction was otherwise much the same: until 1850 or so the boards dividing the central portion from the end ones were tenoned through the boards of the back, and the ends of the tenons can be seen. After that date, the backboards were usually screwed on – a useful, if not infallible, guide to detecting the high-quality reproductions made 1890-1910.

TABLES AND SIDEBOARDS

About

1840-1890

American Renaissance walnut dining-table, about 1860.

Mass production and popularization of furniture in many styles, much of it made in suites, with a different 'period' for each room, for example Renaissance in the dining-room, Louis XV in the parlour.

STYLE AND APPEARANCE

Dining tables: Late-Empire type with pillar supports remained fashionable until 1850. From 1840, a 'Gothic' version designed by Alexander Davies was made by Byrnes of New York, Jelliff of Newark, New Jersey and others, but without any serious attempt at re-creating the medieval trestle table. Something much nearer to that was still being made in rural areas, for example the saw-buck table in Pennsylvania or the trestle tables of the Shakers. From 1870, heavily turned legs replaced pillars on sophisticated dining-tables.

Sideboards: No longer a side-table on legs, but a structure with cupboards down to ground level and a mirror above reaching for the ceiling, the sideboard was devised as a temple dedicated to meals as heavy as itself. The favoured style in the 1870s was Renaissance, adapted for machine production by manufacturers including Pabst of Philadelphia, who later became a convert to the neo-Gothic Eastlake style.

Sideboard by Pabst, about 1870.

Card and supper tables: Pillar-and-scroll types, based on designs of J. Hall (Philadelphia, 1840) remained popular until around 1850; ousted by revivals of Louis XV (rococo curves, cabriole legs) and Louis XVI (geometric shapes, straight, tapering legs). Baudouine of New York designed and made a 'multiform' table – a pair of rococo card tables that fitted together to form a supper table (see **MATERIALS**).

Centre ('parlour' or 'loo') tables: Basically oval or circular tops, often with scalloped edges; usually pivoted (see **TABLES**, tripod, 1790-1840, **p. 175**) on lumpy pillars with scroll feet or round bases. ('Loo' derives from lanterloo, a 19thC card game.)

Ladies' work ('bag') tables: Made with a great variety of supports, including tripod bases with elaborately scrolled feet. Many had lift-up tops with compartments for silks inside, in place of drawers. (For 'cottage' types, see **FINISH** below).

Ladies' 'dressers' (dressing-tables): Although a few tables with hinged tops concealing mirrors had been produced during the Federal and Empire periods, a kneehole chest of drawers or a lowboy (see **CHESTS, HIGHBOYS AND LOWBOYS, p. 307**) with a small toilet mirror standing on it had generally served as a dressing-table. In the mid-19thC, the new-fangled bedroom suite included a purpose-built model on the lines of the *Duchesse*, made 1850 by P. Mallard in the French Restauration style, with cabriole legs, marble work-surface and large oval mirror.

MALLARD

Prudent Mallard came to New York from Paris in 1829, settled in New Orleans in 1838, and became a leading cabinet-maker in rococo and Renaissance styles. First name given as 'Prudence' in some reference books, implying female authorship for feminine French dressing table.

The American Museum

Duchesse mahogany dressing-table, mid-19thC.

Etagères (what-nots): Tables with two or three tiers, originally for serving refreshments but appropriated as display stands (what-nots) for bric--brac and taking on different forms – more in the nature of shelves, often fitting into corners.

Rosewood rococo etagère, about 1855.

Sotheby's

MATERIALS

Mahogany, oak, maple, poplar, walnut; rosewood, satinwood and other exotic timbers used mainly for veneers. Baudouine of New York perfected a method of making a form of laminated wood, without infringing Belter's patent for a similar material.

CONSTRUCTION

Steam-driven machines were used to prepare timber cheaply for assembly by traditional methods – not to replace them. A mortise-and-tenon joint did not change its nature by being cut by machine. New principles were mainly developed for 'patent' pieces, for example a late-19thC dining-table with legs attached to sliding bearers so that the whole frame could be extended for insertion of extra leaves by turning a handle connecting with a steel worm. This type is known in trade parlance as a 'winder'.

DECORATION

Carving in imitation of various styles, for example pointed arches, tracery, on pillars of 'Gothic' dining-tables – a style taken up in Cincinnati and New York by amateur wood-carvers who decorated mass-produced furniture.

FINISH

Marquetry inlay in various woods on veneered tops of centre tables. Ladies' work tables made of poplar in Eastlake 'cottage' style were painted with flowers in bright colours and gilt on a black ground.

RELATIVE VALUES

Pillar tables command high prices for boardrooms as well as dining-rooms, so you are competing with company money. Winders, though no longer cheap, are still good value. Ladies' work tables are now expensive luxuries.

WINDERS

Thousands of winders have been dismantled and made into Empire style pillar tables, or to provide missing leaves for genuine ones. The latter practice rates as legitimate; the former, unless it is declared by the seller, does not. It can usually be detected by turning the table up and looking for marks of rails and bearers where they should not be.

TABLES AND SIDEBOARDS

About

1890-1940

Sotheby's

Oak library table by Stickley, about 1910.

The age of revolution; rebels seek to topple *l'ancien régime*. About 1890-1920, the war cry is 'honesty' – solid wood rather than veneers, exposed joints, few curves. Some produce hand-crafted Mission furniture, others favour machines to make functional pieces. From 1920-40, conflict continues between austere industrial design and luxurious Art Moderne (see *p.275*). Theories are ultimately sacrificed to demand for family furniture with real or pseudo-traditional features.

STYLE AND APPEARANCE

Dining-tables: Apartment-dwelling increased the need for space-saving dining-tables. One based on early draw-leaf table was mass-produced from 1920-40. (See **TABLES**, 1620-1700, **p. 319**, and **CONSTRUCTION** below.)

Art Moderne: Rectangular with slab ends, or circular with cubist supports. Some glass-topped with chromium-plated tubular **Sideboards:** Massive, high-backed type out of fashion by 1920, giving way to a longer, lower shape, typically with a central bank of drawers flanked by cupboards; appeared in many guises from neo-Chippendale with claw-and-ball feet to a streamlined model with curved ends, on a flat plinth.

***Below**, streamlined sideboard, about 1935.*

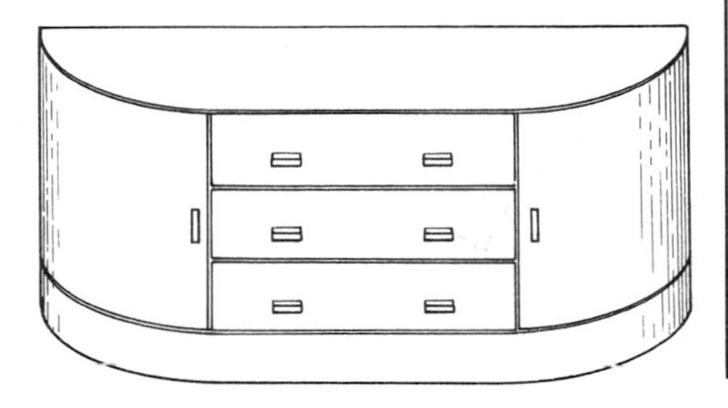

Dressing-tables:

1890-1920: Part of bedroom suite; varied arrangement of drawers, including small ones for jewels grouped around a triple mirror fixed to main structure but adjustable.

1920-40, Art Moderne: Angular, often asymmetrical, all glass and glitter.

Pseudo-traditional: Free-standing triple mirror on a kidney-shaped dressing-table, cheaply constructed but glamorized with draped chintz.

Coffee, bedside and end tables:

1890-1920: Reproductions of the original coffee-table, octagonal and inlaid with minute pieces of bone (not ivory), that was being imported from the Middle East to furnish the 'Turkish cosy corner' – a mini smoking-room.

1920-40: Low divan beds, sofas and easy chairs demanded tables in proportion.

Mission style: Solid oak with projecting tenons secured with key wedges.

Art Moderne: Anything goes – tops of wood or glass, marble or Bakelite, square or rectangular, circular or oval, large or small; conventional legs or cantilevered metal frames. The type has now declined into a dumping ground for publications known as coffee-table books.

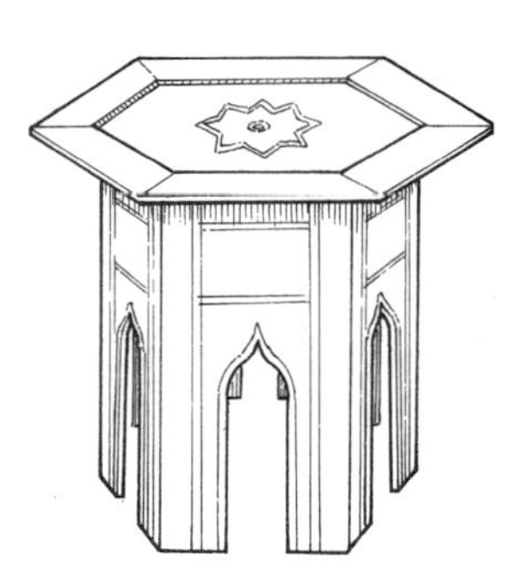

Reproduction of an imported Moorish occasional table, about 1890.

MATERIALS

1890-1920: Wide variety of native and imported timbers used; a in the solid; b as veneers; c as plywood.

1920-40: Woods as before, supplemented by tubular steel for frames, plate glass and early plastics, for example Bakelite.

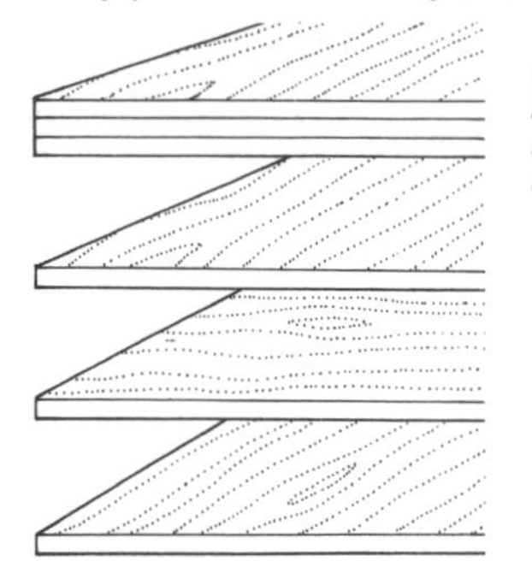

Plywood sandwich, alternating grains of laminate.

Veneer, plywood and plastics became dirty words, synonymous with nasty furniture. The fault was mainly with the makers, not the materials (for details of veneering, see **ENGLISH CHESTS, p. 86**). Plywood is a sandwich of at least three sheets of thick veneer, with the grain of the filling being at right angles to that of the breadth, for strength and resilience. The early plastic Bakelite (phenol formaldehyde), patented 1907, was developed in 1926 into a form that could be coloured (urea formaldehyde), and into decorated laminates, for example Formica (melamine formaldehyde) in 1935.

CONSTRUCTION

Joints: Screws, nails and glue often take the place of traditional joints in cheap furniture.

Draw-leaf table (see illustration): Top made in three sections, solid or panelled, one large and two small, resting on frame. Leaves fixed to bearers that slide in and out under main surface, which drops into position when table is extended.

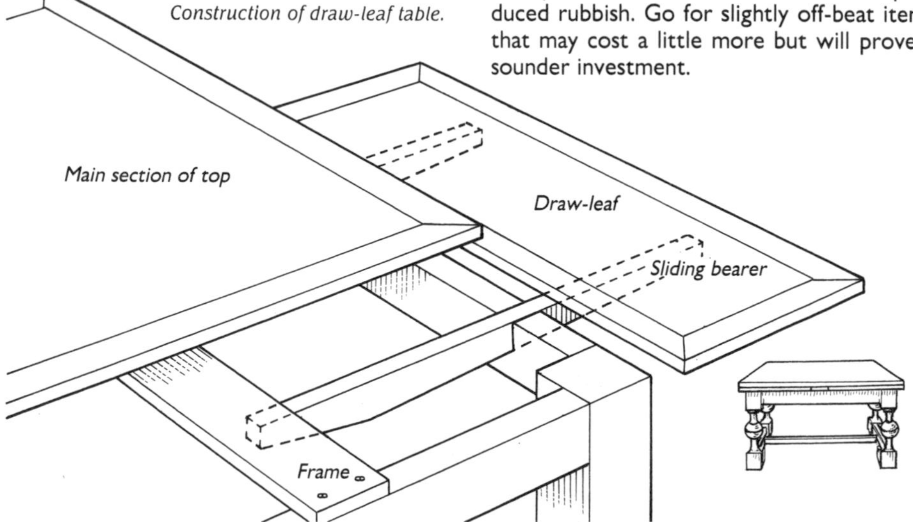

Construction of draw-leaf table.

VENEERS

Although veneers, whether on solid wood or plywood, are perfectly satisfactory in their place, that place is not the top of a dining-table. They react badly to hot dishes and spilt liquids, and are often not thick enough to withstand re-finishing. If in doubt as to whether a table top is solid or veneered, compare the grain on the upper and lower surfaces; if they differ materially, the top is veneered.

DECORATION

Craft furniture: Occasionally some rather flat carving of birds and flowers.

Art Moderne: High grade; marquetry. Low grade; effects created with applied beadings, mouldings and machined carving.

FINISH

Craft furniture: Coloured stains.

Art Moderne: High grade; polished or painted. Low grade; varnished or sprayed with cellulose.

RELATIVE VALUES

Plenty to choose from but much mass-produced rubbish. Go for slightly off-beat items that may cost a little more but will prove a sounder investment.

Bold indicates that an entry appears elsewhere in the glossary

acanthus classical leaf ornament
amorini winged cupids
antefixae stylized leaf or half-leaf ornament fashionable on top of cornices during the Regency
anthemion honeysuckle motif
apron decorative structure suspended between furniture legs
arcading arched decoration
astragal small semi-circular moulding used to disguise joints
aumbry medieval food cupboard often with pierced doors

balloon-back see illustration on **p. 66**
baluster turned vase-shaped member
banding strip of inlaid wood
  cross-banding see 1
  feather banding see 2
  herringbone banding see 3
bearers strip of wood supporting a drawer, table-top, or other part
bentwood wood steam-bent to shape
Berlin woolwork 19thC wool needlework
blind not pierced right through
boiserie carved wood panelling
bombé bulging shape, with horizontal and vertical **serpentine** outline
bonnet-top American term for a broken and scrolled pediment
boulle brass and tortoiseshell inlay
bow front horizontal convex curve on drawer or cupboard fronts
breakfront projecting central section to break line
brushing-slide pull-out surface in chest or dressing furniture

candle slides small pull-out supports for candles, on 18thC secretaries
carcase basic framework
cartonnier 18thC French cabinet
cartouche scrolled-edge motif
carving patterns cut into solid material
  carving in the round three-dimensional carving
chip-carving geometrical shapes cut into a flat surface
relief-carving surrounding wood cut back from carved decoration
caryatid female figure of classical derivation as decorative support
cassone large Italian chest
certosina inlay of polygonal pieces of bone, ivory, wood or metal
chamfer smoothed-off edge, also canted bevelled
chinoiserie European adaptation of Oriental designs
clamp strut on underside of surface to prevent warping
cock-beading narrow moulding on edges
collar horizontal moulding around upright member
compo putty-like medium for moulding
cornice moulding surmounting frieze or carcase
countersunk screw-head flush with or below surface
credenza sideboard with drawers above doors
cresting decorative top rail
crocket Gothic projecting foliage ornament
cyma curve double curve of convex and concave parts

demi-lune semi-circular shape
dished slightly hollowed-out
dovetails see illustration
  lapped dovetails front slots cut only partway through
  through dovetails side dovetail is flush with outside surface
dowelled fastened by wooden pins
drop-in seat see **p. 228**

ébéniste French general term for cabinet maker
ebonised wood stained black and polished to resemble ebony
escutcheon ornamented plate surrounding keyhole

fall-front lowered writing-surface of desk
farthingale 17thC chair without arms to accommodate large skirts
feet
  bracket feet see 1
  Braganza feet see 2
  bun feet see 3
  claw-and-ball feet see 4
  hairy paw feet see 5
  ogee feet see 6
  pad feet see 7
  scroll feet see 8
  splay feet see 9
  stump feet see 10

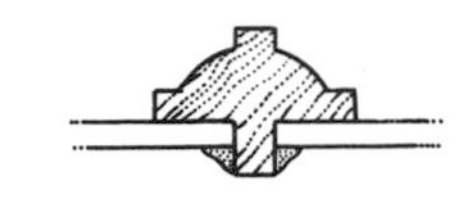
astragal

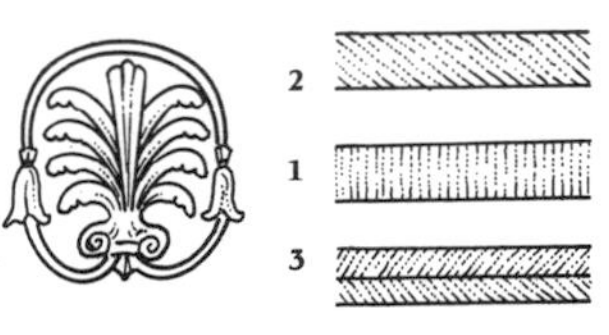

anthemion banding

cartouche

cock-beading

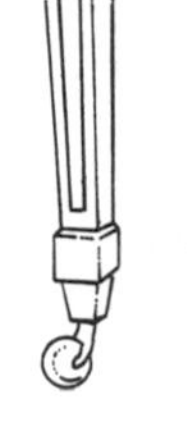
collar moulding

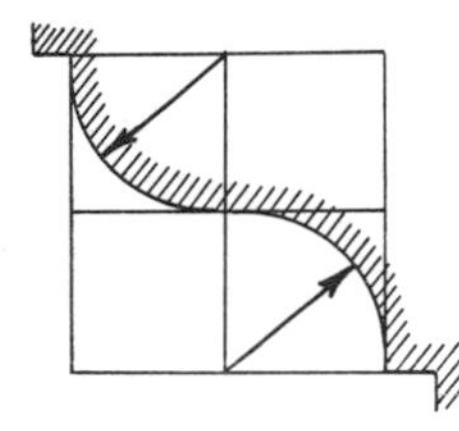
cyma

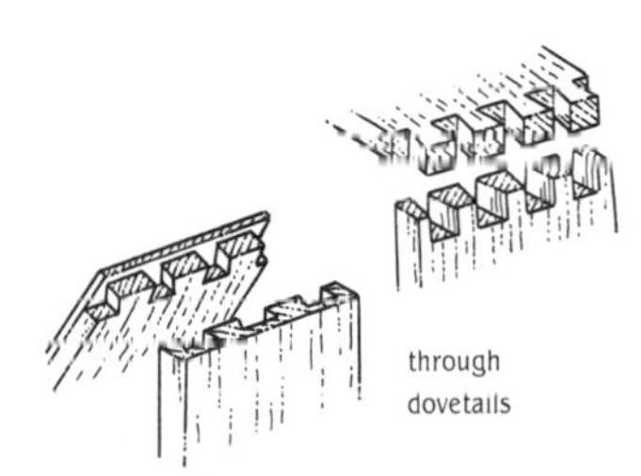
through dovetails

lapped dovetails

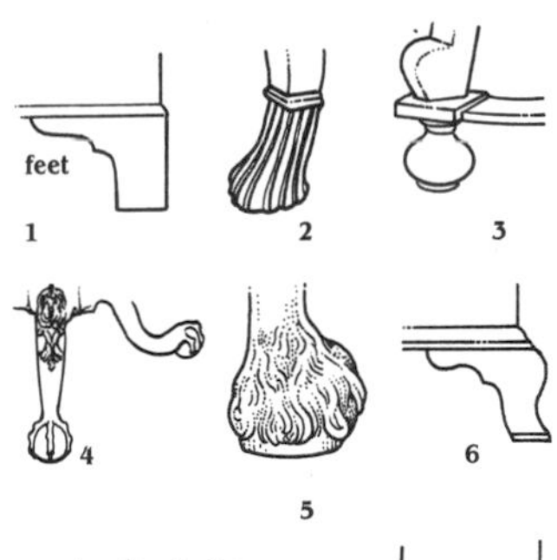

feet

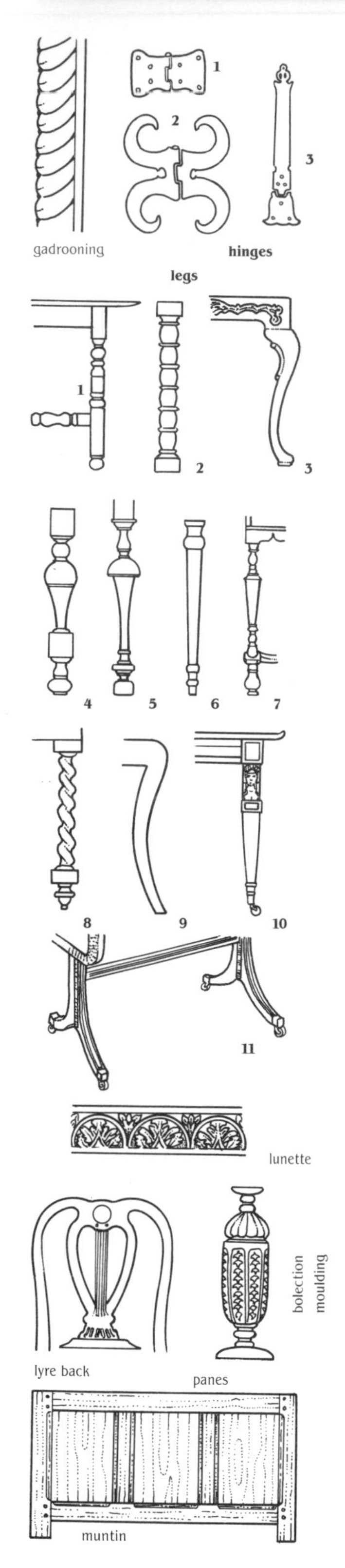

fielded panels fitted into grooved frames, can be extracted
fillet narrow band between mouldings
finial projecting ornament
fluting parallel vertical grooves
fretting open carving cut with fretsaw
  blind fret fretting on surface only
frieze horizontal section below cornice; often decorative

gadrooning carved convex lobes or concave flutes
gallery miniature brass or wood railing on edge of shelf or top
gesso gilded or silvered plaster-like material
gilding gold leaf decoration
gimp 19thC woven upholstery trimming
glazing bars framing to hold glass in glazed doors
grisaille painting intended to imitate marble relief
guilloche decorative motif, two intertwined bands forming continuous circles

highboy American term for chest on stand, with elaborate pediment
hinges
  butterfly hinge see 1
  S-hinge see 2
  strap hinge see 3
hipping extension of leg above seat rail
husk stylized wheat head or bell flower motif
hutch early food cupboard, see **aumbry**

inlay shapes of ivory, metal, tortoiseshell, mother-of-pearl, or wood, inset into timber to form decorative patterns
intarsia pictorial marquetry
ionic capitals upper part of support or decorative column

japanning imitation of oriental lacquer

kas large two-doored cupboard if Dutch origin in US
klismos classical Greek chair
knees top part of cabriole leg

lacca 18thC Italian lacquer
lacquer painted resin
laminated layers of timber glued together for strength
legs
  balluster leg see 1
  bobbin-turned leg see 2
  cabriole leg see 3
  cup and cover leg see 4
  inverted cup leg see 5
  taper leg see 6
  trumpet leg see 7
  twist leg see 8
  sabre leg see 9
  sphinx leg see 10
  splay leg see 11
linenfold panelling carved to resemble folded drapery
lion's mask stylized lion's face as decoration
lockplate metal plate covering lock
lopers narrow pull-out supports for flaps or table-tops
lotus stylized Egyptian motif
lowboy small side table with drawers
lozenge diamond-shaped ornament
lunette semi-circular motif
lyre back see ill. this page

marquetry a pre-formed picture made up of contrasting, coloured veneers, glued into a sandwich and cut through as in a jigsaw puzzle. The resulting pieces are juxtaposed for colour and contrast, and applied as a veneer for decoration.
  seaweed marquetry box or holly with walnut
mitre line bisecting the angle of a diagonal joint
monopodium pedestal support comprising animal head above single leg
mortise-and-tenon see **p. 236**
mouldings decoration worked from solid wood
  applied mouldings decoration fixed to surface of wood
  bolection mouldings see ill. this page
  dentil moulding regular crenellated border
  ovolo moulding quarter-round convex moulding
muntins upright wooden member between panels or drawers see ill. this page

ormolu gilt bronze

palmette stylized palm leaf
panel construction see ill. this page

papier mâché moulded paper pulp
parcel gilt partially gilded
parquetry a geometric pattern of veneers laid one to another so as to form a panel. Not pre-formed, as is **marquetry**.
paterae neo-classical oval or circular motif, often enclosing a flower-head
patina see **INTRODUCTION, p. 8**
pediment architectural structure above cornice
pietre dure decorative panels comprising semi-precious stones
pilaster flattened decorative column
plinth base of piece of furniture
putti cupids without wings

quatrefoil Gothic motif formed of four symmetrical leaf shapes

rebate joint formed by groove
reeding parallel convex lines of moulding
rexine artificial leather
rocaille shell and rock motifs
romayne medallion decoration of profiled head
roundel circular decorative motif

saddle seat chair seat shaped to prevent sitter sliding forward
scagliola composition material imitating marble
scalloped edge with scallop depressions
scrolls see ill. page 331
seat rails frame to support chair seat
serpentine convex curve flanked by two concave curves, **see p. 241**
shield-back see p. 62
shoe see p. 59
show-wood wood exposed to view on upholstered furniture
size gelatinous substance used to seal or stiffen a material
spandrel a decorative corner bracket
splat central support between chair seat and top rail
  Prince of Wales feathers splat see 1, p. 331
  vase-shaped splat see 2
  wheel-back splat see 3
split turnings turned member split lengthwise to form two matching pieces
stile upright supporting post
strapwork interlaced decorative bands or repetitive carved designs
stretcher horizontal rail between chair and table legs
  box stretcher see 1
  cowhorn or crinoline see 2
  double-H stretcher see 3
  X-frame stretcher see 4
stringing thin inlaid lines of contrasting wood
stuff-over seats see illustration on **p. 228**
stumpwork 17thC relief embroidery
swags stylized motif of suspended loop or garland
swan-neck see ill. this page
sunburst see ill. this page

tallboy chest on chest
tambour front narrow strips of wood glued to canvas to make roll door or desk front
tang pin to secure handle
top rail surmounts chair back
tongue-and-groove joint see ill. this page
trefoil Gothic motif formed of three symmetrical leaves

veneer thin layer of decorative wood glued to thicker timber
carcase
  figured veneer natural patterns revealed by cutting
  oyster veneer see ill. this page
vernis Martin 18thC translucent lacquer
vitrine display cabinet
Vitruvian scroll repeated pattern of C-scrolls

waisted back chair back with concave curve on stiles
wainscot panelling

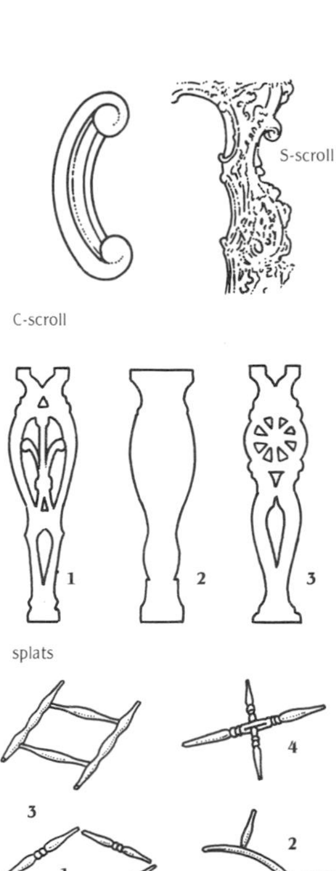

S-scroll
C-scroll
splats

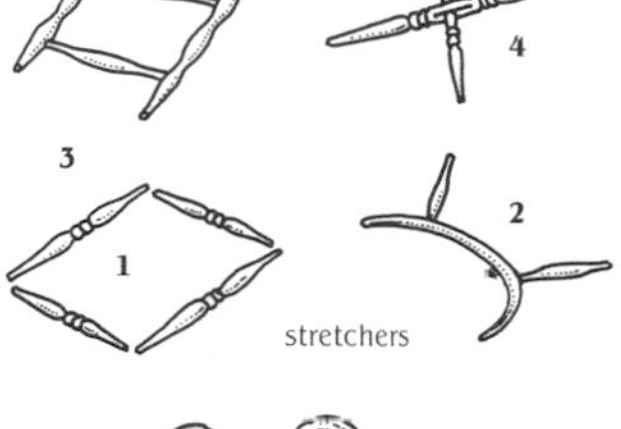

stretchers

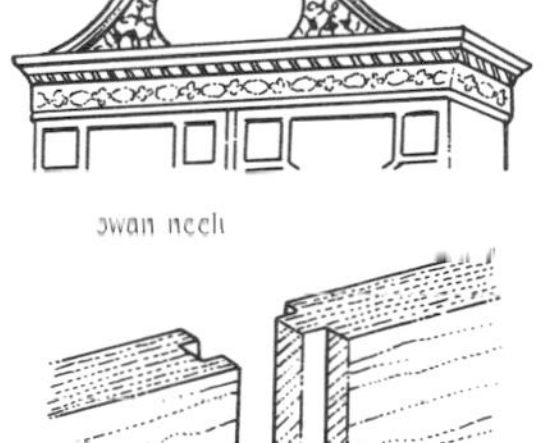
swan neck

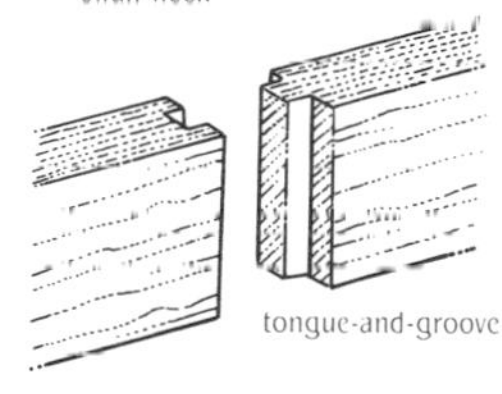
tongue-and-groove

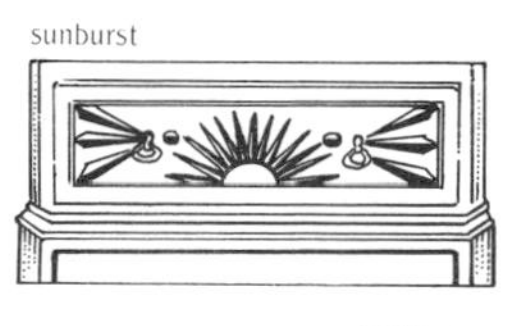
sunburst

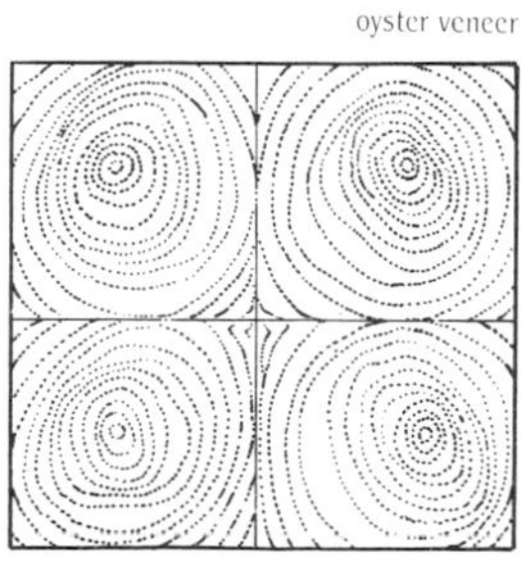
oyster veneer

PRICES

This book is an identification guide, not a price guide; but it would be incomplete without giving some idea of the cost of the furniture it features.

The following lists are, therefore, necessarily selective, and they should be approached with caution. They show, for the main types of furniture in each period, only what has been paid, not necessarily what you might expect to pay. Furniture prices can change quickly and dramatically.

Some early pieces, typically before 1500 or sometimes before 1600, are not given prices because they are so rarely available to the ordinary buyer.

ENGLISH FURNITURE

Unless otherwise stated, all sales took place in London.

Beds and Bedroom Furniture
Before 1500-1690
17thC oak bed; Christie's, May 1990, £1,760.
1700-1800
George III mahogany tester bed; Christie's, July 1990, £1,400.
19thC brass and iron
Victorian brass four-poster bed; Sotheby's Sussex, March 1990, £3,600.
1825-1900, brass and iron
Victorian brass and iron bed; Sotheby's Sussex, March 1990, £480.
Bedsteps, 1790-1900
William IV bedsteps; Sotheby's, November 1990, £1,870.
Close-stools, 1700-1890
Mahogany close-stool; Christie's, September 1990, £600.
Wash-stands, 1740-1915
Georgian mahogany enclosed washstand; Phillips, December 1990, £400.
Clothes horse, 1750 onwards
Edwardian mahogany towel horse, inlaid and painted; Phillips Oxford, October 1990, £170.

Bookcases
Breakfront and library, 1730 onwards
George III mahogany breakfront bookcase; Christie's, February 1991, £5,500.
Dwarf bookcases, 1800 onwards
Pair of Victorian burr elm and parcel gilt book cabinets; Sotheby's, May 1990, £9,020.
Hanging shelves, 1750 onwards
George III mahogany hanging shelves; Christie's, November 1990, £5,200.
Revolving bookcases, 1790-1915
Regency revolving bookcase; Sotheby's New York, April 1990, $25,300.

Cabinets and Cupboards
Cabinets, side and display, 1580-1915
George III harewood and mahogany side cabinet; Christie's, February 1991, £4,000.
Chiffonier, 1800-1880
Regency rosewood chiffonier; Christie's, November 1990, £6,000.
Credenza, 1850-1880
Victorian credenza; Sotheby's Sussex, March 1990, £1,250.
Corner cupboards, 1690-1800
George III mahogany corner cabinet; Christie's October 1990, £1,870.
Canterburies
George IV rosewood canterbury; Christie's, February 1991, £1,700.

Chairs
Wainscot, 1550-1660
Late-17thC panelled oak chair; Christie's, May 1990, £1,045.
Backstools, farthingales, 1615-1700
Late-17thC Derbyshire carved oak backstool; Phillips, September 1990, £250.
Queen Anne, 1700-1730
George I walnut open armchair; Christie's, October 1990, £3,400.
Pre-Chippendale, 1725-1730
Pair of George II walnut dining-chairs; Christie's, February 1991, £1,600.
Chippendale, 1750-1780
Chippendale mahogany stool; Phillips, November 1990, £3,300.
Hepplewhite, 1775-1790
Set of eight George III shield-back mahogany dining-chairs; Christie's, July 1990, £19,000.
Regency, 1800-1840
Pair of sabre-legged Regency open armchairs; Christie's, February 1991, £4,500.
Victorian balloon-backs, 1840-1885
Set of six balloon-back dining-chairs; Sotheby's Sussex, May 1990, £950.
1840-1915
Pair of Morris & Co. ebonised side-chairs; Christie's, February 1991, £1,050.
Upholstered, wing or easy chairs
George II mahogany wing armchair; Christie's, July 1990, £950.
Upholstered, 1720-1840
Set of six Regency mahogany dining-chairs; Christie's, October 1990, £3,800.
Victorian upholstered, 1840-1900
Victorian easy chair; Sotheby's Sussex, May 1990, £520.
Corner chairs, 1710-70; 1890-1915
Mahogany corner chair; Christie's, October 1990, £700.
Reading, writing, desk, library; 1700-1900
George IV rosewood library armchair; Christie's, February 1991, £450.
Hall and Porter's chairs, 1750-1850
Pair of mahogany Regency hall chairs; Christie's, February 1991, £1,200.
Ladder-back chairs, 1700-1939
Six ladder-back chairs; Sotheby's Sussex, March 1990, £600.
Country Windsor, 1700 onwards
Pair of Windsor armchairs; Sotheby's Sussex, May 1990, £90.

Chests and Chests of Drawers
1200-1800
Georgian oak chest; Christie's, May 1990, £418.
Mule or dower chest, 1630-1800
George III oak mule chest; Christie's, October 1990, £2,420.
Early panelled oak, 1650-1730
Charles II fruitwood chest; Christie's, May 1990, £1,100.
Veneered chest of drawers, 1680-1740
Queen Anne oyster-veneered chest of drawers; Sotheby's, July 1990, £3,100.
Chest on stand, 1680-1730
Queen Anne walnut chest; Sotheby's, March 1989, £1,050.
Mahogany chest of drawers, 1730-1830
George II mahogany chest; Christie's, February 1991, £650.
Victorian/Edwardian chest of drawers, 1840-1915
Miniature Victorian mahogany chest of drawers; Phillips, December 1990, £250.
Tallboys, 1710-1820
Mahogany George III tallboy; Christie's, October 1990, £4,000.
Military chests, 1810-1915
Small early-19thC military chest; Phillips, September 1990, £650.
Wellington chests, 1810-1900
Burr walnut secretaire-Wellington chest; Sotheby's Sussex, May 1990, £1,600.
Drawing-room commodes, 1750-1800
George III commode; Christie's, July 1990, £6,000.

Cots
Cots 1500-1900
17thC elm cradle; Phillips, September 1990, £240.

Desks
Escritoires, 1680-1720
William & Mary walnut escritoire; Christie's, May 1990, £9,900.
Bureaux on stands, 1670-1760
William & Mary burr elm bureau; Christie's, February 1991, £2,800.
Bureaux and bureaux cabinets, 1740 onwards
George III mahogany bureau; Sotheby's, May 1990, £6,820.
Secretaries and secretaire bookcases, 1710-1830
George III mahogany bureau bookcase; Christie's, November 1990, £4,500.
Kneehole desks, 1700-1780
Mid-Georgian padouk kneehole desk; Christie's, February 1991, £2,600.
Pedestal desk, 1750 onwards
Regency mahogany pedestal desk; Christie's, November 1990, £4,000.
Bonheurs du jour and cheverets, 1770-1915
George III mahogany bonheur du jour; Christie's, July 1990, £7,500.
Carlton House desk, 1785-1915
Regency mahogany Carlton House desk; Christie's, November 1990, £9,000.
Cylinder and tambour, 1780 onwards
Regency mahogany cylinder bureau; Christie's, October 1990, £1,500.
Davenports, 1795-1885
Rosewood Regency Davenport; Christie's, November 1990, £3,600.
Dressers, 1650-1915
George I dresser; Sotheby's Sussex, March 1990, £1,350.
Dumb Waiters, 1750-1830
George III mahogany dumb waiter; Christie's, February 1991, £1,900.
Screens, 1700-1900
George III mahogany 2-leaf folding screen; Christie's, July 1990, £250.
Sideboards, 1770-1915
George III breakfront mahogany sideboard; Christie's, February 1991, £5,000.
Sofas, 1700-1915
William IV rosewood sofa; Christie's, February 1991, £1,800.

Stools
Joint stools, 1600-1700
Charles I oak joint stool; Christie's, November 1990, £1,430.
Upholstered, 1660-1900
George III mahogany footstool; Christie's, November 1990, £900.
Window, 1750 onwards
George III satinwood and beech window seat; Christie's, July 1990, £6,000.

Tables
Refectory, 1580-1700
Oak refectory table; Christie's, May 1990, £4,620.
Sofa tables, 1790-1840
Regency brass-inlaid rosewood sofa table; Christie's, February 1991, £6,000.
Sutherland tables, 1850-1900
Early Victorian mahogany Sutherland table; Christie's, February 1991, £1,100.
Dining-table, gate-leg, 1640 onwards
Queen Anne gate-leg dining-table; Christie's, October 1990, £1,980.
Dining-table, drop-leaf, 1735-70
George II drop-leaf dining-table; Sotheby's Sussex, May 1990, £1,050.
Dining-table, extended with legs, 1750 onwards
Regency mahogany extending dining-table; Christie's, February 1991, £3,200.
Dining-table, extended with pedestals, 1780-1840
Regency mahogany twin-pedestal dining-table; Christie's, November 1990, £14,000.
Breakfast tables, 1780-1820
Regency mahogany breakfast table; Christie's, February 1991, £2,500.
Centre or Loo tables, 1820 onwards
William IV rosewood and parcel gilt centre table; Christie's, February 1991, £13,000.
Tripod tables, 1730 onwards

George III tripod table; Christie's, February 1991, £10,000.
Pembroke table, 1770-1830
Oval mahogany George III Pembroke table; Christie's, February 1991, £1,700.
Drum or rent tables, 1790-1860
Early-19thC mahogany drum table; Christie's, February 1991, £4,000.
Library tables, 1790-1900
Mahogany Regency revolving library table; Christie's, November 1990, £5,000.
Work table or tea-poys, 1775-1880
Regency rosewood work table; Christie's, February 1991, £1,200.
Wardrobes, 1750-1950
Walnut Art Deco wardrobe; Christie's, February 1991, £700.
What-nots, 1790-1900
Regency simulated bamboo what-not; Christie's, February 1991, £1,900.
Wine-coolers
Pair of George III brass-bound mahogany wine-coolers; Christie's, February 1991, £2,200.

EUROPEAN FURNITURE

Unless otherwise stated, all sales took place in London.

Bedroom Furniture
1620-1730
Early-18thC carved baroque cradle; Christie's, June 1990, £10,450.
1730-1770
Lit la polonaise; Christie's, June 1990, £7,700.
1770-1800
Louis XIV three-sided bed; Christie's, December 1988, £1,400.
1800-1870
Lit en bateau; Christie's, June 1990, £16,500.

Cabinets, Cupboards and Armoires
1300-1630
Spanish oak dwarf cabinet; Christie's, May 1989, £4,400.
1625-1725
Late-16thC French walnut armoire-è-deux-corps; Christie's, May 1989, £5,000.
1725-1775
French provincial fruitwood buffet, mid-18thC; Christie's, May 1989, £2,640.
1775-1800
Dutch mahogany side cabinet, late-18thC; Christie's, November 1990, £1,800.
1800-1850
Dutch Empire mahogany side cabinet, early-19thC; Christie's, November 1990, £1,800.
1850-1890
South German painted marriage armoire, mid-19thC; Christie's, June 1990, £2,420.
1890-1940
French bibliotheque; Sotheby's Sussex, November 1990, £3,630.

Chairs
Before 1630
Italian walnut hall chair, late-16thC; Christie's, October 1990, £1,430.
1630-1770
Spanish certosina X-frame open armchair; Christie's, November 1990, £1,400.
1770-1815
Empire mahogany *bergère-de-bureau*; Christie's, June 1989, £6,380.
1815-1860
Pair of Charles X mahogany *fauteuils*; Christie's, November 1990, £1,100.
1860-1890
Dutch walnut and marquetry armchair; Sotheby's Sussex, March 1989, £800.
1890-1920
Louis XIV-style carved armchair, 1900; Sotheby's Sussex, March 1989, £380.

Chests and Chests of Drawers
1450-1600
Italian walnut cassone, late-16thC; Christie's, November 1990, £4,000.
1600-1675
German 'Armada' chest, early-17thC; Christie's, May 1989, £715.
1675-1760
Polychrome boulle commode; Christie's, December 1989, £28,600.
1760-1800
Louis XV tulipwood and kingwood commode; Christie's, November 1990, £6,000.
1800-1850
Biedermeier walnut chest of drawers; Christie's, June 1990, £3,850.
1850-1890
Swedish pine chest of drawers, mid-19thC; Christie's, May 1989, £440.

Desks
Before 1630
17thC bone-inlaid cabinet; Christie's, May 1989, £4,950.
1630-1715
Louis XIV boulle *bureau Mazarin*; Christie's, June 1990, £16,500.
1715-1770
Louis XV kingwood *bureau plat*; Christie's, December 1989, £6,050.
1800-1850
Charles X mahogany secretaire abattant; Sotheby's Sussex, March 1989, £850.
1850-1890
French cylinder bureau; Sotheby's Sussex, November 1990, £19,800.
1890-1940
French secretaire vitrine; Sotheby's Sussex, November 1990, £4,620.

Tables and Stands
1500-1630
Swiss walnut draw-leaf table, 17thC; Christie's, May 1990, £9,350.
1630-1730
French ebonised walnut torchère; Christie's, May 1990, £825.
1730-1770
Portuguese side-table, mid-18thC; Christie's, March 1989, £9,350.
1770-1790
Louis tricoteuse; Christie's, December 1989, £12,100.
1790-1850
Swedish birchwood centre table, 1830; Christie's, November 1990, £1,800.
1850-1890
Dutch marquetry table, 1870 in 17thC style; Christie's, June 1989, £4,400.
1890-1920
Gall walnut and marquetry table; Christie's, July 1988, £550.
1920-1940
Art Deco walnut dining-table; Christie's, July 1988, £660.

NEW WORLD FURNITURE

Unless otherwise stated, all sales took place in New York.

Beds and Cradles
1760-1790
Federal maple four-poster bedstead; Sotheby's, October 1990, $2,500.
1790-1820
Federal birchwood bedstead; Sotheby's, February 1991, $3,500.
1820-1890
Turned curly maple cradle, early-19thC; Sotheby's, January 1990, $950.
1890-1940
Tent bed; Sotheby's, January 1989, $12,650.

Cabinets, Cupboards, Bookcases and Wardrobes
Press and Court Cupboards 1670-1700
Oak cupboard; Sotheby's, January 1991, $6,875.
Dutch *kas* 1700-1850
William and Mary gumwood *kas*, 1730-60; Sotheby's, February 1991, $6,250.
Cupboards 1680-1800
Chippendale walnut *shrank*, 1770; Sotheby's, October 1990, $3,000.
Corner Cupboards 1720-1850
Queen Anne hanging corner cupboard, 1750; Sotheby's, February 1991, $2,900.
Dish Dressers
Federal mahogany sideboard; Sotheby's, October 1990, $15,000.
Bookcases and Cabinets 1760-1840
Chippendale bonnet-top secretary bookcase, 1765; Sotheby's, February 1991, $17,000.
Cabinets and Wardrobes 1890-1920
Craftsman cabinet; Sotheby's, March 1989, $3,850.

Chairs
1620-1690
Early American chair; Sotheby's, January 1990, $715.
1690-1725
Pilgrim turned ash and maple armchair, 1700-50; Sotheby's, January 1991, $650.
1725-1790
Painted and turned Windsor comb-back armchair, 1785; Sotheby's, February 1991, $2,250.
1790-1810
Turned Windsor settee, 1810; Sotheby's, February 1991, $5,000.
1810-1840
Federal mahogany sofa, 1815; Sotheby's, February 1991, $2,200.
1840-1890
Classical mahogany recamier sofa; Sotheby's, January 1991, $3,250.

Chests and Chests of Drawers
1620-1740
Pilgrim oak chest; Sotheby's, February 1991, $9,000.
1700-1790
Chippendale mahogany chest of drawers; Sotheby's, February 1991, $9,500.
1790-1890
Federal mahogany and satinwood chest of drawers, 1805; Sotheby's, February 1991, $5,500.
1890-1940
Pilgrim-style oak and pine chest, 20thC; Sotheby's, January 1991, $5,250.

Desks
1680-1760
Chippendale mahogany slant-front desk; Sotheby's, January 1991, $50,000.
1760-1785
Chippendale mahogany fall-front desk, Rhode Island; Sotheby's, February 1991, $14,000.
1785-1810
Chippendale mahogany slant-front desk; Sotheby's, February1991, $5,750.
1840-1890
Wootton desk; Sotheby's, September 1990, $9,990.
1890-1940
1920s desk; Christie's, September 1990, $4,400.

Tables
1620-1700
William and Mary trestle base table; Sotheby's, October 1990, $7,500.
1700-1790
William and Mary gate-leg dining-table, 1740; Sotheby's, February 1991, $4,000.
1790-1840
Federal three-part dining-table; Sotheby's, February 1991, $3,500.
1840-1890
Late-19thC American table; Sotheby's, September 1990, $4,950.

INDEX

INDEX